TERRORISM
and
U.S. FOREIGN POLICY

TERRORISM
and
U.S. FOREIGN POLICY

PAUL R. PILLAR

BROOKINGS INSTITUTION PRESS
Washington, D.C.

To Cynthia

Copyright © 2001
Paperback edition copyright © 2003
THE BROOKINGS INSTITUTION
1775 Massachusetts Avenue, N.W., Washington, D.C. 20036
www.brookings.edu

Library of Congress Cataloging-in-Publication data
Pillar, Paul R., 1947-
Terrorism and U.S. foreign policy/Paul R. Pillar.
 p. cm.
Includes bibliographical references and index.
 ISBN 0-8157-0004-0 (alk. paper)
 ISBN 0-8157-7077-4 (pbk. : alk. paper)
 1. Terrorism. 2. Terrorism–Prevention. 3. United States–Foreign relations.
I. Title: Terrorism and US foreign policy. II. Title.
 HV6431 .P56 2001
 327.73–dc21   00-013070
                                                                              CIP

9 8 7 6 5 4 3 2 1

The paper used in this publication meets minimum requirements of the
American National Standard for Information Sciences—Permanence of
Paper for Printed Library Materials: ANSI Z39.48-1992.

Typeset in Sabon

Composition by AlphaWebTech
Mechanicsville, Maryland

Printed by R. R. Donnelley and Sons
Harrisonburg, Virginia

Contents

Introduction to the
Paperback Edition

The most significant event in international terrorism since this book, in its hardcover edition, was first printed in the spring of 2001 is obvious.

The hijacking of four commercial airliners by Usama bin Ladin's al-Qaida on September 11, 2001, and the flying of two of them into the World Trade Center towers in New York and one into the Pentagon outside Washington, with the fourth plane crashing into a field in Pennsylvania after an in-flight struggle between passengers and hijackers, immediately overshadowed every other terrorist incident Americans had previously experienced.

The sheer lethality of the operation, with a death toll of more than 3,000, was far greater than what had been achieved in any previous attack during the era of modern international terrorism, ensuring its tremendous impact. The event became known simply as "September eleventh," or even more briefly "9/11," partly because the multiple targets in different cities precluded an appropriate place-based name but also because it was one of the few events in American history that immediately became so large a part of the national consciousness that a shorthand reference to the date was all that was needed to identify it.

9/11 has had more extensive effects than any earlier terrorist attack on popular thinking in the United States about terrorism, official policy priorities and attention to terrorism, and decisions affecting programs and resources. It has spawned a plethora of commentary and analysis about terrorism. And it has generated much talk about "sea changes" and "new eras" and how the United States must make major changes in dealing with new security challenges.

Any consideration of what 9/11 *ought* to mean for thinking about terrorism and for counterterrorist policy should revolve around the following questions: What really did change, and what did not? And what are the opportunities and the pitfalls of the surge of interest in counterterrorism? Despite the shock and emotion of this one event, there is remarkable continuity, pre- and post-9/11, in the nature of the challenges that international terrorism poses and in the principles for meeting those challenges. On both of those fronts, much has not changed. For the general public and for others who had not previously focused intensively on the realities of international terrorist threats, 9/11 was an eye-opening event. But the realities were already in place.

If *Terrorism and U.S. Foreign Policy* were being written now, the attack and, even more so, the responses to it obviously would provide plentiful material. But almost all of the material would illustrate principles this book presents in its original hardcover printing. With few exceptions, the analysis in the original—on the nature and costs of modern international terrorism, the elements of countering it, the strengths and weaknesses of each counterterrorist instrument, the roles of states and groups, the importance of public understanding and support, and the ways counterterrorism and broader foreign policy intersect—stands as written, as do the lessons, recommendations, and projections at the end of the book. Accordingly, this paperback printing consists of this introduction— a comment on the most important aspects of 9/11 and its aftermath—and a main text that is unchanged from the original book.

The Threats: Continuing Patterns

The 9/11 attacks were manifestations of trends and patterns that international terrorism has been exhibiting for a decade. The audacity and enormity of the attacks made the threat seem new to many. But the who, what, why, where, and even most of the how of the attacks were not new.

The perpetrators of the 9/11 attacks were radical Sunni Islamists, who had emerged several years earlier as the most immediate threat to U.S. interests, were part of a larger trend toward religiously inspired terrorism, and were driven by the mixture of motives chapter 3 discusses. Even the specific group (al-Qaida) and leader (bin Ladin) behind the attacks already had reached the top of the list of terrorist threats to U.S. interests by the late 1990s and became even more prominent after the attacks on U.S.

embassies in Africa in 1998, for which they were also responsible. The larger network of radical Islamists of which al-Qaida has been a part also has been around since the early 1990s.[1] The continuity is personified by the close relationship between Ramzi Yousef, who led the bombing of the World Trade Center in 1993, and his colleague and uncle Khalid Shaykh Muhammad, the apparent mastermind of the 9/11 attacks.

9/11 illustrated another important trend of the past decade: the increasing role of groups rather than states in international terrorism. Initial reactions to the attacks included speculation that an operation so big, sophisticated, and deadly must have reflected help from some regime's clandestine service. But two years of investigation have revealed no state role in it.

9/11 also illustrated the increasingly transnational nature of international terrorism. The attackers were Arabs but of many nationalities. The operation was planned, financed, coordinated, and prepared on three different continents. The plotters took advantage of the ease of movement and efficient long-distance communications associated with globalization as they traveled, transferred funds, and issued instructions over thousands of miles.

The trend toward greater lethality in terrorist operations was clearly demonstrated by 9/11, as the number of fatalities graphically proved. The numbers had already been heading upward, and the trend is even more apparent if one considers what terrorists had been attempting to do before September 11 and not just what they had succeeded in doing. Yousef's goal in bombing the World Trade Center in 1993 was to topple the twin towers and kill thousands. That he failed to do this and the 9/11 plotters succeeded had to do partly with the better financing of the later plot but also with technical issues such as the design of skyscrapers and the effects of burning jet fuel on steel girders. It did not reflect a difference in terrorists' intentions or motivations, or in the overall shape of the developing terrorist threat against the United States. If Yousef had solved his technical problems, national trauma comparable to 9/11 would have occurred eight and a half years earlier.

Even though the shock of 9/11 was followed by exclamations that this type of operation had been "unimaginable" and by recriminations that those officials with counterterrorist responsibilities should have imagined it, the tactics were not far removed from what terrorists were already

1. The development of this network through the 1990s is traced in part one of Daniel Benjamin and Steven Simon, *The Age of Sacred Terror* (Random House, 2002).

doing. Hijacking of commercial aircraft is one of the most time-honored terrorist methods—it was the tactic used in some of the most spectacular terrorist operations of the 1970s and 1980s. Even the idea of using a hijacked aircraft to strike high-profile targets on the ground has come up before; Algerian extremists who hijacked a French airliner in December 1994 reportedly intended to do exactly that against the Eiffel Tower in Paris, but French security forces stormed the plane when it was on the ground in Marseilles. Ramzi Yousef and his colleagues, while working on a different type of attack on commercial aviation in the Far East, also discussed crashing a plane into CIA headquarters outside Washington. In any event, the same security measures would be needed to prevent hijacking regardless of what terrorists intend to do with an airplane once they seize it.

Another attribute of the tactics used by the 9/11 terrorists is that—despite the heavy attention in recent years to possible chemical, biological, radiological, or nuclear (CBRN) terrorism—their operation used nothing more unconventional or exotic than pilot training and box-cutter knives. The attacks underscored the point made in this book that the attention given to CBRN terrorism has been out of proportion to its part in the larger panoply of terrorist threats. The attacks also demonstrated that mass casualties are not to be equated with use of CBRN. An instructive comparison is between 9/11 and the other terrorist attack inside the United States in the latter half of 2001: the mailing to various recipients of letters contaminated with anthrax spores. The attack that used hijacking and knives killed 3,000; the one that used a biological agent killed 5. It is remarkable how often these lessons get lost or even stood on their head as 9/11 is invoked in arguments that go something like: "9/11 showed what a horrible thing terrorists can do to us, and so it shows that terrorists would use CBRN, which is another horrible thing."

The threat of CBRN terrorism is still present and indeed may have risen since 9/11, although for reasons other than the flawed logic of the kind of argument just cited. One reason is that the availability of the relevant materials is probably at least as great as it was two years ago, with the disorder in Iraq following the overthrow of Saddam Hussein's regime being a new cause for worry. Iraqi nuclear facilities were among the sites that were looted, and the International Atomic Energy Agency expressed concern about the loss of control of nuclear materials stored there.[2] A

2. Barton Gellman, "Seven Nuclear Sites Looted," *Washington Post*, May 10, 2003, p. A1; and Walter Pincus, "U.N. Atomic Chief Again Warns U.S. about Iraq," *Washington Post*, May 20, 2003, p. A8.

possible mobile biological weapons production unit came into U.S. hands only after it had passed through the hands of a thief who had stolen the truck.[3] Another reason is the way 9/11 may have raised the bar for other terrorists hoping to make a big impact. It will be difficult for any terrorist to match the death toll of 9/11, but the extra cachet of fear that has become associated with CBRN terrorism may compensate for a smaller body count. Americans have repeatedly displayed that fear. The anthrax letters caused few casualties but major disruptions, including to the operations of the U.S. postal system and Congress. The principal popular response in the United States to heightened concern about terrorism as the war against Iraq was imminent in early 2003 was a run on duct tape and plastic sheeting at hardware stores, as citizens prepared airtight rooms in their homes to seal out any chemical and biological agents. Fifty years from now, this response may seem as curious and feckless as the "duck and cover" drills of the 1950s seem to us now. But terrorists pay close attention—as interrogations of some of the ones captured since 9/11 confirm—to what such responses show about what scares us. They will take these observations into account as they select their tactics.

Another pattern discussed in this book and highlighted by 9/11 is the pre-eminent place that the United States has come to occupy on the list of terrorist targets. Chapter 2 presents an argument that international terrorism inflicts substantial costs on U.S. interests, in the form of numerous effects on U.S. resources, domestic life, and foreign policy, in addition to the pain represented by terrorist-inflicted deaths and injuries even before 9/11. This kind of argument may seem quaint and superfluous now. The huge increase in the body count from 9/11 has brought about nearly unanimous agreement that counterterrorism is important. But before 9/11, arguments were being made in respected publications that terrorism was not a significant threat to the United States and that the costs of it were low and manageable.[4]

Presumably, it will be a long while before that kind of argument is made again. But someday it may be made, resting on the same fallacy that the previous versions of the argument did—namely, equating the level of threat from terrorism with the number and severity of terrorist attacks

3. Walter Pincus and Michael Dobbs, "Suspected Bioweapon Mobile Lab Recovered," *Washington Post*, May 7, 2003, p. A1.

4. Larry C. Johnson, "The Declining Terrorist Threat," *New York Times*, July 10, 2001, p. A19; and John Mueller and Karl Mueller, "Sanctions of Mass Destruction," *Foreign Affairs*, vol. 78 (May–June 1999), p. 44.

that are taking place, or have taken place, recently. The threat from terrorism is instead the *potential* for terrorists or would-be terrorists to inflict harm. That threat manifests itself in highly discontinuous ways, with some attacks being the sudden culmination of operations that, like the 9/11 plot, were in the making for years.

If an uninformed visitor had observed what Americans were saying and doing about terrorism before September 2001 and then again afterward, he would have concluded that the terrorist threat to the United States had suddenly and drastically increased. But it was public awareness of the threat, not the threat itself, that had gone up. Americans were no less threatened on September 10, 2001, than they would be on September 12. Similarly, if the United States were successful enough and lucky enough to avoid a major terrorist attack for several years, it would not mean the threat had gone away.

States: Still Part of the Problem and the Solution

The outsider who intermittently looks in on us might also mistakenly conclude that state sponsorship of terrorism had increased. The attention to state sponsorship that would give that impression has resulted not from the 9/11 attacks themselves but from other policymaking purposes that have exploited the post-9/11 public mood. The reality of state sponsorship over the past two years has been—as with the nature and shape of the terrorist threat overall—largely one of continuity.

The one relatively recent (although now three years old) piece of bad news about state sponsorship was the reaction of Iran to the Palestinian *intifadah* that broke out in September 2000. Tehran's assistance to a variety of Palestinian groups, secular and Islamist, that confront Israel probably increased, although at the same time Iran appeared to have reduced its involvement in other forms of terrorist activity.[5] The aid to the anti-Israeli groups has reflected the strong sentiment on the issue of Palestine that seems to exist across much of the Iranian political class. It also reflects the continued control of the terrorist support apparatus (found mainly in the Islamic Revolutionary Guard Corps) by hardline elements in the Iranian regime, despite the advances that more moderate, reform-minded leaders have made in recent years in winning popular support and elections. Acquiescence of, or even collusion with, elements of the Revolu-

5. Department of State, *Patterns of Global Terrorism 2001* (2002), p. 64.

tionary Guard may lie behind the presence of some of the members of al-Qaida reported to be in Iran. The nature of that presence is unclear, however. Some al-Qaida members, after crossing the long and porous borders with Afghanistan and Pakistan, probably have lived and operated in Iran unbeknownst to the Iranian regime. Tehran has announced the arrest of some al-Qaida operatives; its refusal to hand them over to the United States clearly is a bargaining ploy intended to gain Iranian custody of members of the anti-Tehran terrorist group Mujahedin-e Khalq (MEK).

The story with other regimes on the U.S. list of state sponsors has been little changed from two years ago, with some dollops of good news. The disincentives to sponsoring terrorism that are discussed in this book—having mainly to do with the high price of being a pariah in a globalizing world—still are shaping policies. Syria maintains the same relationships with several Palestinian groups and with Hizballah and for the same reasons—as levers in its confrontation with Israel over the Golan Heights—while continuing to restrict the operations of those groups. Libya, North Korea, and Cuba still have nothing more than the residual (or mediatory) relationships with terrorists that they had before. None of these countries is currently providing material assistance to a terrorist group, and none has been implicated in any additional terrorist attacks. Libya has been trying to resolve open issues left over from the Pan Am 103 incident and by mid-2003 was on the verge of doing so through talks with the United States and the United Kingdom.[6] Terrorism-related talks also had been taking place between the United States and Sudan, with Khartoum's efforts to clean up its behavior having been good enough for the State Department's report on terrorism for 2002 to state that "the United States is pleased with Sudan's cooperation and the progress being made in their antiterrorist activities."[7]

The biggest news of the past two years relevant to state sponsorship of terrorism—and it is good news—was the ouster of the Taliban regime in Afghanistan through the U.S.-led intervention (Operation Enduring Freedom) in the civil war between the Taliban and the opposition Northern Alliance. The Taliban's activities did not involve state sponsorship in the classic patron-client sense, because the help that Usama bin Ladin and al-Qaida gave to the Taliban (financial and development assistance and

6. Felicity Barringer, "Libya Admits Culpability in Crash of Pan Am Plane," *New York Times*, August 16, 2003, p. A6.
7. Department of State, *Patterns of Global Terrorism 2002* (2003), p. 81.

fighters on the front lines of the civil war) was at least as significant as what the Taliban gave in return (safe haven). Nonetheless, the deep logistical, financial, and ideological partnership between the Taliban and al-Qaida was unquestionably one of the strongest relationships ever between a regime and a terrorist group. The defeat of the Taliban was not only a major blow to al-Qaida but also a setback to other radical Islamists who have made use of Afghanistan as a training ground and safe haven.

Whether the good news in Afghanistan endures depends on what progress is made in stabilizing and developing that strife-torn country. The prognosis as of mid-2003 is not bright. A transitional government struggles to establish authority in the face of warlords who collectively have control over more guns and more money. Remnants of the Taliban and elements of al-Qaida continue to pose security problems. Much of the economy and infrastructure is still in ruins from more than two decades of civil war. Tensions over the structure of a new government, the role of Islamic law, and the distribution of power among ethnic groups and between center and periphery threaten a collapse of the whole process of peace and reconstruction. If the process were to break down, Afghanistan would again become an inviting base of operations for transnational terrorists.

Afghanistan illustrates an important point about states and terrorism in the years ahead: terrorism is likely to be aided less by state sponsorship than by an absence or weakness of state authority. Lawless conditions are the international terrorist's friend. The inability of a government to exert authority over large parts of its territory has been a major factor in recent terrorist activity in places such as Somalia, Yemen, and the southern Philippines. It may become increasingly significant in the months ahead in Iraq.

Iraq has been at the center of the evolution of public perceptions of state sponsorship of terrorism since 9/11. This evolution did not occur because of any changes in the terrorism-related policies of the former regime of Saddam Hussein. Those policies had included for many years sponsorship of three Palestinian groups—the Palestinian Liberation Front (PLF), the Arab Liberation Front (ALF), and the Abu Nidal Organization—as well as the Iranian Mujahedin-e Khalq. The one new twist in the Saddam regime's policies, beginning in early 2002, was the giving of $25,000 in cash payments through the ALF to families of Palestinian suicide bombers. The Iraqi policies are unlikely to have made an appreciable difference to the level of Palestinian terrorism, which has been carried out chiefly by

Hamas, the Palestine Islamic Jihad, and the Fatah-affiliated al-Aqsa Martyrs Brigade and fueled by hatred of Israel's policies toward the West Bank and Gaza. Of the Iraqi clients, the PLF has made some largely unsuccessful attempts to add to the *intifadah* violence. There are no data on what role the payments to families may have played in individuals' decisions to commit suicide bombings; cash to one's heirs has never been known to be the decisive factor in taking such a drastic step. Saudi Arabia had already been giving cash payments to the families of all Palestinian "martyrs," including suicide bombers, as the Saudis openly acknowledged.[8] In any event, Hamas has always had an ample supply of aspiring suicide bombers, and the organization has steeled its young perpetrators through a well-honed regimen of indoctrination and isolation.

What was new about Iraq and terrorism was the U.S. administration's use of the militant post-9/11 mood of the American people to win support for the toppling of Saddam Hussein through military force. Such a military expedition had been a long-standing goal of some senior members of the Bush administration and like-minded opinion makers outside it, chiefly for reasons other than terrorism.[9] What 9/11 did was to so outrage Americans that the public was willing to entertain aggressive and forceful measures in the name of national security that it would not have accepted earlier. This made it politically feasible for the first time to launch an offensive war against Iraq even in the absence of a specific Iraqi provocation. Since the post-9/11 mood was created by a terrorist act, seizing this political opportunity meant emphasizing whatever association could be made between Iraq and terrorism. More specifically, it meant uncovering and highlighting any possible connections between Iraq and al-Qaida—even if without this policy imperative the connections would barely rise above the level of background noise amid the plethora of reported contacts and "links" among individuals, groups, and state agents that characterize the daily flow of intelligence on international terrorism.

Such links range from the most incidental (or coincidental) contacts to full-blown alliances or sponsorship. Much of the public discussion of Iraq and terrorism during the year and a half preceding the launching of the war in March 2003 overlooked the key question about any relationship between a state and a terrorist group: is the state making the group more

8. See the Saudi press release (www.saudiembassy.net/press_release/00_spa/11-29-mideast-aid.htm [October 2003]).

9. Joseph Cirincione, *Origins of Regime Change in Iraq*, Carnegie Endowment Proliferation Brief, vol. 6 (March 19, 2003).

capable of conducting deadly attacks or even instigating such attacks? The discussion treated the existence or nonexistence of a link, however inconclusive or inconsequential, as if it were the question that mattered most. Some of the least edifying contributions to the discussion were on the editorial and op-ed pages, where the standards of evidence tend to be looser than in official statements. This was where suggestions were made that the links between the Saddam regime and al-Qaida may have extended to the 9/11 operation itself—a tantalizing proposition that, if it had been confirmed, would have provided the strongest possible argument for going to war. Added to all the minutiae on empirical links was a constant rhetorical linkage between the "war on terrorism" and the war on Iraq. Proponents of the war used every opportunity to depict it as "part of the war on terrorism." Much press coverage—whether for editorial convenience or for other reasons—followed suit, with "War on Terrorism" being a banner caption for television reports on Iraq, and newspaper stories on both Iraq and terrorism being placed in the same special sections.

An important pertinent statement was a presentation on Iraq by Secretary of State Colin Powell to the United Nations Security Council in February 2003.[10] The statement was based on intelligence and made heavy use of hitherto classified information. It was carefully prepared, with the White House and several agencies participating in the preparation. It also admittedly was advocacy—an effort by the United States to make the best possible case for doing something about Saddam Hussein. As such, it could be expected to use material that would support the case, to omit material that would undermine the case, and to convey ambiguous material in a manner favorable to the case.

Secretary Powell's comments about Iraq and al-Qaida came in the last few minutes of the statement, after a much longer presentation of intelligence about Iraq's programs to develop weapons of mass destruction and efforts to conceal those programs from UN inspectors. Most of those few minutes were about a terrorist network headed by Abu Musab al-Zarqawi, who was not part of al-Qaida itself but described as an "associate and collaborator" of bin Ladin. Zarqawi's activities were centered in an area in northeastern Iraq that Saddam's regime had not controlled for more than a decade. The only connection between the regime and that area that

10. See the text of Secretary Powell's statement (www.state.gov/secretary/rm/2003/17300.htm. [October 2003]).

was mentioned was that Baghdad had an "agent"—which usually means a source of intelligence, although it can mean an agent who exerts influence—within the Islamist group (Ansar al-Islam) that controlled that corner of Iraq. According to the statement, Zarqawi spent two months in Baghdad for medical treatment in mid-2002, at which time nearly two dozen other "al-Qaida affiliates" also came there. This would have placed Iraq in the same category as several dozen other countries, in the developing world as well as the West (including the United States, as with the 9/11 plotters), in which al-Qaida or its associates have operated. The secretary said another government had approached Baghdad about extraditing Zarqawi, but there was no other indication that the Iraqi government was aware of the presence of any of the extremists, and no indication at all that Zarqawi or any of the others had ever had contact with the regime.

The statement mentioned that representatives of the Iraqi regime and al-Qaida had met at senior levels "at least eight times" since the early 1990s. Nothing was said about the subjects of those meetings apart from one report (evidently dating from the early to mid-1990s) that al-Qaida would "no longer support activities against Baghdad." Finally, the secretary mentioned al-Qaida's (already well-documented) interest in acquiring a CBRN capability. A single al-Qaida detainee had referred to Iraq "offering" chemical or biological weapons training for two al-Qaida associates, to the separate dispatch of a militant to Iraq to seek help in acquiring poisons and gasses, and to that militant's mention of a "successful" relationship with Iraqi officials. The secretary offered no reports, however, that Iraq had provided CBRN-related assistance. The only item in the statement that came close to being a report of Iraqi assistance of any kind being given to al-Qaida was from an Iraqi defector who said that "sometime in the mid-1990s" Saddam had sent agents to Afghanistan to provide training (with the recipients unspecified) in document forgery. On the 9/11 attacks—the event that had given rise to the whole debate, and about which so much speculation and innuendo about an Iraqi role had been written during the previous year—the secretary was silent.

The American public's understanding of most issues involving U.S. foreign and security policy does not rest on detailed perusal of what a secretary of state says at the United Nations. And in this case it did not reflect careful analysis of what the available information indicated about whether Saddam Hussein's regime had made al-Qaida more able or willing to attack the United States. It rested instead on a much vaguer sense of whether the concepts "Iraq" and "al-Qaida" go together. That sense was acquired through the public's exposure to repeated mention of the two subjects in the same breath, to the many hints and suggestive references to links, and to the larger conceptual blurring that resulted from applying the term "war on terrorism" to the fights against both al-Qaida and Iraq. The impact of that exposure has depended more on the quantity than on the quality of what the public heard.

By the time Secretary Powell spoke in New York, a year of exposure had already damaged the public's understanding of the role of Iraq in particular and state sponsors in general. The initial public perception of responsibility for the 9/11 attacks appeared to vindicate the optimism expressed in chapter 7 that the American public had come to comprehend that international terrorism today is more a problem of nonstate actors than one of states. In a poll taken in the first week after 9/11, 57 percent of Americans surveyed named Usama bin Ladin as the one most likely responsible for the attacks. Fourteen percent did not know or did not answer, and no other response received more than 4 percent. Only 3 percent named Iraq or Saddam Hussein as the leading suspect.[11] In a poll in August 2002—after months of a rhetorical drumbeat in which Iraq, "war on terrorism," and 9/11 had repeatedly been blended together in words and thus in people's minds—53 percent of respondents said they believed that Saddam Hussein had been "personally involved" in the 9/11 attacks.[12] In a poll in August 2003, after another year in which Iraq and 9/11 were linked in pro-war rhetoric but not in any new evidence, 69 percent of Americans believed Saddam Hussein had a role in the attacks.[13] This result represented one of the greatest misperceptions about terrorism that the American public has ever displayed, and it was largely the consequence of efforts to manipulate public perceptions to sell a policy undertaken for other purposes.

The damage to public understanding of this subject may slowly be repaired as Saddam Hussein's regime fades into history and anti-U.S. terrorism continues. The mounting doubts, amid postwar problems in stabilizing Iraq, about the administration's prewar case for toppling Saddam could help to repair that damage. Most of the doubts have had to do with weapons of mass destruction, but a by-product seems to have been a growing recognition in American public commentary—mirroring what had been

11. Wirthlin Worldwide poll, 2001.
12. CNN/*USA Today*/Gallup poll, August 19–21, 2002.
13. Dana Milbank and Claudia Deane, "Hussein Link to 9/11 Lingers in Many Minds," *Washington Post*, September 6, 2003, p. A1.

the prevailing perception all along in Britain—that the administration's effort to portray Saddam's regime as an ally of al-Qaida had been weak at best.

Paradoxically, however, some of the very problems of the postwar occupation that have fed doubts about the administration's policies may help to sustain a perceived link between Iraq and terrorism. The administration has tried to turn the growing terrorist violence in Iraq to its rhetorical advantage by using it to sustain the theme that "the war in Iraq is part of the war on terrorism." President George W. Bush had good reason to say—near the end of the long, hot Iraqi summer of 2003, amid a series of increasingly deadly vehicle bombs in Iraqi cities—that the effort to erect a new political order in Iraq was "turning out to be a continuing battle in the war on terror."[14] Such words may have more of an impact on popular perceptions than the fact that the terrorism in question was not anything the Saddam regime would have done if the United States had not gone to war, but instead something that terrorists were doing because it had.

In the meantime, public misunderstanding about the role of states in terrorism entails costs to counterterrorism. An informed public is still important for the reasons discussed in the book, and leveling with the American people is still a prudent recommendation. Public misunderstanding of terrorism means misplaced support for policies undertaken in the name of counterterrorism. It can mean a false sense of confidence that terrorist threats are being reduced. And it can mean disillusionment when subsequent terrorist attacks demonstrate that the threats have not been reduced.

An aspect of state sponsorship that got a particular boost in attention during the debates about Iraq was the specter of a regime giving CBRN weapons or matériel to a terrorist group. This fear has been around much longer than the past two years. But the possibility of a state-to-group transfer of CBRN matériel fit neatly into the task of mustering support for the war to topple Saddam Hussein. Unconventional weapons were the subject of the repeated resolutions on Iraq that the United Nations Security Council had passed and that Iraq had violated. As Secretary Powell's presentation to the council showed, it was a subject on which there was substantial intelligence. Tying this issue to terrorism—despite the non-CBRN nature of 9/11—through the fear of a hypothetical future transfer of weapons thus became a major theme. Supporters of the war repeatedly stated that

14. Amy Goldstein, "Bush Cites 'Foreign Element' in Iraq," *Washington Post*, August 23, 2003, p. A16.

the Saddam regime "could" give CBRN weapons to al-Qaida or other terrorists. The statements usually were coupled with references to the resulting horrors if such weapons were used to attack American cities.

That kind of "could" statement is not very amenable to either support or refutation through facts and analysis. To those who suggest that a CBRN transfer is unlikely, the usual response is that the potential consequences of CBRN weapons getting into the hands of terrorist groups are so severe that the possibility must be countered no matter how low the probability. Keeping CBRN weapons out of the hands of terrorist groups necessarily is a high concern, mainly because deterrence applicable to states does not work the same way, or work at all, with groups. But any policy departures predicated on the possibility of a state-to-group CBRN transfer—as distinct from a terrorist group acquiring a CBRN capability through some other means—needs to take account of the following three points.

First, probabilities shape policy all the time, even with what would be catastrophic contingencies. There are all sorts of high-cost possibilities, ranging from asteroids striking earth to nuclear-armed allies suddenly becoming enemies, that the United States does relatively little to counter precisely because the probabilities of occurrence are low. Probabilities matter because there always are trade-offs, including expenditure of resources as well as undesirable consequences of trying to counter the hypothetical threat, or of trying to counter it in a forceful or direct way. The war against Iraq is itself the most glaring recent case in point. A military campaign launched partly in the name of preventing the possibility of a CBRN transfer to terrorists is entailing substantial expenditures of blood and treasure as well as the risk of other untoward consequences to U.S. alliances and other interests overseas. It also probably has increased, rather than decreased, the chance of anti-U.S. terrorism (see below) and possibly even has increased, rather than decreased, the chance of CBRN matériel falling into terrorists' hands (see above).

This point also was recently illustrated, with a different policy response, by North Korea, which inconveniently rose on U.S. policymakers' screens during the run-up to the Iraq war, as Pyongyang announced its withdrawal from the Nuclear Nonproliferation Treaty and took several steps to reinvigorate its efforts to develop nuclear weapons. North Korea is still designated a state sponsor of terrorism, its regime has directly committed major terrorist acts in the past, its nuclear program is more advanced than Iraq's ever was, and it is ruled by a dictator at least as mercurial as Saddam Hussein. But the Bush administration wisely sought diplomatic means of dealing with North Korea because use of force would risk severe consequences, including possibly a new war on the Korean Peninsula and use of nuclear weapons that North Korea may already have.

Second, the reasons adduced in chapter 6 for why CBRN transfers to terrorist groups would be self-defeating are still relevant. Counterarguments to those reasons could take either of two forms. The first, which did not play a significant role in the debate over Iraq and which would not find much support in the overall behavior of state sponsors, is that a regime may engage in that kind of self-defeating behavior because it is irrational or undeterrable.[15] A second possible argument—suggested by the penury of the North Korean regime and the funds that have been available to al-Qaida—is that a regime might sell a CBRN capability because it needs the money. Fortunately, North Korea seems to be the only regime for which the pecuniary motive could be sufficiently strong to consider such a drastic step. Other states of concern, such as Iran, Libya, or Saddam's Iraq, have had CBRN programs partly because they have had the petroleum-based or other wealth to pay for them.

Third, there is no known instance of any regime transferring CBRN weapons to any terrorist group. The historical record is now substantial. It includes the former Soviet Union, which had comprehensive CBRN programs and gave abundant assistance to extremist and revolutionary groups worldwide. It includes the behavior to date of all the currently listed state sponsors of terrorism. And with the war in Iraq having been waged, it now includes the entire history of Saddam Hussein's dictatorship.

There still is good reason to expect that any acquisition by a terrorist group of a CBRN capability is more likely to result from the group stealing or indigenously developing the capability rather than from a regime transferring it willingly. Although few groups may have the wherewithal to put together their own CBRN programs, the interest—sustained in part by the numerous indications of the potential for sowing fear and disruption in the United States—clearly is there. What has been learned over the past two years about al-Qaida's operational objectives and efforts has confirmed that it has a strong interest in all the types of unconventional weapons represented by the CBRN label.

15. Such an argument is applied to Saddam's Iraq in Kenneth M. Pollack, *The Threatening Storm: The Case for Invading Iraq* (Random House, 2002). A case that Saddam was in fact deterrable is presented in John J. Mearsheimer and Stephen M. Walt, "An Unnecessary War," *Foreign Policy*, no. 134 (January–February 2003), pp. 50–59.

The events and policy debates during the past two years are a reminder that terrorism is not necessarily the most important U.S. policy concern, even with regimes that are state sponsors of terrorism. Weapons of mass destruction are most often the top concern. That clearly is the case with North Korea and by most measures was true as well of Saddam's regime, although other non-counterterrorist motives also underlay the decision to launch the war against Iraq. With the distinctions between the issues of weapons proliferation and terrorism increasingly blurred in the rhetoric of the past two years, it is more important than ever to recognize that they are different issues, involving different security challenges. This is not just because of the low probability of state-to-group CBRN transfers. Unconventional weapons and support to terrorism are different tools that serve different purposes for the states concerned. Different levers and incentives would be germane to changing a state's policy on each issue. Perhaps most important, conflating the two issues undermines counterterrorism by weakening its moral (and legal) clarity: *all* terrorism is unacceptable, regardless of who uses it and regardless of the cause being pursued. That is not true of weapons of mass destruction. To describe someone else's missiles or nuclear weapons as "weapons of terror" leaves unmentioned the fact that the United States and some of its allies have such weapons too.

The United States will be tested in the coming years on how well it can handle terrorism and other security concerns without one issue getting in the way of another. The main hazard, as it was when this book was first published, is that the disingenuous use of the fight against terrorism and the labeling of states as terrorist in order to pursue other objectives risks creating a *disincentive* for nations to get out of terrorism, since regimes will realize that the United States will penalize them whether they sponsor terrorism or not. The persistence of the problem is underscored by the fact that the official U.S. list of state sponsors remains unchanged—even though ten years have gone by since the last addition and no deletion has ever been made because a state improved its behavior on terrorism. The label "state sponsor" has already shown signs of complicating renewed dialogue with North Korea on nuclear weapons. Libya will be a clear test case once compensation and acceptance of responsibility for the Pan Am 103 bombing are resolved—a test that the United States would fail if it were to move the goal posts (because of weapons of mass destruction or other issues) and thereby show not just the Libyans but the rest of the world that it did not mean what it said about terrorism. The counterterrorist success story of Libya—involving one of the few really successful uses of sanctions—calls more strongly than ever for engagement rather than simply more isolation.[16]

Iran will be another important case, for somewhat different reasons. The differing purposes and incentives germane to terrorism and to weapons of mass destruction are especially important to remember with Iran. Probably most Iranian leaders see advanced weapons as a necessary and appropriate accoutrement of Iran's status as a regional power and as a valuable deterrent. Weapons-related policies will, for that reason, be difficult to change. Iran's terrorist-related policies probably are more changeable. Much will depend on the course of the Israeli-Palestinian conflict, because most Iranian support to terrorism revolves around the Palestinian issue. Getting action from Iran on terrorism also requires the United States to take seriously Tehran's own counterterrorist concerns. It would be a mistake to keep in business the Mujahedin-e Khalq—Saddam Hussein's biggest and most active terrorist client—as a lever against Iran, as some officials reportedly have favored doing.[17] The administration appears to have backed away from flirtation with the MEK, but Tehran will look for evidence that the United States is firmly committed to treating the MEK as a terrorist group rather than a means of leverage.

The greatest change for the Iranians during the past two years has been the overthrow through U.S. military force of regimes to their east (Afghanistan) and west (Iraq). This has increased Iran's suspicions of U.S. intentions. It also has created new U.S. dependency on Iran, since Iranian cooperation, or the lack of it, will be a major factor in determining whether peace and stability ever come to Afghanistan and Iraq. Pursuing those objectives, as well as the counterterrorist objective, are reasons for engagement and dialogue with Tehran. The dialogue on Afghanistan was initially good, with Iran playing a constructive role at the conference in Bonn in late 2001 that led to the establishment of the interim Afghan administration. Dialogue on Iraq so far has been less conspicuous. Future historians looking back at the U.S.-Iranian relationship probably would see it as a big missed opportunity if, after the United States used its military to topple two regimes—the Taliban and Saddam Hussein—that were adversaries of both the United States and Iran, relations did not improve.

16. See the recommendations in the report of the Atlantic Council of the United States, *U.S.-Libyan Relations: Toward Cautious Reengagement* (Washington, May 2003).

17. Glenn Kessler, "U.S. Seeks Surrender of Iranian Group," *Washington Post*, May 9, 2003, p. A1.

Another of this book's major themes about states—that there is no clear division between the white hats and the black hats, and that many regimes present both terrorist problems and opportunities for counterterrorist cooperation—has been very apparent since 9/11. U.S. officials were able to make good use of the phrase "you're either for us or for the terrorists" when they were appealing for enhanced counterterrorist assistance in the wake of the attacks, but as a description of reality rather than a diplomatic device it is no more accurate now than it was before 9/11. One of the best indications of this is the help that even state sponsors, several of whom have had their own serious worries about al-Qaida and radical Islamists, have offered. An outstanding case is Syria, which, following the U.S.-Iraq war in the spring of 2003, was the target of rhetoric from Washington so harsh that it stimulated speculation that a U.S. invasion of Syria might be imminent. At that same time, the State Department was releasing its latest annual report on terrorism, which stated that "the Government of Syria has cooperated significantly with the United States and other foreign governments against al-Qaida, the Taliban, and other terrorist organizations and individuals."[18]

Chapter 6 of this book mentions two states in particular as posing significant problems as enablers of terrorism even though they are not designated as state sponsors and are important allies or partners of the United States. With one of those states, Greece, the recent news has been good. In 2002 Greek authorities finally arrested several suspected core members of the group November 17 and appeared hot on the trail of other members of the radical underground left responsible for dozens of terrorist crimes dating back to the 1970s. The reasons for this sudden progress after a quarter century of ineffectiveness probably include the need to get more serious about domestic security as the 2004 Olympic games approach, the increased U.S. priority given to counterterrorism worldwide, and the dynamics of police investigations in which one lucky break that cracks a case provides leads for a series of arrests.

The other state, Pakistan, continues to be one of the best examples of a state that is both an important terrorist problem and an important counterterrorist partner. Operation Enduring Freedom in Afghanistan left the United States as dependent as ever on Pakistan for help, or at least acquiescence, in tracking down the remaining Taliban and al-Qaida members (including perhaps Usama bin Ladin) in the Pakistan-Afghanistan

18. *Patterns of Global Terrorism 2002*, p. 81.

border area. The problems partly involve lingering questions—despite Pakistan's official break with the Taliban—about possible continued Pakistani ties with Afghan extremists. They also involve Pakistan's support to Kashmiri militants fighting against India and using terrorist tactics in Kashmir and elsewhere. Some of these militants are part of the wider network of Sunni extremists of most worry to the United States. An attack on the Indian parliament in New Delhi in December 2001, which India attributed to the Pakistan-based groups Lashkar-e Tayyiba and Jaish-e Mohammed, caused the two South Asian nuclear powers to mobilize their armies, go to the brink of war, and step back from the brink only after energetic diplomacy led by the United States and United Kingdom—a reminder of how terrorism can be a serious U.S. policy concern even if Americans are not killed.

9/11 drew attention to terrorist problems of other U.S. partners, especially Saudi Arabia. The Saudi nationality of fifteen of the nineteen hijackers caused U.S. commentators to focus more intently than ever before on the nature of Saudi society and how it can affect U.S. interests beyond the supply of oil and access for U.S. military forces. That attention is healthy; there are major issues involving the export from Saudi Arabia of money and ideology that help the terrorists, and even more so of societal patterns within the kingdom that can readily produce young men inclined to conduct the sort of mission that those fifteen did. At the same time, U.S. policy does not treat Saudi Arabia as an adversary, nor should it. There is no good way of addressing these problems that includes writing off the al-Saud. Managing the relationship with Saudi Arabia in a way that encourages beneficial change in Saudi society without making things worse will be a delicate task for Washington.

The transnational nature of the 9/11 operation showed how large numbers of countries must be directly involved in countering modern international terrorism. It also showed how incorrect it is to consider automatically any country in which terrorists operate as a problem state to be confronted rather than engaged. Preparations for the 9/11 plot took place in far-flung locations in Europe, Asia, and the United States—where the pilot-hijackers spent months living and training. Each of these activities represents a terrorist problem for the individual country in which it took place, and one is entitled to ask why the authorities in that country could not or would not stop the terrorists. But the plot also demonstrated the strong need for international cooperation and the strong dependence of counterterrorism on the foreign relationships within which that cooperation takes place.

Responses: Uneven Intensity

The sense that a distinct "war" on terrorism began in September 2001 has been strong enough for some official circles to bestow the ultimate Washington recognition of an acronym: the GWOT (pronounced gee-watt), for Global War on Terrorism. But anyone who believes that a "war" on terrorism began with 9/11 can refer to page one of this book, which notes that the metaphor of war was applied to earlier U.S. counterterrorist efforts, albeit without an acronym and without the ubiquity of its current usage. The now widely forgotten fact that the United States had major counterterrorist efforts under way well before 9/11 underscores one of the shortcomings, discussed in the book, of the war metaphor: that unlike most wars, counterterrorism does not have a definite beginning, and it will not have a definite end.

The response to 9/11 points to a couple of other respects in which the war on terrorism imagery is misleading and unhelpful in designing a comprehensive and effective counterterrorist strategy. Because most wars in U.S. history have been against states, the metaphor accentuates the misperception that terrorism is a threat coming from states more than groups. And because war naturally brings to mind armed force, the metaphor encourages an emphasis on the military instrument over other counterterrorist instruments, regardless of which combination of tools would be most effective. Both of these factors were in play for Iraq, of course, but they also have affected discourse about counterterrorism beyond Iraq. Much commentary about the "war on terrorism" seems to be dominated by an image of armies driving through one state after another, with speculation about which country (Syria? Iran? North Korea?) would be the "next target" in the war.

The conceptual leanings of the war metaphor are reflected in U.S. policies since 9/11, which have placed far greater emphasis on some counterterrorist tasks rather than others. Chapter 2 of this book outlines four basic elements of counterterrorism: cutting the roots of terrorism, reducing the capabilities of terrorist groups, manipulating the intentions of those groups, and erecting physical security measures against terrorist attack. The United States has made major efforts in the past two years with the second and fourth of those elements—the clearest forms of offense and defense in the "war." It has done far less with the first and third.

Defensive countermeasures since 9/11 naturally have stressed security of the U.S. homeland. Those measures have included consolidation of several agencies into a new Department of Homeland Security, the biggest reorganization of the federal government since the Department of Defense was established more than half a century ago. Improvements have gone well beyond the reshuffling of boxes on the government's organization chart. Special emphasis has been placed on enhancing aviation security, with the previous system of contract security screeners being replaced by a new Transportation Security Administration (now part of the Department of Homeland Security).

This book is not primarily an analysis of defensive security measures, and questions about the effectiveness of the new steps will not be fully and fairly answerable until much more time has passed. It is almost certainly more difficult, however, for international terrorists to operate inside the United States now than it was two years ago. This is partly because of the direct enhancements in governmental security programs. It is partly because of the increased vigilance of both the government and American citizens. And there probably is an additional deterrent effect as some terrorists, having read and heard so much about the new U.S. emphasis on homeland security, perceive that it would be even more difficult to mount an operation in the United States than it actually is.

The emphasis on enhancing aviation security is appropriate, and not only because the 9/11 attacks targeted civil aviation. Civil aviation always has been an especially tempting target because of its inherent vulnerabilities and usefulness to terrorists. Having dozens or even hundreds of people in a single thin-skinned container at 30,000 feet means they are far away from any help and could all be killed by an explosive charge that on the ground would kill only one or two. The long-range mobility of airliners gives terrorists several options that they have used through the years, including making demands to be flown to a friendly location, destroying an aircraft when it is over an ocean and the physical evidence would be lost, or—as with 9/11—using an airliner as a large cruise missile. The increased professionalism in aviation security is apparent to anyone who has passed through a U.S. airport since the Transportation Security Administration took over screening responsibilities. Terrorists will still look for ways to defeat the new procedures, but enhancing security in this area, despite the large expense, was one of the more cost-effective defensive countermeasures that could have been taken.

Defensive countermeasures overall still face the limitations discussed in chapter 2. Terrorists choose the tactics they will use and the targets they will strike; defenders do not know what the choice will be, and it would be infeasible or prohibitively expensive to cover all the possibilities. Terrorists will adapt their tactics and targeting decisions, as they always have, to the defenses that are thrown up against them. Even in the now-better-protected U.S. homeland, the tactical possibilities are seemingly endless. And even the lowest of low-tech tactics, especially with suicidal individuals to carry them out, can wreak havoc. A suggestion of this problem came in 2002 when the Washington, D.C., area became fixated on a series of sniper-style shootings of random individuals, carried out by two misfits with an old car and a rifle. If the same number of men as carried out the 9/11 attack were to conduct similar shootings simultaneously in one or more American cities until they were captured or killed, the resulting disruption and fear would be enormous.

The strong focus on homeland security has risked giving inadequate attention to overseas vulnerabilities, even though those vulnerabilities are likely to be at least as great during the next few years as in the past, given the size and geographic spread of the U.S. overseas presence. Terrorists still have U.S. embassies, U.S.-owned businesses, and residences to consider as targets—as with multiple car bombings in May 2003 against residential compounds in Riyadh, Saudi Arabia—and they also have an expanding menu of U.S. military targets. This menu includes, despite announced plans to withdraw the U.S. military from Saudi Arabia, a large continuing presence in the Middle East.[19] U.S. military personnel and facilities, especially in Iraq and elsewhere in the Middle East, are likely to be attractive targets not only because of their number and relative accessibility compared with the American homeland but also because of the symbolic value of striking what is for some a hated embodiment of U.S. power.

The offensive side of counterterrorism—reducing the capabilities of terrorist groups—has used the same counterterrorist instruments since 9/11 as were used before, although in some cases more intensively or with greater domestic or foreign support. Many of the strengths and weaknesses of each instrument, as discussed in chapter 4, have been demonstrated in the efforts since 9/11.

Diplomacy has facilitated the application of each of the other instruments, and that has been its principal advantage. A very large share of what has been accomplished in counterterrorism since 9/11, including the capture of senior terrorists and other disruption of their operations, has

---

19. Thom Shanker and Eric Schmitt, "Pentagon Expects Long-Term Access to Key Iraq Bases," *New York Times*, April 20, 2003, p. A1.

been done by foreign governments acting with the support and encouragement of the United States. The principal limitations have been that commitments made in diplomatic discussions do not necessarily mean that a foreign government will keep its promises (as seems to be true of some of Pakistan's commitments), and that even earnest efforts by a cooperating foreign government may not be enough to bring about the necessary reduction in a terrorist group's capabilities.

The criminal justice system probably has gone down a notch on most Americans' lists of counterterrorist tools, because it is now even more in vogue than before to think of terrorism as war rather than crime and because of the generally greater emphasis on military measures. The factors that have made law enforcement one of the favored counterterrorist instruments of the past, however, are still in evidence. Bringing terrorists to justice for their crimes is still one of the official tenets of U.S. counterterrorist policy.[20] The urge to see justice done underlies much of the heavy attention, especially during the first year after 9/11, to finding and capturing Usama bin Ladin—attention that could not be justified solely on the basis of the operational threat that one man posed. Most Americans probably now see death in a firefight or bombing raid as an even more appropriate fate for a terrorist like bin Ladin than a criminal prosecution. But most Americans probably still value the sense of closure that comes from a successful prosecution, and prosecutions still have some counterterrorist value beyond that emotional reason. Moreover, the creation by the Department of Defense of a system of military tribunals to try captured suspected terrorists shows that the military and criminal justice instruments are not entirely separate counterterrorist tools.

Some of the limitations of the criminal justice system as a counterterrorist instrument have been in evidence since 9/11. One is the difficulty of finding and capturing some of the biggest fish, as the failure to nab bin Ladin demonstrates. With all of the hijackers killed in their own attack, there was as of mid-2003 only one person yet brought to trial in a U.S. court for complicity in 9/11. The prosecution of that one suspect, Zacarias Moussaoui, has been slowed by much pretrial wrangling over access to witnesses and other issues, thus serving as a reminder of another limitation—the frequent practical difficulties of developing a legally sound criminal case against a terrorist.[21] It remains to be seen whether the military

20. *Patterns of Global Terrorism 2002*, p. xi.
21. Jerry Markon, "Moussaoui Is Spinning a Legal Web," *Washington Post*, May 27, 2003, p. A1.

tribunals will be able to sidestep some of those problems and whether the procedures and results coming out of that system will stand up to future legal challenges.

The other new development relevant to criminal prosecutions is the creation of the International Criminal Court (ICC). The statute of the court received enough ratifications to enter into force in July 2002. The difficulties—particularly having to do with the use of sensitive intelligence—that always have made the ICC an unpromising venue for terrorist prosecutions are still relevant. In any event, the Bush administration shows no inclination to reverse the Clinton administration's rejection of the court for that purpose.

The interdiction of terrorist finances evidences one of the biggest post-9/11 improvements of any of the counterterrorist instruments. In contrast to the pittance of funds belonging to terrorists and terrorist groups that had been frozen before the attack, more than $121 million in terrorist-related financial assets had been frozen by governments worldwide as of the end of 2002.[22] Executive Order 13224, signed twelve days after the 9/11 attacks, expanded previous legal powers for freezing of assets. The haul of terrorist money suddenly got larger not just because of expanded legal powers but because the much higher priority that the U.S. government was now giving to the problem elicited more cooperation from foreign governments.

The 9/11 operation drew increased attention to terrorist funding because it clearly was more expensive than almost any previous terrorist operation known to Americans. The effectiveness of the financial instrument, however, is still limited in that money often is not the main constraining factor for terrorist groups. Even an operation as expensive as 9/11, which ran up a bill of a few hundred thousand dollars, could easily be bankrolled by a single wealthy donor. And plenty of deadly mayhem can be carried out far more cheaply than that. Moreover, the difficulty of finding and tracking the movement of terrorist money is still another major limitation. Although significant progress has been made since 9/11, partly through capture of some of the money-handlers, the use by terrorists of couriers and the informal transfer arrangements known as *hawala* still constitute a largely impenetrable money-moving network.

The past two years have seen the biggest and most successful counterterrorist use of the military instrument: Operation Enduring Freedom in

22. *Patterns of Global Terrorism 2002*, p. v.

Afghanistan. That operation's ouster of the Taliban, rousting of al-Qaida's headquarters, and closing of training camps made it one of the more significant blows against radical Islamist terrorism, even bearing in mind the tenuousness of the reconstruction of Afghanistan. The operation demonstrated some of the strengths of the military instrument, especially its display of determination to combat terrorism and the direct damage that it can inflict on certain terrorist capabilities. Enduring Freedom also demonstrated some of the weaknesses. Despite the use of overwhelming firepower and high-tech weapons, U.S. forces found it difficult to find and destroy many well-disguised and well dug-in al-Qaida positions.[23] Some of the occupants of those positions still are being chased along the Afghanistan-Pakistan frontier. Although the reaction of most Afghans to the U.S. intervention has been more positive than negative, there is resentment over collateral damage to Afghan civilians as some U.S. munitions have gone astray.

Despite the drawbacks, Enduring Freedom is widely and appropriately seen as having been the right thing to do. Both the American public and foreign governments understood it as a direct strike against those responsible for 9/11. Given the successes of Enduring Freedom, it is fair to ask whether a military operation like it should have been undertaken earlier, even if this had meant less foreign support for it and even if the operation might not have prevented 9/11. After all, al-Qaida's presence in Afghanistan, its activities there, the nature of its alliance with the Taliban, and its intention to inflict deadly harm on the United States were known to U.S. policymakers and intelligence analysts before 9/11. But missing was not only the support and understanding of foreign publics but also the support of the American public. Without the 9/11 disaster there would not have been the political base for undertaking a seemingly unprovoked military expedition to a half-forgotten land thousands of miles away. This reality confronted the Clinton administration and the Bush administration during its first seven and a half months in office. The closest thing to a previous window of opportunity for military intervention in Afghanistan was the aftermath of the attacks on the embassies in Africa in August 1998. As a *casus belli* for a foreign war, however, this event did not resound nearly as loudly with the American public as the much deadlier and closer-to-home 9/11. And President Clinton's political difficulties at the

23. Stephen Biddle, "Afghanistan and the Future of Warfare," *Foreign Affairs*, vol. 82 (March–April 2003), pp. 31–46.

time (associated with the Monica Lewinsky affair) meant that even the limited cruise missile strikes that the United States conducted two weeks after the embassy bombings were subjected to significant questioning and skepticism. Making something like Enduring Freedom politically feasible was one of the biggest changes wrought by 9/11.

Afghanistan under the Taliban was a unique case. No other country has come close to it, as the home of the terrorist group most threatening to the United States, the seat of a regime in close partnership with that group, and an operational base and training ground for anti-U.S. terrorists generally. Accordingly, the judgment (in chapter 4) still holds that the military instrument should be used only rarely. The farther one gets from the sort of strong, direct connection to terrorist attacks and terrorist threats that characterized Operation Enduring Freedom and earlier U.S. uses of military force for counterterrorist purposes, the more the drawbacks of the military instrument—particularly resentment against the United States for using its military muscle—will outweigh the benefits. Moreover, the 9/11 plot demonstrated one of the most fundamental limitations of using military force against terrorism: most terrorist preparations that matter do not present good military targets. The 9/11 attacks were prepared not in training camps that could be bombed, but rather in apartments in foreign cities such as Hamburg and Kuala Lumpur, and in apartments and flight schools inside the United States.

Another possible departure in the counterterrorist use of U.S. military force was the killing, by a missile fired at their vehicle from an unmanned aircraft, of six suspected al-Qaida members in Yemen in November 2002. Just how much of a departure is unclear. Although the operation seemed consistent with much that the Bush administration has said about the need to use force more aggressively to combat terrorists, the United States has not staged any other comparable operations since 9/11, at least none that became known to the press. Probably the absence of similar strikes reflects the point just made about the difficulty of identifying good military targets. Any further use of this tactic—targeting killings in a country in which the United States is not otherwise conducting combat operations—would need to consider the same issues of unexpected consequences, hostile responses, and the possibility of costly mistakes or collateral damage that have arisen with Israel's use of similar tactics, as discussed in chapter 4. For the United States, use of military forces for such strikes would raise unresolved issues of how military covert actions should be controlled and approved (although the Yemen operation reportedly was conducted by the CIA). As the Israeli experience suggests, the tactic may be of more use for the extrajudicial execution of terrorists wanted for past attacks than for preemption of future attacks (one of those killed in the Yemen missile strike was believed responsible for planning the attack on the U.S.S. *Cole* in October 2000). It needs to be discussed in those terms if the United States is to go down the path that the Yemen operation represents.

Of all the counterterrorist instruments, intelligence received perhaps the most public attention in the wake of 9/11.[24] The initial postmortem inquiry into the event was conducted by the congressional intelligence committees. This reflected a tendency discussed in chapter 4: an overreliance on intelligence as the "first line of defense" against terrorism, based on a wish that by making intelligence good enough to uncover any terrorist plot directed against us we could avoid disasters like 9/11 and costly investments in other instruments and other lines of defense. Much commentary on 9/11 defined the problem primarily as one of "intelligence failure." Many commentators did not stop to consider, however, that a world without intelligence failures, in the sense in which they generally used that term, would be a world without terrorism (because the purpose of predicting an attack is to prevent it). Nor did they ask whether that sort of world is achievable.

There is no question that effective intelligence is critical to reducing the likelihood that terrorism, including high-casualty terrorism like 9/11, will hit Americans in the future. There is no question that the United States must explore every possible avenue for improving counterterrorist intelligence. The tasks, challenges, and limitations that face the U.S. intelligence community are basically the same now as they have been for most of the past decade, but the vastly increased public and congressional interest, in the wake of 9/11, in making whatever changes might offer hope of reducing the terrorist threat provide an opportunity for initiatives that may have had insufficient political or budgetary support in the past.

The appetite for change to improve counterterrorist intelligence, and the need to be open to change, are crystal clear. Not clear are exactly *what* changes ought to be made. What organizational, procedural, or other alternatives would be not only different from how the U.S. intelligence com-

---

24. For a more extensive post-9/11 analysis of the role of intelligence in counterterrorism and how the issue has been addressed since the attacks, see Paul R. Pillar, "Intelligence and the Campaign against International Terrorism," in Audrey Kurth Cronin and James M. Ludes, eds., *Attacking Terrorism: Elements of a Grand Strategy* (Georgetown University Press, forthcoming).

munity addresses terrorism now but also better? And exactly how would such changes be expected to reduce the likelihood of Americans falling victim to terrorism, especially major terrorist attacks like 9/11, while avoiding or minimizing any drawbacks? Unless those questions are answered satisfactorily, any "reform" of the intelligence community in the name of counterterrorism would be change for the sake of change—which might satisfy a public appetite but would not reduce the risk of terrorists killing Americans. Besides entailing a possible waste of resources, there could be other negative consequences, including feeding a misperception that Americans had been made safer when they really had not. More serious still would be counterproductive effects making the intelligence community less effective than before—a danger if a quest for the perfect (the unattainable world without terrorism) becomes the enemy of the good. For counterterrorist policymakers as well as for physicians, the first principle should be the Hippocratic oath of doing no harm.

Unfortunately, the opportunities for doing harm are considerable. One reason is that most of the steps worth trying in counterterrorist intelligence already have been tried. Most of the bureaucratic crockery that needed to be broken has been broken, and the fires that had to be lit under agencies have been burning for some time—something often forgotten given the widespread belief that the "war on terrorism" began on September 12, 2001. The current counterterrorist intelligence apparatus is the product of an evolution that goes back to the 1980s, the first period of heightened American concern about terrorism, when Hizballah was attacking U.S. interests in Lebanon. That evolution has included the creation in 1986 of CIA's Counterterrorist Center (CTC), which at the time was a bureaucratic revolution. It has included such innovations as the establishment in the mid-1990s of a center-within-a-center concerned solely with Usama bin Ladin. And it has included greatly increased interagency integration through such measures as cross-assignments between the FBI and CIA. 9/11 was followed by a plethora of commentaries on what the intelligence community needs to do better—put more human agents in the field, develop better language capabilities, and so on. But almost all of this advice echoes efforts already being made or is based on lore rather than the reality of how the intelligence community operates. In short, the past application of ideas for reform has depleted the supply of good ideas for further change.

Another factor contributing to the hazard of well-intentioned changes possibly doing more harm than good is that post-9/11 discussion of intelligence issues has displayed patterns typical of public and congressional responses to major shocks, which is to say that emotion has sometimes been more in evidence than deliberation. A related tendency has been to focus on whatever specific errors were related to the recent disaster (uncovered with all the blinding light of hindsight) and to jump to the conclusion that those errors reveal a broader pattern that must be corrected. An example is the inference based on a couple of well-publicized mistakes in the 9/11 case (CIA's tardiness in placing two of the hijackers on a watch list, and resistance by FBI headquarters to letting an FBI field office check some names with CIA) that "the FBI and CIA don't talk to each other." In fact, the errors were a tiny fraction of what has been, since increased integration in the mid-1990s, a huge daily flow of terrorist-related leads and other information between those two agencies and between the larger intelligence and law enforcement communities. The objective—even if unattainable—should be zero errors and zero impediments to the interagency flow of information. But exactly what additional changes, given what has already been implemented, would further that objective?

That question is related to the widely voiced demand for some kind of organizational change in hopes of "connecting the dots"—in what rapidly became a hackneyed phrase in post-9/11 discussion—and uncovering terrorist plots in the making. The Bush administration responded partly to that demand by creation of a Terrorist Threat Integration Center (TTIC), which began work in May 2003 and reports to the director of Central Intelligence but incorporates FBI personnel. TTIC represents only a minor change from integrative analytical work that had already been done in the Counterterrorist Center. To the extent that TTIC evolves into something more, with a more distinct organizational identity and a physical location separate from existing agencies (as is already planned), it risks incurring the disadvantage of such integrative efforts discussed in chapter 4. Reducing the separation between selected counterterrorist elements of agencies such as the CIA and FBI could *increase* the separation between those elements and the field offices and stations that conduct investigations and collect intelligence. The new component can become one more stovepipe bordered by a new set of bureaucratic lines. Designed to enhance the intragovernmental flow of counterterrorist information and insights, the change may in some respects impede the flow. The possibility of this sort of counterproductive effect must be carefully assessed before undertaking any organizational change, not just the one embodied by TTIC.

It would be unreasonable to expect major improvements in working with the "dots" of fragmentary intelligence on possible terrorist threats, the connections among which typically become apparent only after an actual attack provides a context for interpreting them. The daily reality that counterterrorist analysts will continue to face—no matter how they are organized—is that there never is just one set of dots waiting to be connected in one correct way, but rather many sets of dots that can be connected in many different, equally plausible, ways. Analysts will have to employ the same meticulous methods they have used for years, such as tracing names and following up leads that may associate one suspected terrorist with another, and they will still do so with information from all available sources.

The most comprehensive official study into the implications of 9/11 is still the joint inquiry of the congressional intelligence committees. The inquiry was a professionally conducted investigation that raised many useful questions. It produced a list of nineteen recommendations (many of them with several subpoints).[25] Most of the recommendations are unobjectionable, and they constitute a useful guide in considering any further legislative or executive changes. Most of the list, however, reads less like an agenda for change than a checklist of existing programs and criteria for measuring their effectiveness. That the intelligence community should have a strategy for developing human sources to penetrate terrorist organizations, that it should deal with financial support for international terrorism, that the FBI should clearly designate national counterterrorism priorities, that the National Security Agency (NSA) should be a full collaborating partner of the FBI and CIA in counterterrorism, that enhancement of foreign language capabilities should be emphasized, that Congress should exercise vigorous and informed oversight, and many other items mentioned are commendable objectives; but what is different about them from what agencies do now, or at least are endeavoring to do?

In some respects the list has the value of adding congressional endorsement, and thus presumably some additional oomph, to ongoing efforts to correct already recognized shortcomings (such as improving antiquated information technology systems at the FBI). Some recommendations already are implemented, or are well on their way to being so (such as making the intelligence community's priorities more amenable to updating,

25. The recommendations are at www.intelligence.senate.gov/recommendations.pdf. (October 2003).

recreating the position of a national intelligence officer responsible for terrorist issues, and disseminating more promptly to intelligence analysts the results of searches and surveillance under the Foreign Intelligence Surveillance Act). On several subjects the committees simply call for an additional study or report. All of this is reasonable, but it also is testimony to the difficulty—even after the joint inquiry's intense study of the 9/11 case—of coming up with new and promising ideas for preventing a recurrence.

The intelligence committees did offer some ideas for real change, and these suggestions deserve careful consideration. Their lead recommendation is to create a director of national intelligence with management, budgetary, and personnel responsibility for the entire intelligence community. This is an old—and important—idea and involves issues that have been discussed off and on since the original National Security Act of 1947. Such a change would be beneficial for reasons beyond the scope of this book and beyond counterterrorism, but its effect on the prospects of heading off another 9/11, while positive, would be only tangential. It is hard to see how, for example, day-to-day cooperation between analysts at CIA and NSA would be appreciably affected by changing NSA's location on the executive branch's organization chart. A related suggestion from the committees that might have at least as much beneficial effect at the working level is for Congress to enact legislation, modeled on the Goldwater-Nichols Act of 1986, to instill the concept of "jointness" across the intelligence community. This could be a useful legislative imprimatur to continue, and extend where possible, the existing cross-agency collaboration.

Another recommendation is to create an "all-source terrorism information fusion center" in the Department of Homeland Security. Most of the desired attributes the committees listed for such a center (for example, having full and timely access to all relevant intelligence, participating in levying tasks on collectors, and having a reporting mechanism for sharing lead information with other analysts) are descriptive of what already takes place in the CIA's Counterterrorist Center. The Bush administration's creation of TTIC could be seen as a partial response to this recommendation, and it still is unclear what shape the intelligence apparatus in the Department of Homeland Security will have. Some of the same questions just raised about TTIC could be raised about a fusion center within the new department. Terrorist threats to U.S. interests are not just threats to the homeland—and some of the information that needs to be "fused" concerns terrorists who could attack at home or abroad—raising another question of whether this function belongs in the new department.

A separate recommendation is for development of a "national watchlist center," which the Bush administration appears to be implementing with the establishment in September 2003 of a Terrorist Screening Center administered by the FBI. It is unclear how such a center would have prevented the most noted watchlist-related error in the 9/11 case, which occurred not because there was not an appropriate list or because the list that did exist was insufficiently integrated or available to the right users, but rather because there was a slip-up at the working level in not promptly following an established procedure. The committees did provide a hint of how terrorist watchlists could be used more extensively and effectively when they referred to possible use by the "private sector." The most relevant parts of the private sector are the transportation and hospitality industries. Terrorist use of aliases always will be a problem, but one is entitled to ask why the 9/11 hijackers, including ones on watchlists, were able to buy tickets and board airplanes under their true names. This is not really an intelligence issue but instead an issue of how much scrutiny and expense the citizenry and relevant industries are willing to bear in implementing a system that could more effectively monitor the movements of suspected terrorists.

The committees allude to another possible set of innovations related to collection and analysis of intelligence that now may be worth trying even though the cost would be high and the expected payoff very low: more comprehensive "data-mining" using such sources of information as travel and immigration records. The acquisition of some of the data would be difficult, and developing useful algorithms to exploit the data would still pose major challenges. But with the vastly heightened national priority now being given to counterterrorism, the threshold for high-cost, low-payoff projects has been lowered.[26]

The one possible major initiative raised by the joint inquiry with at least a hope of significantly affecting the chances of catching the next major terrorist plot against the United States would be the creation of a domestic intelligence and security service.[27] The United States is atypical among industrialized nations in not having one, comparable to MI-5 in

26. Statement of Paul R. Pillar to the Joint Inquiry of the Senate Select Committee on Intelligence and the House Permanent Select Committee on Intelligence, October 8, 2002, 107 Cong. 2 sess. (www.cia.gov/nic/speeches/testimony/paul_pillar.pdf [October 2003]).

27. For further discussion see Pillar, "Intelligence and the Campaign against International Terrorism."

the United Kingdom or the Federal Office for the Protection of the Constitution (BfV) in Germany. The principal arguments in favor of creating a new agency are that it would be one of the bolder possible departures from old ways of dealing with terrorist threats against the U.S. homeland, and that the intelligence-collection function could never be done well enough by the FBI, which will always be at heart a law enforcement organization. The principal arguments in the other direction are that the FBI already has reoriented itself (especially since 9/11) toward counterterrorism and toward collection of intelligence, and that creation of a new organization would risk drawing new bureaucratic lines that could impede the free flow of information. Moreover, a domestic intelligence agency would culturally be something of an anomaly in the United States; Americans do not like the idea of their government spying on them. This last consideration probably is the main reason the United States does not have that kind of agency, why the chance of one being created is still small, and why the intelligence committees shied away from recommending that one be created, instead only calling for more study of the subject. 9/11, however, has brought the topic up for at least limited discussion. Whether it gets considered further will be a mark of how serious Americans are about being willing to make major changes—even ones contrary to their customs and traditional preferences—in the interest of improving intelligence on the next terrorist plot against the U.S. homeland.

The scope of the congressional inquiry into 9/11, which was conducted by the intelligence committees, was limited largely to intelligence issues. Any useful prospective changes in the intelligence community's work on counterterrorism, however, necessarily would be connected to other aspects of counterterrorism and counterterrorist policy. A welcome development was thus the establishment in late 2002 of a national commission of inquiry with a broad charter, chaired by former New Jersey governor Thomas Kean.

The principal lesson of the 9/11 plot for intelligence activity is the same one that could be drawn from most prior terrorist attacks against U.S. interests and is discussed in chapter 4: that it always will be difficult to uncover tactical information specific enough to roll up a terrorist plot, even with good strategic intelligence about the threat that a terrorist group poses. The strategic intelligence about the threat to the United States from al-Qaida in the months leading up to 9/11 was strong. Director of Central Intelligence George Tenet, in his statement to Congress in February 2001—seven months before the attacks—on worldwide threats to U.S. interests, placed international terrorism and specifically al-Qaida at the top of the list of dangers.[28] Tenet said that "the threat from terrorism is real, it is immediate, and it is evolving." He described bin Ladin and his global network of lieutenants and associates as "the most immediate and serious threat," stating that they were "capable of planning multiple attacks with little or no warning." During the subsequent summer, information that the intelligence community collected led it to conclude that the threat from al-Qaida was even more immediate and serious. Tenet was described as "nearly frantic" with concern over the danger, and he repeatedly conveyed his warnings to senior administration officials.[29]

As for tactical intelligence, the 9/11 conspirators seem to have taken the few simple but effective steps needed to keep the plot hidden. They do not appear to have communicated the existence of the plan, let alone details of it, to anyone beyond a few individuals directly involved. Bin Ladin, in the most candid of his videotapes, said that even some of the hijackers were unaware of the nature of the operation.[30] Probably only bin Ladin, operational chief Khalid Shaykh Muhammad, a few other of bin Ladin's senior lieutenants, and Muhammad Atta and the other pilot-hijackers knew what was going to happen. It is hard to disagree with President Bush's judgment that the attack was not preventable, or with the conclusion of some members of the congressional intelligence committees that there was no single piece of information that, if properly analyzed, could have prevented it.[31]

No matter how assiduous, pathbreaking, and wise the United States is in taking steps to improve its counterterrorist intelligence, the improvements probably will be substantially less dramatic than what most Americans expect.[32] This prospect stems mainly from the nature of terrorist groups

28. "Worldwide Threat 2001: National Security in a Changing World," statement by Director of Central Intelligence George J. Tenet before the Senate Select Committee on Intelligence, February 7, 2001, 107 Cong. 1 sess. (www.cia.gov/cia/public_affairs/speeches/2001/UNCLASWWT_02072001.html [October 2003]).

29. Barton Gellman, "A Strategy's Cautious Evolution," *Washington Post*, January 20, 2002, p. A17.

30. Karen DeYoung and Walter Pincus, "In Bin Laden's Own Words," *Washington Post*, December 14, 2001, p. A1.

31. Speech by President George W. Bush, June 6, 2002 (www.whitehouse.gov/news/releases/2002/06/20020606-8.html [October 2003]); and Dana Priest and Juliet Eilperin, "Panel Finds No 'Smoking Gun' in Probe of 9/11 Intelligence Failures," *Washington Post*, July 11, 2002, p. A1.

32. Richard K. Betts, "Fixing Intelligence," *Foreign Affairs*, vol. 81 (January–February 2002), pp. 43–59.

and their operations, as well as from the inherent limits of trying to further refine institutions and procedures that already have undergone considerable refinement. This truth is uncomfortable to most Americans, who would prefer to believe that with enough determination, ingenuity, and accountability, a mission as noble and important as uncovering future terrorist plots can be accomplished. It is uncomfortable to those responsible for other aspects of counterterrorism, who continue to look to intelligence to carry the biggest share of the load. (The most recent manifestation of the latter outlook is in Iraq, where U.S. officials hoping to avoid a politically and economically painful increase in the troop presence look to "better intelligence" to stem the rising terrorism.)[33] The truth needs to be accepted, however, to avoid unintended damage to intelligence itself in trying to get it to accomplish the impossible and to put in proper relief the share of the load that other instruments and elements of counterterrorism must carry.

Counterterrorism since 9/11 has underscored the importance of an approach emphasized in this book: the cell-by-cell, terrorist-by-terrorist disruption of terrorist infrastructures, mainly accomplished through raids, arrests, interrogations, and other measures by foreign police and security services acting in cooperation with the United States. The approach has been the dominant and most effective use of covert action. But the method also has required the coordinated use of all the counterterrorist instruments—even military force, which in the case of Operation Enduring Freedom not only damaged some physical infrastructure and killed some terrorist operatives (most notably senior bin Ladin aide Muhammad Atef) but also flushed out of Afghanistan other terrorists who subsequently were captured in Pakistan or elsewhere. Disruption of al-Qaida since 9/11 has been substantial. Although bin Ladin and his second in command, Ayman Zawahiri, have remained at large, a major segment of the second- and third-tier leadership has been captured. The biggest catch so far is Khalid Shaykh Muhammad, arrested in March 2003. Al-Qaida is now an organization on the run and markedly less capable than it was two years ago—although still capable enough, as attacks such as the bombings in Riyadh in May 2003 demonstrate, to conduct well-planned operations.

The damage inflicted on al-Qaida since 9/11 has highlighted and accelerated the trend, discussed in chapter 3, away from hierarchical groups

33. Anthony Shadid and Daniel Williams, "U.S. Recruiting Hussein's Spies," *Washington Post*, August 24, 2003, p. 1.

and toward more diffuse networks and more decentralized initiative for terrorist attacks. Even with attacks properly labeled "al-Qaida operations"—including the Riyadh bombings—the impetus may be coming less from bin Ladin in hiding somewhere in South Asia than from lower levels of the organization. The disruption that has put senior al-Qaida leadership on the run probably has made it physically more difficult for the leadership to exert control and issue directions. An even bigger part of post-9/11 terrorism has been operations by other radical Islamist groups that can only be described as "affiliated with" or to some degree assisted by al-Qaida. The deadliest terrorist attack since 9/11—the bombing of a tourist area in Bali, Indonesia, in October 2002, with almost 200 persons (including 7 Americans) killed—almost certainly was the work of the Indonesian Islamist group Jemaah Islamiya, probably with some assistance from al-Qaida.[34] A set of suicide bombings in Casablanca in May 2003 evidently was carried out by Moroccans belonging to a local jihadist group called al-Assirat al-Moustaquim that, according to Moroccan officials, had received financial assistance from al-Qaida.[35] Smaller attacks in the Middle East may have fit a similar mold. Secretary Powell, in his statement to the United Nations, attributed the murder of U.S. Agency for International Development official Lawrence Foley in Jordan in October 2002 to the organization led by Abu Musab al-Zarqawi.

This is the shape of terrorism that the United States will face over the next several years. The threat will continue to come principally from radical Islamists, but as al-Qaida is further disrupted it will come less from the al-Qaida organization as we have known it and more from fragments of, or successors to, al-Qaida. It will also come from a variety of Islamist groups around the world that have never been part of al-Qaida proper but share many of its perspectives and are plugged into the same radical networks. Some of these will be groups with an established identity, such as Jemaah Islamiya; others will be smaller, nameless cells. Some will be focused mainly on local issues and will be targeting the authorities in their own countries. But they also will exhibit the antipathy toward the United States that al-Qaida has taken the lead in articulating, an antipathy that will motivate some of these groups to strike more directly at U.S. interests.

34. *Patterns of Global Terrorism 2002*, pp. 2, 18, 118.
35. "Synchronised Crime," *Economist*, May 24–30, 2003, p. 50; and Elaine Sciolino, "Moroccans Assert Al Qaeda Financed Suicide Bombings," *New York Times*, May 23, 2003, p. A16.

The U.S. counterterrorist response since 9/11 not only has helped to shape the terrorist threat (or accelerated trends already under way); it has shaped the costs of terrorism to the United States. Chapter 2 discusses how those costs entail not only the direct damage inflicted by terrorists but also the costs of measures taken in response to terrorism, including expenditures of resources and impediments in the daily lives of U.S. citizens. Most of the costs are incurred whether or not terrorist attacks are occurring. That chapter cites the example of aviation security, which already involved substantial costs even though the United States had been virtually free of attacks on civil aviation for many years before 9/11. The point is even stronger now, with the major additional costs connected with the creation of the Transportation Security Administration—costs that the United States will incur even if another several years should go by without more attacks on aviation. The same is true of the other large expenditures now being made on counterterrorism, which will constitute a budgetary legacy of 9/11 for years to come.

At least as important as monetary costs are the potential costs to civil liberties or personal privacy. This book discusses the American tendency to "do something" following significant terrorist incidents by rushing through legislation and other initiatives that, had they been considered with cooler heads and less urgency, probably would have taken a different shape. The aftermath of 9/11, given the enormous shock of that event, provides a fresh example, with much of the hasty response having implications for civil liberties and privacy. The omnibus counterterrorist legislation, called the USA Patriot Act, which was enacted a month after 9/11, contained some provisions—such as giving the CIA access to grand jury testimony—that would have seemed unthinkable earlier.[36] Using new powers granted in the Patriot Act, as well as changes in the attorney general's guidelines on investigations, the Justice Department has taken in the name of counterterrorism a much looser and more expansive approach than before on a wide range of matters, from the mingling of information from intelligence and criminal investigations to the detention of material witnesses.[37] Some in the administration and Congress have proposed expanding investigative powers even further, such as by giving the CIA and the

---

36. P. L. 107-56, sec. 203.

37. Eric Lichtblau, "Justice Dept. Lists Use of New Power to Fight Terror," *New York Times*, May 21, 2003, p. A1.

military the ability to subpoena personal and financial records of persons in the United States.[38]

Many of the new measures are warranted, and some of them may at least marginally increase the chance of uncovering the next foreign terrorist plot in the United States. But the issues to be considered are not just near-term efficacy (and even less the urge to "do something") but the long-term acceptability to the American people of expanded investigative powers. There is no specific reason to expect abuses, but there were valid reasons for creating such restrictions as keeping the CIA out of domestic investigations and drawing a line between the intelligence and criminal justice operations of the FBI. As the public mood changes, what seems acceptable now may become less so. A question worth asking is whether any of the new powers contain the seeds of future recriminations and investigations such as those of the Pike and Church committees of the 1970s, and whether they risk undermining one of the most important U.S. counterterrorist assets: the confidence of the American public in its intelligence and law enforcement agencies.

Roots: Uncut and Growing

Influencing the intentions of terrorist groups understandably has received much less attention since 9/11 than other elements of counterterrorism because it is largely irrelevant to the task of countering a group like al-Qaida. As discussed in chapter 2, there are no compromises to be made or negotiations to conduct with terrorists whose goals are so extreme and revolve around destruction and hatred rather than governance.

With other groups, however—ones that have a more legitimate claim to represent larger populations and that aspire to a peaceful political role— the past two years have demonstrated the continued relevance, and indeed the necessity, of peace negotiations to resolve conflicts to which those groups are parties. The pattern has been one of fits and starts and formidable difficulties in reaching agreements, but also of a lack of alternatives to the conference table if the violence is ever to be quelled. In Northern Ireland, the five-year-old Good Friday agreement has encountered more problems, with disagreements over the disposition of the IRA's weapons and suspension of the provincial government. But all of the parties, in-

38. Eric Lightblau and James Risen, "Broad Domestic Role Asked for C.I.A. and the Pentagon," *New York Times*, May 2, 2003, p. A18.

cluding the republicans, unionists, and British and Irish governments, keep coming back to the agreement as the only hope for bringing a lasting end to Ulster's "troubles." In Colombia, the peace efforts of former president Andres Pastrana have been superseded by the more forceful approach of his successor, Alvaro Uribe, but with no indication that the government is closer than before to subduing the leftist insurgents. In Sri Lanka, the peace talks that got under way have developed little momentum but nonetheless have continued as a recognition that a purely military solution to the two-decade-old Tamil rebellion is not feasible. In Kashmir, there are no peace talks but also no more indication than two years ago that Kashmiri terrorism will be controlled without an agreement among Islamabad, New Delhi, and the Kashmiris themselves.

In the Israeli-Palestinian conflict, the peace process begun a decade ago at Madrid and Oslo has unraveled, with the *intifadah* and subsequent reoccupation by the Israeli military of previously vacated Palestinian land having undone almost all of the earlier diplomatic gains. But the events in Palestine—with about 800 Israelis and 2,000 Palestinians killed since September 2000—have also demonstrated the bankruptcy of any attempt to bludgeon the Palestinians into submission. The overwhelming majority of Palestinians will not accept it. The Palestinian terrorists, especially those of Hamas, show no sign of becoming less able or less willing to continue their attacks. And the alternatives to a negotiated two-state solution—a costly and unstable apartheid system with Palestinian Bantustans, an unnegotiated separation of Israelis and Palestinians on Israeli terms, or a unified state in which Jewish Israelis would soon be in the minority—are unstable over anything but the short term. The work of the United States, European Union, United Nations, and Russia in developing a "road map" for reaching a settlement is a recognition of those realities.

The Israeli-Palestinian conflict is important not only for its impact on Palestinian terrorism. Because of the tremendous resonance that the Palestinian issue has in the Arab and Muslim worlds, it is one of the most prominent issues fueling Islamic radicalism overall, the brand of extremism most threatening to the United States. And this gets back to the first of the elements of counterterrorism listed in chapter 2: cutting the roots of terrorism.

The roots of Islamist terrorism are almost certainly at least as strong now as they were at the time of the 9/11 attacks. The United States has been winning the campaign to cripple al-Qaida's capabilities. It has not been winning the campaign to cripple the willingness of other angry

Muslims to do the sorts of violent things against the United States that al-Qaida has been trying to do.

One aspect of roots—the unpromising economic and political conditions in which would-be terrorists live and that leave them susceptible to extremist messages—has received additional attention since 9/11, and some beneficial steps have been taken. Many questions were raised about why the nineteen young men who hijacked the airliners could have been motivated to do what they did. The Bush administration has taken some useful initiatives intended to nudge Middle Eastern countries toward more democratic political systems and more open economies. These have included the Middle East Partnership Initiative, announced by Secretary of State Powell in December 2002, which is intended to encourage economic and educational reform and the development of civil society.[39] They also include a proposal by President Bush to create a U.S.–Middle East free trade zone.[40]

These initiatives are a worthwhile but very modest chipping away at what is a huge set of structural problems in most Arab countries and, to varying degrees, some other Muslim countries. The challenge is not simply one of poverty, as discussed in chapter 2 and as demonstrated by the backgrounds of the 9/11 hijackers, who were not conspicuously poor. Rather, it is one of closed, state-dominated economies and undemocratic, unresponsive political systems, which deny citizens the opportunity to realize their full potential and to effect peaceful political change when they are dissatisfied with their lack of opportunities.[41] People in such circumstances become alienated from the economic and political systems in which they live. And once populations are alienated, it becomes harder to develop the entrepreneurial spirit needed for economic growth and the civic culture needed to make a democracy work. It will take a long time, probably at least a generation, to break this vicious circle.

Because it will take so long, and because the United States must deal with terrorism right now, it is important to pay attention to the other

39. Speech by Secretary Colin Powell, December 12, 2002 (www.state.gov/secretary/rm/2002/15905.htm [October 2003]).

40. Commencement speech by President Bush at the University of South Carolina, May 9, 2003 (www.whitehouse.gov/news/releases/2003/05/20030509-11.html [October 2003]).

41. One of the most important recent statements of these problems is the Arab Human Development Report, a study by Arab scholars published in 2002 by the United Nations Development Program (www.undp.org/rbas/ahdr [October 2003]).

aspect of roots: the grievances and causes that extremists voice directly. With anti-U.S. terrorism, this means the sources of anger—justified or not—that are directed against the United States. On this front, the United States not only may not be winning, it may be losing.

An indirect but quantifiable indication of this animosity comes from polling. One of the clearest patterns to emerge from recent polls is strongly negative opinion toward the United States in the Middle East and in certain other Muslim countries, such as Pakistan. In forty-two countries surveyed in 2002 by the Pew Global Attitudes Project, six out of the seven countries that showed more people with an unfavorable than with a favorable opinion of the United States were Muslim states in the Middle East and South Asia.[42] Some of the results were striking, such as only 6 percent of Egyptians polled having a favorable view and 69 percent an unfavorable view of the United States, with similar results in Pakistan (10 percent favorable, 69 percent unfavorable) and Jordan (25 percent favorable, 75 percent unfavorable). The Pew survey found evidence that the antipathy toward the United States is grounded, as discussed in chapter 3 of this book, both in what the United States stands for and in what it does. The strongest correlations, however, were with opposition to what it does— that is, to U.S. policies. Large majorities in the Middle Eastern countries (77 percent in Lebanon, 74 percent in Turkey, 71 percent in Jordan) said they believed that U.S. foreign policy ignores the interests of their own countries. There was strong opposition to the U.S.-led "war on terrorism" —in whatever way respondents may have understood that phrase (those opposed included 85 percent in Jordan, 79 percent in Egypt, and 58 percent in Turkey).[43]

The newness of reliable polling in most Middle Eastern states makes the tracking of opinion over time difficult, but what evidence there is suggests that disapproval of the United States has increased during the past two years. A separate Pew study showed that favorable opinion of the United States among Turks, for example, dropped from 52 percent in polls taken in 1999–2000 to 30 percent in 2002 and 12 percent in March 2003.[44] Other Pew polls have indicated that the modest support the U.S.-led "war

42. *What the World Thinks in 2002* (Washington: Pew Research Center for the People and the Press, 2002), pp. 53–55. The countries with a plurality of unfavorable opinion were Egypt, Jordan, Lebanon, Turkey, Pakistan, Bangladesh, and Argentina.
43. Ibid., pp. 59, 69.
44. *America's Image Further Erodes, Europeans Want Weaker Ties* (Washington: Pew Research Center for the People and the Press, 2003), p. 1.

on terrorism" has had in Muslim countries declined from 2002 to 2003 (for example, those supporting it dropped from 38 percent to 30 percent in Lebanon, from 31 percent to 23 percent in Indonesia, and from 13 percent to 2 percent in Jordan).[45] Similar trends are suggested by unscientific but numerous other observations across the Middle East and elsewhere in the Muslim world, ranging from the content of Friday sermons to commentary in the independent press.

Although polls and press commentary do not directly count terrorists, the trends exhibited by the broad spectrum of Muslim opinion are likely to be true as well of the radical end of the spectrum. If there are millions in a particular country who resent the United States, probably there are tens of thousands who would subscribe to radical anti-U.S. ideologies, thousands who would support anti-U.S. violence, and hundreds who would be willing to engage in terrorism themselves.

The Pew surveys have provided some evidence of the extent of support for Islamic radicalism by asking for opinions of Usama bin Ladin. In polls taken in May 2003, those saying they had "a lot" or "some" confidence in bin Ladin "to do the right thing regarding world affairs" included 45 percent in Pakistan, 49 percent in Morocco, 55 percent in Jordan, 58 percent in Indonesia, and 71 percent in the Palestinian territories. In each of these populations, bin Ladin ranked first, second, or third among eight leaders about whom this question was asked.[46]

Chapter 7 discusses the importance of shaping foreign public opinion and recommends applying the skills of Madison Avenue to public diplomacy on counterterrorism. The Bush administration appeared to have followed this advice by putting a prominent advertising executive in charge of its public diplomacy effort.[47] The lack of success indicated by the polling results above may be partly because of shortcomings in the public diplomacy strategy but also reflects the principle that ultimately the success of public diplomacy depends on the product being sold. The U.S. posture toward the Israeli-Palestinian conflict unquestionably will con-

45. *Views of a Changing World, June 2003* (Washington: Pew Research Center for the People and the Press, 2003), p. 28.

46. The other leaders were President Bush, British Prime Minister Blair, French President Chirac, Israeli Prime Minister Sharon, Palestinian President Arafat, Saudi Crown Prince Abdallah, and United Nations Secretary General Annan. *Views of a Changing World, June 2003*, pp. 3, T153–59.

47. Charlotte Beers, formerly head of the J. Walter Thompson and Ogilvy and Mather advertising agencies, was undersecretary of state for public diplomacy and public affairs from October 2001 to March 2003.

tinue to be one of the most important influences on the opinions of Arabs and Muslims, given its demonstrated ability to stir their emotions and color their interpretations of almost anything the United States does. But also important will be whatever other U.S. policies seem pertinent to the widely held jaundiced view of the United States as anti-Muslim, imperialist, and insensitive. Justified or not, many Muslims are quick to believe the worst about what the United States does overseas.

It is in this climate that the United States initiated what is perhaps the biggest event in the Arab and Muslim worlds in a decade and probably the most significant international event since 9/11: the invasion and occupation of Iraq. The effects of this event on the roots, and the amount, of anti-U.S. terrorism will take a long time to become apparent—perhaps even a generation, because the war may turn out to be for many Arab youth the kind of generation-defining, coming-of-age event that shapes attitudes for a lifetime. How the occupation and reconstruction of Iraq are handled will have major effects on Arab and Muslim opinion. But however skillfully those tasks are performed, the war already has played into the radical Islamists' portrayal of the United States as out to kill Muslims, subjugate the ones it does not kill, plunder their wealth, and be as intent as the Israelis are on occupying Arab lands. Despite the falsity of that portrayal, the radicals' message has been reinforced by the narrowness of the regional coalition that supported the United States and the lack of any Iraqi attack to which the United States was responding—both contrasts to Operation Desert Storm, the U.S.-led reversal of Iraq's seizure of Kuwait twelve years earlier.

The prevailing Arab and Muslim opinion of the 2003 war was decidedly negative, even though Saddam Hussein was widely despised. Arab press coverage reflected the negative themes in that opinion, such as likening the war to the sacking of Baghdad by the Mongols in the thirteenth century—the first of several traumatic defeats in Arab history that were followed by extremist political responses.[48] Perhaps most telling about the radicals' exploitation of opinion on the U.S. operation was Usama bin Ladin's effort to play up the Iraq issue in audiotapes he released in November 2002 and February 2003, just as he had earlier endeavored to

---

48. Susan Sachs, "Arab Media Portray War as Killing Field," *New York Times*, April 4, 2003, p. B1.

associate himself with the Palestinian issue.[49] He knows what themes strike a chord in his audience.

It would be difficult to make a net assessment of whether Americans are more, or less, likely to fall victim to terrorism today than they were two years ago. The progress made on such matters as improving homeland defenses and dismantling al-Qaida would have to be weighed against the likelihood that the number of angry Islamists who are ready and willing to use terrorism against the United States has increased. Suffice it to say that it is uncertain whether Americans have become safer from terrorism than they were in 2001.

More useful than a net assessment are a couple of observations about which elements of counterterrorism are most likely—with additional effort—to make Americans safer during the next several years. The discussion in chapter 2 notes that each element offers diminishing returns. With the heavy attention already being devoted to defenses and to attacking the capabilities of terrorist groups (not to mention the very heavy attention to state sponsors), the biggest potential return on future investment involves the other elements of counterterrorism—particularly cutting the roots of terrorism and, especially in the near term, addressing the reasons for the hatred that motivates people to become terrorists. How many Americans die from terrorism during the next several years will depend most of all (assuming counterterrorist measures already taken stay in place) on how U.S. policies affect the level of anger of foreign Muslims against the United States.

A second and related observation is to remember one of the most basic attributes of terrorism: it is the quintessential weapon of the weak against the strong. To focus narrowly on making the weak even weaker, and to exercise our strength in the areas in which we already are overwhelmingly strong, will never be enough to stop those who wish to do us harm.

These observations lead back to the main theme of this book: that minimizing terrorism against U.S. interests depends on the health and wisdom of overall U.S. foreign policy. Countering terrorism requires not only fortitude in going after our enemies but also skill in getting foreign partners to help in that task and care in pursuing our interests overseas in ways that do not unnecessarily make enemies to begin with.

---

49. On the November tape, see James Risen and Neil MacFarquhar, "New Recording May Be Threat from bin Laden," *New York Times*, November 13, 2002, p. A1. A BBC transcript of the February tape is at news.bbc.co.uk/2/hi/middle_east/2751019.stm (October 2003).

Acknowledgments

I am indebted to many officials in the departments of Defense, Justice, State, and Treasury, and the CIA, Federal Aviation Administration, Federal Bureau of Investigation, and Immigration and Naturalization Service for their time and insights during numerous discussions. In several cases they were helpful in pointing to information that could be used in the book. As officers still serving in government, they must be thanked collectively and anonymously.

Richard Betts, Richard Haass, Brian Jenkins, and Robert Oakley read the entire manuscript and made many comments that helped to improve the final product. Stephen Cohen, Bruce Hoffman, James Lindsay, Suzanne Maloney, Michael O'Hanlon, and Meghan O'Sullivan read parts of the manuscript and offered many useful suggestions. I also profited from discussions with Daniel Benjamin, Steven Simon, and participants in the national security roundtable at Brookings.

Jason Forrester was helpful in providing some of the source material. Theresa Walker edited the manuscript, and Todd DeLelle verified it; Joanne Lockard proofread it, and Shirley Kessel prepared the index.

Abbreviations

AEDPA	Antiterrorism and Effective Death Penalty Act
ANFO	ammonium nitrate and fuel oil explosive
ATA	Antiterrorism Training Assistance program
CBRN	chemical, biological, radiological, or nuclear
CIA	Central Intelligence Agency
CIPA	Classified Information Procedures Act
CSG	Counterterrorism Security Group
DCI	director of central intelligence
DFLP	Democratic Front for the Liberation of Palestine
ELN	National Liberation Army
ETA	Basque Fatherland and Liberty
FAA	Federal Aviation Administration
FARC	Revolutionary Armed Forces of Colombia
FBI	Federal Bureau of Investigation
FTO	Foreign Terrorist Organization
GAO	General Accounting Office
G-8	Group of Eight
ICC	International Criminal Court
IEEPA	International Emergency Economic Powers Act
ILSA	Iran-Libya Sanctions Act
INR	Bureau of Intelligence and Research, Department of State
INS	Immigration and Naturalization Service
IRA	Irish Republican Army
JRA	Japanese Red Army

JSOC	Joint Special Operations Command
LTTE	Liberation Tigers of Tamil Eelam
MEK	Mujahedin-e Khalq
MRTA	Tupac Amaru Revolutionary Movement
NATO	North Atlantic Treaty Organization
NGO	nongovernmental organization
OFAC	Office of Foreign Assets Control
PFLP-GC	Popular Front for the Liberation of Palestine-General Command
PIJ	Palestine Islamic Jihad
PKK	Kurdistan Workers' Party
PLO	Palestine Liberation Organization

CHAPTER ONE

Introduction

Combating international terrorism is—now, as at times in the past—a major objective of the United States. There is broad support for this effort within different branches of government, across the political spectrum, and among the American public. The commitment to the fight against terrorism, which is often spoken of as a "war," is reflected in the statements of national leaders about the persistence and fortitude that the fight will require. President Bill Clinton stated in 1998 that the United States was in "a long, ongoing struggle between freedom and fanaticism, between the rule of law and terrorism."[1] The president later told the United Nations General Assembly that "terrorism is at the top of the American agenda—and should be at the top of the world agenda."[2] The breadth of the commitment has been reflected in the resources provided to counterterrorism, including two supplemental appropriations for that purpose during the past five years.

Opinion polls have shown the strength of public support for counterterrorism. In the most recent survey by the Chicago Council on Foreign Relations of public opinion regarding foreign affairs, Americans cited international terrorism more often than any other issue as a "critical threat to U.S. vital interests." In the same poll, 79 percent of the public (and 74 percent of a smaller sample of opinion leaders) said that combating international terrorism should be a "very important" goal of the United States.[3]

This consensus for counterterrorism is made possible by the nature and clarity of the counterterrorist mission, which involves the prevention of malicious and sometimes lethal harm against innocent and unsuspecting people. Saving innocent lives is about as noncontroversial as issues of public policy ever get. There are fewer credible grounds for challenging this counterterrorist objective than for challenging some of the other objectives on behalf of which the United States has mobilized a "war" effort. Although assertions about the magnitude of the terrorist threat are sometimes questioned, the counterterrorist goal of saving innocent lives by reducing terrorist attacks is not. This makes counterterrorism different from, for example, the "war" on illegal drugs—in which thoughtful and serious critics (albeit ones still in the minority) have challenged the goal of interdicting the supply of drugs and have even suggested legalizing much of what is now illegal.

The clear counterterrorist mission and the support it has engendered underlie significant counterterrorist success in the past several years. Partly because Congress has granted increased resources to the relevant departments and agencies to do this job, and largely because dedicated men and women in these departments and agencies share a common perception of, and commitment to, the core of that job—that is, saving lives, especially American lives—lives have been saved. Attention needs to be focused, of course, on failures and remaining shortcomings. There are many possible standards by which to measure success in counterterrorism, and by no means are all the trends in terrorism favorable. But in a business in which the most widely recognized failures are dramatic and traumatic, it is worth remembering some of what has been accomplished.

The frequency of international terrorist incidents worldwide, for example, was cut in half from its level during the mid-1980s to the rate that existed for most of the 1990s. This reduction resulted partly from broader changes in international politics. But enhanced counterterrorist efforts of the Western democracies, led by the United States, unquestionably also played a major role. Increased security cooperation among the democracies was a significant part of that and will continue to pay dividends in fighting international terrorism in the years ahead.

Another measurable success has been the solving with remarkable speed of some of the most egregious terrorist crimes against the United States in the 1990s, including the bombings of the World Trade Center in New York in 1993, the Murrah Building in Oklahoma City in 1995, and the U.S. embassies in Nairobi and Dar es Salaam in 1998. Nearly all of the perpetrators of the first two incidents have been arrested and convicted, and U.S. intelligence was able to establish with certainty within the first few days of the embassy bombings that Usama bin Ladin and his organization were responsible. These results occurred not only because of simple diligence, brilliant detective work, and good luck but also because of the U.S. investment in enhanced counterterrorist capabilities. The case against bin Ladin, for example, could not have been made with such speed and certainty if U.S. intelligence had not focused special collection and analytical efforts against him during the previous three years.

The crime-solving successes also owe much to excellent interagency cooperation—particularly between law enforcement and intelligence—which rests on a shared vision and commitment to the counterterrorist mission. That cooperation is reflected most visibly in the success during the last few years in tracking down and apprehending fugitive terrorists overseas. FBI Director Louis Freeh stated in September 1998 that in the previous decade thirteen terrorists had been brought from foreign countries to the United States to stand trial.[4]

Finally—and related most directly to the ultimate goal of saving lives—there has been significant success in disrupting terrorist operations and preventing attacks from occurring in the first place. Unfortunately, apart from a few instances such as the FBI's well-known use of an informant to stop a plot to bomb several New York City landmarks in 1993, there can be no public scorecard of this type of accomplishment. One reason is that nearly all such successes that take place overseas (as most of them do) involve intelligence sources or foreign contacts that must remain secret. Another reason is that with most successful counterterrorist operations it is difficult to say exactly how many bombs did not thereby explode and how many people did not consequently become terrorist victims. Much of the most effective disruption occurs early in the terrorist cycle of planning and preparation, before plots against particular targets are even hatched. Although accurate measurement of this type of success is infeasible, many lives—including many American lives—have unquestionably been saved as a result.

This is but a sample of U.S. counterterrorist accomplishments in the past few years. Any attempt at a more comprehensive scorecard would have to consider far more items, ranging from security countermeasures that have deterred attempts to attack U.S. government installations, to diplomatic efforts that have energized foreign officials to act more effectively against international terrorism. Stacked up against the inherently more visible counterterrorist failures, the record of success is remarkable. And the success is possible because all those involved—including law enforcement officers, intelligence officials, senior policymakers, members of

Congress, and the great majority of the American public—although they approach the topic from different perspectives, are in fundamental agreement about the goal of saving people from harm at the hands of terrorists and about the high priority that goal should have.

Beyond this basic goal and the benefit that comes from consensus on it, however, prevailing thinking in the United States about terrorism has certain less beneficial traits. One is a tendency to treat the whole subject of terrorism solely in terms of body counts and to focus not just mainly but exclusively on the number of people (and more specifically, the number of Americans) whom terrorism kills or might kill. Dead, or potentially dead, Americans are obviously the most important aspect of the problem for American policymakers but not the only aspect. Such a narrow perspective overlooks other costs of terrorism (particularly when non-American victims are involved) and other effects of measures taken to counter it. It also encourages one to forget that even the protection of innocent American lives—noble though that cause is—cannot always be an overriding objective but instead must be weighed against other important interests on behalf of which the United States accepts physical risk to its citizens. (The United States orders its military servicemen and women to do certain dangerous things, for example—thereby resulting in the loss of some innocent American lives, even just in training—because this action supports other national security interests.) There are always trade-offs, always other priorities to consider.

The narrow focus on body counts has encouraged a common view that what is really worth worrying about concerning terrorism is whatever could produce very large numbers of deaths. This in turn has led to an often sensational public discussion of seemingly ever-expanding ways in which terrorists could use chemical, biological, radiological, or nuclear (CBRN) terrorism to inflict mass casualties in the United States. This subject, particularly the possible use of biological or chemical substances, has been a hot topic in policy and serious journalism circles as well as in the mass culture. Many plots for movies, novels, and other fiction—a reliable indicator of what has captured the American public's fear or fancy—have involved terrorists using biological or other unconventional means of attack. The fictional world came full circle back to the real world when President Clinton, disturbed by a novel whose plot entails a terrorist attack on New York City with a genetically engineered virus, instructed government experts to evaluate the story's plausibility.[5]

The underlying paradigm—that terrorism is to be measured in numbers of dead Americans, and that counterterrorism is thus largely a matter of preparing for attacks (particularly CBRN attacks) that could cause many such deaths—is shared by people with widely differing appraisals of the terrorist threat and of the priority and resources that should be devoted to countering it. The Clinton administration and probably most commentators on the subject have believed that the danger of mass casualties inflicted through unconventional terrorist methods has grown in recent years, that it is now significant, and that substantial efforts to counter this particular danger are justified. Others have questioned the attention devoted to terrorism in general and have pointed out that fewer Americans die from it than drown in bathtubs (or are struck by lightning, or—choose your favorite comparison). Still others use the same yardsticks to downplay the significance of terrorism as we have known it to date but believe that the most catastrophic conceivable scenarios of CBRN terrorism deserve heightened attention even if the more conventional forms of terrorism do not.

There are real dangers in CBRN terrorism and important issues to consider in any effort to defend against it. But the intense preoccupation with this one contingency (not just CBRN attacks but mass casualty CBRN attacks) has left a host of other important issues in counterterrorism starved for attention by comparison. These include questions related not just to conventional terrorism specifically but to the effectiveness, cost, and consequences of measures taken (or that could be taken) to reduce all forms of terrorism, conventional and unconventional. Overheated rhetoric that has spun out ever more frightening and unusual ways in which terrorists might inflict large numbers of casualties has also elevated the emotional content of discussions of terrorism and as such has not promoted balanced and temperate consideration of what to do about it. Dwelling on the outer limits of potential terrorist destruction is no more helpful in formulating sound counterterrorist policy than discussions of "nuclear winter" and other dire consequences of a nuclear war were helpful in developing sound policies on strategic arms.

Another prevalent pattern of thinking and discussion about counterterrorism is a tendency toward absolute solutions and a rejection of accommodation and finesse. If counterterrorism is conceived as a war, it is a small step to conclude that in this war there is no substitute for victory and thus no room for compromise. The nature of terrorism and of how

American public attention to it has evolved in recent years have made the topic prone to this simplistic pattern of thought. Americans have had little reason to come to terms with the causes or issues associated with the terrorism that has struck closest to their homes and been emblazoned most prominently in their newspapers and their memories. They have had more reason to think of terrorism simply as an evil to be eradicated, rather than a more complex phenomenon with sides that may need to be reckoned with differently.

The only two large terrorist attacks in the United States in the 1990s—the bombings of the World Trade Center and the Murrah Building—encouraged this outlook. The cliché "senseless" that is often applied to terrorist attacks (even ones that were carefully calculated, achieved some of their aims, and therefore made sense from the terrorists' viewpoint) did seem, from the perspective of the American public, to describe these two incidents. For the terrorists, the bombings were well calculated, with carefully chosen targets and identifiable issues (an antigovernment, antilaw enforcement creed for the Oklahoma City bombers; alleged U.S. oppression of Muslims in the Middle East for the World Trade Center group) that provided the rationale for each attack. But for most Americans, it was hard to imagine how the attacks could ever have advanced even the interests on behalf of which the perpetrators claimed to be acting. Moreover, none of the terrorists involved could credibly claim to represent anyone other than themselves. They were correctly viewed not as political or social forces to be reckoned with (although the causes with which they wished to associate themselves involve such forces) but rather as monstrous vermin to be locked up or stamped out.

With many other terrorists and terrorist incidents, however, there *are* larger forces to be reckoned with. A simple, absolute, confrontational approach means the rejection of some policies that, although they might appear to be a less-than-resolute prosecution of the "war" against terrorism, would better serve not only the other U.S. interests involved but also counterterrorism itself. This pattern has been most apparent with U.S. policies toward state sponsors of terrorism, in which unyielding hard lines have sometimes been favored over strategies of engagement that—although they might be better suited to elicit further improvements in behavior from the states involved—are avoided as being soft on terrorism.

Because counterterrorism is so widely accepted as an objective in its own right, it too often is regarded *only* in its own right—as a thing apart, not as something that bumps up against other important U.S. interests and programs. To the extent that other affected interests and objectives have entered into debates on counterterrorism, they have most often been domestic concerns about how an expansion of the authorities of law enforcement agencies might affect civil liberties.[6] The effects of counterterrorist measures on foreign policy interests get discussed much less frequently. This was demonstrated, for example, during deliberations on the omnibus counterterrorist legislation that became the Antiterrorism and Effective Death Penalty Act of 1996 (AEDPA). The sharpest debates were over the domestic law enforcement provisions. Less attention was paid to the foreign provisions of the bill, even though it had diverse effects on such foreign policy matters as relationships with state sponsors, the U.S. posture toward local conflicts involving terrorist groups, and cooperation with allies on regulatory matters.

This portrayal of contemporary thought and discussion on counterterrorism—as narrowly focused, intolerant of nuance, and in general simplistic—is admittedly somewhat of a caricature, presented that way to make the points clear. One can find more sophisticated thinking about terrorism, both inside and outside government. Government officials with responsibility for counterterrorism perforce have to take a more sophisticated approach in implementing policy, because they wrestle every day with complexities and competing priorities. But the broader contours of U.S. counterterrorist policy, like the discourse on terrorism overall, do exhibit some of the traits and tendencies outlined above.

The most recent formal review of U.S. counterterrorist policy—the one undertaken by the National Commission on Terrorism, which issued its report in June 2000—was mostly in the mainstream of American thinking on the subject. The main themes of the commission's report were that terrorism poses an increasing danger to the United States; stepped-up efforts are required to meet this danger; intelligence and law enforcement agencies must use all their authorities to learn of terrorist plans and methods; the United States should "firmly target" states that support terrorists, the "full force and sweep" of law should be applied to terrorist financial and logistical activity; and more should be done to prepare for possible CBRN terrorist attacks.[7] The commission performed a valuable service in underscoring the importance of the subject, and it offered a number of sound recommendations. It left unmentioned, however, most foreign complications and consequences of executing counterterrorist policy—a detailed understanding of which is essential to fully evaluating the policy itself.

The officially expressed tenets of current U.S. counterterrorist policy, which have remained largely unchanged through several administrations, are as follows:

—Make no concessions to terrorists and strike no deals.

—Bring terrorists to justice for their crimes.

—Isolate and apply pressure on states that sponsor terrorism to force them to change their behavior.

—Bolster the counterterrorist capabilities of those countries that work with the United States and require assistance.[8]

The first three of these tenets are very much in the confrontational, fight-don't-finesse stream of American thinking about terrorism. Their thrust is to pressure and prosecute terrorists and not to do anything that could be construed as pandering to them. The longevity of these principles attests to their firm grounding in an American political, moral, and legal tradition that places high value on the rule of law and on the idea that malevolence should be punished, not rewarded. And as principles, they make a lot of sense. But their application, and specifically their application overseas, raises a myriad of questions.

What effect, for example, does observing the "no deal" dictum have on the proclivity of terrorists to conduct terrorism? Given the enormous variety of terrorist groups and objectives, are there some cases in which (even ruling out a direct caving in to terrorist coercion), agreements with terrorists might reduce terrorism, as well as advance other U.S. interests? The principle of bringing terrorists to justice raises similar questions about actual effects on terrorist behavior, as well as questions about the limits of the U.S. criminal justice system as a counterterrorist instrument. What does application of this principle mean when most of what international terrorists do operationally (including some terrorist attacks) is not a U.S. crime, when many of the most senior terrorists are out of reach, when it is difficult to construct prosecution cases against many who are caught, and when foreign governments whose cooperation is essential for catching or prosecuting a terrorist have different views on how a case should be disposed? Additional questions arise from the fact that criminal law is but one of several counterterrorist instruments that the United States has and has used. Should this one instrument take precedence over the others? Are there instances in which the others are more effective, more feasible, or less damaging? Does the application of criminal law conflict with the use of other instruments? The most obvious question about the tenet on state sponsors is whether isolation and pressure really do "force" offending states to change their behavior. There are many others, including what constitutes a "state sponsor" in the first place, what alternative postures might have at least as great a chance of eliciting improved behavior, what complications are posed by allies having different policies toward state sponsors, and what other U.S. interests are affected when the issue of terrorism sets the limits on a bilateral relationship.

The fourth tenet, on counterterrorist assistance to cooperative countries, is the most broad-minded of the four, in implicitly recognizing that counterterrorism is more than just confrontation, that the threat terrorism poses to non-Americans matters to the United States, and that U.S. counterterrorist efforts rely on foreign help. But this tenet, too, begs a host of more specific questions. How much does a state have to "work with" the United States to be considered a counterterrorist partner? What kinds of counterterrorist assistance do other governments need from the United States, and does it need from them? And what factors affect the willingness, not just the capability, of foreign governments to help the United States in counterterrorism? As with the other tenets, this is but a sample of the many germane (and collectively, very important) questions about counterterrorism applied in an international milieu.

Given such questions, the aspect of counterterrorism that has had the greatest analytic shortfalls—and where additional analysis could most help to make what has been a largely successful counterterrorist policy even better—is the fitting of counterterrorism into the larger context of U.S. foreign policy. Terrorism is primarily a foreign policy issue, as well as a national security issue. Most of the terrorism that has damaged U.S. interests is foreign, as are most of the significant terrorist threats that confront the United States today. (Seventy-eight percent of the Americans who died from terrorism during the past two decades were killed by foreign terrorists.)[9] Most of the issues underlying that terrorism are to be found overseas, as are most of the things that the United States can do to combat terrorism. In fact, almost everything the United States does in counterterrorism, beyond physical security at domestic sites, has significant foreign dimensions, even if such action involves tools or techniques not commonly thought of as foreign policy tools. And most progress in the fight against terrorism ultimately depends on the perspectives and behavior of foreign governments, groups, publics, and individuals. One implication of all this is that U.S. foreign policy overall has significant effects on counterterrorism, and, conversely, that counterterrorist measures significantly affect other U.S. interests overseas. A further implication is the central premise of this book: counterterrorist policy must be formulated as an integral part of broader U.S. foreign policy.

The purpose of this book is to explore in detail the ramifications of that statement and the policy complexities, compromises, and pitfalls that it implies. The chapters to follow discuss the means available to the United States to reduce international terrorism, the ways in which the relevant policy tools can be expected to work (or not work), and the impact that counterterrorist policies constructed in Washington tend to have at the real points of application, which are most often overseas. The picture that emerges is in large part one of inherent limits, practical difficulties, unintended side effects, and devils in the details. The book offers no "solution" to international terrorism and no single recommended redirection of counterterrorist policy that promises to greatly ameliorate the problem. The principal substantive conclusion is the more cautionary one that what may seem to be the strongest (that is, the most determined, most hard-hitting, or most inclusive) counterterrorist policies are not always the best ones. Sometimes they are not the best because of damaging effects on other U.S. interests. But often they are not even the best at reducing terrorism. When all of the foreign reactions and repercussions are taken into account, some measures taken in the name of counterterrorism—be they criminal prosecutions, economic sanctions, military strikes, or something else—may, in certain ways and in certain circumstances, be not only ineffective but counterproductive. In this regard the book is an argument that counterterrorism requires more finesse and, if not less fight, then fighting in a carefully calculated and selective way.

The book is intended as a guide to constructing and executing counterterrorist policy. It is not a comprehensive blueprint. Indeed, one of its further themes is the need to adapt counterterrorist policy to many different situations, each of which entails other policy equities and has complexities too numerous to examine in this volume.

Several counterterrorist-related issues are not analyzed in this book, not because they are unimportant but simply because they fall outside the foreign policy–oriented perspective (and most of them have been well treated elsewhere). The book will not examine domestic law enforcement and intelligence-gathering authorities and the related issues of civil liberties. It is also not primarily about physical security and other defensive countermeasures (*anti*terrorist programs, in official parlance), except for some discussion of how those countermeasures relate to broader, more active, efforts to curb terrorism (*counter*terrorist programs, the present subject). Security countermeasures have been the focus of fact-finding panels (and of programs that the panels' recommendations have spawned) following major incidents such as the bombings of Khubar Towers in 1996 and the embassies in Africa in 1998.[10] The book also does not address consequence management (that is, how to handle the aftermath of a major terrorist incident that has already occurred), which is an issue more of emergency preparedness than of combating terrorism, except for a few observations on how consequence management may relate to issues of counterterrorism itself. Finally, there is no intent to duplicate the work of the small community of scholars who have painted informed and detailed portraits of international terrorism itself.[11] There will be enough said about the size and shape of terrorist threats, however, to provide a basis for appreciating both the importance of the problem and the effectiveness of the policy responses.

Chapter 2 considers what terrorism is and why one should worry about it, as well as identifying the necessary elements of any counterterrorist policy. Chapter 3 places terrorism in the larger context of world politics, with particular attention to why the United States is a prime target and what it can (and, for the most part, cannot) do to be less of a target. Chapter 4 examines the counterterrorist instruments available to the United States and what they are capable of doing, separately and together. Chapter 5 discusses the wide variety of terrorist groups and the corresponding variety of approaches that must be used in dealing with them. Chapter 6 is a comparable discussion of how to deal with states, ranging from sponsors of terrorism to close counterterrorist partners. Handling publics—both foreign ones and the American one—is the subject of Chapter 7. Chapter 8 concludes with a recapitulation of principal lessons and a reflection on the future.

CHAPTER TWO

The Dimensions of Terrorism and Counterterrorism

Delimiting a subject is the first step in dealing with it intelligently, and this is especially true of terrorism and counterterrorism. Terrorism has often been conceived in intractably broad ways, while the costs of terrorism and the ways to combat it tend to be construed too narrowly.

What Terrorism Is

Efforts to define terrorism have consumed much ink. A recent book on terrorism, for example, devotes an entire chapter to definitions; the chapter documents previous definitional attempts by earlier scholars, some of whom gave up the effort.[1] Many students of terrorism clearly consider its definition an important and unresolved issue.[2] The concern about definitions, besides reflecting any scholar's commendable interest in being precise about one's subject matter, stems from the damage done by the countless twisted and polemical uses through the years of the term "terrorism." The one thing on which every user of the term agrees is that terrorism is bad. So it has been a catch-all pejorative, applied mainly to matters involving force or political authority in some way but sometimes applied even more broadly to just about any disliked action associated with someone else's policy agenda.

The semantic quagmire has been deepened not only by indiscriminate application of the term terrorism but also by politically inspired efforts *not* to apply it. This was most in evidence in the 1970s, when multilateral discussion of the subject in the United Nations General Assembly and elsewhere invariably bogged down amid widespread resistance to any condemnation—and hence any labeling as terrorism—of the actions of groups that had favored status as "national liberation movements" or the like. Variations on this pattern have continued to frustrate efforts to arrive at an internationally accepted definition of terrorism.

Another, less frequent, tendentious approach to defining terrorism is to define it in ways that presuppose particular policy responses. For example, define it as a crime if you want to handle it mainly as a law enforcement matter, define it as war if you intend to rely on military means, and so on. Arguing semantics as a surrogate for arguing about policy is a confusing, cumbersome, and ultimately poor way to arrive at a policy.

A reasonable definition of terrorism would capture the key elements of what those leaders and respondents to opinion polls who have expressed concern about terrorism probably have in mind, without being so broad as to include much else that is not in fact the concern of those whose job descriptions mention terrorism. As good a definition as any, given some clarification and minor modification, is the statutory one that the U.S. government uses in keeping statistics on international terrorism: terrorism, for that purpose, means "premeditated, politically motivated violence perpetrated against noncombatant targets by subnational groups or clandestine agents, usually intended to influence an audience."[3] This definition has four main elements.

The first, premeditation, means there must be an intent and prior decision to commit an act that would qualify as terrorism under the other criteria. An operation may not be executed as intended and may fail altogether, but the intent must still be there. The action is the result of someone's policy, or at least someone's decision. Terrorism is not a matter of momentary rage or impulse. It is also not a matter of accident.

The second element, political motivation, excludes criminal violence motivated by monetary gain or personal vengeance. Admittedly, these latter forms of violence often must be dealt with in the same fashion as terrorism for purposes of law enforcement and physical security. Criminal violence can also have political consequences if it is part of a larger erosion of order (as in Russia). And ordinary crime is part of the world of many terrorists, either because they practice it themselves to get money or because they cooperate with criminal organizations.[4] Terrorism is fundamentally different from these other forms of violence, however, in what gives rise to it and in how it must be countered, beyond simple physical security and police techniques. Terrorists' concerns are macroconcerns about changing a larger order; other violent criminals are focused on the microlevel of pecuniary gain and personal relationships. "Political" in this regard encompasses not just traditional left-right politics but also what are frequently described as religious motivations or social issues. What all terrorists have in common and separates them from other violent criminals is that they claim to be serving some greater good.[5]

The third element, that the targets are noncombatants, means that terrorists attack people who cannot defend themselves with violence in return. Terrorism is different from a combat operation against a military force, which can shoot back. In this regard, "noncombatant" means (and has been so interpreted for the government's statistical purposes) not just civilians but also military personnel who at the time of an incident are unarmed or off duty (as at Khubar Towers or at the U.S. Marine barracks in Beirut).

The fourth element, that the perpetrators are either subnational groups or clandestine agents, is another difference between terrorism and normal military operations. An attack by a government's duly uniformed or otherwise identifiable armed forces is not terrorism; it is war. The requirement that nongovernmental perpetrators be "groups" is one point, however, on which the statutory definition could usefully be modified. A lone individual can commit terrorism. Mir Aimal Kansi's shooting spree outside the Central Intelligence Agency was politically motivated, and the four-year manhunt for him was always rightly regarded as a counterterrorist operation. Because there was no indication that he had acted at anyone else's behest, however, his attack never counted in the government's statistics on terrorism. For the present purposes, Kansi and any others like him may be considered one-person terrorist groups.

There is one other respect in which terrorism must be conceived somewhat more broadly than the statutory definition above. Terrorism as an issue is not just a collection of incidents that have already occurred; it is at least as much a matter of what might occur in the future. The threat of a terrorist attack is itself terrorism. Moreover, the mere possibility of terrorist attacks, even without explicit threats, is a counterterrorist problem. Indeed, one of the most vexing parts of that problem concerns groups that have not yet performed terrorist operations (or maybe have not even yet become groups) but might conduct terrorist attacks in the future. There is no good way to record this potential or to quantify it, and it would be pointless to manipulate formal definitions to try to embrace it. But counterterrorist specialists must worry about it. It is part of the subject at hand.

The conception of terrorism given above excludes some things that have occasionally been labeled as "terrorism" and are themselves significant national security issues—in particular, certain possible uses by hostile regimes of their military forces, such as ballistic missiles fired at civilian populations. To be sure, there are some similarities to terrorism, involving the motivations of the perpetrators, the impact on the target populations, and even the identity of some of the governments involved. These other security issues, however, have their own communities to deal with them, both inside and outside government. The relationships between different security issues must be noted and analyzed, but that does mean expanding the concept of an issue beyond workable limits. Counterterrorist specialists have enough on their plates without, say, weighing into debates on ballistic missile defense.

The concept of terrorism delineated here is not just reflected in a U.S. statute. It is also in the mainstream of what most students of terrorism seem to have in mind, despite their collective definitional angst. Moreover, it also is in the mainstream of what modest international consensus has evolved on the subject, at least the farther one gets from large multilateral debating halls and the closer to rooms where practical cooperation takes place. The latter point is important, given the necessarily heavy U.S. dependence on foreign help for counterterrorism (discussed in chapter 6). It is also important that whatever concept of terrorism the United States uses not be capable of being twisted to apply to actions the United States itself may take in pursuit of its security interests.

About the latter point, two distinctions are critical. The first is the one between terrorism and the overt use of military force. As the world's preeminent military power, it is in the United States' interest to keep that distinction clear, but this is not just a unilateral U.S. interest. The distinction has a broader moral and legal basis, as reflected in international humanitarian law on armed conflict and its rules requiring combatants to identify themselves openly.[6] The second key distinction is between actions that are the willful result of decisions taken by governmental or group leaders, and actions that result from accidents or impulsive behavior by lower-ranking individuals. The latter are bound to happen, and have happened, in incidents involving the United States, just because of the number of circumstances in which U.S. personnel find themselves in which it could happen. One's concept of terrorism must distinguish clearly—as the definition above does—between, for example, the alleged bombing by Libyan agents of Pan Am 103 and the accidental shooting down of Iran Air 655 in the Persian Gulf by the U.S. cruiser *Vincennes*. Despite the similarities of these incidents (290 people perished in the downing of the Iranian flight in July 1988; 270 people died in the Pan Am incident in December of the same year), and even though Tehran was still calling the Iran Air incident a "crime" more than a decade later, these were fundamentally different events. One was a government's deliberate use of its agents to murder scores of innocent travelers; the other was a tragic case of mistaken identity by a warship's crew that believed itself to be in a military engagement.

The place of clandestine agents and subnational groups in the definition of terrorism requires a bit more reflection, because the United States has used many of both. Not only that, but such use has sometimes involved lethal force, and some of that force has caused civilian casualties. But the real question is whether the intentional (that is, premeditated) infliction of civilian casualties through agents or sponsored groups—say, to undermine a hostile regime—is an option that the United States can safely forswear. It is. For one thing, the irregular use of lethal force against civilians would likely be counterproductive, by enabling the targeted regime to rally popular support in the face of a presumed external threat. Just as important, such methods are contrary to what the American public would support as being consistent with American values (a key test to be applied to any proposed covert action, even ones never likely to become public knowledge). Recent operations such as air strikes against Yugoslavia or Iraq have shown the great emphasis the United States has come to place on *avoiding* civilian casualties, even as collateral damage in a conventional military campaign.[7]

The conceptual lines between terrorism and other forms of politically driven violence are blurry. They would be blurry under any definition. The definition given above is at least as clear as any other, but it still leaves uncertainty as to whether certain specific incidents are acts of terrorism. The U.S. government has an interagency panel that meets monthly to consider such incidents (for the sake only of keeping accurate statistics, not of determining policy). The panel debates such questions as whether a particular target or intended target should be considered a noncombatant. Split votes are not unusual.

Good policy on terrorism does not, however, require hand-wringing about how exactly to define it. For the great majority of counterterrorist activities, the late Justice Potter Stewart's approach toward pornography will suffice: that it is unnecessary to go to great lengths to define it, because one knows it when one sees it.[8] Even though the U.S. government itself has several other definitions of terrorism written for different purposes, definitional discussions are seldom part of intragovernmental deliberations on the subject, beyond the statistic-keeping panel just mentioned. Lawyers do sometimes have to inject precision about whether certain statutory criteria have been met. This usually revolves around not the meaning of terrorism itself, however, but rather, for example, whether certain conditions (such as U.S. citizenship of the victims) are present that would permit a criminal prosecution. In most situations in which a counterterrorist response may be required, government officials simply recognize terrorism when they see it and do what they need to do. Any uncertainty about whether a given incident is terrorism is due not to semantics but rather to incomplete information.

The blurriness of the definitional lines is a salutary reminder that terrorism is but one form of behavior along a continuum of possible political behaviors of those who strongly oppose the status quo. Alternative forms include other types of violence (such as guerrilla warfare), nonviolent but illegal actions, regular partisan or diplomatic activity, or simple expressions of opinion that never even crystallize into something as specific as a political party, resistance movement, or terrorist group. Sound counterterrorist policy does not focus narrowly only on terrorism itself (however defined) but instead takes into account that terrorists have a menu of other tactics and behaviors from which to choose, and that the conflicts underlying terrorism invariably have other dimensions that also affect U.S. interests.

The distinction between terrorism, as defined here, and other forms of violence by subnational groups is apt to be faint in the eyes of some of the people directly involved. The Muslim fight against Indian control of Kashmir, for example, has been a blend of terrorist attacks against civilians and guerrilla warfare against Indian military forces. At least some of the insurgent leaders recognize the distinction publicly and deny attacking civilians. "We are a legitimate freedom movement," said a leader of one of the larger groups, "and we do not want to be stigmatized with the terrorist label."[9] But attacks in Kashmir against cinemas and parliamentary candidates continue, along with ambushes of Indian army patrols. The course of the conflict in Kashmir, and how each side privately views it, will not depend on the exact proportion of attacks against civilian rather than military targets. Both kinds of attack are unjustified in Indian eyes;

both kinds are part of an overall struggle for self-determination, in the eyes of the militants. The selection of targets has probably depended in large part on such tactical factors as the physical vulnerabilities of the targets and the local capabilities of the groups.

For most Americans, however—and for many others—the distinction between terrorism against civilians and warfare (including guerrilla warfare) against an army entails an important moral difference. The warrior who dons a uniform is understood to be assuming certain risks that the civilian does not, and the guerrilla who fires at someone who is armed and can fire back is not regarded as embracing the same evil as one who kills the helpless and the unarmed. While the United States must be cognizant of the tendency of many to gloss over such distinctions, it should not let the distinctions be forgotten. Its message should be that terrorist techniques, in any context, are unacceptable.

Which gets to the most important point to remember about definitions: terrorism is a *method*—a particularly heinous and damaging one—rather than a set of adversaries or the causes they pursue. Terrorism is a problem of what people (or groups, or states) *do*, rather than who they are or what they are trying to achieve. (If Usama bin Ladin, for example, did not use or support terrorist methods, he would be of little concern to the United States—probably receiving only minor notice for his criticism of the Saudi government and his role in the Afghan wars.) Terrorism and our attention to it do not depend on the particular political or social values that terrorists promote or attack.[10] And counterterrorism is not a war against some particular foe; it is an effort to civilize the manner in which any political contest is waged.

Why It Matters

Terrorism has many different costs. The direct physical harm inflicted on people and property is the most obvious, but it is by no means the only, or even the most important, cost. It is the most measurable one, in that deaths and injuries can be counted and property damage can be assessed. The significance of even these direct physical costs can be a matter of debate, however, involving disagreements over exactly what should be measured and against what standard the measurement should be compared.

Start with the question of whose casualties to count. In any discussion of U.S. policy, U.S. citizens are clearly the primary concern. Six hundred and sixty-six American citizens died from international terrorism in the

1980s and 1990s.[11] During the same period 190 Americans died from domestic terrorism within the United States, for a total of 856 American deaths from terrorism during the past two decades.[12] Going beyond U.S. citizens, however, greatly expands the numbers. Deaths of all nationalities from international terrorist incidents during the same twenty years totaled 7,152. (There were also more than 31,000 wounded.) The scale of death and suffering expands yet another order of magnitude if one takes account of terrorism that is not "international" because it takes place within a single nation's borders and directly involves only that country's nationals. There are no statistics on this type of terrorism worldwide, but consider just one of the bloodier examples: Algeria. Most published estimates of the number killed in Algeria by the extremist violence that broke out in 1992 are around 100,000. Many of these deaths were not from terrorism, but many others were, including particularly gruesome mass throat-slittings in villages. Even without U.S. citizens being involved, and even without considering the indirect effects that might be more significant for U.S. interests, this scale of bloodshed warrants attention. The death toll has certainly been at least comparable to that of many natural disasters to which the United States has felt obliged to respond. The deaths in Algeria did, in fact, lead the counterterrorism community in the U.S. government to examine ways in which it might help.

Returning to the more direct U.S. concern with American casualties, what is the right frame of reference for assessing their magnitude? To any contention that the victims of terrorism are many—or few—one is entitled to ask, "compared with what?" Against some possible standards of comparison, such as highway deaths (more than 40,000 annually in the United States), the number of victims of terrorism seems tiny. And the number is less than the bathtub drownings, lightning strikes, and some other standards that critics have used. A more appropriate basis for comparison might be other deaths from foreigners committing political violence—that is, warfare. Even there, American fatalities from terrorism are minuscule compared with such major efforts as World War II (291,557 U.S. battle deaths), Korea (33,651) or Vietnam (47,378).[13]

U.S. military activity since Vietnam, however, provides a different perspective. U.S. deaths from nonterrorist hostile action in military operations during the 1980s and 1990s (including the Iranian hostage rescue attempt, peacekeeping in Lebanon, the bombing of Libya, the escorting of Kuwaiti tankers, and Operations Urgent Fury in Grenada, Just Cause in Panama, Desert Storm in the Persian Gulf, Restore Hope in Somalia, and

Uphold Democracy in Haiti) totaled 251. Even adding the 263 deaths from nonhostile causes (most of which were incurred in Desert Shield and Desert Storm) yields a total of 514, less than the number of Americans killed by terrorists during the same period. The biggest single inflictor of casualties on the U.S. military during this period was a terrorist attack: the bombing of the U.S. Marine barracks in Beirut in 1983, which killed 241. Besides, some of the other military deaths (the eight who died in the attempt to rescue hostages in Iran in 1980, and the two who were lost during the air strikes against Libya in 1986) were casualties of U.S. responses to terrorism. The nature of the hazard that Americans face in carrying out official duties overseas has evolved over the past quarter century to the point that a commission studying the U.S. overseas presence could state in 1999 that "since the end of the Vietnam War, more ambassadors have lost their lives to hostile actions than generals and admirals from the same cause."[14]

There has been an underlying evolution in how U.S. policymakers view casualties, and this also affects how the consequences of terrorism are likely to be viewed. Since Vietnam, the United States has expended lives, or put them in harm's way, more reluctantly than before. The casualties that the U.S. military suffered in Somalia in 1993 (and their graphic and wrenching coverage in the media) appear to have accentuated this trend. Survey research suggests that policymakers and other civilian and military elites may be overestimating the American public's aversion to casualties in military operations incurred in performance of missions that have at least the potential to be successful.[15] Whether or not that is true, policies and strategies, including warfighting strategies, now place very high priority on minimizing casualties. The remarkable phenomenon of a major military campaign without any U.S. battle casualties—the air war against Yugoslavia in 1999—was the apotheosis of this trend. The trend can only accentuate the significance that Americans will place on whatever American lives are lost to terrorism in the future.

Two other dimensions of what terrorists have been doing lately, or appear poised to do in the future, bear on how to think about the direct physical costs of terrorism. One is that terrorism in recent years has become increasingly lethal. More terrorist attacks than before are designed to inflict high casualties. Deaths from international terrorism more than doubled from the first half of the 1990s to the latter half of the decade, even though the number of incidents declined 19 percent. This trend is associated (as will be discussed in chapters 3 and 5) with the nature of some of the terrorist groups that have come to the fore during this time, and there is no reason to expect a reversal of the pattern anytime soon.

The other dimension is the much-ballyhooed danger of chemical, biological, radiological, or nuclear (CBRN) terrorism inflicting mass casualties. There are some legitimate reasons for concern about this to be greater now than a few years ago. The just-mentioned increased lethality of international terrorism is one reason; the more that terrorists use conventional means to kill large numbers of people, the less of a conceptual leap it is that they would use unconventional means to try to accomplish the same objective. Related to that is the increased role of small, religiously driven groups like the World Trade Center bombers, who are less likely than many larger groups (or states) to be deterred by the consequences of their own escalating violence—because they have no constituent populations to abhor their methods and no fixed assets to be the target of retaliation. The availability of materials and expertise relevant to CBRN weapons is another basis for concern. The focus has been on what might come out of the former Soviet Union (not just "loose nukes" but also substances related to biological or chemical weapons, as well as the knowledge and skills of displaced Soviet weapons scientists) and on weapons-related information that is now readily available on the Internet. Intelligence that shows some terrorist groups to be interested in CBRN capabilities is another concern. So is the precedent set by Aum Shinrikyo's attempt in 1995 to use sarin in a Tokyo subway to inflict mass casualties. Finally, the enormous public attention given to the danger of CBRN terrorism has itself probably increased the danger by pointing out to terrorists some of the possibilities—not only how such weapons might be used but also how much they frighten people.

Public discussion of CBRN terrorism has tended to stress many of these concerns—and the vulnerabilities of the United States to conceivable mass-casualty CBRN attacks—but has given less emphasis to reasons that such attacks may still be unlikely. The General Accounting Office has noted this pattern and emphasized the important distinction between conceivable terrorist threats and likely ones. The GAO observes that some of the public statements of U.S. officials about the CBRN threat have omitted important qualifications to the information they have presented.[16] The qualifications can be found not only in the classified material that the GAO reviewed but also in what is now a sizable scholarly literature on

CBRN terrorism.[17] Experts who have studied the subject in depth have found numerous reasons to doubt whether CBRN terrorism is as much a wave of the future as is widely perceived.

Some of those reasons involve technical and other difficulties that any terrorist would face in acquiring the capability to inflict mass casualties with CBRN devices or agents. Some of the substances in question (for example, virulent forms of pathogens that would be needed to make biological weapons, as distinct from other forms that might be used in the production of vaccines) are not as easy to obtain as is commonly supposed.[18] Even with raw material in hand, there are formidable challenges in converting it into an effective and deployable device. Some toxic agents are difficult to keep both potent and stable. Dissemination is a major challenge, with both biological and chemical agents. Airborne particles containing anthrax, for example, can easily be either too large or too small to infect people through inhalation. Chemical agents need to be produced in large quantities and dispersed over wide areas to have hope of causing large numbers of casualties. Given such challenges, development of a CBRN capability to cause mass casualties would require a major, sophisticated program that is well beyond the reach of the great majority of terrorist groups. Aum Shinrikyo demonstrated this point. Despite being unusually well endowed in money and technical talent and going to great lengths to develop CBRN capabilities, Aum's biological program failed completely, and its attempt to use sarin to kill hundreds or thousands on the Tokyo subway instead killed only twelve.

Other reasons for doubt involve terrorist intentions. Terrorists have generally been tactically conservative and have favored proven methods. The hazards and uncertain effects of using CBRN materials are not likely to be attractive to many of them, particularly given the proven effectiveness of old-fashioned truck bombs—in places as diverse as Beirut and Oklahoma City—in causing casualties numerous enough to be considered "mass." The fear-inducing aspect of an unseen killer like a biological pathogen may have appeal to some terrorists, but the theatrical aspect of an event that makes a loud explosion is apt to appeal to even more. Moreover, the large and well-organized groups that have the best chance of obtaining a CBRN capability are also the ones that—because they have the most to lose by outraging their constituencies or inviting forceful retaliation—are most likely to be deterred from using such a capability. Aum Shinrikyo was an exception, but what may be most significant (with more than five years having passed since the incident in the Tokyo subway) is that Aum did not start a trend.

The foregoing leads to the following conclusions about CBRN terrorism. First, it is a legitimate cause for concern; it represents one more way in which terrorism can entail major costs, and one more reason to be serious about countering it. Second, the actual threat of CBRN terrorism—which is impossible to gauge with anything approaching precision—has probably risen somewhat over the last few years but is much less than the alarmist treatment of the subject in the United States would lead one to believe. Third, actual CBRN attacks would (as with such attacks in the past) be more likely to cause few, rather than many, casualties. Their impact would be less a matter of the direct physical effects than the indirect psychological effects on the target population. How a government conditions its public to think about such an attack—a subject addressed in chapter 7—is thus critical in determining what the impact will be.

A fourth conclusion (bearing in mind the preceding two) is that the specter of CBRN terrorism should not be the main basis for shaping thinking about terrorism overall or for organizing efforts to confront it. It would be a mistake to redefine counterterrorism as a task of dealing with "catastrophic," "grand," or "super" terrorism, when in fact these labels do not represent most of the terrorism that the United States is likely to face or most of the costs that terrorism imposes on U.S. interests. A CBRN incident that causes very many casualties is the sort of high-impact, low-probability event that, because of the high impact, policy must take into account. The potentially high consequences may be reason enough to devote more attention and resources to preparing for such an event. But the low-probability aspect of the scenario should also be remembered, and the scenario should not be allowed to distort or downgrade the attention paid to more probable forms of terrorism.

Similar considerations apply to cyberterrorism, about which high concern is even more recent, and the uncertainties even greater. Some terrorist groups have indeed demonstrated considerable sophistication with computers and computer networks. Presumably some groups that lack the necessary expertise for conducting electronic sabotage could purchase it from venal and adventurous individuals. Electronic attacks to date that have been associated with terrorist groups have been few and simple, such as "spam" attacks in which large numbers of messages overload a government's server. The capability of terrorist groups to conduct electronic attacks more damaging than these incidents, or than the nonterrorist sabotage that has occasionally disabled major web sites, is more questionable. Terrorist intentions regarding cyberterrorism are even more problematic. Linking the objectives of actual terrorist groups to scenarios of electronic sabotage that would serve those objectives is conjecture.

To express such skepticism is not to deny the worth of security measures that would protect against unconventional terrorism, not only because of the potentially high consequences of such terrorism but also because many of those measures would also guard against other dangers. Almost all of the steps being taken to safeguard the nation's electronic infrastructure from terrorist groups, for example, would also help to protect it against attacks from the sources that, based on recent experience, seem to pose the main threat of electronic sabotage: individual hackers, and perhaps others driven by nonterrorist motives. This last point is true as well of some measures to defend against biological terrorism, which might include a strengthening of the public health system (including, perhaps, the additional acquisition of vaccines or antidotes) that would be needed anyway to deal effectively with natural or accidental outbreaks of disease.[19]

Terrorism in general, even when conducted with conventional means, tends to have greater psychological impact relative to the physical harm it causes than do other lethal activities, including warfare. In this regard, the earlier comparisons with casualties from past military operations understate, in a sense, the significance of terrorism. The distinction between the fair fight of an open military engagement and the unfair one of a terrorist attack on helpless victims comes into play. Ask the average American if the life of a soldier who dies in battle is worth the same as the life of a countryman who has died from terrorism, and the answer will be yes. But ask after each type of event how much shock and revulsion that American is feeling, and the reaction will be stronger after the terrorist incident. That the felt impact of terrorism tends to be disproportionate to the material damage has led some to argue that if government (and others who comment on terrorism) would only play down its significance and treat it more like ordinary crime, its actual importance and usefulness to the terrorist would lessen.[20] How government publicly portrays terrorism does indeed matter. But however much one might try to talk down the subject, some of the special shock of a terrorist attack will always be there; it is in the nature of the event.

The indirect costs of terrorism are, overall, significantly greater than the direct physical ones. The indirect costs are many and varied. They start with the fear instilled in individual citizens, and what it leads those citizens to do. The fear itself—the sheer mental discomfort—is a cost. So is the economic effect of fearful citizens not taking trips or not patronizing certain businesses. And so is the social effect of those citizens arming themselves or ostracizing fellow citizens of particular ethnic backgrounds that are associated with terrorism, or doing any of a number of other dysfunctional things that less fearful citizens would not do.

Countermeasures against terrorism are also a major indirect cost. Price tags can be placed on some of them but capture only part of the expense. What was labeled as the terrorism-related portion of the Clinton administration's budget for fiscal year 2000, for example, amounted to about $10 billion, although that is a malleable figure depending on what one includes under the counterterrorist label. To take a single type of expense as a more tractable example, the panel chaired by retired Admiral William Crowe that studied the bombings in East Africa estimated that $14 billion would be required over ten years to implement its recommendations for improving the security of U.S. diplomatic missions.[21] Federal expenditures are only part of the picture, because many security countermeasures against terrorism are expenses of state or local governments or of the private sector. And the cost of many measures cannot realistically be estimated at all, although they have innumerable second- and third-order effects that, aggregating them over the entire nation, are surely huge. Every time someone empties his pockets and takes a detour through a metal detector to gain access to a public building, there are costs—which may include not only inconvenience to an individual but also the time and thus the expense involved in transacting a piece of business.

The expenditures made in responding to a problem beg the question, of course, of how many of those expenditures have been necessary and effective. Most of the success stories about countermeasures against terrorism are fragmentary and anecdotal, and it is impossible to calculate how much trouble would have occurred in their absence. But the very fact that so many resources are consumed—however necessary or unnecessary, effective or ineffective, any particular countermeasure may be—is itself a reason for the subject to command policy attention.

With some antiterrorist programs—including some big, expensive ones—past effectiveness and the future need to spend substantial resources are easier to see. Aviation security is an example. A major success story over the past quarter century has been a drastic reduction in skyjackings. Although some other factors affecting terrorists' choice of methods have been involved, the chief reason for this welcome development has been a comprehensive security system that has made it much harder to bring on board an aircraft the wherewithal to hijack it. This system is costly, including the visible costs of x-ray machines, metal detectors, and the staff to operate them, as well as less visible costs such as lengthening the time required to make business trips. The Federal Aviation Administration is now endeavoring to reduce the vulnerability of civil aviation in the United States to the other terrorist threat it faces—in-flight bombings—by enhancing procedures for screening checked baggage on domestic flights. The FAA estimates that this single change would cost $2.8 billion over ten years.[22]

Finally, the costs of terrorism embrace a host of other political and policy effects. They include the governmental equivalent of fear among individual citizens—that is, the government does not do certain things (which could be anything from a trip by a VIP to the holding of a New Year's celebration), or does them in a more gingerly or less effective manner, than it otherwise would because of fear of terrorist attacks. Costs also include the shaping of the political environment in unfavorable ways. Any challenge to government's monopoly on the use of force (which terrorism and other politically motivated violence necessarily entails) affects citizens' views toward government itself, including the trust they place in it to meet their needs for order and security.[23]

The costs of terrorism also include major effects on U.S. foreign relations and foreign interests, especially the following.

First, the possibility of terrorist attacks inhibits, or at least complicates, a wide range of U.S. activities overseas and the maintenance of an official U.S. presence abroad. This includes the necessary concern that almost any official American working overseas must have with security (and in some places it is a high concern), which means a distraction from that official's primary job. It also includes major security-driven operational decisions having significant impact on other missions. For example, the United States vacated its embassy in Sudan in February 1996 (without formally breaking diplomatic relations) because of terrorism. The specific concerns were not only with the terrorism-related policies of the Sudanese government but also with whether U.S. officials living and working in Khartoum would be safe, given the presence in Sudan of a rogue's gallery of international terrorist groups.[24] The absence of a resident diplomatic mission in Sudan, which has the largest territory of any African country and touches on numerous conflicts in the unstable northeastern and East Africa regions, unavoidably hinders support for U.S. interests in the area. One of the things it has hindered is collection of intelligence, including intelligence on terrorist threats that could materialize elsewhere. (It is worth remembering that most of those arrested in June 1993 for plotting to bomb the Hudson River tunnels and other landmarks in New York City were Sudanese.)

A similar security-driven redeployment was the move, following the bombing of Khubar Towers in 1996, of nearly 4,000 U.S. troops in Saudi Arabia from the urban areas of Dhahran and Riyadh to the isolated (and hence less vulnerable to terrorism) Prince Sultan Air Base. The move itself cost $200 million (which the U.S. and Saudi governments agreed to split). Perhaps more costly was the impact on morale, training, and readiness of the isolation and accompanying changes in deployment policy, including the withdrawal of command sponsorship for dependents and the cutting in half (from ninety days to forty-five) of the tours of the fighter pilots who overfly Iraq.[25]

Besides the impediments to official U.S. activity, there are also security-related complications for the private sector. If a U.S. business decides to brave the risk of terrorism in making a direct investment in a hazardous area, it will have expenses for security that will be an added cost of doing business. If the risk dissuades it from making the investment, then an opportunity for making and repatriating profits, and for enhancing employment in the local economy, will have been lost.

A second cost of terrorism in terms of foreign policy is the undermining of peace processes, including ones in which the United States has invested heavily and which, absent the disruption of fresh terrorist attacks, might otherwise be ripe for progress. The series of suicide bombings in Israel by Hamas and the Palestine Islamic Jihad in early 1996, for example, caused popular support for the Labor Party's peace policies to crumble, paved the way for Benjamin Netanyahu's upset election victory, and retarded progress toward further Arab-Israeli accords. In Northern Ireland, attacks in August 1998 by the republican splinter group calling itself the "Real IRA" (especially a car bomb in Omagh that killed 29 and injured at least 330) led to an unraveling of the Good Friday peace accord to the point that, later in the year, the agreement seemed close to collapse. More recently, it has been the main IRA's retention of its means of terror (the issue of "decommissioning of arms") that has been the principal reason for setbacks in the Northern Ireland peace process, such as the temporary suspension of the provincial government in February 2000.

Third, terrorism risks enflaming other regional conflicts that are already closer to war than to peace. (The spark that ignited World War I—the assassination of Archduke Francis Ferdinand—was a terrorist act.) The hijacking by Kashmiri militants of an Indian airliner in December 1999, for example, led to a new round of recriminations between India and Pakistan and raised the temperature of their dispute. Neither this incident nor most others like it have led to a war, but they at least temporarily increase the danger of one breaking out.

Fourth, the concern of an otherwise friendly government that it will become a target of terrorism may dissuade it from cooperating with the United States. Sometimes it fears being perceived as doing Washington's bidding. Sometimes what Washington asks it to do is unpopular for other reasons. In either case the specific fear is that extreme opponents of the requested cooperation will strike back with violence. The cooperation in question may range from diplomatic support to the hosting of a military deployment.

And fifth, terrorism can destabilize friendly governments. This is much less common than merely influencing the policies of such governments, and terrorism itself seldom topples regimes. It has sometimes caused major damage to the social or economic fabric of important countries, however, and as a result has called regimes' political stamina into question. This was true of Peru at the height of Sendero Luminoso's campaign of violence, and to a lesser degree of Egypt when terrorist attacks devastated that country's economically vital tourist industry in the early 1990s.

None of these costly consequences for U.S. foreign relations results *only* from terrorism. Numerous other political, economic, military, diplomatic, and cultural dimensions of the global environment (or regional environments) also affect them. Many of these dimensions involve the United States directly or are subject to U.S. influence. This is part of why counterterrorist policy must be considered and formulated as an integral part of U.S. foreign policy. Counterterrorism is one means by which to pursue the objectives implied above—stable and cooperative allies, effective regional peace processes, and so forth—and others as well. The means, including counterterrorism, used to pursue these objectives must be employed as part of a consistent, well-integrated strategy. And in the judgment of history, whether these objectives are achieved is likely to be at least as important as the means used to achieve them.

Of course, the basic counterterrorist goal of saving lives and property from terrorist attack is a worthy end in its own right and not just a means.

Indeed, some of the objectives posited above, such as effective regional peacemaking, could just as appropriately be viewed as means toward, among other things , the end of reducing violence, especially terrorist violence. The permutations of ends and means relationships between counterterrorism and other foreign policy goals are innumerable. That is the point. Counterterrorism is part of a larger, complicated web of foreign policy endeavors and interests, with numerous trade-offs and unintended consequences that should not be ignored.

The Elements of Counterterrorist Policy

No single approach makes an effective counterterrorist policy. The policy must have several elements. In that respect, counterterrorism is similar to many other policy problems, including other ones that involve the physical well-being of the public.

Consider, for example, highway safety. Highway deaths and injuries are a function of the highways themselves, the vehicles that travel them, the traffic laws, the enforcement of those laws, and the drivers. Government can reduce deaths and injuries somewhat through action on each of these fronts (for example, installing guard rails, raising crash resistance standards for cars, lowering speed limits, putting more police on patrol, tightening licensing requirements for drivers). Each type of measure addresses only part of the problem. Each has diminishing returns. Each entails compromises with other interests, such as competing demands for use of tax dollars, ease and efficiency in getting people where they want go, or environmental concerns. So some measures are taken in all of these areas, rather than concentrating safety efforts in only one of them.

The major fronts on which the problem of terrorism can be addressed are the root conditions and issues that give rise to terrorist groups in the first place and motivate individuals to join them; the ability of such groups to conduct terrorist attacks; the intentions of groups regarding whether to launch terrorist attacks; and the defenses erected against such attacks. Each of these corresponds to a phase in the life cycle of terrorism, from simmering discontent to the conduct of an actual terrorist operation. As with the example of highway safety, important and useful work can be done on each front. But also like that example, efforts on any one front are insufficient to manage the problem and are necessarily limited by competing objectives and equities. Effective counterterrorism requires attention to all four areas.

Roots

Cutting the roots of terrorism is not commonly thought of—or officially expressed as—an element of U.S. counterterrorist policy, for a couple of reasons. One is that it is farther removed than any of the other elements from the here-and-now worries of imminent threats, actual attacks, and what to do about them. It is not as pressing a concern as other counterterrorist work, the links between roots and people actually getting killed or maimed are often tenuous and twisted, and cause-and-effect relationships are difficult to prove. The other reason is that doing something about roots involves the management of numerous foreign policy matters that are not primarily the responsibility of people who call themselves counterterrorist officials. In fact, it embraces a huge swath of U.S. foreign policy on such things as regional and local conflicts, political instability within states, and social and economic conditions in countries in which terrorist groups have arisen or could arise.

Just because a cause-and-effect relationship is difficult to measure, however, does not make it nonexistent. Conditions do matter. Terrorists and terrorist groups do not arise randomly, and they are not distributed evenly around the globe. Scholars who have examined the origins of subnational political violence in general have pointed to the need to consider the perceived deprivation and other grievances that provide motives for violence, as well as the calculations and political opportunities of dissident leaders who mobilize such discontent, to understand better when and where violence breaks out.[26]

Two types of antecedent conditions are germane to the emergence of terrorists. One consists of the issues expressed directly by the terrorists and those who sympathize with their cause: political repression, a lack of self-determination, the depravity of their rulers, or whatever. People who are angry over such issues are more likely to resort to extreme measures, including terrorism and other forms of violence, than ones who are not. Palestinian support for violence against Israeli targets, for example, has to some extent varied inversely with progress in the peace process aimed at realizing Palestinian self-determination. This is true even though most Palestinians realize that Islamist terrorism against Israel has been counterproductive in the sense of retarding the peace process itself, boosting electoral support for harder-line Israeli leaders, undermining the economy of the Occupied Territories, and causing the Palestinian Authority to be preoccupied with security rather than with political development.[27]

The other type of root condition includes the living standards and socioeconomic prospects of populations that are, or may become, the breeding stock for terrorists. Terrorism is a risky, dangerous, and very disagreeable business. Consequently, few people who have a reasonably good life will be inclined to get into that business, regardless of their political viewpoint. Those who have more desolate lives and little hope of improving them will have fewer reservations about getting into it. The majority of terrorists worldwide are young adult males, unemployed or underemployed (except by terrorist groups), with weak social and familial support, and with poor prospects for economic improvement or advancement through legitimate work. To take the Palestinian example, most members of the extremist Palestine Islamic Jihad are of low social origin and live in poverty in the bleak neighborhoods or refugee camps of the Gaza Strip.[28] Hamas also does its most successful recruiting in Gaza.

The connection between lifestyles and proclivity for terrorism has been the basis for a technique that has been used successfully to get low-level members of certain terrorist groups to leave the terrorist business and to stay out of it. Tell the young man that if he cuts all ties with his current organization he will receive assistance in finding a job and a new place to live. Tell him also that the financial assistance he receives will depend partly on his getting married (and, preferably, having children). Settling down into a stable family life with some means of supporting it makes a return to terrorism very unlikely. For such reclamation cases, the principal roots of terrorism have been severed.

Obviously not every terrorist or potential terrorist can be bought off in this way. Policy initiatives on a larger scale do affect the roots of terrorism, however. Peace processes that lead to some measure of self-determination may do so. Political reforms that open up peaceful channels for dissent may do so. And economic development that improves prospects for a better standard of living may do so. The possibilities for snipping away at the roots of terrorism in these and similar ways should be noted and made part of the policy deliberations. But there are three major constraints on what can be done by focusing on roots alone.

The first constraint is the complexity of the relationship between antecedent conditions and the emergence of terrorists. It is not nearly as simple a matter as giving disgruntled people votes or a higher income. No one has produced a good algorithm for the many variables that, in combination, breed terrorists. In the nineteenth century, terrorism frequently emerged in direct response to repression, but the correlation between political grievances and terrorism in more recent times is less obvious.[29] In fact, terrorism today appears more often in free than in unfree societies.[30] Peace processes that realize the aspirations of a majority may, at least in the short term, enflame a minority that opposes a settlement for other reasons. As for economic conditions, one must take account of cases such as the emergence of Islamic terrorist groups in some wealthy Muslim societies like Kuwait but not in some poor ones like Niger.[31] The tearing of traditional social fabrics by economic development may have actually encouraged terrorism in some places.

The second constraint is that counterterrorism can never be the only consideration, or sometimes even the chief one, in determining U.S. policies that affect the economic well-being of certain foreign populations or self-determination for certain ethnic groups. Resource limitations obviously weigh heavily on decisions regarding economic assistance. On the political side, U.S. support for even so long-standing a principle as self-determination has always been limited by a variety of interests and concerns.[32] Some things that an unhappy, potentially terrorist-breeding, population may consider unjust may be viewed by the United States, for politically and ethically sound reasons, as not unjust and in no need of major change. The likely effect on emergent terrorism should be one factor, but only one of many, that is brought to bear on policies that affect these sorts of political and economic conditions overseas.

And third, no matter how much effort is expended on cutting out roots of terrorism, there will always remain a core of incorrigibles—and these will include the terrorists about whom the United States must worry the most. They will remain because for some individuals (even though they are sane and political, not pathological), terrorism also serves personal needs—self-fulfillment, making a big mark, or following some other inner demon—that have little to do with the order of the outside world.[33] They will also remain because the viewpoints of some are simply too extreme to be accommodated. And they will remain because once terrorist groups and terrorist leaders emerge, they develop their own goals and dynamics that go beyond the causes that may have bred them in the first place. The second and third of these factors, and probably the first, apply, for example, to Usama bin Ladin and his inner circle. As former State Department counterterrorism coordinator L. Paul Bremer has put it: "There's no point in addressing the so-called root causes of bin Ladin's despair with us. We are the root cause of his terrorism. He doesn't like America. He doesn't like our society. He doesn't like what we stand for. He doesn't like our values. And short of the United States going out of existence, there's no way to deal with the root cause of his terrorism."[34]

Capabilities

Reducing the ability of terrorist groups to conduct attacks—or to conduct them effectively, or in many different places—is at the heart of U.S. counterterrorist programs (especially in the narrow sense of counterterrorism as offensive efforts against terrorists, as distinct from defensive antiterrorism programs). This work involves a variety of intelligence, legal, and other counterterrorist instruments, which will be examined in chapter 4. Reducing capabilities is properly the focus of policy toward some (though not all) of the groups that have been labeled "terrorist," as will be discussed in chapter 5. And it is the principal focus of cooperation between the United States and its counterterrorist partners, as addressed in chapter 6.

Attacking terrorist capabilities has been an effective way of reducing many brands of terrorism. Most of the successes have been unpublicized, piecemeal acts of disruption—a cell rolled up here, a terrorist operative arrested there. A more visible and dramatic example of how effective even a single blow against a group can be was the Peruvian raid in April 1997 at the Japanese ambassador's residence in Lima, which had been seized four months earlier by the Tupac Amaru Revolutionary Movement (MRTA). The raid not only freed all but one of the seventy-two remaining hostages; it also crippled the MRTA's capability to conduct further terrorism. Several of the group's most able operational leaders died in the raid.

As with the other elements of counterterrorist policy, however, a focus on degrading the capabilities of groups has inherent limitations. One limitation, as the bombing in Oklahoma City demonstrated, is that even the infliction of mass casualties does not always require much capability. That horror was accomplished with two men, a truck, and homemade fertilizer-based explosives. A prior detention (or just investigation) of Timothy McVeigh and Terry Nichols conceivably could have prevented the bombing, but there was nothing else that authorities could have done before the incident to reduce terrorist capabilities to conduct it. Infrastructures and networks of cells—which are critical to the ability of many foreign terrorist groups to conduct attacks—were not present in this case.

Too little capability for U.S. authorities to go after is one limitation; too much capability is yet another one. A major transnational terrorist group such as Lebanese Hizballah is simply too large and widespread an organization to wipe out with a few well-conceived counterterrorist operations. Using such operations to chip away at Hizballah's capabilities is, and should remain, a priority task for U.S. counterterrorism. Such operations can be effective at least in curtailing the group's ability to strike in certain regions. But such a group is not as vulnerable as a smaller one like the MRTA. It must be assumed that, even in the face of vigorous counterterrorist operations, the group will retain a capability that must be negated through the other elements of counterterrorist policy.

Intentions

There is indeed an enormous amount of terrorist capability around the world, in the hands of groups as well as hostile states, which could inflict major harm on the United States (or others) if those who control that capability decided to do so. This includes not only avowedly anti-American groups such as Lebanese Hizballah (which has not directly carried out a confirmed terrorist attack against a U.S. target since at least 1996) but also highly capable groups (such as Hamas or the Tamil Tigers) that have directed their violence elsewhere. Having less rather than more terrorism is thus a function not only of degrading terrorist capabilities but also of terrorist leaders *choosing*—for whatever reason—not to use what capabilities they have to attack. In short, terrorist intentions matter.

The intentions of terrorist groups (what the leaders of groups that already exist choose to do) raise some of the same motives and issues that are related to terrorism's roots (why terrorist groups arise in the first place and people join them). The status of the Arab-Israeli peace process, for example, affects Palestinian terrorism through its influence on intentions (decisions by Hamas's leadership on whether, when, and against what targets to stage attacks) as well as on roots (the emergence of Hamas and the Palestine Islamic Jihad in the first place and the willingness of young Palestinians to be recruited for suicide missions). Again, the issues involved go well beyond counterterrorism, and policy decisions on them necessarily also reflect other objectives and equities.

Measures that are more commonly regarded as counterterrorism also affect terrorist intentions. Punishing terrorists through prosecution or retaliatory strikes, for example, might have some deterrent effect. These instruments, and the extent to which they can be expected to deter, are discussed in chapter 4. The posture that the United States takes toward the political aspirations of groups it has officially branded as terrorist (a subject of chapter 5) affect the intentions of those groups. The same could be said of state sponsors of terrorism (addressed in chapter 6).

One of the longest standing and most frequently expressed tenets of U.S. counterterrorist policy also has to do with terrorist intentions: that the United States will make no concessions to terrorists. The principle is simple: that not rewarding terrorism will give terrorists less incentive to try using it again. It would be difficult to prove that the principle always works in practice, but some analysis has pointed to past patterns of how terrorists have attempted to coerce different states at different times to suggest it has some validity.[35]

The U.S. part of the record is clouded by the fact that the United States has at times made concessions to terrorism. The most notorious instance was the Iran-Contra affair, in which the United States secretly sold arms to Iran in 1986 as part of an effort to gain release of hostages held by Iranian-backed terrorists in Lebanon. That episode certainly tarnished the U.S. image of steadfastness against terrorism, but in some respects terrorists still have good reason to view the United States as one of their most obdurate opponents. Even Israel—despite being a famously hard-line fighter against terrorism that has refused to make concessions while hostages were held—has struck deals with extremist opponents, including ones in which large numbers of prisoners were released in return for much smaller numbers of Israeli nationals. It is with regard to the classic type of terrorist coercion—holding the target country's citizens hostage to obtain a release of prisoners—that the United States has stood most firm. Even Iran-Contra did not involve opening any U.S. jail cells.

A benefit of that firmness was seen after the MRTA's capture of the Japanese ambassador's residence in Lima. The six U.S. officials who were at the reception when the terrorists struck were among the first to be released. The kidnappers let them go five days after the incident began while keeping 140 other hostages, including many foreign officials as well as Peruvians. The MRTA probably calculated (correctly) that to the extent the United States stayed directly involved, it would counsel a harder line to the Peruvian leadership than would many of the Asian and Latin American governments whose officials the MRTA had also seized.

An obvious limitation to firmness in any hostage incident is the immediate risk to the lives of the hostages. No government, the United States included, can promise itself or anyone else that it would never, under any circumstances, make concessions to save the lives of its citizens. Its management of the incident would have to take into account the magnitude and credibility of the harm being threatened, along with its own longer-term credibility and reputation. Accordingly, the rhetorical emphasis of this aspect of U.S. counterterrorist policy perhaps should be less on "no concessions" and more on the slightly more flexible "terrorism will not be rewarded." A concession made in the face of an immediate threat of great harm need not constitute a reward unless the terrorists were demanding some irreversible act, and there are few of those (even released prisoners can be recaptured).[36] Once the immediate peril is over, the terrorists can be hunted to the ends of the earth and appropriate action taken to ensure that when the books on the incident are closed, it will not count as a reward for terrorism.[37] Certainly no government need feel obliged to observe commitments made under duress. Consider the repatriation of the crew of the USS *Pueblo*, a U.S. Navy ship that North Korea seized in 1968; the United States repudiated the "admission" (of violating territorial waters) demanded by the North Koreans even as it was signing it.

A broader limitation on how much can be expected from this kind of firmness is that the classic hostage-and-specific-demand incident is simply not as big a part of international terrorism as it used to be. Although U.S. citizens have been bit players in a few such incidents in recent years (such as the Lima event and the hijacking of the Air India jet), U.S. crisis managers have not for a long time had to wrestle directly with dramatic, well-publicized, hostage situations in which lives are staked against a need to stay tough on terrorism. The great majority of terrorist attacks today (and most of the best-known recent incidents) involve terrorists going right out and killing people, rather than making specific demands and putting themselves in a position to kill people if the demands are not met. The very U.S. firmness discussed above (and stronger backbones grown by some other governments) probably has had something to do with this, and to that extent it is another endorsement for a policy of firmness. But this pattern has also had other causes, including security measures (such as the antihijacking safeguards in civil aviation) and developments in the motives of terrorists that are noted in the next chapter.

Terrorists who suddenly detonate a bomb may still be looking for a concession, even though there are no apparent hostages and no explicit negotiations. Hizballah's bombings of the U.S. and French embassies in Beirut in April 1983, for example, and its attacks later that year on the U.S. Marine barracks and a French military base, were aimed largely at expelling from Lebanon the multilateral peacekeeping force of which the U.S. and French contingents were a part. In such circumstances, the United

States is in a sort of bargaining relationship with the terrorists, whether or not it wants to be or says it is. It cannot ignore the public demands of the terrorist group, and its own policies regarding the subject matter of those demands are in effect part of the negotiation.[38] So there is yet an opportunity to demonstrate firmness, but one with even more potential problems and complications than in the traditional hostage incident. Refusal to act the way the terrorists want not only risks further attacks along the lines of what has already occurred (which was certainly an implicit threat in Lebanon) but also may mean continuing a policy that is unwise or unsustainable for other reasons. The alternative is to do what the terrorists would wish (which the United States and its allies did in Lebanon, pulling their troops out in early 1984), which—regardless of how the move is billed and the other reasons for it—may be seen as a concession to terrorism.

Other terrorist attacks are conducted without any particular concessions in mind; the destruction is more of an end in itself, motivated by hatred or revenge. With those who would wage this brand of terrorism (exemplified by the bombing of the World Trade Center by Ramzi Yousef's group), there is no way to influence intentions over the long term—whether by being steadfast in not rewarding terrorism, or being forceful in punishing it, or through any other means. The incorrigibility of such people is the main limitation of this element of counterterrorism. An ad hoc terrorist such as Yousef, who was not part of any permanent organization, is particularly unlikely to be deterred for long or to be coaxed on to a less violent path. Yousef was out to kill as many Americans as he could, he and his colleagues did not have fixed assets that could be bombed in retaliation, and he showed no sign of caring about his cohorts being caught and prosecuted.

Defenses

The one way in which the bin Ladins and Yousefs can be deterred is at the short-term, tactical level, by erecting security countermeasures that persuade them that a contemplated attack would fail. Some security measures that the United States has used overseas have had this effect. In at least one recent instance, a plot to attack a U.S. embassy was called off in the planning stage because the terrorists concluded that the security they had observed there could not be overcome. Antiterrorist defenses, therefore, are another way to influence terrorist intentions.

Physical defenses are also an element in their own right in saving lives from terrorism, even where they do not deter. And lives are saved even when attacks are not defeated entirely. The security measures at Khubar Towers, which kept the explosive-laden truck from penetrating the perimeter of the compound, prevented a death toll that would have far exceeded the nineteen U.S. servicemen who were killed. Similarly, in both Nairobi and Dar es Salaam in 1998, physical barriers and the refusal of guards to admit onto embassy grounds the trucks used by the terrorists greatly minimized U.S. casualties. Besides, the bigger the bomb the terrorists have to build, and the larger and more complex their operation has to become to defeat the defenses, the greater the chance that their operation will be compromised and discovered.

Antiterrorist defenses constitute a very large proportion of the U.S. fight against terrorism, certainly in resources but also in leadership attention. At the state and local level and in the private sector defenses are virtually the entire effort. Efforts at the federal level include defensive measures at both home and abroad. The two major overseas defensive programs— protection for U.S. diplomatic and military installations—have each received renewed emphasis in response to attacks in recent years.

On the diplomatic side, the bombings in Nairobi and Dar es Salaam highlighted the failure to meet standards for embassy security that had been established after earlier tragedies in Lebanon (the so-called Inman standards, after Admiral Bobby R. Inman, who chaired an Advisory Panel on Overseas Security in 1985). As of mid-1999, 229 of the 260 U.S. diplomatic posts worldwide still lacked the 100-foot setback (from the compound perimeter) specified in the Inman standards.[39] The funding level that the Crowe panel recommended is unlikely to be reached, but the Clinton administration in its last year budgeted more than $1.1 billion for embassy security in fiscal year 2001 and requested $3.4 billion in advance appropriations for fiscal years 2002 through 2005.[40]

Protection for military forces received a comparable fillip from the attack at Khubar Towers. In September 1996, Secretary of Defense William Perry issued a fresh directive on defending against terrorism (DoD Directive 2000.12) and initiated numerous enhancements to U.S. force protection efforts. A new section, headed by a general officer, within the Joint Staff was given responsibility for coordinating and promoting the military's antiterrorism efforts, promulgating doctrine on the subject, implementing a comprehensive training program, and conducting vulnerability assessments of installations around the world. The annual military antiterrorist budget is now about $3.5 billion.

The cost of defensive measures—particularly in dollars but also in re-strictions on freedom of movement—is their main limitation. Compre-hensive protection for everything in the terrorists' sights would be pro-hibitively expensive. As the Crowe panel acknowledged, "We understand that there will never be enough money to do all that should be done. We will have to live with partial solutions and, in turn, a high level of threat and vulnerability for quite some time."[41] A related limitation is that ter-rorists sometimes respond to security countermeasures by shifting their attention to more vulnerable targets. In some cases this means—given the terrorists' own limitations on where and how they can operate—that no attack occurs. But in others it means that a target with less robust defenses gets hit. The shift can be from one specific target to another (for example, from an embassy in South Asia to one in Africa), or from a whole category of targets to a different category that tends to be less well defended (for example, from military bases to private businesses).[42]

Another limitation is that some terrorists are remarkably resourceful in adapting to, and overcoming, antiterrorist defenses. The Irish Republican Army (IRA), for example, has cleverly changed its methods for detonating bombs, using devices ranging from radar guns to photographic flash equip-ment, to stay ahead of the British use of electronic measures to prevent detonations.[43] Yousef demonstrated comparable operational cleverness with the method he devised for bombing U.S. airliners over the Pacific (and which he successfully tested, with a small amount of explosive, on a Philippine Airlines plane in December 1994). The technique involved bring-ing on board innocuous-looking items (including a prepared digital watch and a bottle for contact lens solution that really contained a liquid explo-sive), assembling them in a lavatory, and leaving the assembled device hidden on the aircraft when the terrorist got off at an intermediate stop.

Such ingenuity points to the limitations of using technology to defend against terrorism. It is not as if good minds have not been put on the problem. The federal government has a Technical Support Working Group that oversees a vigorous program of research, development, and rapid prototyping of antiterrorist technologies; the program has grown rapidly in recent years to reach an annual budget of close to $40 million. The Defense Science Board, an advisory body that includes some of the nation's leaders in applying technology to problems of national security, devoted its 1997 summer study to transnational threats, including terrorism, and how to respond to them.[44] The threat itself is not, at bottom, technological. Technology is useful in limited ways in defending against it but is not itself a solution.

All counterterrorist work—regardless of the instruments employed, the particular partners enlisted, or the specific enemies confronted—involves one or more of the elements just described. The limitations of each are patent; the need to address all of them together is strong. But the challenges facing U.S. counterterrorist policy reflect not just the limitations of counterterrorism itself. That policy must be adapted to a real world in which both the terrorist threat and the place of the United States as a terrorist target have evolved in important ways. It is that world that the next chapter addresses.

CHAPTER THREE

Terrorism, the United States, and the World Order

Competing grand visions of global politics since the end of the cold war have yet to develop into a consensus. The place of international terrorism in the current world order, however, is somewhat easier to describe. This chapter looks at how international terrorism at the outset of the third millennium has been shaped by larger political events, how terrorism does (or does not) play a part in global political competition, and particularly how it bears on the preeminent position that the United States occupies. It is a wide-angle snapshot taken in the knowledge that counterterrorism is but one part of a broader effort to maintain national security.

Old Problems in a New Era

A frequently voiced post–cold war catechism is that terrorism is one of several transnational issues (along with narcotics trafficking, proliferation of advanced weapons, and certain other problems) that must receive more attention now that the Soviet military and political threat has dissipated. Naturally, the passing of any concern that was as dominant and long-standing as the competition with the USSR will inevitably mean a release of time if not resources to devote to other matters. But terrorism itself (considering for a moment the issue as a whole and not its subelements) did not become a significantly greater problem once the Berlin Wall and the Soviet Union collapsed. Statistics on international terrorism for the decades before and after those epochal events bear this out. In the 1980s there had been 5,431 international terrorist incidents, in which 4,684 people died; the figures for the 1990s were 3,824 incidents and 2,468 deaths. The United States also devoted considerable policy attention to terrorism while it was still waging the cold war. Such attention in the 1980s was manifested in special studies like those of the Inman panel and a task force on terrorism chaired by then vice president Bush.[1] Partly in response to the recommendations of the Bush group, the Central Intelligence Agency created its DCI Counterterrorist Center in 1986, consolidating work that had been done in a more disaggregated fashion for many years earlier.

Although the overall magnitude of the problem may not have expanded, international terrorism has changed in some significant ways during the past decade. The principal change associated with the collapse of the USSR and the end of the cold war has been the precipitous decline of leftist terrorist groups. Most notable among these were such once-lethal European organizations as the Red Brigades in Italy, the Red Army Faction in Germany, Direct Action in France, and the Communist Combatant Cells in Belgium. The decline of these groups actually began before the end of the cold war, thanks to more effective police work (sometimes using expanded legal authorities) by several European states.[2] But the West's winning of that war sealed their fate. The groups lost both a credible ideology and the material support they had received from communist states to the East. As an unusual punctuation mark to this development, one of the groups took the trouble of formally announcing its demise. In a letter to news media in April 1998, the Red Army Faction (which had not carried out a terrorist attack in five years) declared that it was "stuck in a dead end," that it was ending its project, and that the group was now history.

The cold war's end had ripple effects for some other terrorist groups, even ones that did not call themselves communist or have material links to Soviet bloc states. The Irish Republican Army, for example, had considered itself part of a larger "anti-imperialist struggle"; when that struggle waned, the IRA's foreign friends began questioning why its own campaign of violence should continue. In addition, the IRA perceived Britain no longer to have a strategic stake in Northern Ireland (which, the reasoning went, had helped to keep in check a neutral Republic of Ireland that might otherwise have caused problems in Britain's backyard while it and NATO confronted the Warsaw Pact). In the IRA's perception, London should have become more willing than before to reach a deal on Northern Ireland that would be acceptable to the IRA. For both of these reasons, the IRA became more inclined to try a cease-fire and see what it could accomplish on a political track rather than a terrorist one.[3]

A further beneficial effect of the USSR's collapse was retrenchment by some Soviet client states that have themselves been sponsors of terrorism. The withdrawal of Soviet support led these regimes, for economic as well as political reasons, to cut significantly their support to terrorists. One such state was Cuba, which became too broke to do just about anything overseas, including terrorism. Another was Syria, which continues to host several terrorist groups as leverage against Israel but has not been directly involved in any terrorist attacks since the late 1980s. A third was South Yemen, which went out of existence altogether when it merged with the more moderate North Yemen in 1990.

An offsetting negative effect of the Soviet implosion, the end of the cold war, and the related events in eastern Europe has been the eruption into violence—including terrorism—of a host of ethnic or religiously based conflicts throughout the former Soviet empire that now-dissolved controls had previously kept in check. The immediate issues in these conflicts are local, but many of them have transnational dimensions that are cause for wider worry. Terrorism has rocked several of the now-independent republics of the former Soviet Union, from Tajikistan to Georgia. Georgia's stability, for example, has been brought into question by terrorist attempts to assassinate President Edward Shevardnadze, on whom the United States has placed considerable importance as an island of strength and reason in the turbulent Caucasus. Terrorism has played a role in inter-republic conflicts, including the one between Armenia and Azerbaijan. And then there is the Chechen terrorism that has appeared not only in Chechnya but elsewhere in the Russian Federation. Some of the Chechen violence involves radical Islamic elements with links to like-minded extremists in South Asia and elsewhere who are also strongly anti-American.

Conflict in Yugoslavia—the other multiethnic, now disintegrated, formerly communist state—has also had an external terrorist dimension. The war in Bosnia, and to a lesser extent the subsequent conflict in Kosovo, became popular jihads that attracted radical Islamists from diverse countries to fight on the Muslim side. Some had governmental sponsorship (specifically that of Iran). Others went in units organized by extremist groups that have committed terrorism. Most went as freelancers, although many of them have had ties to extremist groups in South Asia, the Middle East, or elsewhere.

Throughout eastern Europe, as in the former Soviet Union, the loosening or breakdown of formerly tight internal security controls enhanced the organizational and operational opportunities for foreign terrorist groups. Even where violence did not erupt and terrorist attacks did not occur, those groups were better able than in the days of the old communist empire to go about their quiet business of building cells and doing the work that such cells do. Those opportunities opened up widest in Albania. One reason was that Albania experienced the most precipitous change in its security environment: from what was once a rigidly controlled, self-isolated Stalinist state to what at times has been outright anarchy (particularly after the collapse of financial pyramid schemes in the spring of 1997). Another reason is that Albania—the only majority Muslim country among the former communist states of eastern Europe—has been a magnet for Islamic extremists owing to the religious factor. Postcommunist Albania has embraced its Islamic heritage, joining the Organization of the Islamic Conference and welcoming Islamic nongovernmental organizations that have performed much-needed charitable and reconstruction work. The downside has been that some of these NGOs have also served as vehicles for violent extremists. The danger was demonstrated in August 1998 (the month of the bombings in East Africa) when police raids broke up an apparent Islamist plot to attack the U.S. embassy in Tirana.[4]

These events associated with the collapse of communism have underlain some of the principal changes in the face of international terrorism in recent years. There have been other changes, with other causes. Any picture of international terrorism is only a snapshot of a phenomenon that is constantly evolving, with some parts of it waxing and other parts waning. A simplified picture of it at the millennium's beginning would show the following parts.

First, there are still some leftist groups that warrant attention, despite the depletion of their ranks worldwide. Among those that have attacked American interests, these include a few in Europe, particularly November 17 in Greece. They also include Latin American groups, especially the large Colombian organizations—the Revolutionary Armed Forces of Colombia (FARC) and the National Liberation Army (ELN)—and the remains of Sendero Luminoso in Peru. These groups may lack both an external patron (some never depended on one anyway) and a resonant ideology, but a mix of die-hard beliefs, organizational inertia, governmental weaknesses, and diversification into criminal activity has kept them going.

Second, there are remnants of what was, a quarter century ago, the main face of international terrorism: secular Palestinian militants opposed to Israel. The watershed event for this segment of the terrorist world was the Declaration of Principles that Israel and the Palestine Liberation Organization (PLO) signed in 1993. Bumpy though the subsequent peace process has been, this agreement and later accords leading to establishment of the Palestinian Authority took the mainstream of the PLO, including the groups responsive in some degree to Yasir Arafat's leadership, out of the terrorist business. There remain a few extreme secular groups opposed to the Arab-Israeli peace process, such as the Popular Front for the Liberation of Palestine—General Command (PFLP-GC) and the ever-notorious Abu Nidal Organization.

Third, there are ethnic separatist organizations that use terrorism as one of several methods to pursue autonomy or independence. These groups have not figured prominently in American discussions of terrorism, but (as will be discussed in chapter 5) they account for a large proportion of the terrorist capability and activity worldwide. Examples are the Kurdistan Workers' Party (PKK), the Liberation Tigers of Tamil Eelam (LTTE) and Basque Fatherland and Liberty (ETA).

Finally, there is the category that has become the biggest concern: religiously based terrorist groups. This means religion not just as one characteristic that distinguishes the group from its enemies (as might be said of the Irish Catholic IRA or the Hindu Tamil LTTE), but as an avowed *raison d'etre* and principal motivator. Religious groups have constituted a larger proportion of terrorist groups generally, and have been responsible for a larger proportion of terrorist incidents, during the past decade than they did in the 1980s.[5] The category includes groups identified with various major religions (such as the Jewish extremist groups Kach and Kahane Chai) as well as idiosyncratic cults (specifically Aum Shinrikyo in Japan). But by far the most significant segment of this category—by several measures, including terrorist capabilities, level of concern in the United States, and actual degree of threat—consists of terrorist groups claiming to act in the name of Islam.

Islamist terrorism has gained such prominence for several reasons. Its rise has accompanied the decline of other brands of terrorism, in a number of respects. As leftist terrorism causes less worry, there is understandably more worry about the Islamic variety. The discrediting of leftist ideologies within the Muslim world, like the earlier loss of respect for Nasserite pan-Arabism in the Arab portion of that world, has also meant that political Islam has become the main vehicle there for expression—including violent expression—of strongly held dissent. A young man in a Muslim country who wants to make a forceful statement against the existing order has few avenues for doing so except through membership in a radical Islamic group. The removal from combat of Arafat's Fatah and other mainstream secular Palestinian groups after the Declaration of Principles left a banner of violent opposition to Israel that was picked up by Islamists, particularly those in Hamas, who had begun stirring several years earlier. All of this ideological movement has occurred in a Muslim world that, in addition to the Arab-Israeli dispute, has had no shortage of both violent interstate conflicts and acute issues of governmental legitimacy in major countries.

A more specific cause of the rise of Islamic terrorism was the Iranian revolution of 1979. Only a fraction of Islamic terrorism today can be blamed even indirectly on Iran, but the clerical regime's revolutionary zeal and view of terrorism as an instrument of statecraft helped to stimulate the eruption of Islamist terror in the 1980s. Certainly the establishment of Hizballah and its commission of infamous terrorist acts in Lebanon—including bombings in Beirut and seizing of Western hostages—reflected policies and politics in Tehran. Although Iranian attitudes and politics have evolved significantly since then, Iran remained during the 1990s the most able and active state sponsor of terrorism.

Another antecedent of the upsurge in Islamic terrorism—and one whose aftereffects are even more directly related to current terrorist threats—was the mujaheddin war against the Soviets and Soviet-sponsored regimes in Afghanistan. The Afghan war stimulated Islamic terrorism in three ways. First, it provided terrorist-related skills and experience (in the use of firearms and explosives) to large numbers of non-Afghan militants (often called "Arab Afghans," although not all were Arabs) who came to fight in what was the most important jihad of their lifetimes. Second, the war provided these fighters of many different nationalities the ultimate extremist networking opportunity. The connections thus established, and the influence that certain leaders established over followers from different lands, were reflected in later transnational terrorist organizations. And third, the extremists drew from the heady accomplishment of a ragtag, Koran-wielding resistance defeating a superpower (Soviet forces left Afghanistan in 1989, and the Soviet-supported Najibullah regime fell in 1992) the lesson that violence and Islam could defeat anyone, including the remaining superpower. Afghanistan is one place where the USSR's efforts during the cold war to maintain or extend its influence beyond its borders have affected current international terrorism at least as much as the end of the cold war has.

Afghanistan remains an incubator of Islamic terrorists. Najibullah's fall did not end the civil war, and the spillover effects that fighting in Afghanistan has had on the larger terrorist world continue. The advent of the fundamentalist Taliban movement and its seizure of all but a northern slice of Afghanistan by 1996 have only made matters worse. The Taliban is more extreme in its views and policies than any other Islamic regime and more closely connected to active international terrorists than any other regime, Islamic or otherwise. Moreover, the Taliban's dependence on non-Afghan help to prosecute its war against opponents in northern Afghanistan leads it to maintain a home for, and alliance with, Usama bin Ladin and other foreign terrorists. Participation in that war, and training in camps in Taliban-controlled territory, continue to be preparatory experiences for terrorists who have their eyes on targets far from Afghanistan.[6]

The prominence of the Islamic variety of terrorism is also related to the larger question of the Muslim world's overall relationship with the West and the role of violence in that relationship—a subject that has stirred intellectual controversy and will be addressed in the next section. Before turning to that, however, there are two other global developments in recent years that, while unconnected to the end of the cold war, have also shaped the face of modern international terrorism and how terrorists operate.

One is the diffusion of information technology and advanced communications. This has, for one thing, affected the terrorists' menu of possible methods of operations. The concern about "cyberterrorism" is so recent because both the accessibility of the relevant technology and the range of systems potentially vulnerable to electronic attack have expanded so fast. The concern about chemical, biological, radiological, or nuclear (CBRN) terrorism is based partly on the increased ease of finding pertinent technical information on an exponentially expanding Internet. The principal impact of the new electronic technologies, however, has not been to move the terrorists toward more exotic methods of attack but rather—as with most legitimate businesses—to improve the efficiency of all of their activities, including mundane administrative ones. Computers and satellite phones have become standard equipment in terrorist groups. This has, fortunately, introduced some vulnerabilities that counterterrorist investigators can exploit. A captured computer disk or hard drive is sometimes a valuable source of information about terrorist plans and capabilities. On balance, however, the new electronic technologies have aided the terrorists. They have facilitated the conduct and control of operations over long distances while minimizing the need for a large, fixed, physical presence. The headquarters element of even a major terrorist group today may consist of the leader, a few bodyguards and acolytes, and a satellite telephone. Such an element is highly mobile, can operate from remote areas, and consequently is hard to find and to track.

Another global development that has aided terrorists in similar ways is increased movement, and ease of movement, across international boundaries. This has partly resulted from the breakdown of restrictions on travel in the former communist world. It has also partly involved the deliberate dismantling of border controls to facilitate commerce and economic integration—particularly the Schengen agreement that has ended such controls among several European states. Moreover, the sheer volume of international travel that has accompanied globalization, with more planes flying to more places and more people flying on them, has made it easier for terrorists to slip into the bigger stream. What is good for international business executives is, unfortunately, also good for international terrorists.

The terrorists' greater ability to operate over long distances has manifested itself in two ways. The first has been the building by several terrorist groups of globe-circling infrastructures. Lebanese Hizballah now has cells on every continent except Antarctica. Several Sunni groups, such as bin Ladin's al-Qaida organization, the Egyptian al-Gama'at al-Islamiyya, and Palestinian Hamas, have shown similar geographic growth in recent years. Overseas cells sometimes are based in expatriate communities; Hizballah's presence in South America, for example, is anchored in a large cluster of mostly Shia Arabs who live in the area where the borders of Argentina, Brazil, and Paraguay converge. The cells in such networks perform a variety of functions, including recruitment, raising of money, procurement, movement of operatives, and other support tasks such as production of false documents. The infrastructures are also available to support terrorist operations far removed from the home base. Hizballah demonstrated this ability when it bombed the Israeli embassy in Buenos Aires in 1992 and a Jewish cultural center in the same city in 1994, two major operations that killed 116 people and were conducted on short notice in retaliation for Israeli actions that had taken place thousands of miles away in the Middle East.

The other manifestation of modern globalized international terrorism has been the rise of ad hoc terrorists—small cabals of extremists who do not belong to any larger, established, previously known group. Although the individuals involved may gravitate toward particular political or spiritual leaders, they do not become a group until they become one for the purpose of conducting a particular terrorist operation. After the operation, they may dissolve and disperse. The archetype of this breed of terrorism was the group that bombed the World Trade Center in 1993. The men who conducted this attack were followers to varying degrees of the "Blind Sheik," Umar Abd al-Rahman, an Egyptian cleric who preached his extreme views in mosques in the New York City area. But they had come to the United States as individuals and did not coalesce until the Trade Center bombing itself began to be plotted. The global trends just mentioned facilitate this kind of terrorism by helping like-minded extremists to find each other without the aid of a larger organization and by enabling individual extremists with the necessary leadership and operational skills to travel to where the operational opportunities are. The travels and personal history of Ramzi Yousef—the mastermind of the Trade Center bombing—demonstrate the transnational aspect of this phenomenon. Yousef was of Palestinian extraction, was raised in Kuwait, acquired some of his skills at a camp in Afghanistan, received formal education at a technical institute in Britain, came to New York and organized the Trade Center bombing, left the United States on the day of the attack, and later turned up in the Philippines, where he prepared his planned attack on airliners. He was finally captured in Pakistan, where he was working on other terrorist operations in south and southeastern Asia.

This section has pointed to several aspects of modern international terrorism and its place on the larger world stage. First, it is constantly changing. The end of the cold war has indeed altered it in several ways—mostly favorable, some unfavorable—but that is just one of the more recent chapters in a long-running story. Second, the threat is a supple and nimble one that adapts to larger global trends (and thus so must counterterrorism, particularly by being as geographically far-flung as the terrorists are). Third, the religious extremism, and more particularly the radical Islamic variety of it, that has garnered much of the attention toward terrorism has indeed become the single most threatening facet of it. But fourth, international terrorism is still a highly variegated phenomenon, with many different roots, ideologies, and objectives, and connections to many different conflicts around the world. This means any generalization about what makes terrorists tick and what they are out to achieve will have limited applicability. It also means that any preoccupation with the prevailing threat *du jour* risks giving insufficient attention to other varieties that could rise up and strike. A fifth and related point is that even within a single variety of terrorism such as the radical Islamists, the threat has become very diffuse. The people calling the shots (and the bombs) are more numerous and thus harder to identify in advance. With the rise of ad hoc terrorism, threats lurk not only in states or even in established nonstate organizations but also in individuals and tiny protogroups.

The Absence of a Terrorist International

The main change in the world order associated with the ending of the cold war is that the United States has become the only remaining superpower. Indeed, debates in the United States over grand strategy have centered around this preeminence—how long it will last, and how to take advantage of it as long as it does. So a further terrorist-related question about the current world order (besides what is new and different about terrorism itself) is, what does this preeminence mean in the context of a terrorism-prone world? Is there anything about the position of the United States as first among unequals that one should keep in mind while thinking about terrorist threats and responding to them? There are two such things.

The first is that current international terrorism—although it has certainly evolved in some worrisome ways—does not add to the power of any adversary that is challenging the United States for world predominance or that has a realistic chance of revising the global hierarchy of power. That is not a trivial statement; it would not have been true during the cold war. The documentary evidence about the clandestine activities of the USSR and its satellites (particularly East Germany) that has become available in the past decade has shown that assistance to terrorist groups (and to revolutionary socialist organizations that conducted terrorism, among other things) was a significant instrument of Soviet statecraft.[7] Some of the accusations made in the 1970s and 1980s about Moscow's hand in terrorism were exaggerated; the Soviets aided some terrorists, not all of them. Nonetheless, one valid reason (among several) for being concerned about some of the terrorism during the latter part of the cold war was that it was designed to advance the influence of the communist superpower at the expense of the West. There is no comparable situation now.

There are plenty of reasons to worry about current international terrorism (as enumerated in chapter 2), but checking the influence of a rival major power is not one of them.

There is no hint of support for terrorism by any of the power centers that come closest to the United States in the global hierarchy (present-day Russia, China, the European Union, Japan). The closest thing to a major power supporting terrorism is India, because of what it may be doing in Pakistan in reprisal for Pakistani-supported activity in Kashmir. But whatever it is doing is on a small scale and aimed solely at Pakistan, not at U.S. power and influence. Meanwhile, the remaining leftist terrorist groups are nobody's client. Some of them, like Sendero Luminoso, are vociferously autarchic.

There are still state sponsors of terrorism, but they are all at least another tier lower in the global hierarchy of power. They are a handful of countries that have often been labeled "rogue states"—a term that has been replaced in the State Department's official lexicon by "states of concern."[8] They may be trying to change the status quo, but only within their regions, not as challengers to the U. S. position of global predominance.[9]

Moreover, the overall part that state sponsorship plays in international terrorism has been declining. The chief reasons for this are the receding of the end-of-colonialism era of "national liberation movements," which had lent respectability to some uses of terrorism; the previously mentioned disappearance of Soviet support for some state sponsors; the passing of the true revolutionary moment—the time of zeal for exporting revolution—of some regimes; the recognition by those regimes of the costs and negative consequences of their earlier support for terrorism; and their further recognition, particularly in an era of globalization, that integration and accommodation with the West offer a more promising road to strength and stability than does confrontation.[10] There remains, however, the question of whether militant Islam—in the name of which so much current terrorism is committed—collectively constitutes a major challenger to the United States, even though it does not manifest itself in state power outside of Iran, Sudan, and Afghanistan. Is either Islam as a whole, or the more militant side of it, a force that has a global rather than merely a regional reach, that is capable of appreciably reducing U.S. influence in much of the world, and whose own influence is expanded through terrorism? In other words, does Islamist terrorism represent something powerful, hostile, and unified (even if it is not a state), the containment of which is an additional reason to counter the terrorism?

Islamist terrorism is sometimes perceived in this way in the United States, for several reasons. The fact that so much anti-American terrorism is of this one type leads naturally to the thought that the fight against this terrorism is ultimately a fight against some one opposing force (which would make it similar to the cold war, which, despite all the local variations on different fronts of that war, was ultimately a struggle for worldwide influence between Moscow and the West). Islamists were responsible for all of the major anti-U.S. terrorist attacks in the 1990s except Oklahoma City and for several of the most salient ones of the 1980s. The emergence of Usama bin Ladin as a single, widely recognized, terrorist leader has further encouraged the unitary view of Islamist terrorism. Here was someone who, by personifying the threat, by being directly responsible for a pair of major terrorist attacks on the United States (the bombings in Nairobi and Dar es Salaam), and by wielding broader influence through his wealth and charisma, could easily be perceived as a single prime mover who is pulling strings that weave throughout a single Islamist terrorist network.

There is, in fact, some basis for thinking in terms of such a network. There are a multitude of links and cooperative arrangements that extend beyond the infrastructure of any one group. The acquaintances made in the camps of Afghanistan have become the basis for countless bits of assistance extended by one Islamist to another. Globe-trotting independent operators like Yousef do get help. Memberships in radical groups overlap, with some individuals having ties both to a single-nationality group and to a transnational organization. There is much practical cooperation among groups—such as in procuring false documents, facilitating travel, and performing other support functions—even if they do not conduct joint terrorist operations.

The cooperation extends beyond terrorist groups to a number of Islamic nongovernmental organizations, such as the Pakistan-based Maktab al-Khidamat. Many of these NGOs perform legitimate social service work. The senior officers of some of the NGOs are unwitting of the use that terrorists make of them. But that use has become an important part of the support system of many Islamic terrorists. The NGOs provide cover for the movement of money and materiel. They also provide day jobs (and an excuse for traveling to certain areas) to extremists for whom terrorism is not a full-time occupation.

The unitary view of Islamist terrorism has been encouraged (perhaps sometimes unintentionally) by a broader concept of the Muslim world as a whole being on a collision course with the Judeo-Christian West—with terrorism being just one, particularly nasty, front in this confrontation. A decade ago Bernard Lewis described the confrontation as being nothing less than a "clash of civilizations."[11] This phrase did not catch on until Samuel Huntington made it the title of a much-noticed and highly controversial article (later expanded into a book) that addressed relations among all world civilizations.[12] Huntington contends that Islam and the West are engaged in a "quasi war" that is being waged over fundamental issues of power and differing views of right and wrong. Militarily, this quasi war has been "largely a war of terrorism versus air power," with Islamic militants exploiting the open societies of the West to plant car bombs, and Western militaries exploiting the open skies of the Islamic world to drop smart bombs. Huntington stresses that the adversary is not just the militants. "The underlying problem for the West is not Islamic fundamentalism," he argues. "It is Islam, a different civilization whose people are convinced of the superiority of their culture and are obsessed with the inferiority of their power."[13]

The perspectives on which Lewis and Huntington focused do go a long way to explain the posture of Islamist terrorists toward the United States as will be discussed in the next section. But an unfortunate by-product of a civilizationwide focus is a tendency to emphasize what unites people in the other civilization rather than what divides them, even though the divisions may be at least as important. Most of the many criticisms of Huntington's entire thesis have stressed the importance of intracivilizational national differences.[14] Huntington himself notes the disunity of Islamic civilization and the absence of a "core state" in it. Indeed, he even suggests that the absence of a dominant power to regulate behavior within that civilization is one reason for the disproportionate amount of violence involving Islamic countries.[15]

Few serious students regard the militant (or radical, or fundamentalist) part of the Islamic world as monolithic. The fault lines are numerous. Ethnic, national, and socioeconomic differences have impeded efforts at unity, as have differing security perspectives. Sectarian differences are also significant—particularly, but not solely, the split between Sunni and Shia. There are several competing centers of Islamic religious activism, including the Egyptian Muslim Brotherhood, the Jamaat in Pakistan, and the Saudi-based World Muslim League. As the French scholar Olivier Roy has concluded, "The great ethnic, religious, and national divisions of the Muslim world are turning out to be stronger than all the calls to Islamic solidarity."[16]

The advent of Usama bin Ladin requires a further look at the issue of Islamist disunity, because he has been regarded, with some justification,

as a unifying force. Certainly no other figure in the radical Sunni world
has acquired the prominence that bin Ladin had attained by the end of
the 1990s. His persona and personal history (including an admired,
though exaggerated, record in the Afghan war against the Soviets) have
been factors in this rise, along with his mostly inherited bankroll (which
at one point was probably close to $250 million, although much of it has
been expended). Bin Ladin's influence is thus in large part personal, but
he has endeavored to institutionalize it by building and strengthening
alliances across group lines. Leaders of Egyptian, Pakistani, Kashmiri,
and Bangladeshi Islamist groups have been listed as signatories to statements issued by bin Ladin's International Islamic Front for Holy War
against Jews and Crusaders. Bin Ladin has functioned as a sort of nonstate
state sponsor in providing assistance to numerous allies. This has included help to the Taliban in Afghanistan, where fighters under his control have constituted a significant part of the frontline forces confronting the northern opposition. The Taliban's dependence on bin Ladin in
this fight has been the principal reason for its refusal to surrender or
expel him.

The limits to bin Ladin's influence, however, are just as important. For
one thing, he has very little sway among Shia extremists. Although he
shares some enemies with Iran—the center of Shia radicalism—he and
Iran have opposing interests in the fight in Afghanistan, which is important to both of them. Within the Sunni world, bin Ladin's actual control is
much narrower than the range over which he has some minor influence or
evokes admiration or sympathy. He is at the center of concentric circles of
Sunni radicalism that represent decreasing degrees of influence for him. In
the innermost circle is his own organization, al-Qaida ("The Base"), over
which he has direct operational control. The next circle out includes groups
so closely allied with, or beholden to, bin Ladin (most notably the Egyptian Islamic Jihad) that their operations can be assumed to reflect his wishes
or at least to closely parallel them. Farther out still are groups (such as the
Kashmiri Harakat ul-Mujahidin) that are allied to bin Ladin in some way
but are driven chiefly by their own local or regional imperatives. In the
circle beyond them are groups or cells to which some link to bin Ladin can
be drawn through the intricate extremist networks of the Middle East and
South Asia, but without any real alliance. And in the farthest circle are
individuals who admire bin Ladin and his rhetoric and may be stimulated
by it to act violently, even though there may be no organizational links to

him whatsoever. Possible examples of the last category were the four Saudis who confessed to bombing the U.S.-Saudi military program office in Riyadh in 1995 and in the confessions that were made public said they had been "inspired" by bin Ladin.

The labyrinthine network of Islamic extremists, particularly on the Sunni side, thwarts any attempt to draw clear and simple lines of responsibility for Islamic terrorism in general (as well as complicating efforts to assign responsibility for some specific acts or attempted acts of terrorism). Bin Ladin does have strings running through much of the network, but most of what goes on in the network is not the result of him (or any other influential figure) pulling them. There is much more practical, low-level back scratching than string pulling. The organizational picture is even more complicated due to the frequent splitting and merging of groups, the factionalism in many groups, the alliances, and the cross-memberships. Adding the NGOs to the mix makes it still more complex. This network is something like the Internet: it is a significant transnational phenomenon that has grown in recent years and that some determined people have used to their advantage, but nobody owns it or controls it.

Just as it would be a mistake to regard Islamic terrorism as if it were a unitary foe, so would it be a mistake to regard it as an integral part of a larger Islamic civilization in whose interests it conducts its violent operations. The Islamic terrorists do sound some chords that have resonance among other Muslims (more on this shortly), and this affects what other Muslims sometimes say (or do not say) about their operations.[17] But sympathy for a cause does not mean support for violent and inhumane methods in pursuit of it. Nor does it mean that the violent methods of the minority really do support the interests of the majority. Islamist car bombs set off against Western targets are not really the front line of a war waged on behalf of all Muslims, particularly since some of the same people setting off the bombs are also violently opposed to so much of the existing political and social order inside the Muslim world.

In sum, counterterrorism is not a war against any one major foe, the hand of which lies behind most of the terrorism being countered and the influence of which must be checked. This is true even of the Islamist brand of terrorism alone; it is all the more true of modern international terrorism as a whole. This is one of the respects in which the fight against terrorism differs from the cold war. There are transnational structures involved, as there once were with communism. But the structures do not point in one direction and do not have a supreme source. There is no Khomeinitern and no BinLadintern.

This has two implications beyond the general one of how to think about counterterrorism. The first is that the heterogeneous and fractured nature of the threat is a reason for flexibility in counterterrorist strategy and policy. True, constancy and inflexibility sometimes have their advantages, particularly in upholding one's reputation for firmness. But the likelihood of any particular terrorist group killing people at a particular time and place will depend more on the peculiarities of the specific situation, and on how those specifics affect the group's capabilities and intentions, than it will on worldwide reputations. Global terrorism is the sum of many such specific situations, rather than the product of someone's grand strategy. The United States also must stay attuned to the many different roots of terrorism—because there is no one taproot— and to how its own foreign policy affects those roots, for better or for worse. Some of the roots do involve whole civilizations bumping into each other, but many others involve local conflicts and conditions that are more amenable to U.S. influence.

The other implication is that counterterrorist programs should not become preoccupied with the *bete noire* of the moment. There are always other terrorist foes about whom one must worry, and still others yet to emerge. To a large degree bin Ladin became such a preoccupation for the United States following the East African bombings. Capturing him has been a grail whose pursuit has overshadowed other counterterrorist efforts and accomplishments. Certainly bin Ladin is a significant foe, whose call to kill Americans (whether military or civilian, officials or private citizens) is backed up by considerable ability to do just that. Taking him out of action would be a positive development; there is no one else who could quite fill his shoes. But his removal would not demolish his own organization (one of his senior lieutenants would probably keep some version of it running), let alone come close to ending even the Sunni extremist portion of international terrorism. Fixating on a single such foe not only has undesirable effects on how the terrorist himself is perceived overseas (a subject addressed in chapter 7); it is also a misallocation of attention and resources. Having counterterrorist managers and many of their officers concentrating on a single enemy may be an unaffordable luxury when the same people have to handle other current terrorist threats as well as staying ahead of the next bin Ladin (or next Aum Shinrikyo, or whomever) to emerge.

The Superpower as Target

The other terrorism-related observation about U.S. preeminence in the current world order is that the United States—as the sole superpower, the leader of the West, and the only country with truly global impact and presence—is, and will remain, the leading target of terrorists. One-third of international terrorist incidents recorded during the past two decades involved attacks on U.S. interests (either American property or American citizens). That proportion has been rising, from 31 percent in the 1980s to 37 percent in the 1990s. Three factors account for the United States being so often in terrorists' gunsights: the nature of terrorism as a tool of the weak against the strong, the physical exposure of U.S. interests, and special resentments against the United States.

The first of these reasons reflects not only the ways in which the United States is stronger than anyone else—including military power, economic vitality, and other measures—but one in which it is not: terrorism itself. Each successful terrorist operation against the United States demonstrates that its defenses are not impregnable. Offensively, the United States does not use terrorism at all. Even if it did, it might not be any better at mounting, say, a good car bomb operation than any of several highly capable terrorist groups. Because terrorism is one of the few dimensions on which the United States does not have an advantage, it is a promising tool for those who feel strongly about interests they believe have suffered because of other dimensions of U.S. power.

Terrorism may be used to counter any of those other dimensions. Its role as an equalizer is most vivid in countering military power. With force pitted against force, terrorism is the one weapon of the weak that has a chance to be decisive. It played that role in the bombings in Lebanon in 1983, particularly of the U.S. Marine barracks, as a weapon to get the U.S. military out of the country. During Desert Storm, the militarily overwhelmed Iraq tried to strike back not just with Scud missiles but with terrorism. It failed because U.S. counterterrorist efforts were able to exploit the weaknesses of Iraqi tradecraft, which was much more inept than what most established terrorist groups and state security services demonstrate. Since Desert Storm, the only forceful ripostes to the U.S. military presence on the Arabian Peninsula have again been terrorism: the bombings in Riyadh in 1995 and at Khubar Towers in 1996.

The second major reason the United States is the prime target of terrorists is the sheer number and accessibility of U.S. interests that can be targeted. The physical vulnerability starts at home, with a large and open society. That condition is not unique to being a superpower, of course, but the United States has more to worry about in that regard than most countries, even with two oceans as partial moats. Only India is at least as populous and just as open. The United States has, with Canada, the world's longest undefended border, and a border with Mexico that is another 2,000 miles long. The United States also receives a disproportionate number of international travelers (a reflection in part of its economic supremacy). In fiscal year 1999 there were 520 million admissions to the United States. Seventy-five million of these people arrived by air, 10 million by sea, and the rest by land. Two-thirds of the total admissions were aliens.[18]

Given this exposure, the U.S. homeland has been remarkably free of terrorism by foreigners, with the World Trade Center bombing and the rolled-up New York City plot of 1993 the only significant exceptions. A couple of the previously mentioned trends in international terrorism may be heightening the danger of foreign attacks in the United States, however. One is the increased geographic reach of terrorists—in terms of both the infrastructures of groups and the travels of individuals—which extends more deeply through the United States than it did several years ago. The other is the emphasis on inflicting pain, motivated by hatred or revenge, as distinct from more finely calibrated uses of terrorism to gain leverage or to achieve some other specific political or tactical objective (such as expulsion of the United States from Lebanon). There would be no better place to inflict pain on Americans than in the American homeland. The risk of attack probably has also risen because events have demonstrated that it is not as difficult to pull off a major operation in the United States as foreign terrorists may have once thought. The World Trade Center was one such demonstration. Oklahoma City was perhaps an even better one (even though it was the work of domestic perpetrators), because it showed how low-tech methods could cause mass casualties even in the heart of America. The fact that both cases were quickly solved and most of the culprits are now imprisoned may make less of an impression on some terrorists than the fact that bombs went off and Americans were killed.

The vulnerability that sets the United States as a superpower even more apart from lesser countries, however, is its exposure overseas. Its foreign physical presence is greater than that of any other country, and—notwithstanding any increased danger of attacks against the U.S. homeland—foreign terrorists are probably still most likely to strike in foreign lands.

The official U.S. presence overseas includes diplomatic representation in 162 countries. In addition to embassies, there are dozens of separate consulates, delegations to international organizations, and other missions, for a total of 290 diplomatic posts overseas as of late 2000.[19] More than thirty U.S. government agencies operate overseas, employing more than 14,000 Americans and about 30,000 foreign nationals.[20] Added to the civilian representation is a substantial overseas military presence. As of the end of fiscal 1998, out of 1.4 million U.S. military personnel on active duty, about 260,000 were serving outside the United States and its territories.[21] And added to the official presence (which will usually offer the most significant potential targets for terrorists) is the enormous overseas commercial presence of U.S. business, as well as individual Americans traveling for business or pleasure.

The number of potential U.S. targets overseas may seem to go well beyond the range of relevant distinctions. After all, a terrorist needs only one good target. But the magnitude of the presence, and how it sets the United States apart from even other major powers, has two significant effects on vulnerability. First, it brings more local terrorist cells into the picture. Local cells (or more informal groups of sympathizers) usually play important supporting roles in terrorist operations, even if the shooters or bombmakers come from elsewhere. That support includes identification and evaluation of targets, procurement of materiel, transportation, establishment of safehouses, and other functions. The quality of the support, and the potential of targets that are developed, are apt to vary considerably from one locale to another. Hizballah selected Buenos Aires for attacks not because that city had any symbolic value to Hizballah or because of any grievances with Argentina, but rather because its support structure in the region (and a relatively mild security environment) made such operations especially feasible there. Keeping such considerations in mind, a terrorist decisionmaker may have to review a long list of possibilities in search of that one good target. The longer the list, the better his chance of finding one.

The other effect involves a principle applicable to contests ranging from football to warfare: namely, that the offense knows where it will strike, but the defense does not. The larger the playing field and the more possible places to attack, the greater is the challenge for the defense. This fact has correctly driven thinking about security for U.S. diplomatic missions since the bombings in East Africa. The Crowe panel noted the worldwide nature of the terrorist threat and recommended that every diplomatic post should be treated as a potential target and that the State Department's standards and policies on physical security should be revised to reflect this concern.[22] Accordingly, the department's Bureau of Diplomatic Security has in some respects laid aside the system of rating posts as facing high, medium, or low threats to their security and instead has properly posited as its admittedly ambitious goal the upgrading of all posts to standards appropriate for a high threat location.

The special place that the United States occupies on terrorists' hit lists reflects more than just the efficacy of terrorism as a weapon of the weak or the number and accessibility of potential U.S. targets. It also is a product of the special resentment that terrorists hold toward the United States. Terrorists strike this country so often not just because they are able to, but because they want to. Both the operations and the rhetoric of the terrorists make this clear.

This leads to the question of why the resentment exists and what if anything could be done to lessen it. Does the hatred stem from what the United States *does* (which presumably could be changed) or from what it *is* (which is far less alterable)? Some have suggested that the extent of U.S. activity overseas—particularly in certain areas such as the Middle East— underlies the resentment, implying that curtailment of this activity would mean less resentment and hence less terrorism.[23] The truth, as with most truths about terrorism (even confining one's purview to the radical Islamists), is that a mixture of factors is at work. Terrorist hatred involves both the actions and the essence of the United States. Some of the actions, however, are almost intrinsic to being a superpower, and terrorists' sentiments about all of the actions are shaped by their larger, long-standing hatred of U.S. power and what they associate with that power. More than anything else, it is the United States' predominant place atop the world order (with everything that implies militarily, economically, and culturally) and the perceived U.S. opposition to change in any part of that order that underlie terrorists' resentment of the United States and their intent to attack it.

Terrorists do often respond to specific initiatives or interventions overseas, particularly ones involving military force. The intervention could be anything from a retaliatory strike such as the bombing of Libya in 1986 to a primarily humanitarian operation such as Operation Restore Hope in Somalia in 1992–94. Typically there is a burst of small-scale attacks following such an event, partly out of genuine sympathy for the perceived victims of the operation and partly because the event provides an excuse for doing something against the United States. The intervention then becomes an oft-cited grievance that plays a part in the rationales for later, possibly larger, attacks. The Somalia operation was specifically mentioned in a statement that bin Ladin's International Islamic Front for Holy War against Jews and Crusaders issued several days after the East Africa bombings. The U.S. embassies in Nairobi and Dar es Salaam, according to the Islamic Front's statement, were appropriate targets because they had "supervised the killings of at least 13,000 Somali civilians in the treacherous attack led by America against this Muslim country." The actual selection of those embassies as targets probably had more to do with the feasibility of operating in Kenya and Tanzania (given local infrastructures and perceived vulnerability of the targets) than the earlier events in Somalia. Nonetheless, Restore Hope was a genuine issue. Many in the Middle East thought it had more to do with colonialism than with humanitarianism.[24] The mission creep that characterized Restore Hope—in which what started as a humanitarian operation later involved a hunt for Somali warlord Mohamed Farrah Aideed—encouraged such perceptions.

U.S. ties to governments that the extremists hate is another reason the extremists hate the United States. The friend of one's enemy is itself seen as an enemy. U.S. friendship with the Saudi government and with moderate Arab leaders such as Egypt's Hosni Mubarak has been part of this perspective. The relationship that terrorists invoke far more than any other, however, is that between the United States and Israel. The claim of responsibility for the Africa bombings made by bin Ladin's paper front, the "Islamic Army for the Liberation of the Holy Shrines," included a demand for an end to "all American support to Israel." The Islamists (and many less extreme Muslims) look on Israel as a successor to the Crusader states: a creature imposed by the West that has displaced the native civilization and culture.[25] The leader of the Tunisian Islamist movement, Rashid Ghannushi, has said that "Israel represents the projection of this [Western] center into the East to wipe out its specific character, its spiritual wealth."[26] The U.S. role in this picture is both as the current leader of the West that established this Zionist beachhead in the Muslim world and as the principal military supplier and backer of Israel. On the military side, the United States is thus implicated in such events as the humiliating Arab defeat in the Six-Day War of 1967, which radicalized the Islamist movement more than any earlier events and that still, a third of a century later, remains seared in the consciousness of many Muslims and in particular many Arabs.

Besides specific interventions and ties to hated governments, the mere presence of U.S. contingents overseas is an ingredient in terrorist resentment against the United States. This is especially true of a military presence, that most direct and forceful manifestation of U.S. power. The major terrorist bombings in Lebanon in the 1980s were stimulated by, and intended to end, the presence of U.S. and allied forces there, as well as scuttling a U.S.-led peace process. Expulsion of the U.S. military from the Arabian Peninsula has now become a similar cause, though one that the terrorists have found harder to achieve.

Bin Ladin in particular has focused on the U.S. military presence in his former homeland. In a letter he sent to an Arabic-language newspaper in London in 1996, he said it was the "legitimate right" of Saudis to strike at the 5,000 American troops stationed in Saudi Arabia, even though King Fahd had invited them.[27] The claim by the "Islamic Army for the Liberation of the Holy Shrines" included as one of its demands "evacuation of U.S. and western forces from the Islamic countries in general and the Arabian Peninsula in particular." If bin Ladin's organization could have struck those forces directly they undoubtedly would have done so, but that would have been less feasible (particularly given the security-driven U.S. redeployment following Khubar Towers) than hitting embassies in a couple of African capitals.

The presence of U.S. troops in the kingdom angers the likes of bin Ladin in two ways. First, it is seen as a prop holding up the Saudi royal regime. Second, there is the more symbolic concern (implied by the reference to Holy Shrines in the "Islamic Army's" name) of foreign troops staying in the land most sacred to Islam. American boots are seen as contaminating the soil on which the Prophet walked.

A diplomatic presence is less controversial than a military one; overseas diplomatic representation is, after all, a normal attribute of statehood. But embassies can also become symbols—especially big, highly visible embassies, of which the United States has more than anyone else. The accusations against the U.S. embassies in Nairobi and Dar es Salaam in the World Islamic Front's statement plays to an old theme of embassies being centers of machination—or "nests of spies," as the U.S. embassy in Tehran was described when it was seized. The front's statement contained the demand that all U.S. embassies in Muslim lands be closed and their employees expelled.

The U.S. commercial and cultural presence overseas—although it cannot be linked as directly to U.S. policies as diplomatic or military installations can—has also been the target of terrorism conducted solely for reasons of symbolism and hatred (as distinct from more instrumental uses of terrorism such as hostage taking, in which U.S. business has also figured as a target). Leftists, for example, have frequently struck U.S.-owned business as blows against "economic imperialism." Attacks by Greek leftists in 1999 alone included hits against offices of American Express and Chase Manhattan, a General Motors dealership, and a McDonald's. Similarly, when the Tupac Amaru Revolutionary Movement (MRTA) in Peru was still active and capable, it repeatedly attacked American-affiliated enterprises, including branches of Citibank, Kentucky Fried Chicken, and Pizza Hut.

This is where the sources of terrorist resentment against the United States get less into what it does and more into what it is. Very few of the attacks against U.S.-owned businesses in Greece or Peru were stimulated by any particular U.S. initiatives or policies. A branch office of Citibank or a McDonald's restaurant just happens to be among the more accessible, tangible, and attackable manifestations of a much larger U.S.-dominated culture and economy that is the main object of scorn and anger. Other manifestations to which the foreign extremists are exposed include Americanmade or -inspired goods and services, a largely American-created mass culture, and mass media through which the goods are advertised and the culture is conveyed. Globalization has increased the exposure to each of these. And the reactions to each of these—including the hostile reactions of extremists—are responses not just to the substance of the object at hand (the good, the service, the branch office, and so forth) but to the kind of America the object represents. As Benjamin Barber has observed about U.S. corporations marketing consumer goods overseas, "Selling American products means selling America: its popular culture, its putative prosperity, its ubiquitous imagery and software, and thus its very soul. Merchandising is as much about symbols as about goods and sells not life's necessities but life's styles."[28]

The leftists have opposed this America violently because to them it is the font of economic exploitation. The Islamists oppose it violently because to them it is the font of a torrent of dirty water that is polluting the pond where they live. There is so much about American culture for the Islamists to hate, from its overall materialism to the role of women to the more sensual aspects of popular entertainment. And the cultural torrent is not only polluting the pond, it is making waves that are destroying old and fragile structures that were built along it. The American-originated changes in what people throughout the Muslim world are seeing and hearing, on the airwaves and on street corners, is tearing down mores on the obedience of children, the relationship between the sexes, and much else. The Islamists see these changes as wrecking a traditional social fabric without putting anything in its place that offers self-respect and stability, or even—for most Muslims—a more prosperous life.

The face of America that much of the world sees through the global mass media is not its best face. It is a face that reinforces some of the worst stereotypes that Islamists hold about the United States. News coverage that naturally focuses on troubles rather than good news can easily leave an impression of an America that is dominated by racism, drug abuse, the breakdown of families, and other societal ills.[29] American popular entertainment, especially some forms of popular music, appalls the Islamists even more. The more debauched parts of this ubiquitous segment of American culture have been targets of social critics in the United States.[30] It should not be surprising that the revulsion an Islamic fundamentalist feels is even greater, to the point in some cases of contributing to a predisposition toward anti-American violence. Many Islamists take the popular entertainment to be truly representative of the United States. A Pakistani fundamentalist group, for example, denounced two stars of American pop music, Michael Jackson and Madonna, as "the torchbearers of American society, their cultural and social values . . . that are destroying humanity. They are ruining the lives of thousands of Muslims and leading them to destruction, away from their religion, ethics, and morality." The group said the two entertainers are "cultural terrorists" who should be brought to trial in Pakistan.[31]

There are, to be sure, countervailing elements in American culture— evoking prosperity and freedom—that have been an attractive rather than a repellent force in much of the world, including the Muslim world. The U.S. dominance both of a propagating culture and of global media that convey it is a source of U.S. influence—part of what Joseph Nye has called "soft power."[32] But the Islamists and other religious extremists focus more on the negative aspects, not only because of the distorting effects of the media lens but because of the impact on those imperiled aspects of their own culture that are most important to them. Besides, the very U.S. dominance of global media is another form of resented U.S. power, as well as another reason for terrorists bent on gaining maximum publicity to attack U.S. targets.[33] And succumbing to the lure of Western consumer goods does not remove hatred of the society that produced them. As Huntington has colorfully put it, "Somewhere in the Middle East a half-dozen young men could well be dressed in jeans, drinking Coke, listening to rap, and, between their bows to Mecca, putting together a bomb to blow up an American airliner."[34] The music may be the Muslim version of rap, but the scene is not altogether implausible.

Most of the Islamists' animus toward the United States does not reflect tenets of Islam (even the more fundamentalist interpretations of them) as it does a more general religious self-righteousness confronting secularism. Islamists share with the extremists of other religions a view of themselves as part of a cosmic struggle, with their religious belief giving a moral sanction to violence. It is a common trait of all such extremists that they deem the lives of individuals who may die in the course of battling a cosmic enemy (including ones who die in terrorist attacks) to be of little importance.[35] Certain aspects of the Islamic world view do, however, lend themselves more than other belief systems to the notion of an inevitable and violent clash with the U.S.-led West. The division of the world in this view between Dar al-Islam (The Realm of Islam) and Dar al-Harb (The Realm of War), the obligation of Muslims to try to expand the faith (the idea of jihad), and the lack of a clear distinction between temporal and spiritual matters all contribute to this. These and other tenets of Islam are subject to multitudinous interpretations, and for the great majority of Muslims they do not dictate violence, let alone terrorism. Jihad can take many peaceful forms. That is why Huntington's concept of a religiously based clash does not describe the interactions that most Muslims, and most Muslim states and organizations, have with the United States and the West. It does describe, however, the view of the Islamist terrorists. If bin Ladin or someone of his ilk were to read Huntington's work, the reaction would not be surprise or shock but rather acknowledgement that this indeed is the conflict in which they believe themselves engaged. In the terrorists' perception, it is a conflict that is based on religion, involves resistance to cultural intrusion, is inevitable, includes their own terrorist operations as a leading part, and in which the enemy is the West, whose core state is the United States of America.

The U.S. role as leader of the West entails a further reason for special resentment against it, beyond it being the source of the current cultural contamination that troubles the Islamists. The United States has inherited the baggage from centuries of conflict between the Islamic world and the West, going back to the Crusades and including the Christian reconquest of Spain and later colonization by European powers. Some of this history, despite its antiquity, remains prominent in many Muslim minds (including, but not only, the extremist ones), and underlies a sense that the Islamic world has been losing power at the hands of a hostile, relentless West.[36] That the United States had responsibility for almost none of this history does not seem to absolve it from being its principal legatee. So for the Islamists, the contest is about not only a collision of cultures but also a need to restore lost power. To restore it, as Martin Kramer has written, "It must be subtracted from the Western powers, led by the United States, which dominate the Islamic world through instruments as diverse as movies, news networks, banks, and cruise missiles."[37] And for the terrorists, the symbolic value of striking the paramount Western power is at least as important as any details of either the history or the actual reasons for their current problems.

To return to the question posed earlier: how much could the United States, by modifying its policies and postures throughout the world, become less of a target of terrorism? Reduction of some commitments in some places would probably help at least in the short term, by lowering either physical vulnerability or resentment or both. Terrorists do get stimulated or angered by certain things the United States does overseas, such as the military deployments in Lebanon, Somalia, and the Arabian Peninsula. For several reasons, however, any attempt to reduce the worldwide terrorist danger to U.S. interests through withdrawal or retrenchment would have only limited results. In some respects such an attempt would be counterproductive.

The first and most important reason is, as discussed above, that the United States is the principal terrorist target mainly because of largely unchangeable attributes of being the world's preeminent power. The cultural and historical factors and the sheer impact of the United States in the world arena are not readily manipulable. Being at the top of the terrorists' hit list is an unavoidable price of superpowerdom.

Second, any withdrawal from current commitments to reduce the danger of terrorism risks being seen as exactly that and being interpreted by terrorists as a success. Therefore, although it may remove an immediate point of contention it also risks encouraging future terrorism, elsewhere and over other issues.

Third, even limiting one's perspective to any single trouble spot, there are so many sides to international terrorism that pulling back to reduce the danger from one direction may only increase it from a different direction. Conflicts such as those over Northern Ireland, Palestine, or the Balkans have had ample violent extremists, each with their peculiar bones to pick, on each side of the dispute. Placating one side is apt to antagonize the other. The same goes for mediation, peacekeeping, or other U.S. efforts to manage or resolve local disputes. Such efforts raise the ire of (and may increase U.S. vulnerability to) extremists with terrorist capabilities, especially extremists with a stake in indefinite continuation of the conflict. But for the United States to shun a role as a helpful third party may, in some instances, lessen the chance of a peaceful resolution that in the long run would reduce the violence, including terrorism, associated with the conflict.

The U.S. partnership with Israel illustrates the same general point in a different way. As noted above, that partnership is one of the most frequently voiced terrorist complaints against the United States. But continuation of the partnership is also important in influencing Israeli policies (including policies toward terrorism) and in sustaining the Israelis' confidence in their security when contemplating the kind of bold steps needed to reach agreements with their Arab interlocutors. The partnership is thus critical to the type of comprehensive settlement that offers the best long-term hope of reducing violence, including terrorism, associated with the Arab-Israeli conflict. Drastic reduction of U.S. support for Israel would check a box on the grievance lists of many terrorists, but it would not reduce terrorism. It would probably increase terrorism over the longer run.

Fourth, the United States is the prime terrorist target not only because of what it really is like or really is doing, but because of what the terrorists *believe* it is doing. Those beliefs are often mistaken, based on gross misreading of U.S. goals and the sources of U.S. conduct, and are not easily altered by changes in actual U.S. policy. Such misperceptions are prevalent in (but by no means limited to) the Middle East, where they influence the thinking not only of terrorist groups but others who might become, or sympathize with the actions of, terrorists.[38] The central misperception is that the United States is anti-Islamic, and that virtually everything it does in the Islamic world is part of an effort to weaken, control, or destroy Muslims. It is this mindset that led, for example, many commentators in the Middle East to interpret U.S. policy toward both Persian Gulf wars as an effort to divide Muslims and plunder their wealth.[39] The possibility of violent responses to even an absurd falsehood was demonstrated in 1979, when a rumor spread that the United States was somehow involved in a takeover by religious extremists of the Grand Mosque in Mecca. The resulting anti-American violence in Muslim countries included the burning of the U.S. embassy in Pakistan, where four persons, including two U.S. citizens, were killed.

Even more pertinent to the possibility of retrenchment as a strategy for reducing the risk of terrorism is that U.S. *noninvolvement* overseas can be subject to malignant misinterpretation every bit as much as U.S. interventions can. Many Muslims believe that the United States stayed as aloof as it did, as long as it did, from the war in Bosnia because of an anti-Muslim bias, and that it was glad to have Serbs do the dirty work of killing and expelling Bosnian Muslims. As a commentary in a pro-Islamic Karachi weekly put it, "The extermination of Muslims in Bosnia would never have been possible if the international community headed by the United States had interfered in time." The later air war on behalf of Muslims in neighboring Kosovo did little to erase this perception. The same commentator continued, "If someone thinks that the United States and its stooges are spending billions of dollars on attacking Serbs to help or restore the rights of Muslims, he is mistaken."[40]

Such misperceptions about the United States stem at least as much from its largely unchangeable characteristics and place in the world order as from its more alterable policies and actions overseas. Robert W. Tucker has observed, "The rising indictment . . . of a dominant America is the result not of what this nation has done in the world, but of what it is, for what it is may be expected to determine what it sooner or later will do. And even if this view misreads the American disposition, other nations will still be only too ready to believe that it does not."[41] The extremists of the world, and among them the terrorists, are even more disposed to so believe.

A fifth reason that reducing U.S. commitments abroad would be of limited value in reducing anti-U.S. terrorism is that—as will be discussed later, especially in chapters 4 and 6—some of the most effective counterterrorist measures require extensive foreign engagement. This includes not only involvement in conflict management and peacemaking that addresses some of the roots of terrorism but also close cooperation with foreign counterparts to uncover the intentions and attack the capabilities of terrorist groups. Foreign help is critical because of the transnational nature of the threat and because the United States simply does not have the information, resources, access, or authority to do by itself what needs to be done. Even with those aspects of international terrorism that directly involve threats to U.S. interests, the United States is dependent on foreign partners for everything from arresting an individual terrorist to maintaining a consistent diplomatic stance toward a state sponsor. Counterterrorist activity overseas includes the first line (and the next several lines) of defense against foreign terrorist threats even if the terrorists' ultimate target is within the United States itself. And the cooperation of many foreign partners will depend not only on what the United States does with them on counterterrorism but also on what the United States does *for* them in support of their other political, economic, and security interests. Much of the latter depends on the United States acting, committing, or otherwise exposing itself overseas.

Managing Vulnerability

Even focusing narrowly on terrorism, therefore, U.S. activities overseas have both upsides and downsides. The United States must operate abroad to fight terrorism effectively, but every element of its presence abroad involves one more potential terrorist target, and may involve one more motivation for terrorists to attack. These conflicting factors have borne on issues such as whether to reopen the embassy in Khartoum, where the hazards that caused the embassy to be closed are just as real as the important monitoring capabilities that were lost when it did close.

Physical defenses against terrorism need to be considered in conjunction with the roots of terrorism. That is, security measures at U.S. installations abroad should be assessed with an eye not only to how well they would foil an attack but also to how they may affect broader perceptions of, and resentment toward, the United States. Sometimes these considerations all fortunately point in the same direction. The redeployment of U.S. troops in Saudi Arabia, for example, not only reduced their physical vulnerability to further terrorist attacks but had the bonus effect of reducing their visibility to the Saudi public. It thus may have marginally lowered the resentment their presence causes. In other instances the elements point in different directions. This is true of embassy security. The most secure embassy designs (walled compounds and forbidding buildings with few windows but many barriers) make attacks more difficult but also project the image of a hostile, unwanted, occupying power.[42] Such conflicts can be minimized or finessed; it gets down to the finer points of embassy architecture.[43] The point to remember is that because terrorist targets are fungible, roots and resentments do not stay local. An image of the United States formed in the Middle East may underlie a terrorist attack in Africa.

The considerations become much more complex, and the trade-offs more numerous, when weighing the many other reasons, besides counterterrorism, that the United States maintains an overseas presence. Perhaps maintaining any troop presence at all in the Arabian Peninsula is unwise as far as the terrorist threat alone is concerned, but that force performs other functions, involving the containment of Iraq and the serving of other security needs in the Persian Gulf, that even the most narrow-minded counterterrorist specialist cannot wish away. These tradeoffs are another reason counterterrorism should be embedded in all foreign policy decisionmaking, rather than being thought of as a thing apart in which counterterrorist officials make their own separate decisions for their own reasons. Just as one of the questions that should be asked about any prospective foreign policy initiative is what effect it is likely to have on the roots of terrorism, so too one should ask what effect the initiative will have on the vulnerability to terrorism of the Americans charged with carrying it out. This does not mean deciding to undertake the initiative on other grounds and then assessing the terrorist threat and seeing how much protection the United States can afford to buy against that threat. It means making vulnerability to terrorism one of the considerations in deciding whether to undertake a mission in the first place, as well as how (and sometimes where) to undertake it. It also means deciding whether the mission can be performed safely *and* effectively—that is, whether any adjustments or measures needed to deal with the terrorist threat would undermine the primary mission. And it means avoiding a Lebanon-type situation in which one cannot end an initiative without appearing to have been pushed out of it by terrorists.

After pondering these questions the right decision may still be to go ahead with the mission, but perhaps with modification to how it is done. Secretary of Defense William Perry acknowledged the need for these sorts of compromises as the Defense Department wrestled with the changes the Khubar Towers bombing provoked. "To stay ahead of the threat," said Perry, "we now see that we must always put force protection up front as a major consideration with key other mission goals as we plan operations, and that that parity must be maintained throughout the operation." So how does the primary mission still get accomplished? "The answer," the secretary continued, "is that we will require tradeoffs in other areas, such as cost, convenience, and quality of life." And that raises still other needs and challenges, including ones involving the maintenance of morale when personnel are told to perform more harsh, lonely tours of duty unaccompanied by their dependents.[44]

Each deployment or initiative, and each aspect of each deployment, must be assessed separately to strike the right balance between security and accomplishment of the primary mission. There are no general formulas worth applying. The redeployments in Saudi Arabia, for example, appropriately distinguished between those elements that could be moved more easily and those that could not without negating their missions. Troops supporting air operations over southern Iraq could still work effectively at an isolated desert air base, but those advising the Saudi military or manning Patriot missile batteries intended to protect urban areas could not. The latter troops thus were not moved to the desert, although they were provided additional security and in some cases consolidated into safer housing.[45]

Diplomatic representation may rouse terrorists less often than military deployments do, but conflicts between maintaining security and performing the primary mission tend to be even sharper with diplomatic facilities than with military installations. Important parts of a diplomat's job are to represent the United States to the people of the host country and to monitor the pulse of that country. Those tasks require more interaction with, and exposure to, the local population, whereas a security perspective would argue for less. The most secure embassies not only look unfriendly; they also (particularly those located on the outskirts of a capital rather than in city center) are not designed for maximum effectiveness in performing the diplomatic function. The same conflicts arise with the tight security procedures that U.S. diplomats in some countries have to observe in their meetings and movements outside the embassy, and which—necessary though the procedures may be in a hazardous country—inevitably affect the performance of their job.

Skilled and creative (and courageous) U.S. diplomats find ways every day to do their jobs at least reasonably well despite the security-related impediments. Moreover, in some dangerous locations the diplomatic jobs to be done are simply too important to forgo a resident mission. Beirut is such a place. The stringent security measures that infuse everything the small staff of the U.S. embassy there does may sometimes make it seem that the presence is not worth the trouble. But some of the matters the embassy addresses—which bear on the Arab-Israeli peace process, among other things—are clearly of high importance. The embassy is there not just for the sake of being there.

Nonetheless, the tension between conducting diplomacy through resident missions and minimizing targets for terrorists is clear enough (and the cost of providing adequate security for all current missions is high enough) that the Crowe panel suggested closing some embassies and giving other ones regional representational responsibilities. Such a step would run against a long and strong tradition of flying the flag worldwide. Admiral Crowe himself observed, "That's a tender subject in the State Department."[46] Moreover, it is not just tradition but an aspect of doing business (especially, a superpower doing business) in the complex and interconnected world of today. A separate advisory panel studying the official U.S. presence overseas concluded in its report, issued a few months later: "Dramatic changes in the world's economic, political, technological, and social landscape have made an on-the-ground overseas presence in virtually every country more valuable than ever before." The panel correctly cited work against terrorist groups as one of tasks for which embassies are required: "Without people on the ground, our efforts to monitor, contain, and eliminate these groups would be severely limited."[47]

The challenge the United States faces from international terrorism is, in a number of ways, enduring and unavoidable. The color of terrorism has changed along with changes in the world order, but the receding of some threats is offset by the emergence of others. The fractionated nature of international terrorism means that terrorist successes do not strengthen any one hostile center of power, but it also means that counterterrorism can never achieve a knockout blow by moving against a single leader or group. The diversity of U.S. activities to which terrorists respond means the United States can shape to some degree their motivations, but the principal drivers of anti-U.S. terrorism are found in the more immutable history and structure of global politics and economics. The breadth of U.S. activities overseas makes it possible to do much that is important (including counterterrorism) but also entails vulnerabilities and resentments that could underlie more terrorism. Terrorism has had different prime targets in different eras. It is now the turn of the United States. The turn could not be shortened unless the United States were to shrink much farther from its present stature than anyone expects and than even the most ardent isolationists hope.

The elements of counterterrorism most pertinent to this chapter have been the mitigation of roots and the erection of defenses. There are useful things that can be done with both, but major limitations to what can be expected from either. Effective counterterrorism requires that at least as much attention be devoted to attacking the capabilities and influencing the intentions of terrorists. To do this the United States has available several instruments, which are examined in the next chapter.

CHAPTER FOUR

Counterterrorist Instruments

Counterterrorism uses several instruments of statecraft. They include diplomacy, the criminal justice system, interdiction of financial assets, military force, and intelligence, as well as possible use of the intelligence apparatus for covert action. Almost every instrument bears on more than one of the elements of counterterrorist policy identified in chapter 2. Each of the elements can be pursued with more than one instrument. Like the elements, each instrument has distinctive possibilities but also significant limitations. None comes close to being a silver bullet. They all need to be employed or at least considered for employment. This chapter examines the use, potential, and limits of each instrument and concludes by discussing the coordination of the instruments as parts of a coherent counterterrorist program.

Diplomacy

Diplomacy touches at least as many aspects of counterterrorism as does any other instrument. Although U.S. diplomats seldom get the opportunity to apply their diplomatic skills directly on terrorists, the essence of diplomacy—articulating policy to foreign interlocutors, persuading them, and reaching understandings or agreements with them—clearly must be part of efforts that necessarily rely so heavily on engagement with foreign groups and states. Diplomacy is linked with all the elements of counterterrorism. Through peacemaking and the shaping of images of the United States, it affects the roots of terrorism. Persuasion of foreigners obviously bears on intentions. Because persuasion of foreign governments may be aimed at curbing the activity of terrorist groups or state sponsors, it also bears on capabilities. And because it is often aimed at getting foreign governments to provide better protection to U.S. interests, it also pertains to defenses.

U.S. counterterrorist diplomacy is not limited to what the Department of State does. Each of the other instruments entails not only unilateral action by the United States but also the enlistment of cooperation from foreign counterparts. The relative importance of this cooperation varies from one instrument to another. It is a very important for intelligence, for example, but somewhat less so for the application of military force. Much practical counterterrorist work is done through U.S. specialists from various agencies and departments cooperating with their opposite numbers in foreign governments. Each of these contacts also represents a potential point of friction. Effective counterterrorist diplomacy, therefore, must be practiced not only by Foreign Service officers but also by immigration officers, FBI special agents, intelligence officers, transportation specialists, defense attachés, and many other kinds of officials.

Much counterterrorist diplomacy takes place in specialized service-to-service or department-to-department channels. A lot is ad hoc, but with the more important functions and the most important foreign partners, regular exchanges occur. The United States also periodically engages several foreign governments in broad, multifunctional counterterrorist exchanges. These are led by the State Department's coordinator for counterterrorism and his or her closest counterpart in the foreign government. The U.S. delegation includes some combination of representatives from the intelligence and law enforcement communities, the departments of Defense, Transportation, and Treasury, the Immigration and Naturalization Service, the Federal Aviation Administration, other components of the State Department, and perhaps other agencies or the National Security Council. The foreign delegation includes a similar assortment of specialists. A picture of each table at these meetings would be an apt portrait of the wide range of functions that bear on counterterrorism and of how many of them depend on foreign cooperation.

Although many agencies are active, and much of the best work takes place in the specialized channels, it is fitting that counterterrorist cooperation with the more important foreign partners should regularly come together in one place in a proceeding led on the U.S. side by the lead agency for foreign relations, the Department of State. Each bit of counterterrorist cooperation—or disagreement—is part of a larger bilateral relationship. Each is affected by, and in turn affects, the overall state of that relationship. It is useful to keep in mind, and at hand, all of the carrots and sticks available to the U.S. side. It is also important to remember the other side's carrots and sticks, as well as its objectives and sensitivities about its relationship with the United States. Moreover, a clear articulation of U.S. objectives and of the principles the United States intends to maintain while pursuing those objectives (which might include, for example, human rights concerns) provides a necessary framework for more specialized cooperation.

Diplomacy supports the other instruments in numerous other ways. The negotiation of treaties on extradition and mutual legal assistance, for example, assists the application of criminal law by facilitating the transfer of fugitive terrorists or the involvement of U.S. experts in the investigation of terrorist incidents. Discouraging other countries from letting a suspect group operate on its territory narrows the intelligence task of monitoring the group. Sometimes U.S. diplomats add weight to a specific request that arises in one of the specialized channels. If a government is being asked to stick its neck out in helping the United States (such as by making an arrest or rolling up a cell), it might not be enough for a CIA station chief or an FBI legal attaché (legat) to talk to a counterpart in the local security services. In such cases the U.S. ambassador may raise the matter with the head of government. Such ambassadorial démarches have led to the stopping of terrorist operations and the saving of lives. (In some instances the station chief may be the most effective "diplomatic" channel on counterterrorist matters; much depends on the internal dynamics of the host country's regime and the clout of officials such as the interior minister or the head of the intelligence or internal security service.)

The counterterrorist diplomacy that matters most is bilateral. Even issues of broader application, such as sanctions against state sponsors, largely come down to the key concerns of key states. Some very effective counterterrorist cooperation does involve more than two states, but usually it is just three or four states and nearly always ad hoc, with diplomacy playing only a supporting role to practical police or intelligence work. Examples are the transfer with U.S. help of a fugitive terrorist from one state to another (not the United States) where he is wanted for his crimes, or the use of information supplied by one country to disrupt terrorist cells elsewhere.

In general, the larger the gathering to address terrorism, the less effective it has been. The nadir of effectiveness was reached by the United

Nations General Assembly in the 1970s, when widespread sympathy for "national liberation movements" led to condoning of their methods and refusals even to condemn terrorism.[1] The passing of that era has appreciably improved the diplomatic climate regarding terrorism, but the United States is still wise to oppose global conferences on terrorism or similar large-scale exercises if they do not focus sharply on particular agreements and mechanisms for cooperation.

In recent years the United States has participated in some smaller multilateral gatherings on terrorism in which at least the atmospherics were favorable. These have included regional conferences as well as discussions within the framework of the Group of Eight (G-8), the major Western industrialized nations plus Russia. A G-8 ministerial meeting on terrorism in 1996 (convened as a follow-up to the G-8 summit of that year) produced a statement with twenty-five recommendations on topics such as sharing of information, vigorous prosecution of terrorists, and development of antiterrorist technologies. Terrorism was also mentioned in a NATO Alliance Strategic Concept that the North Atlantic Council approved at its fiftieth anniversary meeting in 1999. This document called for improvements in NATO's ability to respond to a variety of possible threats to allied interests, including transnational threats such as terrorism. Any practical measures emanating from such multilateral pronouncements will be modest. The limits to what can be accomplished are set by the state that is least willing to cooperate. Also, even within an alliance such as NATO, constraints on sharing sensitive intelligence increase along with the number of participating countries.

Despite such limitations, multilateral diplomacy helps counterterrorism in three ways. First, in a few cases a multilateral resolution can provide a formal structure for making demands and implementing responses (usually toward a state sponsor of terrorism) without the taint of being solely the work of the United States, or the United States and a few of its allies. The UN Security Council has usefully served this role for Libya and the Pan Am 103 case. The council first became involved in 1991 after U.S. and British authorities charged the Libyans Abd al Basit al-Megrahi and Lamin Kalifah Fhima with carrying out the bombing. The council unanimously adopted Resolution 731, which condemned international terrorism and requested Libya to cooperate in determining responsibility for the Pan Am disaster. Libya's refusal to surrender the suspects led the council in 1992 to adopt Resolution 748, which demanded Libyan cooperation and specified several sanctions under article 41 of the UN charter that would be imposed, as in fact they were, if Tripoli did not cooperate. The sanctions included a cessation of air links to Libya and of arms sales to it and a reduction of staff at Libyan missions overseas. Continued Libyan noncompliance led to Resolution 883 in 1993, which broadened the sanctions by freezing Libyan funds other than petroleum-related assets, banning trade in oil-related equipment, and cutting off all dealings with Libya's national airline. The reasons that Muammar Qadhafi finally turned over Megrahi and Fhima in 1999 were complex. That nearly six years had elapsed between the third of three Security Council resolutions and Libyan compliance with the resolutions demonstrates the limitations of this kind of multilateral diplomacy.[2] But the fact that the Security Council was used surely contributed to the favorable, though belated, result. To the extent that widespread observance of the sanctions contributed to their bite, the council's imprimatur was important. Moreover, the fact that compliance meant not just caving to demands from a hostile U.S. and Britain but rather acceding to a broadly supported measure taken under the terms of a charter that Libya itself had signed, made compliance easier to swallow.

More recently the Security Council has taken similar action toward the Taliban regime in Afghanistan. In October 1999 it unanimously adopted Resolution 1267, which demands the turnover of Usama bin Ladin and, failing that, imposes sanctions that include the banning of Ariana Afghan Airlines flights (other than for the hajj and for previously approved humanitarian missions) and the freezing of the Taliban's financial assets. As with Libya in the early nineties, there are countervailing reasons for the target regime not to comply, and rapid compliance was never likely. But the council's involvement cannot hurt, and in the longer run it may well help.

A second and less specific way in which even the vaguer resolutions that are the stock in trade of multilateral diplomacy can be modestly useful is that they reinforce an international norm against the use of terrorism. What had once been a disturbingly widespread notion that terrorist methods are acceptable if used to pursue certain ends has eroded significantly. This favorable trend, which began in the early 1980s and accelerated as the cold war ended, has been reflected in the UN General Assembly's increasingly forthright condemnations of terrorism.[3] Anything that continues the trend and adds to the opprobrium attached to terrorism is beneficial. Much multilateral diplomacy is essentially mood music, but even mood music can be helpful in reaching more specific goals.

A message that the music of multilateral diplomacy can usefully reinforce is that counterterrorism means opposition to certain *methods*, not opposition to certain groups or states, much less ideologies or religions. Terrorism deserves to be condemned and actively opposed by all the world's nations because it involves conduct that offends universal values involving human life and the suffering of innocents. In this regard, counterterrorism is of a piece with international humanitarian law as it has evolved for more than a century and been codified in the Hague and Geneva conventions on the conduct of warfare and is a similarly apt subject for multilateral diplomacy. Indeed, any act of terrorism is a violation of one or more of those conventions, particularly the 1949 Geneva agreement on protection of civilians. One leading scholar has even suggested defining terrorism as the peacetime equivalent of war crimes.[4] The international community has spoken and has declared terrorist methods to be wrong as a matter of *jus in bello* (the method), not of *jus ad bellum* (the cause).

That principle came under indirect attack at the Geneva Diplomatic Conference on the Reaffirmation of International Humanitarian Law Applicable in Armed Conflict, which met from 1974 to 1977 (the heyday of "national liberation movements"). One of the protocols that the conference adopted weakened the requirements that had been established at Geneva in 1949 for an individual to have combatant status (and thus to be treated as a prisoner of war, not a criminal, if captured). The intent of the change was to ensure combatant status for members of the Palestine Liberation Organization and other guerrilla movements. The earlier requirement that combatants wear distinctive insignia recognizable at a distance and carry their arms openly was replaced with a rule whereby a combatant who belongs to the "armed forces of a party to the conflict" needs to distinguish himself from the civilian population only "while . . . engaged in an attack or in a military operation preparatory to an attack."[5] This change unfortunately lessened the legal distinction between military operations and the methods of terrorists who reveal themselves to be armed and hostile only moments before an attack. Even this dilution of the Geneva rules, however, does not remove the fundamental illegality of terrorism under international humanitarian law. A truck bomb that appears to be nothing more than a truck until the moment of detonation does not qualify its driver for combatant status even under the newer rules. More important, all the basic prohibitions against attacking civilians remain in effect. The new rules further specify that "acts or threats of violence the primary purpose of which is to spread terror among the civilian population are prohibited."[6]

Codified international law on terrorism goes beyond the relevant portions of the law of war. A dozen more narrowly focused international conventions on terrorist-related matters have been opened for signature during the past four decades. They include the Tokyo Convention on Offenses and Certain Other Acts Committed on Board Aircraft (1963); Hague Convention for the Unlawful Seizure of Aircraft (1970); Montreal Convention for the Suppression of Unlawful Acts against the Safety of Aircraft (1971); Convention to Prevent and Punish the Acts of Terrorism Taking the Form of Crimes against Persons and Related Extortion That Are of International Significance (1971); Convention on the Prevention and Punishment of Crimes against Internationally Protected Persons (1973); Convention against the Taking of Hostages (1979); Convention on the Physical Protection of Nuclear Materials (1979); Protocol for the Suppression of Unlawful Acts of Violence at Airports Serving International Aviation (1988); Convention for the Suppression of Unlawful Acts against the Safety of Maritime Navigation (1988); Convention on the Marking of Plastic Explosives for Purposes of Detection (1991); International Convention for the Suppression of Explosives (1997); and Convention on the Suppression of the Financing of Terrorism (2000). U.S. diplomats frequently, in consultations with foreign officials on counterterrorism, urge the other government to accede to any of these conventions to which it is not already a party. These agreements make explicit some of the prohibitions that may only be implied in other international law, and extending their effect and visibility helps to maintain the more general consensus against terrorism and the momentum of international efforts to counter it.

The conventions also—and this is the third way in which multilateral diplomacy helps counterterrorism—provide common standards that facilitate cooperation on certain matters. The agreements relating to hijacking of aircraft, for example, help to sort out responsibilities in responding to incidents in which the nationalities of the airports, aircraft, passengers, and hijackers may all be different. As another example, the marking of explosives with "taggants" to facilitate the investigation of bombing incidents is effective only with widespread international agreement on what should be marked and how.

Criminal Law

In recent years the application of criminal law has become an increasingly large part of U.S. efforts to counter international terrorism. Arrests and prosecutions of terrorists are frequently used as a scorecard of success, not just because they are visible and quantifiable but also because they reflect a major emphasis of the U.S. counterterrorist program. Two other trends reflect this emphasis or are related to it. One is a significant increase in the 1990s in the investigative resources that law enforcement agencies devote to terrorism. The number of FBI agents working on terrorism rose from 550 in 1993 to nearly 1,400 in 1999.[7] The proportion of the FBI's budget devoted to counterterrorism (including not just agents but support personnel and other expenditures) increased from 4 percent in 1993 to more than 10 percent in 2000.[8] In a reorganization in 1999, the FBI gave counterterrorism (which until then had been covered along with counterintelligence and espionage in the National Security Division) its own division with its own assistant director.

The other trend, which had begun in the 1970s, is the increased internationalization of U.S. law enforcement overall. The resources, activities, and cases involving criminal prosecutions that transcend international boundaries in some way have increased significantly over the past quarter century. Reasons for this trend include technological advances that have facilitated transnational operations by police as well as criminals and new laws that have turned certain transnational or overseas acts into U.S. crimes.[9] Two laws provide the principal basis for extraterritorial jurisdiction on terrorism. One is the Comprehensive Crime Control Act of 1984, which authorized federal prosecution of hostage taking overseas that involves American citizens or the United States as a target. The other is the Omnibus Diplomatic Security and Antiterrorism Act of 1986, which extended extraterritorial jurisdiction to any terrorist act against U.S. citizens or interests.[10] The FBI's expanded responsibility for investigating terrorist acts overseas has been a major reason for increasing the number of FBI legal attachés, or legats, stationed abroad. As of late 2000 the FBI had agents stationed in forty-four foreign countries—a doubling of what had been its overseas presence seven years earlier.[11]

All of this emphasis on prosecuting terrorists (even ones who operate far from U.S. territory) reflects something more than just a view of the criminal justice system as a counterterrorist instrument. Using criminal laws to punish wrongdoers has a higher status than that in most American minds. That "applying the rule of law" is one of the major tenets of officially expressed U.S. counterterrorist policy—which does not make comparable mention of the other instruments—suggests that the reasons for emphasizing it go beyond counterterrorist policy itself. One possible reason is to uphold respect for the rule of law generally. Another is that seeing justice done to terrorists is valued as an end in itself. If enough Americans value the punishment of wrongdoers for its own sake, perhaps it ought to be accepted as a national objective regardless of any instrumental value it has in pursuing other objectives. But accepting it for this reason should not be confused with counterterrorism (that is, saving lives and limbs by reducing future terrorist attacks). Moreover, one should be aware of how a pursuit of justice for justice's sake may complicate pursuit of the counterterrorist objective of curbing terrorism or the pursuit of other foreign policy objectives. The goal may be worthy, but it can entail costs and trade-offs, some of which are implied in the discussion below.

Looking at the criminal justice system solely as a counterterrorist instrument, there are several ways in which a U.S. commitment to prosecute terrorists may help to reduce terrorism. First, putting a terrorist behind bars obviously prevents him from conducting further attacks. This is most important with the leaders, instigators, and people with the critical skills. That a terrorist as resourceful as Ramzi Yousef is serving a 240-year sentence in a maximum security prison makes Americans around the world a little bit safer. Second, the movements of terrorists still at large are impeded by their knowledge that they are wanted men and that the United States has a demonstrated ability to catch fugitives thousands of miles from its own territory. Third, the drama, publicity, and evidence of U.S. resolve that a terrorist prosecution entails may encourage other governments to act forcefully against terrorism and sustain public awareness of the problem.[12] And fourth, the prospect of being caught and punished may deter some terrorists from attacking in the first place.

The limitations to the criminal justice instrument are at least as numerous as the advantages. To begin with, the deterrent effect is variable and uncertain. Fear of imprisonment no doubt causes some terrorists to hesitate (although it would be hard to point to any evidence of this effect, even using classified intelligence), but for others, accomplishment of their glorious (for them) deed may be more important than the prospect of anyone getting caught. Deterrence through prosecution is obviously irrelevant to suicide bombers, and it may be as well to other low-level people with a comparable degree of desperation. The leaders, who are less likely to be caught, may not care much if the underlings are.

Even worse than not deterring is the possibility that prosecution may stimulate retaliation. The United States has not yet suffered much from this form of terrorist response, but the risk exists. The Egyptian al-Gama'at al-Islamiyya made very pointed threats against the United States when its spiritual leader, "Blind Sheik" Umar Abd al-Rahman, was prosecuted. It has not made good on the threats, but it is unclear why it has not and whether al-Gama'at has abandoned the idea. The growing number of foreign terrorists in U.S. prisons raises the possibility of a terrorist group attempting the classic operation of taking hostages and demanding a release of prisoners, although the expectation that the United States would take a firm line in such a situation probably has deterrent value. (The Islamic extremist Abu Sayyaf group in the Philippines did make the release of Yousef and Abd al-Rahman a demand when it seized non-American hostages in an operation in April 2000.) More likely would be retaliatory attacks that do not entail a specific demand. FBI Director Louis Freeh suggested (without citing evidence) that the killing of four U.S. businessmen and their driver in Karachi in November 1997 was in retaliation for the arrest and rendition earlier that year of Mir Aimal Kansi.[13]

The fact that the leaders of terrorist groups and organizers of terrorist operations are less likely to be caught and punished than the low-level people who execute an attack is a basic limitation of the criminal justice instrument that goes beyond deterrence. Underlings get caught more often because they are the ones who put their fingers on the evidence, expose themselves to witnesses, must try to escape from the location of the incident, and otherwise perform the riskier parts of the operation. Organizers are a step removed from exposure and the evidence and are generally absent from the area at the time of the attack. The senior leaders who make the decisions to attack are the least accessible of all, likely never to come close to the scene of the operation, and very difficult to arrest. So in such cases as Pan Am 103 and the East Africa bombings (until and unless bin Ladin and his senior lieutenants are caught), it is the working-level people who are tried while those most responsible for the crimes are not. Such an application of justice thus involves a form of injustice. Even though all of the underlings are criminals, all deserve punishment, and many of them are true believers, other low-level participants (including the ones most likely to be caught) are more accurately described as hapless recruits. Some (including one of the first arrestees in the East Africa case) provide statements that are important in solving the case. Trying and convicting such people may give a misleading sense of closure to a terrorist problem that is still very much open or that, with the passage of time, was effectively closed earlier.

There is an added dimension when the ultimate terrorist decisionmakers are governments (which, as noted earlier, has fortunately been a diminishing part of international terrorism). The surrender of Megrahi and Fhima to stand trial for the bombing of Pan Am 103 was for years the key demand being levied on Libya to bring that case to closure. With the trial finally convened twelve years after the bombing, it is useful to reflect on exactly what the trial means and what it accomplishes. There is no question that anyone who did what the two Libyans were charged with doing deserves severe punishment, regardless of where they were in the decisionmaking chain. There is also no question that Megrahi and Fhima (who were employees of the Libyan government) were not at the top of that chain. If the trial provides closure to the Pan Am 103 tragedy, it will not be primarily because of the verdicts on these two men but rather because the trial will serve as one vehicle for the Libyan regime to indirectly come clean about this sordid chapter in its terrorist past and to clear the table for a new and better relationship with the United States. (Another vehicle will be Libyan payment of compensation to the families of the Pan Am 103 victims.)

The United States generally does not try to apply its criminal laws to heads of government, nor should it. The one exception in recent years was the capture in 1989 of Panamanian strongman Manuel Noriega and his subsequent conviction and imprisonment in the United States on charges of narcotics trafficking and money laundering. Noriega's capture was technically a law enforcement operation: U.S. marshals arrested him, although 25,000 U.S. troops made the arrest possible, and the trial judge decided Noriega should be considered a prisoner of war and allowed to wear his military uniform in prison. The terrorist states that the United States has faced in the past and to a lesser degree confronts today present no opportunities comparable to that of Panama, which was a weak country with long-standing ties to the United States, a substantial U.S. military presence in place, and reasonable prospects for a legitimate regime to succeed the corrupt military dictator who was the target. Practical problems aside, criminal law is properly conceived as an instrument and not as an imperative that, if applied to a head of government, necessarily sweeps aside all other aspects of U.S. relations with the government in question.

Not only is it difficult to arrest leading international terrorists; it is also difficult to make prosecutorial cases against many of them. A successful arrest creates a risk because the worst possible outcome would be for a terrorist to be tried and acquitted. That would be a bigger and more dramatic blow to counterterrorism than a failure to capture the terrorist in the first place. The prosecutor's assembling of a case that will stand up in court is generally harder than the assembling of information that is sufficient, for policymaking purposes, to determine that someone is a terrorist. A legal case is not the same as an intelligence case. With a low-level participant in a terrorist attack there is often physical evidence and testimony linking the individual to specific steps in the operation. But with senior terrorist leaders, key links in the chain of decisions and orders leading to an operation are almost always beyond the reach of investigators.

These prosecutorial challenges make for some difficult decisions about whether, and when, to indict terrorists. The possibility of an indicted suspect coming into U.S. custody—even without an active manhunt for him, as might happen if he is identified while crossing a border—raises the specter of a dismissal or acquittal if the criminal case against him is weak. This is an argument for delaying indictment until more evidence is gathered. But there may be other reasons for an early indictment—in particular, to preserve legal options before a statute of limitations expires. Sealed indictments may be used to overcome this dilemma, but there is some resistance to using them, especially from those in the law enforcement community who want to show publicly what they have accomplished.

A further complication in decisions about bringing charges against terrorists is that initiation of a criminal case may mean losing a source of intelligence about a terrorist group. Some of the individuals about whom the strongest criminal cases could be made—because they have significant, known roles in the group—are, for the same reason, among the best sources of intelligence (as either witting informants or as people whose activities and contacts can be secretly monitored). Other sources, human or technical, may dry up as an unavoidable consequence of indicting and trying someone. In each case the value of a prosecution must be weighed against the possible opportunities to learn of—and to stop—further terrorist activity.

Difficulty in building a case against a foreign terrorist often includes difficulty in gaining the necessary cooperation from foreign governments. For prosecutors, the need is not just for information but for information that can be used in court. For many foreign governments that is an important distinction. Some foreign security services that willingly share sensitive terrorist-related information (or material) in regular liaison channels have resisted its use in a U.S. trial. The resistance stems from the same concerns about sensitive sources and methods that give U.S. intelligence officers unease when use of their material in court is proposed, and from fears of public knowledge that the country is cooperating at all with the

United States against certain terrorist groups. The Classified Information Procedures Act (CIPA) is useful in some situations, by providing for *in camera* review and unclassified stipulations when information derived from sensitive sources is needed for a trial.[14] U.S. judges are becoming increasingly familiar with CIPA's usefulness in terrorism cases. There is still apt to be nervousness among foreign officials, however, about any use in a U.S. court of material that conceivably could be traced back to them or their sources.

Capital punishment also affects foreign willingness to cooperate in U.S. prosecutions. As its name implies, the Antiterrorism and Effective Death Penalty Act of 1996 (AEDPA) established the death penalty for some terrorist crimes.[15] One reason U.S. prosecutors may try a case as a capital crime is that it avoids statutes of limitations, which for most other cases impose a limit of five years, extendable to eight. Seeking the death penalty for a foreign terrorist, however, would greatly diminish cooperation in the case from foreign governments. Regardless of one's views of capital punishment, the retention of it by the United States puts the nation out of step with many other countries, especially in the West. The statute for the proposed International Criminal Court (negotiated in 1998), for example, provides for no death penalty even though the court would handle such heinous crimes as genocide. Most governments that do not themselves have capital punishment, including members of the European Union, will not extradite fugitives to the United States without an explicit agreement that the death penalty will not be sought.[16] Moreover, many countries will not even provide evidence for prosecution of a terrorist without receiving such assurances.

Even without any problems connected with classified information or the death penalty, extraterritoriality has other, more fundamental, limitations. Authorizing a criminal prosecution under U.S. law does nothing to authorize it under someone else's law, including the someone else who normally has sovereign power in the territory where the crime was committed. Customary international law does provide some basis for extraterritorial prosecution of terrorist acts because most such acts would be covered by the "protective principle" (whereby a nation is free to act if its own security is threatened) or be considered "universal crimes" (ones so threatening to international order they can be tried anywhere).[17] There are conflicting principles in international law on criminal jurisdiction, however, and the principle that the nationality of the victims should determine who prosecutes the crime—the basis for U.S. extraterritorial statutes on terrorism—is by no means one of the better established or widely recognized ones. One legal commentator notes that it has traditionally been viewed as "at the fringes of customary international law."[18] Even accepting the principle, it does not say who should have priority in prosecuting a crime that claims victims of different nationalities.

The practical and diplomatic complications of extraterritoriality are at least as great as the legal ones. Any attempt to apply U.S. criminal law to an overseas crime involves, in theory, a choice between acting unilaterally or seeking the cooperation of the country where the crime was committed (and often also other countries, such as ones to which the terrorists fled after the crime). The challenges to working a foreign terrorist case unilaterally are so formidable, however, that the United States has wisely, in nearly all such instances, tried to work in concert with the other governments. Conducting an investigation and gathering evidence in a foreign land without the full cooperation of the local authorities would be hazardous as well as difficult. Arresting a suspect in a nonpermissive environment would likely mean a major military operation (like capturing Noriega) or a dangerous and uncertain covert action. And even if the criminal case were successful, the fact that unilateral pursuit of it would mean riding roughshod over some other country's sovereignty would almost certainly mean paying a significant diplomatic price. In practice, then, the extraterritorial application of U.S. criminal law to terrorism rests heavily on the cooperation of other states.

It is easy to understand why that cooperation is not always forthcoming, even with a shared commitment to counterterrorism and a shared interest in opposing the terrorist threat at hand. One has only to imagine the roles reversed and to ask what the U.S. response would or should be if a foreign government insisted on jurisdictional primacy for a terrorist crime within the United States in which the foreign state's citizens were among the victims. Of course, there are always other asymmetries, including perhaps that the United States has more and better investigative resources to apply to a case than does the other government. But the fact remains that in implementing extraterritoriality the United States is asking other governments to yield in ways that the United States itself would be unlikely to yield.[19] Some combination of resentment over this basic asymmetry, punctiliousness about one's own law and sovereignty, fear of revealing skeletons in local closets, fear of how the United States may respond to conclusive proof of responsibility, and simple *amour propre* may lead some governments—despite the shared interests with the United States—to be less forthcoming than U.S. investigators and prosecutors require.

The Khubar Towers and African embassy cases illustrate the wide variation in foreign cooperation with U.S. prosecutions of terrorist cases. FBI
Director Freeh has publicly stated his agency's frustration with what it
considered inadequate cooperation in the Khubar case from Saudi Arabia
(which had shut out the United States even more thoroughly from investigation of the bombing in Riyadh the previous year). "We have not gotten
everything which we have asked for," said Freeh in 1997, "and that has
affected our ability to make findings or conclusions."[20] The Saudi behavior was far different from the "exceptional cooperation and assistance,"
as Freeh put it, that the United States received from Kenya and Tanzania
after the East Africa bombings. That cooperation included help in conducting interviews and searches and permission to remove evidence and
suspects to the United States.[21] U.S. prosecutors and investigators were
impressed with how Kenyan officials were both helpful and effective—a
rare combination.

Even in Kenya, however, there developed an undercurrent of resentment related to one of the key aspects of extraterritoriality: that the U.S.
criminal justice system, with all of its impressive investigative resources,
becomes fully engaged only when U.S. citizens are killed or hurt or U.S.
property is damaged. This aspect is noted by foreigners already prepared
to be critical of what they see as American tunnel vision on terrorism.[22] In
the attacks on the embassies in Africa, Africans suffered the most. In Dar
es Salaam, none of the eleven persons killed, and only two of the seventy-
four injured, were U.S. citizens. In Nairobi, the American casualties were
12 out of 213 killed and 13 out of approximately 4,500 injured. Kenyans
openly resented how U.S. rescue and recovery efforts after the bombings
seemed narrowly focused on the American victims. More than a year later
there was still, as one embassy official put it, "a lingering perception that
we didn't do enough" to help the African victims. A trip to Nairobi by
Secretary of State Madeleine Albright in October 1999, during which she
visited some of the Kenyans disabled by the blast, was intended to assuage
that resentment.[23] Such ill feelings have less to do with criminal prosecutions than with other aspects of responding to a terrorist incident, but
extraterritoriality and the U.S.-only orientation of the criminal justice instrument add to the image of a United States that expects everyone else to
defer to it when Americans are involved but that is less sensitive to the
suffering that terrorism inflicts on others.

Image is not the main shortcoming of extraterritorial jurisdiction being
applicable only to terrorism that directly claims American victims. No
nation, after all, should have to apologize for giving priority consider-

ation to its own citizens. The principal shortcoming is that terrorism that violates U.S. law is incongruent with terrorism that affects U.S. interests. The impact of international terrorism on U.S. interests cannot simply be measured in dead American bodies. Whether U.S. citizens have been killed or wounded in a terrorist incident determines whether U.S. criminal law applies; it does not determine, however, whether the incident, or the issues associated with it, warrant significant U.S. attention. Sometimes American casualties are happenstance. Some of the bombings in Israel by Hamas or the Palestine Islamic Jihad, for example, have claimed the lives of Americans who were unfortunate enough to be standing on the wrong street corner when the bomb went off. The FBI (partly at congressional urging) has devoted considerable attention and resources to these incidents. But except for the immediate victims, these attacks affected U.S. interests no more than otherwise similar bombings in Israel that did not happen to catch any unlucky American passersby. In any event, the Israelis have shown no inclination to give up control of the investigations.

The FBI's formidable investigative skills might be more usefully applied to some other incidents in which no Americans are hurt and in which it may even be unclear whether any were targeted. Indeed, the latter question is one that a thorough investigation sometimes might help to clear up. One such incident was an aborted truck bombing in Bangkok in 1994. The incident came to light when the truck, loaded with more than a ton of C4 and ANFO (ammonium nitrate and fuel oil) explosives, collided in traffic with a motorcycle taxi. The driver of the truck, after a brief exchange with the taxi driver, fled on foot. The truck appeared to be headed for the Israeli embassy, but the target might instead have been the U.S. embassy, which was also nearby. The Thai authorities' handling of the case was slipshod. The abandoned truck was parked at a police station for a week, for example, before its contents were examined (leading to the discovery that a dead body—of an employee of the truck rental agency— was mixed in with the explosives). The Thais later arrested several Iranians for possibly being connected with the operation but released most of them for lack of evidence.[24] The full story of this incident has yet to be uncovered. If the FBI (cooperating with the Thais) could have applied its resources to the case from the outset, perhaps the story would have been told long ago. It certainly would have been in the interest of the United States to get to the bottom of it. But there were neither the U.S. casualties nor the clearly identified U.S. target that would have provided the basis for U.S. investigators to weigh in.

The various problems associated with an individual country (the United States or any other) trying in its national courts a crime that is really transnational have led some to suggest prosecution of terrorism in an international forum. The proposed International Criminal Court, a statute for which was completed at a conference in Rome in 1998, is such a forum. The ICC would be a standing court to handle a variety of criminal cases, based partly on the precedent of the limited-purpose international tribunals for the Balkans and Africa. It is unlikely, however, that the ICC will assume an effective role—or any role at all—in prosecuting terrorist cases. For one thing, the creation of the court is uncertain. As of the end of 2000, one hundred and thirty-nine states had signed the treaty to establish it, but only twenty-seven had ratified it. Sixty ratifications are required for the treaty to enter into force and the court to be formed. The most important source of uncertainty is the United States, which had earlier supported creation of an ICC (and eventually signed the treaty) but, disturbed by certain features of the court's statute, voted against it at Rome.

The trying of terrorist crimes was one of the issues behind the negative U.S. vote. The United States and a number of other states had long opposed efforts to include terrorism (and drug crimes) in the court's jurisdiction because this would undermine existing efforts against those problems. This view seemed to prevail until almost the end of the Rome conference, when language was added in a resolution annexed to the main treaty stating that terrorism and drug crimes would indeed come under the court's jurisdiction, subject only to their being defined at a future review conference. The U.S. opposition was well-founded. Distinguishing terrorism in a legally precise way from other crimes of violence that would still be prosecuted only in national courts means traversing an old definitional morass—a difficult feat, as indicated by the failure to arrive at such a definition at the Rome conference. A greater problem is that an international court would not be linked to the police, investigative, and intelligence resources that make it feasible for national courts to prosecute terrorist crimes. Trying terrorist cases would be much different from the work of earlier international tribunals handling war crimes or genocide, in which there was ample evidence because of the defeat of a state in war or the sheer magnitude of the crime, and what was needed was an impartial forum in which to prosecute. Applying criminal law to modern terrorism instead requires long-term investigative work, the exploitation of intelligence sources, and often the handling of sensitive material that is delicate even in a national court but would be next to impossible in an international forum. The criminal justice instrument will, as far as terrorism is concerned, continue to be a national instrument.[25]

That instrument will, and should, also continue to be a major part of the overall U.S. counterterrorist effort, despite its shortcomings. There is still counterterrorist value in applying the rule of law to terrorists, in addition to whatever value is placed on the application of justice for its own sake. The significance of the shortcomings is threefold. First, everyone involved in using the instrument—including policymakers, prosecutors, and investigators—needs to be aware of likely frictions and pitfalls and to adjust tactics and techniques accordingly. This can involve everything from decisions on whether to seek the death penalty (bearing in mind the chilling effect this may have on foreign cooperation) to how an FBI agent comports himself overseas (bearing in mind how foreign counterparts may contribute to a case, even though they may have yielded the principal investigative role to the United States).

Second, the limitations to what criminal law can accomplish against terrorism underscore the importance of the other counterterrorist instruments. "Rule of law" may be mentioned more often than the other instruments, and a successful prosecution may provide a more satisfying sense of finality and accomplishment than do the others, but it is not inherently more important. Decisions about policy and resources should not treat the conviction and imprisonment of terrorists as an overriding goal. There is much counterterrorist work that needs to be done (toward the true overriding goal of saving lives) that is simply beyond the capacity of criminal law.

Third, even when the U.S. criminal justice system *could* be used, decisions *whether* to use it should be made with flexibility and the broadest possible perspective regarding available options. Prosecutors always exercise discretion in deciding whether to bring charges, based on their judgment of whether the law and the evidence in a case are likely to yield a conviction. In international terrorist cases, such decisions should also be based on other pertinent considerations, including the various ways in which the U.S. handling of the case may increase or reduce future terrorism and the possible effects on foreign policy equities that go beyond counterterrorism itself. Even if the chance of a conviction is high, it may make sense not to indict if, for example, doing so would mean losing a source of information about the ongoing activity of a terrorist group (and in some cases charges are not brought for exactly that reason).

The options for handling some cases should include letting another country prosecute. Applying the rule of law does not have to mean applying

U.S. law. Whether this is an option depends on where the terrorist in question is wanted for his crimes; whether it is an option that should be chosen depends on the quality and reliability of the other country's criminal justice system. U.S. courts usually should be employed if political pressures, fear, or corruption keep full justice from being done in the other country's courts. Indeed, the United States has properly brought charges against some terrorists who were already tried elsewhere but who, for some combination of the reasons just given, were not appropriately punished. For example, both Mohammed Ali Rezaq and Mohammed Rashid were prosecuted in the United States despite being tried and convicted in foreign courts. The few years that each had served in a foreign prison (Rezaq in Malta and Rashid in Greece) before being given early release were incommensurate with the seriousness of their crimes, which involved lethal attacks on air passengers. Similarly, the United States has a criminal case against Panamanian Pedro Miguel Gonzalez for the murder of U.S. serviceman Zak Hernandez, even though Gonzalez was tried and acquitted in Panama. The U.S. government has described the trial of Gonzalez—whose father led Panama's ruling party at the time—as subject to "irregularities and political manipulation."[26] The possibility of someday having to correct such miscarriages of justice is one reason U.S. prosecutors may file an indictment even if their own case is less than strong and they do not expect to try it soon.

In other terrorist cases, however, letting someone else mete out the justice may have advantages—not least of which is that the United States would not be the prime target for any terrorist response. Yielding to Israel to handle fully the terrorist incidents within Israel that have claimed American lives is appropriate, not only because the Israelis are best positioned to investigate crimes in their own territory but because they can be relied upon to deliver appropriate justice. A further consideration in these cases, of course, was that most of the victims were Israelis. But a precedent in which most of the victims were Americans (189 out of the 270 killed) is the Pan Am 103 trial, conducted not by a U.S. court but by a Scottish court applying Scottish law.

Similarly, it may make more sense for the United States to defer to a moderate Muslim state to try some of the leading Islamist terrorists (with the goal of a conviction leading to life imprisonment or, if that state's courts so decide, execution) than to try the suspect itself. Several such terrorists are wanted men not only in the United States but in some Muslim states, including one or more that would not shirk from seeing justice done. The United States can still play a supporting role, by providing information to help build the case and/or arranging for the rendition of the suspect to the country where he will be tried. Such a behind-the-scenes role not only reduces U.S. exposure to terrorist reprisals but also reduces the America-vs.-the-Muslim-world connotations that a well-publicized U.S. trial would have in many Muslim minds. And the terrorist can be taken out of circulation, and punished, as surely as if a U.S. court did the job.

Just as a conviction in a U.S. court should not be the only (or even the primary) goal of the U.S. counterterrorism program, it should not be the only goal of U.S. law enforcement officers working on terrorism. Those officers constitute an impressive investigative capability for unearthing and interpreting information about the activity of international terrorists. That capability resides chiefly in the FBI but also includes relevant skills in other law enforcement agencies, such as the Bureau of Alcohol, Tobacco, and Firearms and the Secret Service. The capability can be an important supplement to the other sources of information on terrorism, even without making a criminal case. Decisions to employ the investigative resources of law enforcement agencies should therefore be kept distinct from decisions on whether to prosecute someone. It should be understood by senior managers in those agencies, and those to whom they are accountable, that it is an appropriate use of their resources to assist in counterterrorist work even if the case does not culminate with a criminal conviction in a U.S. court. This might include gathering information in support of administrative actions or simply helping to find out more about a murky terrorist-related situation (such as the Bangkok incident) which it would behoove the U.S. government to understand and to which the law enforcement agencies' talents are well suited. The use of those agencies in foreign cases should be selective to avoid stretching their resources too thin, and some modification of the rules and guidelines for initiating investigations would probably be required to permit this use.[27]

Financial Controls

Money has often been described as a key to international terrorism and thus to counterterrorism. Track it, some have said, and the responsibility for terrorist attacks will become clear. Interdict it, and terrorism will be reduced as its financial "lifeblood" dries up. Financial support certainly has been a principal part of state sponsorship of terrorism, and the most important part of the assistance that some states have given to some terrorist groups. The emergence of Usama bin Ladin as a leading nonstate terrorist has sustained interest in terrorist finances, given the role of his wealth and the fact that he first came to prominence as an extremist financier. More broadly, financial controls have been a focus of attention of those hoping to make international sanctions "smarter" by targeting them more accurately at wrongdoers and not at innocent victims.[28] Financial controls do have a modest part to play in counterterrorism, but the bolder claims for what can be accomplished by going after the terrorists' money are oversold.

The United States has taken two types of action against terrorist finances: the freezing of assets belonging to individual terrorists, terrorist groups, or state sponsors; and the prohibition of material support to terrorists. The blocking of state sponsors' assets has been employed the longest, using authorities in the International Emergency Economic Powers Act (IEEPA) and other statutes.[29] All of the designated state sponsors except Syria currently have assets blocked in the United States. The most recent blockage of a regime's assets—those of the Taliban—was accomplished under Executive Order 13129 in July 1999. The freezing of assets belonging to terrorist groups and individuals began in 1995 with Executive Order 12947, which named twelve Middle Eastern groups and gave the secretary of the treasury authority to designate individual terrorists to be subject, like the groups, to the freeze. The omnibus antiterrorism act of 1996, the AEDPA, extended the blockage of assets to every group that the secretary of state designates as a Foreign Terrorist Organization. The principal device for implementing these laws and orders is simply for the Treasury Department to direct U.S. financial institutions to freeze accounts under their control that are known to belong to the named states, groups, or individuals. The prohibitions on transactions with terrorists were broader than that but did not become criminal offenses until the 1996 legislation, which established penalties of up to ten years' imprisonment for knowingly providing material support or resources to a foreign terrorist organization or for engaging in unauthorized financial transactions with a state sponsor.[30]

Money is also the subject of the newest international convention on terrorism. The Convention on the Suppression of the Financing of Terrorism, which was opened for signature in January 2000, requires governments to criminalize the provision or collection of funds for terrorist acts and to seize or freeze funds known to be allocated for terrorist purposes. It also mandates cooperation on investigations and extraditions in cases involving financial support to terrorism. The United States, through its previous unilateral actions, is well on the way toward compliance with the convention, which comes into effect when twenty-two states have ratified it.

Putting aside grandiose talk about drying up lifeblood, there are several more modest counterterrorist objectives that one might hope to advance through financial controls and prohibitions. First, blocked assets of state sponsors can be bargaining chips in reaching future understandings with those states, including understandings about ending support to terrorism. Second, even small interdictions of money might at least make a dent in a terrorist's ability to operate. A penny seized is a penny earned for the counterterrorist cause. Third, the threat of interdiction may complicate a group's financial operations. Fourth, criminalization of support to terrorist groups may help to deter some potential supporters. And fifth, appearing tough on financial support is one more way for the United States to demonstrate its seriousness about combating terrorism and expectations for what other governments should do. In particular, it helps to keep U.S. skirts clean by showing that the United States is doing all it can to prevent any support to terrorism from its own citizens, institutions, or territory.

Two major limitations prevent the financial instrument from playing more than a secondary role in counterterrorism. First, terrorism is cheap. Granted, some terrorist organizations maintain large and rather costly organizations, which underlies the relationship of some of them with outside sponsors. But the basic act of killing somebody or blowing something up does not require much money. The truck bomb used at the World Trade Center is estimated to have cost $400.[31] Terrorism is fundamentally different from other leading transnational problems—including narcotics trafficking, other for-profit organized crime, and the procurement of advanced weapons systems—in that big flows of money are not intrinsic to the operation. Production of narcotics, for example, would be pointless if large amounts of cash were not moved from the countries where the product is consumed back to where the producers live. The need of drug traffickers and other criminal syndicates to launder money provides a vulnerability and a basis for money-based strategies for countering them.[32] Although money laundering involves much "dirty" cash being converted into "clean" money, the financial side of terrorism involves smaller amounts of money, some of which may have started out as clean, being consumed within the dirty world. The financial vulnerability of the perpetrators is less, and not all of the same strategies for countering them apply.[33]

Second, the money that does flow in the terrorist world is extremely difficult to track. FBI Director Freeh was, if anything, understating the problem when he noted in commenting on the financial provisions of the AEDPA: "Investigations into the financial operations of clandestine organizations on the shadowy fringes of international politics can be particularly complex, time consuming, and labor intensive."[34] One difficulty, which Freeh mentioned, is the routine use by terrorist groups of multiple names and false names. This is even more true of money handling than of other terrorist-related activities, with financial accounts (including accounts in the United States) almost never being in a name that reveals actual ties. The complex organizational links among interlocking and overlapping groups also frustrate efforts to follow any terrorist-related money trail. Legitimate businesses are often involved. So are nongovernmental organizations, which often commingle funds used for charitable work with those destined for nefarious work. Terrorists usually have multiple channels for storing and moving funds (which is one reason a freeze of assets works best the first time it is used against a target, with its utility greatly diminishing after that).

For the United States, an additional limitation is that most of the terrorist financial transactions that might matter take place outside the United States and do not involve institutions subject to U.S. control. Foreign cooperation is thus at least as important in this aspect of counterterrorism as with others, but—for a variety of reasons involving capability and willingness—is even less likely to be forthcoming. Many of the banking and financial practices in areas of the world that leading terrorists inhabit impede investigative efforts, by foreign governments as well as by the United States. Much international movement of money in the Middle East, for example, takes place outside the formal banking system altogether and is accomplished through informal money-by-wire arrangements or the physical movement of currency. Moreover, the whole offshore banking industry, which operates in places as far-flung as Seychelles and the Caribbean and makes a business out of financial confidentiality, is available to terrorists just as it is to others who have reasons to conceal their transactions. When the United States asks a foreign government to clamp down on terrorist-connected financial transactions that are strongly suspected of taking place on its territory, the usual response is an expression of good intentions and a request for exact account numbers. There the discussion often ends. Perhaps a U.S. financial institution in a similar situation, stimulated by the hot breath of the Treasury Department and the FBI, would do the additional digging based on fragmentary information needed to identify terrorist-related assets. But for most foreign governments the exercise seems too difficult, too weakly connected with terrorist attacks, and too likely to ruffle local feathers for it to be worth doing.

All of these limitations are reflected in what the United States has, and has not, been able to do about terrorist money under the laws and executive orders mentioned above. Quantitatively the biggest accomplishment has been blocking the assets of states, whose accounts are much less concealed than those of groups and individuals. As of the end of 1999 there was $2.8 billion in state sponsors' assets frozen in the United States. The biggest portion belonged to Iraq ($1.5 billion) followed by Libya (just under $1 billion). This sum does not include $252 million in Taliban assets blocked under Executive Order 13129, or $566 million in blocked state assets that are in the foreign branches of U.S. banks. Other than with states, the yield has been meager. Only $104,000 in assets belonging to members of Hamas and the Palestine Islamic Jihad are blocked under the IEEPA-based executive orders. No other assets of terrorists or terrorist groups have been frozen, including any assets connected to the Foreign Terrorist Organizations identified under the AEDPA.[35] As for criminal prosecutions, as of mid-2000 there had been three indictments under the AEDPA for providing material support to Foreign Terrorist Organizations, but all three involved the shipment or attempted shipment of goods. None involved financial contributions.

This record suggests that the value of the financial control instrument will always be more the symbolic one of demonstrating U.S. seriousness in countering terrorism on every possible front than the material one of impoverishing terrorist groups. Two steps might marginally improve effectiveness, however.

One would be to provide greater support from within the government to the Treasury Department's mission of finding and freezing terrorist assets, as distinct from the law enforcement mission of prosecuting criminal cases. These administrative actions require a lower standard of proof and can be accomplished much faster than a criminal prosecution, but they may still have some deterrent value. Assistance might include a broader use of the law enforcement agencies' investigative resources, as suggested in the previous section. The Clinton administration took a step in a similar direction with a budget reprogramming, announced in May 2000, that would support the establishment of an interagency National Terrorist Asset Tracking Center, as well as expanding the Treasury Department's own

Office of Foreign Assets Control (OFAC).[36] The center would appear to fill one of the functions envisioned by the National Commission on Terrorism in calling for the creation of an interagency task force on terrorist fund-raising.[37]

Second, the United States can enhance the ability of foreign financial officials to impede terrorist-related transactions, including through formal training. This is one area in which efforts to combat money laundering can help in counterterrorism. During 1999 the United States funded more than seventy courses and seminars, in forty countries, on financial crime and money laundering. Plans were afoot in 2000 to expand this program to include a curriculum on terrorist financing.[38] The latter training will be aimed mainly at investigators, prosecutors, and judges, but it would be useful as well to educate foreign officials on what can be done through seizure and blocking of assets, not just prosecutions. Such an educational effort starts from a low base. Other governments do not have an equivalent to OFAC. Even in some developed countries, the closest counterpart may be only a single official in the justice ministry, finance ministry, or central bank. Besides imparting investigative skills, the task is one of helping foreign officials to think creatively about new ways to apply their own laws.

Military Force

The military instrument, besides being intrinsically the most forceful, has also become less blunt than it once was, owing to the development of precision-guided munitions and other advanced technology. But it is still used less often than any other instrument. One way to employ armed force against terrorism—the rescue of hostages—the United States has not used since a failed attempt two decades ago. Another way—retaliatory strikes following a terrorist attack—it had used only three times through 2000. The rarity appropriately reflects the difficulties involved.

Conceivably another use of military force would be to strike terrorist capabilities preemptively, rather than in response to a specific terrorist incident. States have not used armed forces in this way in modern times, apart from some of the Israeli military operations in Lebanon. All of the limitations of retaliatory strikes discussed below would also apply to preemptive operations, and without the justification of being a response to a terrorist attack. For those reasons, the overt preemptive use of military force against terrorists is unlikely and unwise.

Several other countries were ahead of the United States in developing a dedicated military capability to rescue hostages. The unsuccessful German attempt to rescue the Israeli athletes kidnapped at the Olympic Games in Munich in 1972 led the major West European governments to develop highly skilled commando units with this mission.[39] For the United States, the principal turning point was its attempt in 1980 to rescue hostages at the seized American embassy in Tehran, an operation that ended in flames and failure in the Iranian desert. Because that disaster was attributed partly to coordination problems, the U.S. military subsequently developed a new command structure that evolved into the Joint Special Operations Command (JSOC). The command is now a subordinate element of the U.S. Special Operations Command (SOCOM), which was activated in 1987. JSOC's publicly stated mission is opaque, but numerous published reports have identified it as the center of the U.S. military's capability to apply armed force to an ongoing terrorist incident.

JSOC has never had to rescue a single hostage, although it reportedly made plans for doing so in some incidents that ended peaceably, and its capabilities have been employed in several operations unrelated to terrorism.[40] The previously noted scarcity of classic hostage-taking terrorist attacks, particularly ones against the United States, is the chief reason why JSOC has not been used for this purpose and why this military capability will remain only a minor part of the U.S. counterterrorist picture. But it is worth noting why, even if such an incident were to occur, decisionmakers should think very hard before attempting to resolve it militarily. Such operations are extremely difficult and risky, and their results have been mixed and sometimes tragic. One remembers the dazzling successes, such as the Israelis' raid at Entebbe, Uganda, in 1976 (which saved all but 3 of the 106 people aboard a hijacked airliner), or the Germans' similar operation the following year in Mogadishu (in which all 86 hostages aboard a hijacked Lufthansa jet were rescued). It is perhaps easier to forget the failures, such as the Egyptians' raid on a hijacked Egypt Air plane in Malta in 1985, during which the terrorists threw grenades inside the aircraft and 60 of the 96 passengers and crew died in the resulting explosions and fire.

Some of the variation in results can be attributed to differences in skill of the forces conducting the operations. But success comes hard even to the very best. Consider the record of Israel, which has far more experience in doing this that any other country. Israeli antiterrorist commando forces are second to none. Their officers have included some of Israel's best and brightest (including two who later became prime minister: Benjamin

Netanyahu and Ehud Barak). Along with Entebbe and other successes, Israel has had its share of failures—even on its own territory, where presumably it would be easier to operate than in a foreign country. In 1974, for example, three members of the Democratic Front for the Liberation of Palestine infiltrated the Israeli town of Ma'alot and seized a schoolhouse where ninety teenagers were sleeping. When Israeli commandos stormed the building they killed two of the terrorists but only wounded the third, who fired an automatic weapon and threw grenades for another ten minutes. Before he, too, was finally killed he had slain sixteen of the teenagers and wounded seventy others, six of whom later died. The following year, Fatah terrorists captured ten hostages at a hotel in Tel Aviv. In the ensuing gun battle, seven of the terrorists were killed but so were eight of the hostages and three of the Israeli soldiers attempting to rescue them. A more recent incident involved the kidnapping of an Israeli soldier by Hamas in 1994. The rescue attempt resulted in the death of the hostage and of one of the officers of the assault team, as well as injuries to several of the other Israeli commandos.[41]

These failures were not because of any lack of skill or bravery on the part of the rescue forces. They happened because of the inherent difficulty of using force in a situation in which the terrorists have the advantage of being able—and willing—to use it immediately against their captives. The line between triumph and tragedy in such operations is thin, and luck plays a major role. The Peruvian rescue in Lima in 1997, for example, could easily have taken a terrible turn—if, say, the terrorists had received even a few seconds' warning (by noticing the preassault activity outside the compound), giving them enough time to stop the soccer game they were playing and grab their weapons.

The capabilities of the U.S. military's special operations units are awesome, and they would stand at least as great a chance as anyone else of pulling off a successful rescue operation. (Moreover, the multiple uses to which their capabilities can be put make them a force worth having, even if they are never called upon to intervene in a terrorist incident.) But the operative word is "chance." Any decision to use military force in this mode should anticipate—and be well prepared to deal with the consequences of—failure as a possible outcome.

Retaliation has been the more important counterterrorist use of U.S. military force. The United States first employed it for this purpose against Libya in 1986, in response to the bombing on April 4 of a nightclub in Berlin, La Belle Discotheque, that off-duty U.S. servicemen frequented.

American casualties at the nightclub included two killed and seventy-nine wounded. The U.S. response on April 14 was a strike by one hundred combat aircraft based on carriers or in the United Kingdom. The targets were several military sites in and around Tripoli and Benghazi as well as numerous surface-to-air missile installations. The second retaliatory use was against Iraq for having unsuccessfully attempted to use paid agents to assassinate former president George Bush while he was visiting Kuwait in April 1993. The retaliatory strike on June 26 used twenty-three Tomahawk cruise missiles, all aimed at the headquarters of the Iraqi intelligence service in Baghdad. The third instance was a set of strikes on August 20, 1998 against targets associated with Usama bin Ladin, in response to the bombings thirteen days earlier of the U.S. embassies in Nairobi and Dar es Salaam. Several dozen cruise missiles were fired, mostly against a complex of training camps in eastern Afghanistan and a smaller number against a pharmaceutical plant in Sudan suspected of being connected to chemical weapons.

There were some obvious differences in how military force was applied in these three cases. The cruise missiles used in the latter two permitted accuracy that had not been possible in the attack on Libya, which killed thirty-six civilians even though the intended targets were military. The strike against Iraq was not only the smallest of the three but was intended to inflict few casualties (perhaps reflecting the less serious terrorist offense—a failed assassination—to which it was a response); the missiles struck the intelligence service headquarters at night, when it was presumed that few personnel would be present. In contrast, the targets and timing of the other two attacks were selected to kill people, including possibly the senior leaders involved, Qadhafi in Libya and bin Ladin in Afghanistan.

What the three attacks had in common was at least as important. All three were unilateral actions (although the strike against Libya required British cooperation). And all three were responses to terrorist operations for which there was ironclad evidence about responsibility. In the La Belle Discotheque case, intercepted communications (revealed by the Reagan administration) between Berlin and Tripoli indicated the Libyan hand. With the attempt against President Bush, both the statements of the men arrested in Kuwait and technical analysis of the items they had smuggled across the border from Iraq pointed clearly to Iraqi government management of the plot. For the bombings in Africa, intelligence from a variety of human and technical sources, statements of arrested suspects, and public statements by bin Ladin's organization left no doubt about its responsibility even though it did not claim the attacks directly. These three episodes have set the precedent that a very high standard of proof should be met before military force is employed against those deemed responsible for a terrorist attack.

Military retaliation is commonly motivated by more than a belief that it will reduce future terrorism. A major terrorist incident commonly arouses a desire to "do something," preferably something emphatic, to get back at the perpetrators. (In this respect there is a parallel with the use of criminal law to "see justice done" rather than to curb terrorist attacks.) A punitive military strike may be the only response that is emphatic and, as long as the principal perpetrators are beyond the reach of the criminal justice system, feasible. American sentiments about retaliation were reflected in the poll by the Chicago Council on Foreign Relations on attitudes toward foreign policy: 74 percent of the general public and 77 percent of the smaller sample of leaders said they would support retaliatory airstrikes against terrorist training camps and other terrorist-related facilities. Moreover, 57 percent of the public and 58 percent of the leaders even expressed support for the use of ground troops to respond to terrorist attacks—the only one of several scenarios in which a majority of the public indicated it would back the use of troops.[42] Polls taken after each of the U.S. retaliatory strikes have shown similar support for the individual attacks, even though the public expressed considerable doubt about whether the attacks would reduce terrorism.[43]

Is "doing something" a defensible reason for responding militarily to terrorist attacks, independent of the impact on terrorism itself? Catering to popular urges solely to bolster a government's popularity is not defensible as a matter of foreign policy, of course, however much it may be of interest to political advisers. Revenge for the sake of revenge is not very ennobling either, although some might argue that if enough Americans place value on exacting revenge, it is a legitimate goal for their government. A more justifiable perspective is that striking back may help to sustain national morale. This has probably been the principal consideration in most of Israel's retaliatory strikes against terrorist foes.[44] The United States has not been as physically beleaguered as Israel, but the strength with which Americans see their government standing up to international terrorism might affect their willingness to support other aspects of U.S. foreign policy. Finally, a demonstration of American fortitude might send a message to foreign allies and adversaries, with beneficial effects on nonterrorist issues. A punitive strike is chiefly a message-sending exercise, and as with any other use of military force, the audience includes more than just the immediate adversary.[45] As will be noted below, however, foreign perceptions of strikes against terrorists have had negative as well as positive sides, making the net impact on U.S. foreign policy interests uncertain.

As for the strictly counterterrorist role of military retaliation (that is, its role in reducing future terrorism), there are four possible benefits. First, as the most dramatic possible demonstration of U.S. seriousness in fighting terrorism, a military attack may stimulate other governments to enhance their own efforts to fight it. Second, the strike may directly disrupt the operations and impair the capability of the targeted terrorist organization. Third, the implicit threat of further retaliation may deter the targeted organization from attempting additional terrorist attacks against the United States. And fourth, there may be similar deterrence of other terrorist groups or states.

The attack on Libya certainly realized the first benefit, even among European governments that criticized the strike. Indeed, it was their fear of what additional unilateral actions the United States might take that led some of them to go farther than they had ever gone before in confronting Libya specifically and terrorism in general. European measures included expulsions of Libyan officials, cancellation of some contracts with Tripoli, reduction in purchases of oil and other trade with Libya, and an overall increase in resources and political efforts devoted to counterterrorism. Comparable benefits were not to be realized from the cruise missile strike on Iraq, which was already subject to an assortment of international sanctions since its invasion of Kuwait three years earlier, although perhaps there was a more general intangible benefit of sustaining attention to counterterrorism. The missile strikes in Afghanistan in 1998 possibly helped, in a manner similar to the Libyan episode, to facilitate the Security Council's adoption of sanctions against the Taliban the following year, although a more important factor in securing the council's approval was Russian interest in pressuring the Taliban because of its links to Chechen extremists whom Moscow believed responsible for several terrorist bombings in Russia.

The direct effects of military strikes on terrorist capabilities and operations have been minimal. Although the damage in Libya in 1986 was considerable, it would be difficult to identify any impairment of Libya's capability for conducting terrorism, which was much more a matter of clandestine operatives, relationships with foreign terrorist groups, and money than of military installations in Libya. The same could be said of the smaller attack on Iraq, which was a distraction and expense for the Iraqi security services but not a significant blow against their capabilities. The physical impact of the missile strike in Afghanistan was limited by the primitive nature of the facilities that were hit. U.S. officials described the damage to the training camps as "moderate to severe," but the camps consisted chiefly of such facilities as simple housing, firing ranges, and assembly areas, with few substantial structures that could not easily be replaced or repaired. Probably most of the people killed were trainees and instructors.[46] Apart from the physical destruction, it can be assumed that there was some disruption to the organization's procedures or at least its training activities. This disruption and the organization's heightened focus on security in Afghanistan might have resulted in plans for further terrorist attacks being postponed, although this outcome is uncertain. Worrying about his physical security may also have become a continuing distraction for bin Ladin that has marginally reduced his attention to further terrorist operations. It does not prevent such operations, however. Moreover, any such worry is based not just on the military attack of August 1998 but on all of the other indications that bin Ladin is a prime target of the United States. These include stories in the media (including both the U.S. and Pakistani press) suggesting that the United States might try to reach bin Ladin not only with cruise missiles but with a raid on the ground.[47]

The measures that U.S. action has induced bin Ladin and his organization to take inside Afghanistan may have some counterterrorist value as a distraction, but they undermine the third hoped-for benefit of military retaliation: to deter the terrorist in question from attacking again. Bin Ladin has taken one good shot from the U.S. military, and both he and his organization survived—even though his anticipated presence at one of the targeted facilities was a key consideration in the timing of the strike.[48] Now he is at least as hard to hit (or to capture) as he was before. His movements not only make it difficult to track him; it also means that by the time more missiles are ordered into action and arrive on target, he is likely—as in August 1998—to have already moved on. And of course, if he were to attack the United States again, he could heighten his own security even more in the days and weeks that followed.

One might make a case that the threat of further military retaliation has deterred bin Ladin, but the case is not strong. The fact that more than a year went by after the bombings in Africa without any confirmed attempts by this leading terrorist—who has declared war on the United States and publicly rationalized the killing of any Americans—to strike again suggests that the U.S. response to his earlier attacks may have indeed given him pause. But with the further passage of time it becomes harder to say that he has been deterred, since he may have been involved in attempted terrorist operations that good counterterrorist work elsewhere has preempted. A foiled plot to attack Americans in Jordan in late 1999 is a possible example.

The earlier U.S. retaliatory attacks are also unlikely to have deterred the targets of those attacks from further terrorism. The missile attack on Iraq was a pinprick compared with what the United States and its allies in the Persian Gulf War had already inflicted on it. Besides, ever since Desert Storm—when amateurish Iraqi attempts to conduct terrorist attacks against coalition targets were defeated—Iraqi terrorism has been limited more by capabilities than by intentions. The possible deterrent effect of the attack on Libya has been subject to debate. It is fairly clear, however, that Qadhafi did not get out of the terrorism business in the first couple of years after the U.S. raid. There were several instances during that period of possibly Libyan-sponsored terrorist attacks against U.S. targets, including ones that employed surrogates such as the Japanese Red Army. And there was the bombing of Pan Am 103 in December 1988.

Whether military retaliation has helped to deter other terrorists (not just the targets of the retaliatory strikes) is even more uncertain. There is no intelligence that would indicate that terrorists' plans have or have not been so affected. Statistical analyses of worldwide terrorism following the attack on Libya reveal an upsurge in incidents immediately after the U.S. strike but are otherwise inconclusive; some analysts suggest that terrorism subsided somewhat in the subsequent two years, but others interpret the data differently.[49] Whatever effect the U.S. attack may have had, one way or another, on global terrorism during that period is obscured by the many other influences on the behavior of terrorists. There are three reasons, however, to expect that any deterrence to be had from military retaliation is likely to be limited at best.

First, the terrorists most likely to threaten U.S. interests present few suitable military targets, especially high-value targets whose destruction would be very costly to the terrorists. This is chiefly the result of the threat coming more from groups than from states, with the former lacking the territory and physical infrastructure of the latter. The rudimentary nature of the targets in Afghanistan in 1998—which were the best of any possible targets associated with bin Ladin—are a case in point. With smaller or more transient groups such as the World Trade Center bombers, there are no suitable military targets at all. Even the largest and best organized groups have few physical facilities that would be effective pressure points. Lebanese Hizballah, for example, has known training camps and other facilities in Lebanon that could be struck in the event that Hizballah attacked U.S. interests, but the principal physical effect of such a strike might be to bounce rubble that the Israelis had already created several times over.

Second, the nonphysical effects of a military strike may serve some of the political and organizational purposes of terrorist leaders, and for that reason they may tacitly welcome such an attack. The immediate political effect within Libya of the airstrikes in 1986 appeared to be one of rallying the populace behind Qadhafi.[50] With terrorist groups, for a great power to fire salvos of million-dollar missiles increases the publicity given to the group and its cause, and may bolster the members' sense of importance. It also reinforces the leaders' message that the United States is an evil enemy that knows only the language of force.[51] In this regard terrorism has a dynamic similar to that of guerrilla warfare, in which one of the purposes of the guerrillas' attacks is to goad the government into counterattacking in ways that will alienate the civilian population and increase recruits, resources, and sympathy for the guerrillas.

Third, the terrorists' response to a retaliatory strike may be counter-retaliation rather than good behavior. Some of Israel's military strikes against its terrorist opponents have been part of seemingly endless patterns of action and reaction. The Israeli air raid on the PLO's headquarters in Tunis in 1985, for example, may have stimulated such reprisals, including the hijacking of the *Achille Lauro* (which was intended as an attack on the Israeli port of Ashdod) and an attack on El Al ticket counters in the airports at Rome and Vienna (where a note found on one of the terrorists said the attack was a response to the Tunis raid).[52] If some of the Libyan-sponsored operations in the late 1980s—especially Pan Am 103— were reprisals for the U.S airstrike of April 1986, it was an unsurprising response from a Libyan leader who did not lose his terrorist capability, but did lose his adopted daughter, in the U.S. bombing.

Besides the limitations to such hoped-for results as disruption and deterrence, military retaliation has other problems. A lesser one—but one that still needs to be taken into account in any decision to employ armed force—is the practical challenge (which sometimes becomes a political one) of getting the appropriate ordnance on target and getting it there safely and with surprise. Overflight is a consideration. The U.S. aircraft based in the United Kingdom that were among those that attacked Libya (others were launched from carriers in the Mediterranean) took an exhausting circuitous route because France and Spain had refused permission to overfly their territories during the mission. The more recent reliance on sea-launched cruise missiles has lessened that problem, but striking land-locked Afghanistan still meant overflying Pakistan, which compounded the unfavorable Pakistani reactions to the strike. (The vice chairman of the Joint Chiefs of Staff, who was visiting Pakistan at the time, had the unenviable task of informing his hosts at the appropriate moment that U.S. missiles were violating their airspace.)[53]

A greater problem is more broadly based resentment against the world's only superpower using its military muscle offensively. Many will inevitably see any such operation as contemptible bullying, no matter how strong the case against the terrorists being struck or how skillfully that case is presented. Foreign reactions to the three U.S. retaliations ranged from mixed to decidedly negative. The perception even of most European allies to the strike on Libya was sharply negative (although, as mentioned earlier, it had the indirect benefit of spurring some of these allies to take other counterterrorist measures). Reactions in the Arab world to the missile strike against Iraq included silence from some Arab countries friendliest to the United States and vehement criticism from others. Israel was the only Middle Eastern state to support publicly the missile strikes in 1998, although the reactions of the Arab governments with the closest ties to the United States were again temperate, while others were highly critical. The most favorable reactions were from Europeans to the strikes against bin Ladin: the United Kingdom and Germany strongly supported them, although France's and Italy's reactions were more lukewarm and Russian President Boris Yeltsin said he was "outraged" (partly because he had not been consulted in advance).

Foreign reactions will depend partly on the case against the terrorists but also on whatever political context gives foreigners a basis for interpreting U.S. motives. Cynical interpretations tend to prevail. The strong backing that the U.S. public commonly gives to forceful responses against foreign threats (and that is especially likely with military force against terrorists) leads easily to the belief that boosting domestic support was the real reason for a retaliatory attack. This was how many viewed the missile strikes in 1998, especially given the unfortunate coincidence with President Clinton's political and legal troubles stemming from the Monica Lewinsky affair. (The strikes occurred three days after the president admitted in a televised address that he had misled the public about his relationship with Lewinsky.) Even though bin Ladin's culpability was unassailable, intelligence about a scheduled meeting of bin Ladin and other terrorist leaders at the training site in Afghanistan determined the timing of the attack on August 20 (the meeting evidently did occur but broke up before the missiles arrived),[54] the administration's senior national security officials (including a Republican secretary of defense) unanimously backed the strikes, and the attacks received considerable bipartisan support in Congress (Speaker of the House Newt Gingrich said the president "did exactly the right thing"), there was still suspicion that the decision to fire the missiles had more to do with the president's political problems than with terrorism. The issue surfaced so recurrently that it acquired a shorthand label: the "Wag the Dog" scenario—after the title of a then-popular movie, the plot of which involved the White House concocting a phony war to divert attention from a presidential sex scandal. Well after the event, American critics of Clinton were still alluding to the issue.[55] Such doubts found resonance among foreign critics of America, and among others overseas who might otherwise have believed that the retaliation had to do only with terrorism but were given reason to believe otherwise. The whole affair muddied the message that the missile strikes were intended to send.

The tendency of foreign audiences toward criticism and cynicism in reacting to U.S. retaliatory attacks may extend to the targets as well as the timing of such attacks. That was certainly true of the decision to strike the al-Shifa pharmaceutical plant in Sudan in 1998. Criticism of the decision at home and abroad was long and strong, and the United States was on a public relations defensive well after the attack. The attack struck some of the stronger anti-U.S. propagandistic chords: the United States was castigated not only for using its military might to kill Muslims but for striking at poor dark-skinned Muslims by destroying a factory that made their medicines.

There was nothing about the intelligence that the United States had on al-Shifa that has proved inaccurate; what U.S. intelligence said about the plant in August 1998 was essentially the same as what could be said about it two years later.[56] The elements of that intelligence were that certain aspects of the security of the plant and public information about it suggested that it was engaged in more sensitive activity than just the production of pharmaceuticals; that a sample of soil collected outside the plant—unlike samples collected at other suspicious sites in Sudan—contained a chemical that is a precursor to the nerve agent VX (there are other conceivable reasons for the chemical to exist, but none that was a plausible explanation for it to be present at this location in Sudan); that there were reasons to believe the al-Shifa plant was part of Sudan's larger Military Industrial Corporation, the center of Sudanese work on the development of weapons, including unconventional weapons; that bin Ladin contributed financially to this corporation (part of his substantial ties with the Sudanese regime dominated by Hassan al-Turabi's National Islamic Front); that there were other, more direct, links between bin Ladin and the management of the al-Shifa plant; and that there were other intelligence reports that bin Ladin's organization was attempting to acquire a chemical weapons capability (not to mention bin Ladin's public statements suggesting the same thing). The only respect in which the intelligence picture evolved in the weeks following the retaliatory strike was the emergence of some additional links between bin Ladin and the manager of the al-Shifa plant.

U.S. intelligence did not say that al-Shifa should be destroyed; it did not say that an active VX production program was there; and it did not say that destroying the plant would make a difference in bin Ladin attacking, or not attacking, the United States in the future with chemical weapons. U.S. intelligence performed the same role in August 1998 that it always performs in supporting military targeting: namely, providing everything known about a large number of sites that are associated with the adversary and that could be reviewed by military planners and senior decisionmakers for possible selection as targets. The intelligence did not show what role, if any, al-Shifa may ever have played in any VX program (production, storage, occasional transshipment, or whatever), nor did it point to any specific plans by bin Ladin to use chemicals in a future attack. The intelligence also did not deny that the plant was engaged in the legitimate production of pharmaceuticals (chemical weapons programs elsewhere, as in Iraq, have had such dual-use facilities). The issue was thus not one of bad intelligence but rather whether, based on the partial information and still unanswered questions about al-Shifa, hitting the plant was prudent in view of the costs of doing so.

Those costs included the public relations battering that the United States suffered from the al-Shifa strike itself, as well as the broader blow that the episode inflicted on the perceived integrity of U.S. intelligence and U.S.

counterterrorist efforts generally. It is hard to identify any offsetting benefit from destroying the plant. The strike probably added little or nothing to whatever deterrent effect that strikes in Afghanistan alone would have had on bin Ladin's intentions, and there is no evidence that it prevented or postponed a chemical attack by bin Ladin or anyone else.

The decision to attack al-Shifa illustrates a procedural hazard of employing the military instrument. Decisions to use armed force engage what the late Soviet foreign minister Vyacheslav Molotov (in explaining why Soviet objectives expanded during the Russo-Finnish War of 1939-1940) called the "logic of war": the tendency, once one resorts to arms, to reach for goals that would not by themselves be sufficient reason to use armed force in the first place. Decisionmakers should resist that tendency. The United States would never have struck al-Shifa in the absence of the embassy bombings and the decision to retaliate for them; the evidence about chemical weapons did not come close to justifying that kind of preemptive strike. The United States should not have lowered its evidentiary standards merely because it was resorting to arms anyway by attacking targets in Afghanistan (targets that could be linked much more convincingly to terrorism). Retaliatory strikes in response to terrorist attacks will always be primarily message-sending exercises, rather than a physically significant crippling of terrorist capabilities. The United States should keep the message as clear and defensible as possible by limiting itself to the most credible targets.

Military force should continue to be available as a U.S. counterterrorist instrument—because it is a form of power with which the United States has a clear advantage, and because in some situations it will be the only way to respond publicly and emphatically to a terrorist outrage. It would be more costly for the United States than for other countries to be perceived as doing nothing in such situations, because of the untoward messages this would send about U.S. leadership generally and counterterrorism specifically. But use of this instrument should continue to be rare, because of all of the inherent limitations. The high standard of proof (in establishing responsibility for a terrorist incident) should be maintained. There are enough downsides to using military retaliation without having to contend with serious doubt about whether those truly responsible for a terrorist attack are being hit. The incidents in which that standard is met will continue to be few. Moreover, even in some instances in which the standard eventually is met, if it is not met quickly enough the military option effectively fades away. This would be true, for example, of the bombing of

Khubar Towers, which was still an open case more than four years after the event. Even if it were publicly established that Iran was responsible, far too much time has passed, and far too much of importance has transpired within Iran during that time, for military retaliation to be a sensible or feasible option any more, if it ever was.

Intelligence and Covert Action

The contribution of U.S. intelligence to counterterrorism is necessarily the least open of any of the instruments, but in many respects the most substantial—though not primarily in the way commonly supposed. This section addresses the collection and exploitation of information on international terrorists (which is chiefly, but not solely, the responsibility of the CIA and other intelligence agencies) and the potential for using the U.S. intelligence apparatus more actively as an instrument in its own right to affect the capabilities and intentions of terrorist groups.

The counterterrorist contribution most often expected from intelligence is to detect terrorist plots in time for measures to be taken to remove the threat (suspects are arrested, material is confiscated) or, as the next best outcome, to put the target out of reach (travel is cancelled, events are postponed or relocated). Occasionally this happens, and it is immensely gratifying to counterterrorist officers when a terrorist plot is foiled. It does not happen often, because intelligence on terrorist threats is rarely specific enough to roll up confirmed plots or to put targets out of reach without disruptions so major that they would constitute a different kind of victory for the terrorist. Typical threat-related intelligence includes a report of a plot to attack a traveling VIP that names a country but not a city; a threat report that mentions a whole category of possible targets, such as U.S. embassies in a given region; or an alleged threat to commercial aviation that mentions only an airline, a country, and a month-long time frame rather than a specific flight. Post mortem studies of major terrorist incidents, such as the Downing report on Khubar Towers and the Crowe report on the East Africa bombings, have cited a lack of specific tactical warning even where strategic intelligence (that is, more general information on the level and sources of threat to U.S. installations in a given country) was good.

Specific intelligence on terrorist threats is rare because there are few sources that could provide it, and those sources are very hard to get. That reflects the nature of terrorist groups and how they operate. They are either small (as with ad hoc groups like Ramzi Yousef's) or highly compartmented (as in larger organizations like Hamas). Either way, few people are witting of the details—or even the existence—of an impending terrorist operation. Those who are closest to the center of decisionmaking in a group (and thus most likely to be witting of all its operations) are the ones least likely to betray it and thus most resistant to recruitment as intelligence sources. Besides this problem of motivation, any attempt to recruit such individuals also faces a problem of access—of getting to them and cultivating relationships with them. This is an even greater difficulty with most religiously oriented terrorists of today than it was with, say, leftists who moved within bourgeois circles in Europe. Creative use of intermediaries can sometimes help, but any attempt to penetrate the inner circles of terrorist groups must confront very high suspicion of outsiders and ruthlessness toward anyone suspected of betraying the group. A well-placed human source is the best possible intelligence asset for counterterrorism, but for the reasons just given, such sources will be very few—and always will be, no matter what resources, skill, and dedication are applied to the task of acquiring them.

An additional complication in recruiting terrorist assets is that the individuals with the most information to offer tend to have considerable baggage, including possible involvement in past terrorist acts. Any use of such persons as intelligence assets requires additional checks and safeguards, including approval at high levels (up to the director of central intelligence) and notification as appropriate to the congressional intelligence committees. If the person may have violated U.S. law, the Department of Justice must also review the case and decide whether to seek or to waive prosecution. The National Commission on Terrorism stated that the CIA's guidelines for using such people as sources has hindered the recruitment of terrorist informants by making intelligence officers "risk averse."[57] The commission based this conclusion on testimony from operations officers in the field who criticized the procedures (which are more stringent than earlier ones) and spoke of their inclination to avoid the extra hassles by devoting their energies instead to other matters.

The principal challenge regarding these procedures is one of educating officers in the field—about the need for safeguards, the need to keep trying to recruit sources of information on terrorism even though this task is more difficult and complicated than performing other missions on a station's operating directive, and the fact that a formal approval process decreases risk to individual officers by requiring superiors to buy into potentially controversial recruitments before they are made. In practice, virtually all proposals submitted to headquarters to recruit sources—even ones with blood on their hands—who have at least a reasonable chance of providing useful intelligence on terrorism are approved. The current procedures require extra memorandums to be written and discussions to be held, but the delays are minimal and seldom make the difference between gaining and losing a source.

Technical intelligence plays an important supporting role but also has limitations. Terrorists are well aware of the monitoring capabilities of the United States and other Western governments. The kind of smoking-gun message from Libyans in Germany that was intercepted after the bombing at La Belle Discotheque is thus rare, as are messages that precisely forewarn of impending terrorist operations. The most important preoperational messages are conveyed through noninterceptable face-to-face contact. Exploitation of terrorist messages that do get sent electronically must contend with the proliferation of commercially available encryption technology and, even more so, with the tendency of security-conscious terrorists to disguise who they are and what they are up to.

Terrorist-related intelligence thus provides little direct or conclusive information about terrorist attacks, especially ones that have yet to happen. It does provide a great deal of information that is potentially useful but is indirect, fragmentary, and ambiguous. This includes reporting from human sources who are on the periphery of terrorist groups, reports from volunteers or "walk-ins" of greatly varying credibility, problematic technical intelligence of the sort mentioned above, and other snippets and shreds of information. Making sense of all of this is the job of the intelligence analyst, who must consider the classified intelligence along with such open information as the statements of terrorist leaders, a group's record and what it suggests about when and where it tends to attack, and current events (including especially U.S. initiatives) to which a group might react.

The analysis of terrorist intelligence has challenges that parallel the difficulties in collecting it. The ever-changing, ever-complex nature of international terrorism is one such challenge, particularly for the managers of analytical resources. In what directions should this labor- and expertise-intensive effort be focused? There will always be demand for heavy coverage of the bin Ladins and other threats simmering on the front burner. But it is also a responsibility of U.S. intelligence to monitor threats-in-the-making that have not yet moved to the front burner or even to the stove.

A problem is the sheer magnitude of what there is to cover, including not only the whole lineup of existing terrorist groups but also terrorists who have not yet formed a group (for example, the World Trade Center bombers before they started planning their attack) and groups that have not yet gotten into terrorism (for example, Aum Shinrikyo before its first attempts to use toxic chemicals). The U.S. intelligence community was fairly criticized for not having paid more detailed early attention to Aum (given how large the group had grown even before its first chemical attack), but what about the plethora of other extreme religious cults around the world, many of which could represent future terrorist threats? There are not the resources to cover them all, and culling the ones that are most likely to pose such a threat is an awesome analytical task.

The huge amount of information that is potentially relevant to terrorist threats, and the difficulty of mustering the analytic resources to exploit it all, has led some to propose methods of handling data that are more automatic and seemingly more systematic than what is done now. The Illegal Immigration Reform and Immigrant Responsibility Act of 1996, for example, required (in section 110) the Immigration and Naturalization Service to devise an automated system to track the entry into, and exit from, the United States of all non-U.S. citizens. The Defense Science Board, in its 1997 study, urged greater use of real-time data from international border crossings, cargo manifests, financial transactions, and airline ticket manifests to obtain indications of possible terrorist threats. Recognizing that exploitation of these data would be beyond human resources, the board recommended the development of automated search and recognition techniques that would consider the content and the context of the data being handled.[58] Members of Congress have also called for greater efforts at this kind of "data mining." The underlying idea—that correlating data from diverse sources is needed to warn about terrorism—is sound, and the automation that the Science Board envisioned could theoretically mimic much of a counterterrorist analyst's thought processes. The problem is that this would treat like a science what is far more of an art. Plausible rules for reviewing data could be devised and written into a computer program, but the most useful indicators of terrorist threats tend to be sui generis ones that become apparent not in the application of a rule but in the gut of an analyst who, through experience, has acquired a feel for how a group operates. Besides, large-scale efforts to mine data would run into the practical problems of terrorists habitually using false identities, institutions being reluctant to provide data for use as a dragnet, and other difficulties in implementation. There have already been second thoughts about section 110 of the 1996 immigration law—the Senate has voted to repeal it—reflecting the opposition of Canada and of border-state representatives who argue that it would deter tourists and create back-ups at points of entry.[59]

A related and recurrent idea is that by developing and applying a terrorist "profile," the task of exploiting data could be pared down to a manageable size. For example, do not try to track all foreigners, just the ones who fit the profile. The problem is that there is nothing close to a single profile of terrorists, and any attempt to create one would either exclude too many terrorists or include too many nonterrorists. The one currently effective counterterrorist use of profiling—in security of commercial aviation—illustrates this limitation. Profiling of air passengers is used not to identify possible terrorists, but rather to identify—with sufficient confidence to obviate any scrutiny of their baggage—passengers who are *not* terrorists. The FAA, in estimating the costs of its proposal to protect domestic flights from bombs in checked baggage, assumes that profiling would still leave 5 percent of the traveling public whose bags would need to be examined (or matched with people on board the plane). For domestic U.S. flights that means about 29 million passengers a year.[60]

Intelligence analysts covering terrorist groups face other challenges. The amorphous and often nonhierarchical nature of terrorist organizations is one such challenge. The factions within, and alliances among, terrorist groups often make it unclear who is acting on behalf of whom, and whether a particular action reported in the intelligence resulted from the leader of a group ordering it to happen. Another handicap is that analysts do not consistently receive after-action checks on the accuracy of their analysis; even when steps are taken to counter a possible terrorist threat, there may be no proof uncovered of exactly what kind of threat, if any, had existed. But the greatest challenge is that most of the raw intelligence on terrorism that comes to the analyst is fragmentary or of dubious credibility. The analyst's task is akin to sifting through a large trash bin to reach conclusions about what is going on inside the building from which the trash came—a necessary and sometimes fruitful task, as criminal investigators who have culled the contents of real trash bins can testify—but a messy and time-consuming one as well. Much of what the analyst examines is outright junk. Most of the rest, though possibly meaningful, consists of scraps. The best analysts have an eye for distinguishing the potentially valuable items from the junk, a memory for past discoveries that may be related to current ones, and skill in pattern recognition that enables them to piece the scraps together cogently. Significant counterterrorist successes sometimes do result from analytical successes. But the inherent difficulties in both collection and analysis of intelligence on terrorism mean that there will never be tactical warning of most attempted terrorist attacks, or even most major attempted attacks against U.S. targets.

That is not a welcome conclusion to many security managers. The more that intelligence can be relied on as the "first line of defense" against terrorism—a valid concept, for the most part—the less onerous is the burden on the other defensive lines. There is a tendency among those responsible for those other lines to rely on tactical intelligence more than they should to gauge the terrorist threat at certain times and places. The Accountability Review Boards chaired by Admiral William Crowe found this to be the case with the bombings of the embassies in Africa. "The Boards found," as part of their principal findings, "that intelligence provided no immediate tactical warning of the August 7 attacks. We understand the difficulty of monitoring terrorist networks and concluded that vulnerable missions cannot rely upon such warning." Despite that correct conclusion, the panel discovered that officials "have relied heavily on warning intelligence to measure threats, whereas experience has shown that transnational terrorists often strike without warning at vulnerable targets in areas where expectations of terrorist attacks against the U.S. are low."[61] Intelligence learns of only some of the terrorist plotting that goes on every year. The true threat that the United States faces from international terrorism therefore swings neither as high as a focus on the latest alarming threat report would lead some to believe, nor as low as the absence of such reports over a period of time might suggest.

Focusing heavily on the stream of day-to-day threat reporting not only risks forgetting that the next real threat may go unreported; it also means diversion of attention and resources in responding to many reported threats that never materialize. There are various possible reasons for the latter type of threat report: the source fabricated the information, or he misinterpreted what he heard or saw, or the threat was real but the terrorists for any number of reasons did not proceed further with their plans and preparations. Dissemination within the government of questionable threat reports therefore requires care. The practice of the DCI Counterterrorist Center is to disseminate to all of the relevant departments and agencies any terrorist threat report that cannot be disproved. If the experts in the center nonetheless have doubts about a report (because of its source or its substance), they will add comments reflecting those doubts to the disseminated version of the report. Such caveats reduce, but do not eliminate, the problem of overreaction to the daily flow of reporting on terrorism.

Although tactical intelligence on terrorist threats should not be relied on as heavily as it often has been, strategic intelligence on the subject has been valuable and for the most part reliable. The analyst rummaging through the trash bin of raw information sometimes notices a certain kind of item appearing more often than usual, leading to the conclusion that worrisome activity is taking place in the particular building in question, even if the time, date, and specific place of an event defy prediction. An increase in intelligence reporting that mentions a group, country, or class of target is sometimes a good indicator (when analyzed, as always, in conjunction with openly available information and the context of other events) that a terrorist operation is brewing, even if no single report can be relied on and some of the reports may be spurious. The resulting threat assessments have been useful to security planners (though limited by the previously noted proclivity of terrorists to shift to targets that are not as well protected). This was true in Saudi Arabia before the Khubar Towers bombing. The Downing commission concluded that U.S. intelligence had provided military commanders "warning that the terrorist threat to U.S. service members and facilities was increasing."[62] That intelligence was the basis for the security measures that had been taken at Khubar and that saved many lives from the truck bomb. Both this kind of strategic threat assessment and more basic intelligence assessments on the capabilities, methods of operation, and likely intentions of major terrorist groups (and states) are important inputs to numerous other counterterrorist decisions, ranging from local ones about security countermeasures to broad decisions about allocation of resources to national counterterrorist programs.

Intelligence supports all the other counterterrorist instruments, with specific information as well as strategic assessments. Some of the difficulties have been mentioned in discussion of those other instruments (for example, the problems in following a money trail or tracking a terrorist who may be a military target). One area in which the support role for intelligence has enlarged significantly in the past few years is law enforcement. This reflects the enlargement of the role of criminal law in counterterrorism and the fact that so much of the information about, and links to, the terrorists—most of whom are foreigners—lie overseas, where the intelligence agencies are best equipped to operate. Those agencies are legally barred from directly participating in law enforcement, but Executive Order 12333 states that the CIA may "provide specialized equipment, technical knowledge or assistance, or expert personnel for use by any department or agency" and can "render any other assistance and cooperation to law enforcement authorities not precluded by applicable law." In some counterterrorist cases, that assistance can include almost every step short of flashing a badge and putting handcuffs on a suspect.

Some intelligence support to law enforcement is aimed at preventing foreign terrorists from conducting attacks in the United States. The intelligence agencies routinely pass to the FBI information collected from foreign sources about foreign terrorists that might be germane to terrorist-related activity in the United States. Occasionally such information suggests a current threat, but more often it consists of names, phone numbers, information about commercial transactions, or other data collected in the course of monitoring a foreign terrorist group that may be useful to the FBI in its task of monitoring potentially dangerous foreigners in the United States.

A more formal program aimed at keeping terrorists out of the United States in the first place is called Tipoff; it converts all-source intelligence about foreign terrorists and suspected terrorists into unclassified watch lists used by consular officers in making decisions on visa applications and by INS and Customs officers at U.S. points of entry. Tipoff is managed by the State Department's Bureau of Intelligence and Research (INR), which controls access to the underlying classified intelligence when it must be consulted in making a decision on admitting a suspect person. The program has been an effective way to apply intelligence to the job of keeping dangerous people out of America. Since its inception several years ago, Tipoff has resulted in the rejection of visa requests from more than 500 suspected terrorists. As of August 1999, use of the system by the INS at points of entry had led 168 suspected terrorists to be denied entry and returned to their point of origin, and seven others to be arrested.[63]

Once a terrorist attack occurs, the partnership between intelligence and law enforcement tackles two other tasks. One is to determine responsibility for the crime. Here the intelligence analyst performs her familiar job of sifting through the trash bin of fragmentary information, only this time it focuses on an act already committed rather than one yet to occur. Some of the information examined may be old intelligence reporting that seemed inconsequential earlier but may contain clues to who committed the later attack. This work is performed in close consultation with law enforcement elements doing the more traditional police work of analyzing physical evidence and interviewing witnesses. Information flows back and forth between the intelligence officers (mostly in the DCI Counterterrorist Center) and the law enforcement officers (mostly in the FBI), with leads developed in one area requiring follow-up in the other. Follow-up by intelligence may include research of archival data as well as asking fresh questions of intelligence assets in the field. Major cases that used this approach included the bombing of the World Trade Center (for which the counterterrorist center established a special task force) and the Iraqi attempt to assassinate President Bush (the investigation of which culminated in parallel reports—substantively in agreement—from the attorney general and the director of central intelligence).

Once responsibility is determined, the final task is to locate and capture the perpetrators. Finding a fugitive terrorist overseas is not unlike many other intelligence tasks, and lends itself to some of the same techniques. Once the terrorist is located in a city or country, more detailed information about his situation and movements is usually required to effect an arrest. Intelligence officers, and their sources, on the scene are usually better able to do that than law enforcement officers from the United States. Finally, intelligence, and the CIA, brings to the task established liaison relationships with local security services, whose participation is almost always part of the arrest of terrorists in foreign countries. Those relationships are particularly useful in arranging the quick and informal renditions that are used most often in moving terrorists to where they will face justice. DCI George Tenet stated in February 2000 that the United States had assisted in the renditions of more than two dozen terrorists since July 1998.[64] Some of these were brought to the United States to stand trial; most were delivered to other countries where they were wanted for their crimes.

Foreign liaison is vital to U.S. counterterrorism efforts in other ways, and so the nurturing and use of relationships with foreign counterparts is a further significant contribution that the CIA makes to counterterrorism. Most of the intelligence the United States obtains on international terrorism comes from (or at least is heavily dependent on the participation of) foreign intelligence, police, and internal security services. Those foreign services are often closer than the United States to the front line of conflict with particular terrorist groups, have longer experience in monitoring them, and better access in attempting to penetrate them.

The dependence on foreign liaison is even greater when the task is not just to collect information on international terrorism but to take action to counter it. Here, the CIA makes what is probably not only the U.S. intelligence community's largest contribution to counterterrorism but also the most effective contribution of any of the instruments toward the goal of reducing future terrorism. Then-DCI John Deutch referred to this contribution in 1996 when he said, "We are increasing the U.S. intelligence community's capability to act forcefully against terrorists worldwide . . . What we intend to do now is give the President more options for action against foreign terrorists to further preempt, disrupt, and defeat international terrorism. We want to increase the President's options to act against terrorist groups directly, either to prevent them from carrying out operations or to retaliate against groups we know are responsible for operations."[65] Deutch's comments overstated the newness of this mode of action against terrorism, but they give a sense of the possibilities.

The most effective possibility is a painstaking cell-by-cell, terrorist-by-terrorist, dismantling of terrorist infrastructures worldwide. The antiterrorism act of 1996, although it did not create new authorities in this area, properly highlighted it as an important mission. The language in that law paired such action with military force as complementary ways of going after the terrorists' apparatus: "The President should use all necessary means, including covert action and military force, to disrupt, dismantle, and destroy international infrastructure used by international terrorists, including overseas terrorist training facilities and safe havens."[66] Actions can include questioning, investigating, arresting, deporting, or rendering individual terrorists, and confiscating items in their possession that may relate to their terrorist activity. Local police or security forces are obviously the ones with the authority and wherewithal to accomplish such actions directly. The behind-the-scene U.S. role may be to provide encouragement, prodding, information, advice (including formal training if necessary), and perhaps monetary or logistical support, as well as to coordinate with other countries in a counterterrorist operation. Many, and perhaps most, of the rousted individuals are not shooters and bombers themselves but are part of an infrastructure that provides critical support to the ones who are. Disruption of the infrastructure thus deals a blow to terrorist capabilities and, by sowing various forms of doubt among those not rousted, also affects terrorist intentions.

As with any counterterrorist instrument, there are limitations. Disruption depends on prior intelligence about terrorist activity, which, for the reasons discussed earlier, is invariably incomplete. Success depends heavily on the reliability of the local service, which varies greatly from country to country and even among services within a country; a single untrustworthy individual who is either corrupt or sympathetic to the terrorists can blow a major counterterrorist operation. Cell-by-cell operations are inherently small scale and constitute a chipping away at a larger problem. And the lack of drama and publicity prevents broader deterrent effects and does little to demonstrate U.S. seriousness to the world and to maintain a larger sense of counterterrorist momentum.

There are significant offsetting advantages, however, to this kind of disruption. First, the lack of publicity avoids some of the biggest problems of other instruments, such as making the United States appear to be a bully that steps on other nation's sovereignty and uses its military muscle indiscriminately. The U.S. hand can stay hidden, and the risk of terrorist reprisals is minimal. Second, the United States has the criminal laws of other countries working in its favor. An exploitable vulnerability of terrorists is that most of them commit crimes other than terrorism —such as use of false documents to enter a country, shipment of contraband, or other illegal activity to raise money. The local legal basis for much counterterrorist disruption is that these individuals have committed one of these other violations. U.S. intelligence officers working to facilitate such disruption are in the happy situation not of persuading a foreign official to violate the laws of his own country but of encouraging him to *enforce* those laws. Third, a little disruption goes a long way. Terrorists fear being uncovered. Even just a knock on the door by police and a few questions, without any arrests, is sometimes sufficient to divert terrorists from their plans. There are also ample opportunities to place doubt in the minds of terrorist leaders about who might have betrayed the group. And fourth, success in this business breeds further success, with the information uncovered when a cell is broken up sometimes leading to the rolling up of another cell in another country or even on another continent.

There are certainly other possible ways in which covert action could be applied to counterterrorism. One that requires comment because it has been an issue of public discussion is the possible assassination of terrorist leaders.[67] U.S. executive orders have prohibited assassination for the past quarter century. President Gerald Ford initiated such a ban in 1976 with Executive Order 11905; President Ronald Reagan renewed it in 1981 with Executive Order 12333, which states flatly that no person employed by or acting on behalf of the U.S. government shall engage in, or conspire to engage in, assassination. A renewed interest in assassination as a possible counterterrorist tool stems partly from heightened concern about international terrorism generally and partly from the perceived importance of a single terrorist leader like bin Ladin. It also results from the use of military force in Afghanistan, which (like the use in Libya twelve years earlier) had among its apparent goals the killing of the enemy leader. A valid question is why, if the United States is willing to use armed force—with its collateral damage and casualties—for this purpose, should it forgo the use of more precise and potentially more effective clandestine means for the same purpose?

This involves two more specific questions. One is whether the assassination of terrorist leaders would tend to reduce terrorism. The other is whether, given all the related issues of politics, legality, and morality, it would make sense for the United States to state openly that it was back in the business of assassination. On the first question, the most instructive experience is that of Israel, whose thinly disguised use of assassinations has had mixed results at best. Israel began using this technique in Western Europe in the 1970s against operatives of the Palestinian group Black September—a campaign that may have disrupted some terrorist operations but did not come close to ending Palestinian terrorism in the region. Probably the most effective assassination that Israel is widely believed to have conducted was of Fathi Shiqaqi, principal leader of the Palestine Islamic Jihad, in Malta in October 1995. Shiqaqi was replaced by a much weaker leader, Ramadan Abdullah Shallah, who has been subject to repeated challenges from inside the PIJ and has been unable to restore the group's operational effectiveness. Less favorable were the results of the assassination three months later (using explosives hidden in a cell phone) of Hamas's leading bombmaker, Yahya Ayyash ("The Engineer"). Partly in revenge—and perhaps partly to demonstrate that Hamas's ability to fabricate bombs had not disappeared with Ayyash— Hamas carried out three suicide bombings over the next two months in Jerusalem and Tel Aviv, killing sixty-five people. The difference in results reflected Shiqaqi's especially dominant role in the PIJ and the fact that Hamas, the larger organization, has never been heavily dependent on a single individual.

The results of failed assassination operations can be even worse. The leading examples for Israel were the shooting to death in Norway in 1973 of an innocent Moroccan waiter mistakenly identified as a Black September leader (Norwegian authorities subsequently arrested and convicted several Israeli agents involved in the misdirected killing) and the botched attempt to kill Khalid Mishal, the chief Hamas political officer in Amman, in September 1997. The latter incident caused a crisis in Israeli-Jordanian relations, with King Hussein threatening to break diplomatic ties and Israel having to release from prison the spiritual leader and founder of Hamas, Sheik Ahmed Yassin, as part of a deal with Jordan to get its two arrested agents released.[68] The conclusion to draw from these experiences is that there are particular leaders whose elimination probably would seriously weaken their groups and thereby reduce terrorism, but that there are many other cases in which an assassination—or an attempt to conduct one—is at least as likely to be counterproductive.

Whether assassination of terrorist leaders should be an openly acknowledged tool of the United States (or at least that it should not be expressly denied) has some reasonable arguments on either side. The comparison with military operations aimed at enemy leaders is apt (and the moral case for such operations—given the greater risk of collateral harm to innocent persons—may be even more difficult to make than the case for a clandestine assassination). Moreover, legal scholars have made the case that, although assassination is normally a crime under international law, there are instances involving terrorism in which assassination would be not only legal but a means to enforce the law. Assassination, in this view, would constitute extrajudicial punishment of perpetrators of egregious terrorist crimes who would otherwise go unpunished.[69] Knowledge that assassination is a U.S. policy option might also have some deterrent effect.

Three considerations on the other side outweigh these arguments. First, it would weaken an international norm against assassination of foreign leaders—a norm that is in U.S. interests to preserve.[70] U.S. leaders, being more open and exposed than many others (and certainly more so than most terrorist leaders), would be among those with the most to lose.[71] Second, whatever the moral equivalence to certain military operations, an individual assassination through clandestine means would inevitably be widely viewed as a distinct tactic and as a stooping by the United States, in its choice of that tactic, to the level of the terrorists. It would completely undercut the principle that terrorism is a matter of methods, not just of targets or purposes, and the point that extraterritorial assassinations conducted by Iran and others are themselves terrorism. A third consideration is that assassinations could shake the confidence of many Americans in the relevant governmental institutions, resurrecting old suspicions about what the CIA and other U.S. intelligence and security services were doing.

For these reasons, and because there are few instances in which assassinations would be likely to curb terrorism, assassination should not be relied on as a counterterrorist instrument, nor should it be declared to be such. Executive Order 12333 should not be rescinded. This does not imply an absolute and permanent ban on assassination, however, since whatever is barred by an executive order can, of course, be changed or suspended if the president of the day were to sign a new piece of paper—in this case, a covert action finding, or a memorandum of notification if there were an existing relevant finding. Any move to do so in an exceptional case in which assassination was thought to be useful should be made only after the administration and the congressional intelligence committees (to which covert action findings are reported) had thought carefully about whether the blow struck against a terrorist group's capability would outweigh the downsides suggested above, about the operational risks, and about the possible additional risk of acting contrary to what the American public and foreigners believe to be U.S. policy.

Coordinating the Instruments

The limitations of each of the counterterrorist instruments make it necessary to use—or at least to consider the use of—all of them. Moreover, they must be used in concert. Most counterterrorist work involves more than one instrument. Intelligence has a role in almost every counterterrorist operation, and diplomacy does in most of them. The instruments are complementary, and the value of using them should be—and generally is—more than just the sum of the parts. If the process is not properly managed, the value may be less than the sum of the parts, because of the possibility of different instruments working at cross purposes—a military operation making the arrest of a fugitive more difficult, for example, or an arrest negating a valuable source of intelligence.

Interagency procedures and machinery to accomplish the necessary coordination should have the following attributes. First, coordination should be led by the National Security Council because of the priority of counterterrorism and the need to apply a broad perspective that takes account of the relationship with other national security issues. Second, it should routinely involve all of the departments and agencies that wield the different counterterrorist instruments while drawing in other parts of the bureaucracy as required on specific matters. And third, the communication among the departments and agencies should be sufficiently routine and comprehensive to coordinate the execution of counterterrorist policy and not just the making of it.

That describes the U.S. counterterrorist machinery as it had evolved by the late 1990s. The center of that machinery is the Counterterrorism Security Group (CSG), which is chaired by a senior NSC official, the national coordinator for security, infrastructure protection, and counterterrorism. The other core members of the CSG are the heads of the counterterrorist elements of the CIA, FBI, Joint Chiefs of Staff, and departments of State, Justice, and Defense. Other components, such as the departments of Transportation or the Treasury, are brought in to consider specific matters that bear on their responsibilities. The CSG is possibly the most cohesive and effective subcabinet body of its kind. This is partly because of the consensus surrounding the fight against terrorism and partly because of the regularity of the interactions and the longevity of the working relationships. The CSG meets frequently—face-to-face or by secure videoconference—as often as daily during especially worrisome or fast-moving situations. Although the current charter for the CSG is Presidential Decision Directive 62, which was signed in May 1998, its basic membership and procedures (and even some of the individuals involved) date from several years before that.[72]

Other interagency machinery supplements, and works under the general supervision of, the CSG. The core CSG agencies confer regularly at a more junior level to review possible current threats. There is an Interagency Intelligence Committee on Terrorism (IICT) that includes more than forty federal agencies that have an interest in counterterrorist intelligence as either producers or consumers, ranging from the National Security Agency to the U.S. Capitol Police. Besides regular meetings to discuss substantive issues and other matters of general concern, the IICT has subcommittees on intelligence requirements, technical countermeasures, training, warning, handling of information, CBRN matters, and research and development. The Technical Support Working Group (TSWG) is another active interagency body; more than fifty federal offices participate, with program direction provided by an executive committee consisting of representatives from the departments of State, Defense, and Energy, and the FBI.

Informal working relationships are at least as important as the formal machinery, and are critical to each agency understanding the business and equities of the other agencies. Those relationships have developed greatly in recent years—particularly the one between the intelligence and law enforcement communities, which was strained as recently as the early 1990s. That situation was corrected through a commitment at high levels of the

CIA and FBI to make the relationship work, a commitment at lower levels to learn more about the other organization, and cross-assignments of personnel. The position of deputy chief of the foreign counterterrorist section at the FBI is now regularly filled by a senior CIA operations officer, and one of the deputy chief's jobs at the DCI Counterterrorist Center is reserved for a senior FBI special agent. The CIA and FBI also exchange more junior counterterrorist officers. All of this has turned what had been more of a rivalry into an effective partnership between intelligence and law enforcement that has been in large part responsible for such successes as the increased numbers of captures and renditions of fugitive terrorists. The closer relationship between the CIA and the FBI has enabled each agency to help compensate for the shortfalls of the other, such as the paucity of analytical resources in FBI field offices.

Other cross-assignments of personnel in the counterterrorist community also further that community's cohesion. The first name of the DCI Counterterrorist Center emphasizes the community nature of the enterprise. Besides the FBI, about a dozen agencies have personnel assigned there, including not only intelligence organizations in addition to the CIA but also other law enforcement agencies such as the Secret Service and policy or regulatory agencies such as the FAA.

Interagency coordination on counterterrorism is not perfect, but it is generally effective and probably about as good as can be expected on any subject that cuts across so many functions. Different agencies do approach counterterrorism from the perspectives of their different core missions— such as collecting information, prosecuting criminals or interdicting contraband—and these differences become apparent in the coordination process. But the experience of the past few years indicates that organizational boundaries do not need to be barriers to cooperation.

The principal alternative to the current machinery would be to centralize most of the government's counterterrorist work in a single office or agency. If integration is good, would it be even better to integrate still further, by consolidating as many counterterrorist functions as possible under one roof and one line manager? It would not, for reasons that go beyond the general one of not trying to fix something that is not broken. If centralization meant creation of an altogether new component, it would entail duplication of some work in which existing agencies would necessarily keep a hand, and in effect the addition of one more agency with which counterterrorist policy must be coordinated. If it meant moving all the work to an existing agency, it would involve duplication of a different sort and assigning tasks to an organization that was not the best equipped to perform them. Either way would fly in the face of the reality that a comprehensive counterterrorist program unavoidably includes functions that are part of the core missions of several federal agencies.

Centralization would also mean ripping at least some counterterrorist components out of parent agencies on which they are highly dependent for their effectiveness. It would bureaucratically sever those components from field elements that do so much of the actual implementation of counterterrorist policy, and from regionally organized bureaucracies that support and direct those elements. The DCI Counterterrorist Center, for example, has no overseas stations and bases of its own but instead must operate through the ones managed by the regional divisions of CIA's Directorate of Operations. Similarly, the FBI's detailed investigative work on terrorists and terrorist groups is done by the bureau's field offices, including ones in the United States that have responsibility for overseas cases.[73]

Coordination between Washington and elements in the field is sometimes a concern, but for reasons that have more to do with intra-agency rather than interagency relationships and that greater centralization of counterterrorist functions would do nothing to improve. At most overseas posts three key players work together on counterterrorist matters: the CIA station chief, the FBI legat, and the State Department's regional security officer (who is responsible for safeguarding the embassy itself and, like the legat, is also a law enforcement officer). The importance of a close working relationship among these three officials has made the opening of additional legat offices beneficial, at least as far as counterterrorism is concerned (rather than being, as is commonly supposed, a threat to the turf of CIA station chiefs—who, without a resident legat present, would still have to deal with a circuit-riding one based in another country). At most embassies these officials work together well.

More frequent than problems of disharmony in overseas missions are omissions of reporting from the field to headquarters. The problem varies from one agency to another, partly reflecting the different degrees of independence that the field elements of each enjoy. U.S. attorneys and FBI special agents in charge, for example, conduct largely on their own the sort of business that almost all CIA station chiefs, and many ambassadors, would not think of undertaking without detailed reporting to Washington. The differences also reflect the different missions of agencies. A primary task of CIA stations is to report information of interest to analysts and consumers in other agencies, and so it is second nature to them to pass along material that may have counterterrorist uses. There are "reports officers" in key stations whose job is to do just that, and others at headquarters who nag stations that fail to do so. The FBI has not had reports officers, and sometimes information that a field office collects during an investigation that may be terrorist related but does not contain obvious threats does not get conveyed to counterterrorist analysts in Washington. In addition, military units deployed overseas that observe suspicious behavior near their installations have sometimes not reported it promptly because of an understandable reluctance to get Washington agitated over incidents that may, on further examination, have innocent explanations. These problems have been recognized, however, and steps have been taken to ameliorate them. The FBI, for example, has had under consideration the creation of its own cadre of reports officers—a proposal that the National Commission on Terrorism endorsed.[74]

Given the coordination that has been achieved through the CSG and the other mechanisms noted above, getting the different parts of the counterterrorist community to work together is now probably less of a problem than melding counterterrorism with other foreign policy issues that are the responsibility of offices outside that community. Coordination between counterterrorist elements and components within the same agencies that have country or regional responsibilities is needed to ensure that counterterrorist initiatives do not undermine other U.S. interests overseas and that the counterterrorist perspective is injected into decisionmaking on other foreign policy issues. The Office of the Coordinator for Counterterrorism in the Department of State plays a key role, and its relationship with the regional bureaus and other parts of the State Department is especially important. The influence of the counterterrorism coordinator has varied with different occupants of that job and their different relationships with secretaries of state. The ability of that official to live up to the title of "coordinator" of counterterrorism matters on behalf of the entire department (as distinct from simply managing counterterrorist programs) might be better ensured by institutionalizing his office's participation in foreign policy deliberations generally. Just as it is common in many discussions of policy for a lawyer to be present to insert the legal perspective and a budgetary official to be there to inject the fiscal perspective, the participation of a counterterrorist official would ensure the asking of the question, "how might this contemplated initiative affect the threat from, or U.S. vulnerability to, international terrorism?"

There has been some criticism of how the counterterrorism coordinator's functions mesh with those of other components within the State Department that also deal with terrorism, particularly the Bureau of Diplomatic Security (DS) and the Bureau of Intelligence and Research. The Crowe panel encouraged discussion of this issue by calling for a reexamination of how the department is organized to handle security-related matters and for the appointment of a single senior official with authority over all such matters.[75] It would be tempting to consolidate some of these functions, which might appear not only to streamline the State Department's organization chart but also to respond to concerns that have sometimes been expressed about how terrorist-related information is handled in the department. But the counterterrorism coordinator has a distinctive policy function (much different from DS's mission of safeguarding embassies and erecting other security countermeasures, or INR's job of assessing and distributing intelligence) that should not be downgraded in any reorganization.

A final issue regarding counterterrorist machinery is how the involvement of certain departments or agencies in deciding counterterrorist policy questions tends to lead to particular policy answers. The cohesion of the counterterrorist community, the mutual understanding of different roles within that community, and the underlying counterterrorist consensus have blurred somewhat the usual pattern of "where you stand depends on where you sit," especially at the working level. A decision on whether to initiate a prosecution that would remove a source of intelligence, for example, does not necessarily pit law enforcement agencies against the CIA; it is at least as likely to involve a judgment by FBI agents working on the case that it would be better to forgo for the time being the pressing of criminal charges against a foreign extremist in the United States in order to continue collecting intelligence on his contacts and activities. Process inevitably affects substance in any decisionmaking, however, and major counterterrorist decisions, especially on how to respond to terrorist incidents, reflect institutional perspectives to some degree. Military decisionmakers, for example, are inclined to focus on uses of force that attack terrorists' capabilities (the first priority in any combat operation is to destroy the enemy's ability to strike back). A greater military role in fashioning a response therefore may mean more attempts to hit capabilities, as with the missile strike against al-Shifa, even if they detract from the political messages being sent.

Institutional perspectives in high-level counterterrorist decisions are apt to be even more apparent on the application of criminal law. The criminal justice system is oriented toward prosecuting and convicting, and its leaders naturally will argue for doing just that. The force of any attorney general's arguments in favor of a prosecution in U.S. courts is amplified by what Ethan Nadelmann calls an "increasingly strident and pervasive sense of moralism" about the application of criminal justice domestically and internationally. Nadelmann observes that "the number of government officials willing to oppose an international law enforcement initiative that might be costly to other U.S. foreign policy objectives has diminished," especially since the anticommunist objectives of the cold war no longer have priority.[76] This pattern applies at least as much to the prosecution of terrorists—often seen as the most evil of all criminals—as to other issues of law enforcement that have an international dimension.

There is no good institutional solution to the problem of such institutional leanings. In countering terrorism, all of these perspectives should be voiced and all possible responses considered. The nature of the topic demands it. The attorney general needs to be at the high table of decision-making on terrorism, even if a U.S. prosecution is not the best or primary measure to take in a specific case. The secretary of defense and the chairman of the Joint Chiefs of Staff also need to be at that table, even if military action is not the preferred response in a given situation. Sound policy requires the other players to push other perspectives, even though the prevailing ethos may make it uncomfortable to argue against seeing justice done in one's own courts or against a forceful effort to try to keep chemical weapons out of the hands of terrorists. It also requires the direct involvement, despite all the competing demands on their time and attention, of those who are above departmental perspectives, meaning the national security adviser and as necessary the president. The president has, in the past, had to take a more direct role in counterterrorism than merely endorsing the recommendation of senior advisers—as President Clinton did in agreeing with the British to handle the Pan Am 103 case in a transplanted Scottish court, thereby overruling a recommendation from the Department of Justice that it be tried under U.S. law—and presidents will have to do so again in the future.

CHAPTER FIVE

Groups

Counterterrorist policy is, in large part, policy toward foreign groups—ones that have used terrorism in the past and might do so again in the future. The U.S. interests at stake include not just counterterrorism itself but the stability of countries and regions rent by conflicts in which the groups have taken part.

Heterogeneity

Everything that makes a terrorist group what it is—including its culture, ideology, demographic characteristics, and history—needs to be taken into account in formulating a posture toward it. Sound policy toward a terrorist group requires an understanding of what is and is not important to it, what drives its leaders and members, what its hot buttons are, what would stimulate it to attack, and what would lead it to give up terrorism.

A rather disturbing implication is that the United States needs, in a sense, as many counterterrorist policies as there are terrorist groups. To make thinking about this more manageable, however, one can ask two more basic questions about any terrorist group. The first is, what is the *nature of the objective* that it pursues through terrorism? This does not mean specific beliefs or goals (left or right, secular state or theocracy, and so on). Rather, it means the use to which its terrorist operations are put. Groups employ terrorism for a wide range of purposes, including:

—Gaining leverage for bargaining (for example, seizing hostages and then demanding the release of prisoners);

—Political or diplomatic disruption (for example, derailing a peace process);

—Influencing the behavior of a fearful population (which can be anything from scaring away foreign tourists or investors to scaring residents out of a disputed territory as part of an ethnic cleansing operation);

—Provoking a government into reacting harshly and indiscriminately (and thereby alienating the government from the local population);

—Showing the flag (that is, demonstrating that resentment runs deep, that the government does not have firm control over its territory, or simply that the group itself is still alive and functioning—some of the operations of the Basque Fatherland and Liberty (ETA) for example, have probably been conducted mainly to show that the organization is still kicking);

—Imposing costs on the adversary to increase the chance that the adversary will change its policies (such as attacking U.S. troops in Lebanon or Saudi Arabia to try to get the United States to evacuate the troops);

—Deterrence through punishment of the adversary's actions and the threat that similar actions in the future will also be punished (such as Hizballah's attacks in Buenos Aires in retaliation for Israeli operations in Lebanon);

—Revenge (in practice usually indistinguishable from deterrence but motivated by a desire to "get back" regardless of whether there is a realistic hope of deterring—no doubt part of the motivation for Hizballah's operations in Argentina);

—Simple hatred (often linked to revenge in that the terrorist claims to be retaliating for past injustices but stimulated less by any one action than by a primitive belief that the citizens of the targeted country deserve to die); and

—Carrying out a divine mandate (that is, the terrorist's belief that he is acting in service of, or to reflect the will of, a supreme being).

The distinctions in this inventory of objectives are admittedly blurry. Most terrorist operations serve more than one objective, and the motivations of any one group may shift over time. Nonetheless, different groups tend to be associated with different points along the spectrum of objectives. In general, groups that conduct terrorism for the more carefully calculated, instrumental purposes near the top of this list are more likely to give up terrorism as a result of rational recalculation of changed circumstances (and maybe even of negotiation) than are groups that conduct it for the more visceral purposes near the bottom of the list. The most incorrigible terrorists are ones driven both by elemental hatred and by a belief that they are performing a sacred mission—an outlook that leaves no room for compromise or for abandonment of the mission.[1]

The second basic question is: does the group *represent* something larger than itself? This does not mean "represent" only in the sense of being an extreme manifestation of something. Nor does it mean that the group has been elected to anything, or even that it would win a majority of votes from its claimed constituent public if it were to participate in an election. Rather, the issue is whether the group is a major embodiment, if not the chief one, of some larger political movement or set of unrealized aspirations. The question is significant because it determines what other interests are at stake, and what other forces have to be dealt with, beyond those relating strictly to terrorism and counterterrorism. The answers to the second question tend to parallel those to the first. The most viscerally motivated groups are usually not representative, while the representative groups are the ones that tend to use terrorism in more measured, instrumental ways.

The principal terrorist threats that the United States has faced—and certainly the principal ones about which Americans have been concerned—in recent years have come from groups near the visceral, unrepresentative end of the spectrum (part of the larger trend toward using terrorism less to bargain and more to inflict pain). The bombers of the World Trade Center and the Murrah Building certainly fit that description (as do similar small, ad hoc cabals). With some qualification, so do the attacks against the embassies in Africa and more generally the threat from Usama bin Ladin. Although bin Ladin's operations were intended partly to pressure the United States into pulling its troops out of the Arabian Peninsula, his animus toward the United States is much broader than that.[2] Bin Ladin's organization is also not representative in the sense in which that term is being used here, even though much of what he says resonates with many people outside the organization. And despite bin Ladin's economic and other activity in Afghanistan, al-Qaida is still basically just a terrorist group.

Although the threats from this type of group are more immediate than from other types, the formulation of policy toward them is simpler. The primary goal should be to eliminate the group or, failing that, to eliminate as much of its capability as possible. That means employing the instruments discussed in the previous chapter, particularly the patient, behind-the-scenes dismantling and disruption of the group's infrastructure. Manipulation of intentions plays less of a role, except insofar as disruption or security countermeasures dissuade the group from attacking at particular times or places. Broader political efforts do matter, not in the sense of accommodating the group's demands—much less of negotiating with the group itself—but only in the sense of addressing some of the underlying roots of discontent. Resolving regional conflicts or burnishing the United States' troubled image in the Islamic world, for example, might diminish support and recruitment for some such groups and make potential counterterrorist partners (ranging from individual informants to governments) more willing to cooperate against them. But such measures will not remove altogether the terrorist threat from such a group, which has no better means than terrorism to advance its agenda.

Making sound policy toward the opposite kind of group—representative organizations that have used terrorism in a more instrumental way—is more complicated because the organizations are much more than just terrorist groups, and policy toward them is necessarily far more than just counterterrorist policy. The groups in question are mostly large, ethnically or religiously based (but not necessarily religiously driven) organizations that aspire to political power, either exclusively over a particular territory or as a major participant in an existing state. Leading examples include Palestinian Hamas, Lebanese Hizballah, the Irish Republican Army (IRA), the Kurdistan Workers' Party (PKK) in Turkey, the Liberation Tigers of Tamil Eelam (LTTE) in Sri Lanka, and the Revolutionary Armed Forces of Colombia (FARC) and National Liberation Army (ELN) in Colombia. Several of these groups purvey a variety of social services to their constituents. Many residents of the Gaza Strip have become dependent on such services from Hamas, for example, while Hizballah operates in Lebanon a welfare network of schools, hospitals, and other sources of assistance. The groups' political activities include extensive propaganda (using, among other things, radio and television stations as well as websites) and participation in electoral politics either directly (Hizballah held nine seats in the Lebanese parliament going into elections in 2000) or through allied parties (for example, the IRA's relationship with Sinn Fein). Several of the groups have developed substantial military capabilities (the FARC has an estimated 8,000 to 12,000 armed combatants), which they have employed in guerrilla operations (for example, by both major groups in Colombia, or by Hizballah in its attacks against Israel and its Lebanese allies in south Lebanon) and even maneuver warfare (which the LTTE has used at times). Military successes have made some groups the de facto government over substantial pieces of territory. (The LTTE has sometimes exercised such control on the Tamil-inhabited Jaffna Peninsula in northern Sri Lanka. The Colombian government formally ceded control over a 16,000-square-mile area in southern Colombia to the FARC in November 1998, and agreed in April 2000 to give similar privileges to the ELN in a smaller tract in the central portion of the country.) Clearly there are as many dissimilarities among these groups as there are similarities. But what they have in common—besides having used terrorism—is that they are major, multidimensional forces that have to be reckoned with in a multidimensional way, both because of who they are (much more than small bands of bombers) and what they represent (larger currents of discontent and aspiration that would persist and would manifest themselves in different ways, even if these particular groups did not exist).

Even though the multidimensional groups have not accounted for most of the salient terrorism against U.S. interests in recent years, there are good reasons to give them more attention. One is that further terrorist attacks by such groups against Americans are certainly possible. It is perhaps easy to forget—because it has not hit U.S. interests directly in the last few years—that Lebanese Hizballah has killed more U.S. citizens through terrorism than has any other group, foreign or domestic. Most of those deaths occurred in the bombings in Beirut in the 1980s that were intended chiefly to push U.S. troops out of Lebanon. Having accomplished that goal, Hizballah has focused more on its political activity and its military operations against Israel in southern Lebanon. But Hizballah's terrorist apparatus, led by Imad Mughniyah, is still robust and dangerous. The globe-circling reach of that apparatus (demonstrated by its attacks in Buenos Aires) enhances the danger. The Colombian groups have been harming Americans in an unspectacular but more regular fashion. Ninety-two U.S. citizens were kidnapped in Colombia between 1980 and 1998; twelve of those Americans died in captivity.[3] Thirteen more U.S. citizens were kidnapped in Colombia in 1999, some by the FARC and some by the ELN. In addition to deliberate attacks on U.S. interests, Americans risk becoming collateral victims. This has happened not only in some of Hamas's bombings in Israel but also in PKK attacks against the Turkish tourist industry; a PKK bomb in Istanbul in August 1995, for example, injured two U.S. citizens.

Looking beyond any direct harm to Americans, the operations of multidimensional groups constitute a very large part of international terrorism, in terms of actual operations and, even more so, the groups' ability to ratchet up the violence at will. The PKK launched two major waves of international terrorism (mostly against Turkish targets in Europe) in 1993 and 1995, which constituted nearly 40 percent of international terrorist incidents worldwide in those two years. The Colombian groups continue to account for a substantial proportion of international terrorist incidents. Many of the operations by the PKK and the Colombians caused only property damage, but such groups have at times been far more lethal. A single vehicle bomb that the LTTE detonated in the financial district of Colombo in January 1996, for example, killed 90 civilians and wounded about 1,400.

Terrorism itself aside, several of the groups play large roles in regional conflicts or in the stability (or instability) of their home countries. The LTTE, the PKK, and the Colombian groups have each been the biggest security concerns and challenges to stability of their respective countries. Consider, for example, what the PKK's rebellion has meant to Turkey. At its peak in the mid-1990s the PKK had as many as 10,000 men under arms, with about half of them in Turkey at any one time. To confront them, the government of Turkey was using about a quarter of its sizable land forces plus about 45,000 additional village guards, at an annual cost of $4–7 billion. Total deaths from the insurrection have been between 20,000 and 30,000, with about 3,000 villages destroyed, 400,000 people resettled, and many others emigrating individually to the cities, exacerbating urban social problems. The confrontation with the PKK has colored every aspect of Turkish foreign and security policy, often to the detriment both of Turkey and of states that seek to cooperate with it. It has, for example, complicated U.S.-Turkish relations in dealing with Iraq, given Ankara's opposition to doing anything with the Iraqi Kurds that might stimulate Kurdish separatism. Yes, the PKK is a terrorist group, and U.S. counterterrorist policy must address the terrorist challenge that it presents. But it would be a grave mistake to think of it *only* as a terrorist group and to downplay the other realities that it embodies—including not just the security problem of a (now largely quelled) guerrilla war but also the political problem of a long-standing (and still unrealized) ethnic aspiration, of which the PKK became the most forceful and effective expression.[4]

That said, some of the same methods of attacking the capabilities of smaller, unidimensional terrorist groups can be applied as well to the large multidimensional ones. This includes the monitoring of a group's illicit activities and the encouragement of foreign law enforcement agencies to work against the group's overseas infrastructure. The fact that the terrorist apparatus of some of these groups is organizationally distinct from the political and social structures (as with Mughniyah's terrorist element in

Hizballah and the Izz el-Din al-Qassam Brigades in Hamas) helps to keep the counterterrorist work from appearing to be directed at more than just terrorism.

This does not mean that the different parts of a multidimensional group are ever truly severable. Even the most benign charitable work may indirectly assist the terrorist operation by enhancing support for the group and thereby helping recruitment; Hamas's good works in Gaza, for example, have helped to sustain its supply of suicide bombers. Separate or not, any terrorist activity is fair game for counterterrorist operations. There need be no compromise with the principle that terrorism is unacceptable and that it should always be actively opposed, regardless of any legitimacy that one may give to other things a group does or stands for.

One particularly effective way—if it can be done—of attacking the capability of some multidimensional groups (and possibly also increasing the chance of a peaceful settlement of the underlying conflict) is to capture the group's senior leader. Although this would have little effect on groups with a collective leadership (such as Hamas or the Colombian organizations), several other groups have—despite their large size—been led by a single supreme figure with dictatorial powers. The PKK, for example, is very much the creation of Abdullah Ocalan, around whom a cult of personality grew up. His name was the only one on the PKK's official statements, and he forcefully suppressed challenges to his absolute leadership. The capture of such a figure not only removes the group's source of direction; the opportunism that tends to characterize such leaders—who use their groups primarily as paths to personal power, not as means of national salvation or religious expression—may lead to a jailhouse "conversion" that will further confuse and sap the group. That is what happened after Turkish authorities arrested Ocalan in Kenya in February 1999. Speaking from his prison cell through his lawyers, Ocalan called for PKK fighters to cease their attacks and to withdraw to bases outside Turkey. He also described the PKK's insurrection as a "mistake" and renounced demands for independence or even autonomy for the Kurds, suggesting it would be sufficient for the government to relax bans on uses of the Kurdish language and to grant amnesty to his guerrillas. A desire to be spared execution no doubt motivated Ocalan's statements. But whatever his motives, his words had beneficial effects. Many PKK fighters did apparently withdraw in response, and in October eight members of the organization voluntarily turned themselves in to the government following Ocalan's appeal for them to do so as a gesture of goodwill.[5]

The experience with Ocalan's arrest resembles what happened to Sendero Luminoso in Peru following the capture in September 1992 of its founder and leader, Abimael Guzman. The cult of personality surrounding Guzman was at least as strong as that around Ocalan. To the Sendero faithful he was "President Gonzalo," who was not only their operational commander but the source of "Gonzalo thought," the latest and greatest variant of Marxist ideology. Members of the group swore personal loyalty to him. Although Guzman's initial statement after his arrest was bellicose, he then began writing letters from prison that appealed to the guerrillas to suspend the war. Guzman's mellowing caused confusion, dissension, and despair in the ranks of Sendero. There were disagreements among members over whether Guzman really meant what he had said. His capture was clearly the pivotal event in what became a long decline for Sendero throughout the rest of the 1990s. (Guzman's lieutenant who subsequently took control of the organization, Oscar Ramirez Durand, was himself captured in July 1999.)

The remaining leader who most fits the mold of Ocalan and Guzman is the LTTE's Velupillai Prabhakaran. If anything, Prabhakaran has carried intragroup dictatorship to even greater extremes. Like Sendero Luminoso under Guzman, members of the LTTE make their pledges of allegiance to the leader, rather than to the organization or to larger causes. Prabhakaran's iron-fisted control over the group extends to the smallest details of its members' personal lives. He has responded brutally, including with murder and torture, to even mild criticism of his leadership. Prabhakaran's departure from the scene—with or without a jailhouse conversion—would be the brightest ray of hope to shine upon the conflict in Sri Lanka, which seems far from resolution through either military or political means. It would mean removal of the LTTE's linchpin and could only improve the faint prospects for a negotiated settlement, given that Prabhakaran would probably be satisfied with nothing less than a Stalinist-style reign by himself over the Tamil-inhabited provinces (a disturbing preview of which has been his tyrannical rule over Jaffna when it has been under the LTTE's control).[6]

The United States will have only a modest supporting role in most attempts to capture leaders, particularly ones who, like Guzman and Prabhakaran, remain mostly or exclusively in the home country. With a leader in exile, like Ocalan, there are greater opportunities for U.S. assistance. This includes diplomatic pressure on third countries to deny safe haven and intelligence work to locate the individual.

The capture of a group's leader is a way of attacking a group's capabilities that also (especially given jailhouse conversions and their aftereffects) may affect its intentions. And in general, manipulation of a terrorist group's intentions is a larger part of dealing with a multidimensional, representative group like the PKK or Hamas than it is in countering a unidimensional group like al-Qaida or Yousef's gangs. Because the former type of organization has other ways, besides terrorism, to advance its agenda, the question of intentions goes beyond simple matters of deterrence to the group's larger strategic calculations. This leads to the question of what might cause a group to decide that further terrorist attacks are in its interests; and—from a narrower U.S. counterterrorist perspective—whether such terrorism might include attacks against U.S. targets.

The decisional line between using or not using terrorism (or other forms of violence, for that matter) is apt to be thin for many multidimensional groups. A decision to use it may be tactical, reflecting a calculation that the conditions at the moment—including such factors as the political strength of the adversary government and the attention that international diplomacy is paying, or not paying, to the conflict—are propitious for employing it. The calculations, and the use of terrorism, will change as conditions change, even though the nature and objectives of the group have not. The PKK was not a fundamentally different group between one year and the next during the early 1990s, as it decided either to launch, or to refrain from launching, major terrorist offensives. The Liberation Tigers of Tamil Eelam did not change their stripes from one phase of their campaign to another, even though their use of terrorism has also varied.[7]

Because for such groups the line between using or not using terrorism is so fine and so changeable, it would be very difficult to develop an accurate formula for anticipating its use. One generalization, however, that helps to explain such restraint as these organizations have shown—as well as addressing the question of whether they would attack U.S. targets—is that they have an interest in not spoiling their chance for future international acceptance as legitimate political actors. A key difference between the multidimensional organizations and smaller unidimensional terrorist groups is that the former generally aspire to such acceptance, possibly even as the governing authority over a separate territory, while the latter do not. The need for acceptance is a significant deterrent against terrorist actions that might irreparably scar the perspectives of those governments from whom the acceptance is sought. If this consideration does not turn a group completely away from international terrorism, it at least is a strong argument in favor of moderating it. The PKK's European terrorist offensives, for example, were huge in terms of the number of incidents but relatively mild in terms of lethality; the decision to smash much property but to cause relatively little blood to flow in European streets was no doubt shaped by the organization's concern for minimizing the ill will of West European governments and publics.

This consideration is also a major reason for multidimensional groups to eschew deliberate attacks on the interests of the United States—the country that matters most as far as international acceptance is concerned. This is particularly so for groups that aspire to lead, or at least to be a major part of, independent states, bearing in mind everything that future normal relations with Washington would imply regarding possible economic assistance, trade, and investment, as well as diplomatic recognition. This factor largely explains why attacks by multidimensional groups have accounted for only a modest proportion of recent major terrorism aimed at the United States—despite their capability to inflict far more damage—and why many American victims of terrorism by such groups were only incidentally caught up in attacks directed against someone else. It also has helped to counteract suspicions and resentments of the United States based on Washington's support for governments that are the group's principal adversaries, such as Israel in the case of Hamas or Turkey in the case of the PKK.[8]

A further factor that may make some groups chary of operations that would risk enraging the American government or public is that the groups benefit from private financial contributions from within the United States. This was true for many years of the IRA, which received funds in particular through Irish Northern Aid (NORAID).[9] The cells in the United States of Hamas, Hizballah, and (although it is not a multidimensional group) al-Gama'at al-Islamiyya also are used partly for fund-raising.[10] Any financially based deterrent effect is likely to be weak, however, because many witting contributors probably would not change their behavior in response to terrorist attacks, unwitting contributors do not know they are supporting terrorism, and the U.S. government (for the reasons discussed in the previous chapter), has difficulty enforcing even the financial provisions of antiterrorism law already on the books.

Any group's restraint toward the United States will be conditioned mostly on whatever influence the group sees the United States exerting in the conflict to which the group is a party. That means that the group's posture toward possible terrorist attacks against the United States can change (maybe a lot), and that U.S. policy toward the underlying conflict matters a lot as far as the risk of such attacks is concerned. An important facet of U.S. policy toward multidimensional terrorist groups is thus policy toward peace processes (actual or possible) intended to resolve those conflicts.

Peace Processes

The role that the United States should play (and if and when it should play it) in resolving local and regional conflicts in which terrorist groups take part depends on such factors as the larger interests that the United States has in the country or region in question, whether the conflict has reached a point that makes it ripe for settlement, and whether the impediments to resolution of the conflict are such that intercession by an outside party would be helpful. These and other issues pertinent to resolving such conflicts go beyond the subject of dealing with terrorist groups, and have been addressed extensively elsewhere.[11] This section discusses a few questions about peacemaking that are germane to terrorism itself or that are more likely to arise when a group that has used terrorism is part of the conflict.

Given that the United States is both the number one target of international terrorists and the most prominent (and one of the most committed) forces on behalf of counterterrorism, it might seem unlikely that protagonists that were also terrorist groups (even the multidimensional kind) would accept Washington as an interlocutor. And, indeed, some would not. Hizballah, for example, would probably prefer little or no U.S. involvement in the disputes in Lebanon and the Middle East to which it is a party. But the preferences of other groups are more complex than that. The FARC, for example, has had its lead negotiator publicly proclaim "no more meddling of the North American state in the internal affairs of Colombia," but it sought in 1998 and 1999 to maintain a back channel of communication with the U.S. government.[12] Some other multidimensional groups would also welcome a dialogue with Washington or a U.S. intercession to resolve their conflicts. The extent to which this process can go has been demonstrated by the terrorists or ex-terrorists of the IRA and the Palestine Liberation Organization (PLO), who have met with the president at the White House and have become, to varying degrees, partners in peace with the United States. Merely talking with a group will nearly always be an important card in the U.S. hand.

The relationship between terrorism and peacemaking is complex. Any conflict with a long and violent history will have extremists with an interest in continuing the conflict and thus in opposing a peace process. That opposition may manifest itself in attacks by splinter or fringe groups intended to disrupt progress toward peace, and in that regard such progress may carry a short-term price in the form of increased terrorism. Overall, however, it is not terrorism but rather the absence of it that tends to correlate with progress toward peace settlements. Terrorist attacks at critical junctures can disrupt or retard a peace process by causing the parties to focus narrowly on parochial security concerns, while an absence of attacks builds the confidence needed for taking political risks required for moving toward a settlement. Conversely, lack of movement toward an agreement that would satisfy the political yearnings of a discontented group feeds extremism that often leads to terrorism, while progress toward such an agreement dampens such extremism. And if a peace agreement is finally reached with a group that has practiced terrorism, that is one less group that is in the terrorism business.

Counterterrorism is thus an important adjunct to peacemaking. That is true not only before an agreement is signed but also after, given the potential for groups still in opposition to use terrorism to undermine implementation of the accord. The hazards of postagreement disruption through terrorism were recognized at the summit meeting held at Sharm al-Sheik in March 1996 in support of the Arab-Israeli peace process, following which the United States pledged $100 million in antiterrorist assistance to Israel, to be used in coordination with Israel's new partners in the Palestinian Authority.

But as such agreements are negotiated and signed, as the United States and other outside powers express their support, and as assistance is doled out, a question sometimes arises that cuts to the heart of policy toward terrorist groups: exactly which groups should be made part of a peace process, and which ones stamped out as incurable threats to peace? Which ones, in other words, should be looked on as part of the solution, and which ones as nothing but part of the problem? In the post-Oslo Israeli-Palestinian equation, a portion of the answer to that question is easy, but another part is more difficult. The remaining rejectionist secular groups on the Palestinian side—principally the Popular Front for the Liberation of Palestine-General Command (PFLP-GC) and the Abu Nidal Organization—as well as the Palestine Islamic Jihad, are only problems. None of them is representative of large segments of the Palestinian people. But what about Hamas? As a large multidimensional organization with broad support, it has a claim to a major role in the political future of Palestine, even though it is not now part of the peace process, and its terrorist capability is one of the greatest threats to that process. The difficulty of this part of the question is reflected in the Palestinian Authority's ambivalent posture toward Hamas, as well as Hamas's own ambivalence regarding cooperation with Arafat.

The basic question of whether or not to draw a group into a peace process does not have to be strictly an either-or proposition. To some extent the question can be conditional; renunciation of terrorism and acceptance of Israel are in effect conditions of participation in the Middle East peace process, and much of what has separated a group like Fatah that has entered it from a group like Hamas that has not. Moreover, a government can combat the terrorism and other violence while talking with a group about ways to end it, which is what has been going on in Colombia since 1999. The organizational distinctions between terrorist and nonterrorist elements within an organization can be of help; for example, one can fight the Izz el-Din al-Qassam Brigades while engaging the political leadership of Hamas. But eventually one has to decide whether the ultimate objective regarding a group is to engage it or to exterminate it.

There are usually substantial arguments on either side of this decision. On one hand, eradicating a group that embodies broader popular aspirations may mean that a major political current goes unrepresented, that a blow has been struck against self-determination, or that a defeated rebellion is merely driven further underground, only to re-emerge (possibly in an even more extreme form) in the future.[13] Strong measures needed to crush a group are apt to increase resentment of the government, discredit moderates, and increase support for radical elements and for terrorism.[14] Excluding a group from a political system leaves it free to call for unrealistic but rhetorically appealing "solutions" to national problems and may even increase its mystique among some members of the public.[15] However, an attempt to draw a hard-line group—especially one with terrorism on its resume—into a peace process may complicate to the point of impossibility the reaching of any kind of consensus on a nation's political future. Negotiating with (and making concessions to) such a group is apt to inflame groups elsewhere on the political spectrum, including ones to which "rewarding terrorism" is anathema (as well as possibly encouraging groups elsewhere to use terrorism as a way of getting their demands recognized).[16]

The governments of the countries where the conflicts occur have to make most of these tough decisions, not the United States. But in one respect the U.S. posture is even more delicate than that of the government on the front line. If the United States is not foursquare behind fights against terrorist groups, it could be seen as getting soft on terrorism itself. But if it becomes closely identified with a government's attempt to crush a group that has some strength and popular sympathy, it risks making enemies it did not have before. This could include antagonizing entire ethnic groups as well as enraging the group itself to the point that it strikes back with terrorism against what it sees as its enemy's major supporter. The situation is somewhat like dealing with a bee, which will not sting if left alone but may do so if swatted at and missed.

The United States can influence, but should give considerable deference to, the government that is dealing with the terrorist group firsthand. Washington cannot get too far in front of the host government's own posture toward making peace with a terrorist group if it is to retain influence with that government on the issue and cannot get too far behind if it is to influence either the government or the group. The latter point is germane to Colombia, where the government of President Andres Pastrana has gone to extraordinary lengths to make the FARC a full partner in shaping the country's political future. One way it has done so (besides regular negotiations and granting the FARC its own zone) is to try to shape the group's political and economic thinking in directions that will make it a more compatible part of a new national consensus. It has taken leaders of the FARC on visits to European capitals to absorb modern, post-Marxist thinking about political and economic organization. It has brought business leaders (including the chairman of the New York Stock Exchange and the chairman emeritus of America Online) to FARC-controlled territory to meet with the group's leaders and discuss how foreign investment could improve a peaceful Colombia.[17] It has had representatives of the FARC cochair public hearings on a range of national issues.[18] The road to peace in Colombia is still exceedingly rough. No cease-fire has accompanied the negotiations, and the FARC continued or even increased its attacks after talks began. The government has had to deal with the competing demands and increasing violence not only of the ELN but also of the right-wing paramilitaries in the United Self-Defense Forces of Colombia (AUC).[19] As far as a peace process in Colombia is concerned, however, the train has already left the station.

Elsewhere the United States is less apt to face a decision of whether to catch up with such a train than of whether to nudge a reluctant host government into embarking on a peace process in the first place. In making that decision—and in formulating its own thinking, and influencing the host government's thinking, about whether to embrace or to exterminate a group—several considerations are pertinent. One is how significant a part the group occupies in its nation's political fabric, in the sense of representing substantial social, economic, or political interests. The more substantial the interests, and the more genuinely the group represents those interests, the less sense it makes to try to eradicate the group and the more sense it makes to try to engage it. The fact that an organization has used terrorism (or that much of its constituent public would disapprove of its use) should not ipso facto disqualify it on this score. Ultimately the size, strength, and resilience of an organization reflects to a large degree the support that its constituency chooses to give to it or to withhold from it. "The only reliable standard for judgment by the outside observer," Ted Gurr notes about ethnically based resistance groups, "is that the most authentic organizations—those whose claims have greatest current validity—are those that are largest and most durable."[20]

A second and related consideration is whether the government's security forces have a good shot at wiping out the group. Even if they do, this is not by itself a reason to do so, given the chance that the underlying grievances may reappear in another troublesome form. But effective military and police work has smashed even some large terrorist (or terrorist-*cum*-guerrilla) groups without significant problems in the aftermath. The Fujimori government in Peru came close to doing so with Sendero Luminoso, as well as with the smaller MRTA. The setbacks that the PKK suffered at the end of the 1990s (hastened by the capture of Ocalan) led Turkish military leaders to believe that they were within reach of crushing that group altogether.[21] Maybe the Turks are wrong, or maybe their military assessment is right, but it would be wrong to rely on security measures as heavily as Turkey has in dealing with its Kurdish problem. Nonetheless, if eradication seems feasible, it is at least an option to be considered.

A third factor is the feasibility of a negotiated settlement, given what is known about the group's objectives and its likely bottom-line demands ("bottom line" being not necessarily what a group expresses now, but rather what it is unlikely ever to concede even in long negotiations). If a settlement appears infeasible because of the extremity of those demands or their incompatibility with other major interests in the country, there may be no point in launching a peace process (except possibly as a tactical gambit to weaken or confuse the group and to demonstrate the government's goodwill). The struggle with the LTTE in Sri Lanka is an unhappy example of a conflict in which, although a military solution is not in sight, neither is a political one, as least not without a change in the group's leadership. Sendero Luminoso is another group which—despite its size and strength, which at its height numbered in the thousands—could never have been part of any political accommodation, given its objective of ripping apart Peruvian society.

In some cases a negotiation may be fruitless not because the group's goals are as intrinsically vicious and destructive as Sendero's but because the structure of the issues is such that there is simply nothing to negotiate. This may be true of the ETA. The Basques have already won considerable autonomy during the quarter century since Francisco Franco died, and there would be little more for the Spanish government to concede short of outright independence—which most residents of the Basque country, and possibly even a majority of ethnic Basques—do not want.[22] Another example of a terrorist group to which negotiation was never a feasible or logical response despite the group's size and strength is the religious cult Aum Shinrikyo. Aum had thousands of members at its height and could fairly be described as multidimensional in view of its extensive economic and political activities in addition to its terrorist and religious ones. But its Armageddon-based beliefs had no conceivable role in a larger political process, and there were no "concessions" that Japanese authorities could have made to it even if they had wanted to; before it turned to terrorism the group could and did run candidates for elective office. The only appropriate response to such a group is to suppress it.

The implacability of some groups may be due less to a commitment to the interests on behalf of which the group claims to be fighting, than to a commitment to the fight itself, which over time has become an end in itself.[23] Some groups, whether or not they have an obdurate leader, have a corps of "hard men" who have known no other life than the one of violence. To them, any negotiated end to the violence would be a form of defeat. The conflict itself may also be a source of profit to leaders as well as a livelihood for the rank and file.

A fourth consideration is whether there are viable, nonterrorist interlocutors who represent the same interests the terrorists claim to represent. To the extent there are, this is an argument against dealing the terrorist group into a peace process (or perhaps starting any negotiation that could strictly be called a peace process). Concessions made to defuse discontent that has erupted into terrorism need not be concessions to the group that has conducted the terrorism. A wide variety of political parties have served, or could serve, this role of nonterrorist interlocutor. Sinn Fein in Northern Ireland is, in a sense, one of these, although it is such a thinly veiled surrogate for the IRA that the terrorists have effectively been dealt into that peace process. Other parties have had slightly looser links to the terrorist groups, such as the Basque Euskal Herritarrok, formerly known as Herri Batasuna (which Spanish officials once indicated was an acceptable representative for discussion of political issues) or, still looser, the Kurdish People's Democracy Party or Hadep (which Turkish authorities—perhaps shortsightedly—have not used as an interlocutor, choosing instead to ferret out any links between Hadep officials and the PKK).[24] There may also be moderate leaders with no known links to the terrorists. Reaching understandings with the more moderate leadership of an ethnic or religious community has a counterterrorist multiplier effect, in that it not only may attenuate grievances and demonstrate that moderation works, but also can lead to intracommunity policing of the extremists, which in some ways is more effective than anything the government can do.[25]

In some conflicts, viable nonterrorist interlocutors may be hard to find. A tragic irony is that they tend to be most scarce where the terrorist groups are most brutal, because of what the terrorists have done to eliminate rivals. The archetypal case in point is Sri Lanka, where the LTTE has murdered any actual or even potential moderate Tamil leader it could reach (as well as eliminating rival militants).[26] Even the absence of an alternative negotiating partner, however, does not preclude the sort of concessions to a community's interests that undercut support for a terrorist group that claims to act on the community's behalf. Turkey, for example, would not need a negotiated settlement with anyone to remove remaining restrictions on use of the Kurdish language (a step that would also call Ocalan's bluff). Moreover, an open, competitive political system will breed new moderate leaders even where none existed before. This is what may make Peru's near-subjugation of Sendero Luminoso a lasting success and not just a temporary one. Sendero had tapped into the grievances of Peru's mostly poor Indian and mixed race populations. That current of opinion subsequently found more peaceful expression, particularly in the presidential candidacy in 2000 of Alejandro Toledo, a U.S.-educated economist of Indian descent. In his campaign, Toledo flaunted his ethnic background as a "cholo"—successfully enough to force incumbent Alberto Fujimori into a runoff before withdrawing amid a dispute about the timing of the second vote.

Most terrorist groups will not, and should not, be made a direct part of any negotiation or peace process. Most should be exterminated, not engaged. This is certainly true of the small, unidimensional groups whose goals are incompatible with peace and reason, who genuinely represent no one but themselves, and who have nothing to offer but an end to their violence. For some of the reasons given above, negotiation may also not be a suitable response even to some of the larger, multidimensional groups that have used terrorism. But for some others, it will be. And where it is, the group's terrorist baggage (even if it has suspended terrorist operations) will inevitably be an obstacle, but a surmountable one, to engaging it. Terrorism's illegitimacy makes it politically and emotionally harder (quite apart from any hard-nosed counterterrorist concern about not rewarding terrorism) to sit down and talk with those who have practiced it—more so even than to talk with those who have conducted conventional military operations and who may have actually killed far more people in doing so.[27]

This obstacle will confront both the government that is directly involved in the conflict at hand and the United States, as a friend and perhaps facilitator of the peace process intended to resolve the conflict. The obstacle will be all the greater for the United States if the terrorism involved has claimed American victims. That is the case, for example, regarding communications between the United States and the FARC, which the U.S. side suspended following the murder by a FARC commander of three American humanitarian workers in March 1999. Such actions by a group cannot be ignored, and withholding at least for a while the plum of a dialogue with Washington is an appropriate response. There will be times, however, when the greatest contribution the United States can make to counterterrorism will be to swallow hard and not just to talk with the leaders of a group but to shake hands that carry stains of old blood, possibly including American blood.

That is what the United States has done—to the benefit of counterterrorism as well as other important objectives—in supporting and facilitating the peace process between Israel and the Palestinians of the former PLO, as well as the peace process in Northern Ireland. Those two cases demonstrate both the problems and the possibilities of such endeavors. The setbacks that each of these initiatives has suffered—including the disagreements that led to the temporary suspension of the new Northern

Ireland government in early 2000, the failure of Israeli and Palestinian negotiators to meet deadlines for concluding further agreements, and the breakdown of confidence in the Middle East following the outbreak of violence in the autumn of 2000—are unsurprising problems of the sort that should be expected in any attempt to resolve a conflict in which hostility has been strong enough for terrorism to have been used. The setbacks should not be allowed to overshadow the significance of what has been achieved. The accords reached in Northern Ireland and the Middle East—in addition to whatever they do for self-determination, local prosperity, and other objectives—have been signal accomplishments for counterterrorism; major terrorist organizations have committed themselves to using nonterrorist means, even though this commitment has entailed significant risk for the leaders of those organizations. Supporting such a process is worthy of the United States taking some risks as well.

One possible risk, of course, is a weakening of the U.S. reputation for steadfastness in standing up to terrorists. There has been no appreciable damage in this regard from the Irish and Palestinian negotiations, however, for three reasons. One is a widespread international recognition of the worth of, and need for, peace processes aimed at resolving these two conflicts. A second reason is that the United States has, for the most part, stayed in step with those governments (the United Kingdom and Israel) whose interests have been most at stake and which have carried the biggest and most direct burden of confronting the terrorists in question. (The one exception was when Washington got ahead of London in 1994, inviting Gerry Adams to the White House and permitting him to raise funds in the United States. The infuriated British summoned the U.S. ambassador to Downing Street for a scolding, and Prime Minister John Major did not return President Clinton's telephone calls for two weeks.)[28] A third reason is that curtailment of terrorism and the capacity to conduct it have been intrinsic parts of the agreements reached. These have included the concepts that the Palestinian Authority would actively cooperate with Israel in combating the remaining Palestinian terrorist groups, and that the IRA would eventually "decommission" (that is, give up) its arms.

The issue of decommissioning has been the biggest problem in fully implementing the Good Friday agreement on Northern Ireland. It illustrates both how questions of terrorism are apt to be major challenges after, as well as before, a peace accord, and how die-hard elements most strongly committed to a conflict can undermine efforts to end it even after an agreement is signed. Being an "undefeated army" is a point of pride within the IRA, and however Gerry Adams may view decommissioning, it has been a bitter pill for the hard men of the IRA to swallow. Their resistance always made implementation of this part of the understanding problematic, even before the IRA stated in February 2000 that it would not talk to the commission supervising disarmament, and even after it promised three months later that it would put its arms "beyond use."[29]

The principal terrorist-related, postagreement dispute in the Middle East concerns Israeli dissatisfaction with the Palestinian Authority's counterterrorist efforts. This issue involves not so much the threat of renewed terrorism by one of the parties to an agreement as the effectiveness of measures to curb terrorism from other sources. The effectiveness of the Palestinian Authority's measures has been variable—and became even more questionable amid the turmoil of the *intifada* that broke out in late 2000—but for most of the past several years its efforts have been earnest.

The possibility of further terrorism by rejectionist fringe groups, however, is indeed one of the bigger threats to the peace processes in both the Middle East and Northern Ireland. Additional terrorism in the Arab-Israeli theater could come from the Palestine Islamic Jihad or (despite its ambivalence about possible political cooperation) Hamas, and maybe the PFLP-GC. Jewish extremists affiliated with groups such as Kach or Kahane Chai could stage another incident like the massacre by Baruch Goldstein (who was affiliated with Kach) of worshippers at the al-Ibrahimi Mosque in Hebron in 1994. In Northern Ireland, a threat of disruptive terrorism has come from fringe groups such as the so-called Real IRA, the Continuity IRA, and the Irish National Liberation Army on the republican side, and the Loyalist Volunteer Force on the unionist side.

A final lesson from the Arab-Israeli and Northern Ireland experiences is that supporters of peace processes should not expect perfect compliance from the groups that participate in them, either in cease-fires that accompany negotiations or in implementing the terms of a peace agreement itself. One should instead expect that continued hard-line sentiments within the ranks, together with the imperfect command and control that the senior leaders of many groups exercise and the intragroup political constraints that those leaders face, will result in occasional terrorist operations that, even if they cannot quite be described as "rogue," also do not reflect the policy of the top leadership. The IRA's bombing of Canary Wharf in London in February 1996, which broke a seventeen-month cease-fire, was one such operation. Adams did not condemn the bombing, but he probably had not sanctioned it either. The U.S. response of withdrawing Adams's fund-raising privileges but maintaining lines of communications to him as a peace negotiator was the proper one.[30] The murder of the three humanitarian workers in Colombia (which the FARC's leaders eventually acknowledged was wrong, although they did not deliver the perpetrators to anyone's justice but their own) perhaps was in the same category. Even if the Israeli-Palestinian peace process gets back on track, the Palestinian Authority also will make more mistakes and exhibit more shortcomings in combating Palestinian terrorism. Each such incident or problem should be noted, criticized, and as appropriate penalized. But to allow it to scuttle an incipient or ongoing peace process would be counterproductive counterterrorism.

Lists

The previous sections have shown why policies toward terrorist groups need to reflect the many ways in which the groups, and the conflicts in which they take part, differ from one another. Although some aspects of counterterrorist policy should be constant and global, others need to be tailored to individual circumstances. The current statutory centerpiece of U.S. policy toward terrorist groups, however, stresses uniformity rather than variation: the establishment by the Antiterrorism and Effective Death Penalty Act of 1996 of a formal list of Foreign Terrorist Organizations (FTOs).

The antiterrorism act stipulates three criteria for designation as an FTO: that the group is a foreign organization, that it engages in terrorist activity, and this activity threatens the security of U.S. persons or the national security of the United States (broadly defined to include national defense, foreign relations, and economic interests in addition to the safety of individual Americans). Designations expire in two years unless explicitly renewed, although groups can be added or removed from the list at any time. The designations are subject to judicial review.[31] Thirty FTOs were initially designated in October 1997. The first biennial review of designations in 1999 resulted in one group (al-Qaida) being added to list and three being dropped: the Democratic Front for the Liberation of Palestine (which had moved toward acceptance of the Arab-Israeli peace process, with DFLP leader Nayif Hawatmah shaking hands with Israeli President Ezer Weizman), the Khmer Rouge (which, because of defeats and defections, had virtually ceased to exist), and the Manuel Rodriguez Patriotic Front (a moribund Chilean leftist group). The first out-of-cycle change to the list was the addition in September 2000 of the Islamic Movement of Uzbekistan.

Designation of FTOs was necessary to add legal precision to other provisions of the antiterrorism act that hinged on membership in, or support to, terrorist groups. Chief among those were the financial provisions described in the last chapter. As noted, the results of using those provisions have been meager, with no assets having been frozen under the new legislation, and few prosecutions. Since the prosecutions involved in-kind support rather than money, other criminal statutes generally could be used. In one of the cases, for example, an individual arrested in Michigan in July 1998 was attempting to ship $124,000 worth of sensitive night vision and navigational equipment. He was charged not just with material support to an FTO but with several export violations.[32] A group in North Carolina suspected of raising money for Hizballah was jailed in July 2000 not on the basis of the antiterrorism act but rather for immigration violations, weapons offenses, money laundering, and cigarette smuggling.[33] The success of a criminal statute, of course, cannot be measured only in the number of prosecutions that rely on it. FBI Director Louis Freeh made this point in 1998, urging that the law be given time to work and suggesting that it may have deterrent value. "As investigators build successful cases and prosecutors develop sound prosecutorial strategies" to enforce the law, Freeh said, "targeted groups may decide that fund-raising activities in the United States are not worth the risks."[34] There will have to be a longer and stronger record of prosecutions, however, for there to be any likely effect on the decisions of terrorist groups.

The other provision of the antiterrorism act that relies on the list of FTOs makes membership in a Foreign Terrorist Organization a ground for removing an alien from the United States.[35] This provision appears to have been used more extensively, with approximately thirty deportation cases having been initiated by the Immigration and Naturalization Service by mid-2000 that mention affiliation with an FTO. As with the prosecutions, however, this is often just one of several valid grounds for excluding or deporting an individual. Someone engaged in dangerous terrorist-related behavior can almost always be dealt with by using other statutes. Some of those in the United States who are affiliated with foreign terrorist groups and do the less dangerous things (such as propaganda or proselytization) are U.S. citizens and are not subject to exclusion as aliens.

The programs for which the list of FTOs was explicitly created, therefore, make at most an extremely modest contribution to counterterrorism.

Given that U.S. counterterrorist efforts survived for many years without such a list, it is fair to ask what other advantages or disadvantages the formal designation of terrorist groups may have. Probably the greatest advantages are the symbolic ones of calling attention to terrorist groups as objects worthy of opprobrium, putting the United States formally on record as opposing their terrorist activities, making it clear that the United States is closely monitoring and assessing those activities, and sustaining attention to counterterrorism generally. There are also more practical benefits. It helps to keep counterterrorism an issue of high policy within the government, and in particular to maintain the role of the counterterrorism coordinator in the State Department. It provides a handy frame of reference for international cooperation against terrorist groups. And even if other laws can also be used, affiliation with a formally designated terrorist group can strengthen a variety of legal and administrative cases involving suspected terrorists, including not only deportations and prosecutions but also requests to collect information under the Foreign Intelligence Surveillance Act.

The drawbacks are significant, starting with the fact that the list unavoidably mixes the apples and oranges of terrorism, putting the same label on all of them even though they are actually quite different. The twenty-nine groups on the list at the end of 2000 vary greatly on several dimensions. They include large multidimensional groups based on Islamist ideologies (Hamas, Hizballah), Marxism (the FARC and ELN in Colombia), a combination of the two (the Iranian Mujahedin-e Khalq) or ethnicity (LTTE, PKK), as well as the smaller ethnically based ETA. They include old-line secular Palestinian groups, including one that has at times seemed interested in a peaceful political route (the Popular Front for the Liberation of Palestine) and others that have not (the PLFP-GC, Palestine Liberation Front, and Abu Nidal Organization). Non-Palestinian leftist groups include one that is a shadow of its formerly formidable self (Sendero Luminoso), European groups that have always been small but deadly (November 17 and the Revolutionary People's Struggle in Greece, and the Revolutionary People's Liberation Party/Front in Turkey) and remnants of defeated groups that consist of a few dozen inexperienced fighters (MRTA) or a handful of fugitives (the Japanese Red Army). Radical Islamist organizations include bin Ladin's al-Qaida and several groups cut from the same cloth—and some of which are allied to varying degrees with al-Qaida—which have different mixtures of national and transnational objectives (the Egyptian al-Jihad and al-Gama'at al-Islamiyya, the Algerian Armed Islamic Group, Harakat ul-Mujahidin in Kashmir, the Abu Sayyaf Group in the Philippines, the Palestine Islamic Jihad, and the Islamic Movement of Uzbekistan). The other religious groups on the list are the small Jewish groups Kach and Kahane Chai and the idiosyncratic cult Aum Shinrikyo. The variation is great not only according to the criteria mentioned at the outset of this chapter (representativeness and the type of terrorist objectives) but also in size, strength, activity, ideology, ultimate political goals, outside support, anti-U.S. orientation, and whether the group is waxing or waning. Besides the general drawback of encouraging a truncated view of these organizations by looking at all of them through a single lens, there is the more specific drawback of possibly burning bridges to groups with which the United States might want to deal in the future. In a worst case, such bridge-burning may make a group more inclined to attack U.S. interests directly.

The secretary of state can inject political and diplomatic considerations into decisions on designating FTOs, which is what was done in excluding the IRA from the original list of thirty groups. The IRA certainly qualified for designation under the terms of the statute, and it presented a more significant threat to U.S. interests as defined in the law than did many of the groups that were designated. The decision not to designate it was probably right, given that there was more to gain (in terms of counterterrorism, as well as other objectives) from dealing with it as an interlocutor in a peace process than from branding it formally as a terrorist organization.[36] Each such political exception, however, diminishes the credibility and value of the FTO list itself. Although the law only "authorizes," rather than requires, the secretary to designate any organization that meets the criteria as an FTO, the list has tended to be viewed as a more comprehensive and definitive "A list" of the groups the United States considers terrorist. Any apparent inconsistencies in application of the law risk generating skepticism about the consistency of the overall U.S. commitment to counterterrorism.

Another basic problem with the designation of FTOs is that any list of discrete groups does not accurately reflect the blurred and ever-changing organizational lines that characterize modern international terrorism. The State Department's most recent annual report on international terrorism (which, among other things, lists and describes the FTOs) correctly notes in its introduction "the shift from well-organized, localized groups supported by state sponsors to loosely organized, international networks of terrorists."[37] The system of formally designating FTOs does not capture the ad hoc groups, the fringe groups, and other less well established—but still often dangerous and significant—manifestations of international terrorism. The release of the annual report and the announcement of redesignation of FTOs have been occasions for understandable questions to be raised about why, for example, Irish fringe groups such as the Continuity IRA and Real IRA have not been designated as FTOs.[38] These and fourteen other groups (or more inchoate assemblages of terrorists, such as Zviadists in Georgia) are named (with no legal significance) in the State Department report as a kind of "B list."[39]

Part of the problem is that the designation of FTOs is a large, cumbersome process that is slow to respond to the changes in the gallery of international terrorist groups. That process involves not only several parts of the State Department but also the departments of Justice and Treasury and the intelligence community—necessarily so because of the legal and financial implications and the informational basis for designations. The initial designation of thirty groups was a long and (for the officials involved) painful process that consumed enormous time and attention in each of the agencies involved. Despite nagging from interested members of Congress, the process was not completed until nearly a year and a half after the AEDPA had become law. The fact that al-Qaida was not one of the groups listed in October 1997 (just ten months before the bombings in East Africa) illustrates the difficulty the system has in responding promptly to the emergence even of a group that directly threatens U.S. interests.

The slowness stems in large part from a further basic difficulty of designating FTOs: that it turns into a legal issue what should be more a matter of politics, diplomacy, and intelligence. Designation requires an "administrative record" that assembles intelligence on a group that will not only be sufficient for policy purposes but will stand up in court if the group challenges the designation. The "terrorist activity" in which a group must be proven to be engaged need not be attacks but may instead include recruitment, training, planning, and other terrorist-related work.[40] Nonetheless, it is often tough to prove ongoing activity because of the limitations, described in chapter 4, of intelligence on terrorist groups. With many groups it may be a safe bet that the group is still in business and still a terrorist threat, but difficult to adduce specific evidence about what it has been up to lately.

There have been multiple legal challenges to the designations of FTOs. Both the Mujahedin-e Khalq (MEK) and the LTTE hired prominent lawyers to take their cases to the U.S. Court of Appeals for the District of

Columbia, where they argued that they had been denied due process because of the secrecy of the administrative records and the lack of advance notice of their designations. In June 1999 the court unanimously upheld the designations of both groups.[41] In a separate suit in the Ninth Circuit, plaintiffs wishing to support political and humanitarian activities of the LTTE and the PKK have challenged the constitutionality of the FTO portion of the AEDPA.[42] Even if the government continues to win in court, the vagaries of what is provable or not provable in such cases ought not to be the main determinant of U.S. policy toward foreign terrorist groups.

The problems with designations of FTOs are not sufficient grounds for repealing that portion of the AEDPA altogether. Repeal would end the real advantages of the list and would send its own negative and confusing messages about the U.S. commitment to counterterrorism. The law could profitably be modified, however, to address the issues of flexibility, responsiveness, and inclusiveness. One possibility would be to maintain a formal list of terrorist organizations that would be just as official as the current one (and thus have the same advantages of serving as a frame of reference, sustaining attention to counterterrorism, and so on) but would not be directly linked to the freezing of assets, criminalization of material support, and exclusion of aliens. It would thus be free of the legal impediments that make the current system so ponderous. There would not be an official A list and an unofficial B list but rather a single official list that would represent the U.S. government's best judgment, as a matter of intelligence and policy, regarding which groups are of counterterrorist concern. Such a list could be modified more quickly and easily than the current designations of FTOs. In addition to such a list, the administration could be given discretion (some of which it already has anyway under the International Emergency Economic Powers Act) to apply, through executive order, to *selected* groups on the list such tools as the blocking of assets and the exclusion of members from the United States (in which cases some of the legal requirements associated with FTOs would still have to be met). These tools should be used only where they had a chance of being effective and were specifically determined to support particular U.S. policies.

There is some precedent for such an arrangement The intelligence community, to set priorities for its collection and analysis, already maintains a frequently updated list of terrorist groups (and states and selected issues) that looks much like the comprehensive official list suggested here. And Executive Order 12947 in 1995, which prohibited transactions with twelve groups deemed to be threatening the Middle East peace process, is an instance of selective application of sanctions to support a specific U.S. policy initiative.

This chapter has shown that to identify an organization as a "terrorist group" is only the starting point in formulating sound policy toward it. The groups are diverse, as are the environments in which they operate, the policy tools that are most appropriately applied to them, and the U.S. interests affected by the conflicts to which they are parties. Such diversity, and some of the issues of characterizing, categorizing, and listing terrorist groups discussed above, apply in a similar fashion to state sponsors of terrorism. That is the subject of the next chapter.

CHAPTER SIX

States

Counterterrorism involves policy not just toward groups but toward foreign states—those that support, facilitate, or practice terrorism, or whose help is needed in combating it. The categories of "sponsors," "enablers," and "cooperators" used below are analytical conveniences in organizing the discussion and, particularly with sponsors, reflect a common way of viewing the role of foreign countries in terrorism and counterterrorism. All three categories, however, really constitute a single spectrum, with mixtures of conflict and cooperation all along it. Indeed, a tendency to think too much in distinct categories of states has hampered the making of effective counterterrorist policy. Most countries worth mentioning in any discussion of terrorism represent both part of the problem and part of the means to manage the problem.

Sponsors

The reduction in state sponsorship during the past several years has not meant a reduction in problems of managing relations with state sponsors or of dealing with the legacy of past measures taken against them. In fact, the United States has exhibited more uncertainty in developing relationships with states that have reduced their support for terrorism than it has in standing up to those states when they were still actively supporting it. Unlike many terrorist groups, terrorist states (and sometimes even the same regime) will remain even if the terrorism ends. Extermination is an appropriate goal regarding many terrorist groups; with states it is not an option.

There is always a bilateral relationship to manage, with opportunities for other issues in that relationship to complicate counterterrorism or for counterterrorism to complicate the other issues, as well as opportunities—to be seized or squandered—for developing improved and mutually beneficial ties.

Terrorist states, like terrorist groups, are subject to formal designation under U.S. law. The Export Administration Act of 1979 established the list of state sponsors by authorizing the secretary of state to designate countries that have "repeatedly provided support for acts of international terrorism."[1] Amendments to this law enacted ten years later codified several export controls and prohibitions on military sales or foreign assistance for countries on the list.[2] The legislative history of the amendments indicates that the kind of "support" for terrorism that qualifies a state for designation includes but is not limited to lethal matériel, logistical help, headquarters facilities, safe houses, planning, training, money, documentation, or sanctuary from extradition or prosecution.[3] Other legislation has applied a variety of additional sanctions to any state designated under the 1979 law. These include a prohibition on direct or indirect exports of items on the U.S. Munitions List; a requirement for licenses and advance congressional notification of certain other exports; a prohibition on any assistance under the Foreign Assistance Act, the Agricultural Trade Development and Assistance Act, and the Peace Corps and Export-Import Bank acts; withholding of General System of Preferences designation as a developing country entitled to duty-free treatment; negative votes by U.S. representatives to international financial institutions on any proposed loans or use of funds involving the listed countries; no tax credits for U.S. corporations or individuals earning income in the listed countries; and a prohibition on foreign assistance to any third country that provides lethal military equipment to one of the listed countries. These measures are in addition to further sanctions imposed separately on many of the same states through country-specific legislation, executive orders under discretionary laws such as the International Emergency Economic Powers Act, or administrative action such as the secretary of state's regulation of the use of U.S. passports for travel.

As of 2000, seven states were listed as state sponsors of terrorism: Cuba, Iran, Iraq, Libya, North Korea, Sudan, and Syria. An eighth regime has in effect been added to these seven: the Taliban in Afghanistan, the subject of Executive Order 13129, signed in July 1999, which imposed financial and commercial sanctions because of the Taliban's support to terrorism.

Afghanistan is not on the main list of state sponsors because the United States does not recognize the Taliban as a government.

As with the list of Foreign Terrorist Organizations (FTOs), the legal uniformity imposed by the statutory list of state sponsors disguises much diversity. There are two dimensions especially relevant to counterterrorism along which the listed states differ from one another. One is the extent of the state's current involvement in terrorism.[4] The other—a different question—is the importance of terrorism relative to that of other U.S. concerns about the country.

Iran has been the most active state sponsor in recent years, with its terrorist-related activity taking three forms. One is the extraterritorial assassination of Iranian oppositionists. A second is the provision of money, training, weapons, and other assistance to terrorist groups that oppose Israel, the Arab-Israeli peace process, or the established order in a number of countries in the Middle East, North Africa, and Asia. Lebanese Hizballah has consistently been the largest recipient of Iranian help, although Tehran has extended its largesse to many other groups, mostly Islamist (such as Hamas and the Palestine Islamic Jihad) but some secular ones too (such as the Popular Front for the Liberation of Palestine-General Command [PFLP-GC]). A third type of activity—one that would not by itself make Iran a state sponsor but is perhaps the most worrisome for the United States—is regular Iranian surveillance of U.S. installations and personnel overseas, which would facilitate any future Iranian terrorist attacks against those targets.[5]

Terrorism is one of the major U.S. concerns about Iran but not the only one. Others are Iran's nuclear program and acquisition of advanced weapons, overall opposition to the Middle East peace process, and policies toward moderate regimes in its own neighborhood. The latter two issues overlap with terrorism in that support to terrorist groups has been one of the principal means through which Tehran has opposed the Arab-Israeli peace process and has tried to undermine, for example, the regime in Bahrain. With Iran (and to varying but generally lesser degrees with the other state sponsors), U.S. policy interests also include not only the state's undesirable behavior but also the need for cooperation with it on other issues. In Iran's case this includes, for example, the stopping of unauthorized shipments of Iraqi oil and the containment of the Taliban in neighboring Afghanistan.

As for the Taliban, it is at least as deeply in bed with terrorists as is any other regime. It is a willing and even enthusiastic host to Islamic extremists from around the world who live, train, and plan in Afghanistan. Islamists committing violence in Chechnya, Lebanon, Kashmir, and elsewhere have a base of support in Taliban-controlled territory. Terrorism, and in particular the hospitality that the Taliban extends to Usama bin Ladin, is clearly what concerns the United States most about Afghanistan. Farther down on the list are the export of illegal narcotics and the Taliban's miserable human rights performance.

Iraq qualifies for continued listing because of the safe haven that it gives to Palestinian rejectionists such as Abu Nidal and to the Mujahedin-e Khalq. It also still appears to be involved in assassinating opponents of Saddam Hussein. Terrorism is by no means the main U.S. concern regarding Iraq. The main immediate concern is to limit Saddam's means for military aggression, particularly by curbing his special weapons programs. The longer-term concern is over who rules Iraq, with the ultimate U.S. goal being Saddam's departure.

Terrorism is still the principal U.S. concern about Libya but not because of any ongoing terrorist activity; rather, it is because of unfinished business related to prior terrorism and because of a lack of other pressing concerns. Qadhafi has essentially gotten out of the terrorist business. Libya has not been implicated in international terrorist operations for several years. It has broken completely with its former client Abu Nidal, implemented procedures to prevent terrorists from entering Libya or using its territory, cooperated on counterterrorism with moderate Arab states, acted in accordance with an Arab League agreement to extradite suspected terrorists, and transferred support from Palestinian rejectionists to Arafat's Palestinian Authority.[6] Libya has at most only some residual relations with rejectionist groups with which it had done business for many years, such as the PFLP-GC. As of 2000, the United States' main terrorism-related concern regarding Libya was the tying up of loose ends related to Pan Am 103—specifically, getting continued Libyan cooperation in the trial of Abd al Basit al-Megrahi and Lamin Kalifah Fhima, and obtaining compensation for the families of the victims.

The Islamist-dominated regime in Sudan continues to host elements of several terrorist groups, including Hizballah, al-Gama'at al-Islamiyya, the Palestine Islamic Jihad, Hamas, and the Abu Nidal organization. It provides to these and other groups such practical support as meeting places, training facilities, documentation, and refuge. Khartoum's sponsorship of terrorism is the principal U.S. worry about Sudan. Other concerns include the seemingly endless civil war between the regime and non-Muslims in southern Sudan, abuses of human rights, and Sudan's role in other conflicts in East Africa.

The overriding U.S. interest in Syria is in getting Damascus to make peace with Israel. The issue of terrorism is subsidiary to the peace process. Syria's provision of safe haven and support to several rejectionist groups in Syria and Syrian-controlled portions of Lebanon is a chip in its bargaining with the Israelis over return of the Golan Heights. If Syria and Israel succeed in reaching a peace agreement, Syria's support to the terrorist groups will be dealt with—because the Israelis would settle for nothing less.

Terrorism is not even close to being a significant threat, or the major U.S. concern, with either of the two non-Middle Eastern countries on the list of state sponsors. North Korea shelters a few fugitive Japanese extremists and in recent years has tried to kidnap (and perhaps assassinate) a defector or two, and possibly to assassinate a South Korean official.[7] This behavior pales in comparison with the far greater U.S. worries over North Korea's nuclear program, its development of long-range ballistic missiles, and possible instability on the Korean Peninsula. Cuba's remaining links with terrorism consist of providing a home for a handful of members of the Basque Fatherland and Liberty group (ETA) and other fugitives, and providing some accommodations to the Revolutionary Armed Forces of Colombia and National Liberation Army (which, as noted earlier, the Colombian government has been doing as well). The Castro regime's post–cold war retrenchment has been so extensive that it is doing nothing either in terrorism or other military or external activities that would appear to qualify it for its pariah status.[8] Instead, the U.S. posture toward Cuba is a function of internal politics—those of Cuba as well as of the United States. The officially expressed U.S. goal regarding Cuba is "to promote a peaceful transition to a stable, democratic form of government and respect for human rights as soon as possible."[9]

This quick review demonstrates how great is the variation within even this short list of states, both in the extent to which each state's practice or sponsorship of terrorism is really a problem and in the prominence of terrorism on the U.S. list of worries about each state. As with the designation of Foreign Terrorist Organizations, the pinning of a single label on what is actually a mixed bag has the drawback of promoting uniformity of policy when customization is needed.

Fortunately, the label of "terrorist sponsor" has not been a completely impenetrable barrier to conducting business with some states on the list of state sponsors when the United States has had other interests in doing so. This has been true of the extensive dialogue with Syria (the only state on the list with which the United States has full diplomatic relations with a resident ambassador) on the Middle East peace process. It was also true of the Agreed Framework that the United States negotiated with North Korea in 1994 and was intended to reduce the proliferation hazard of Pyongyang's nuclear power program.

Branding a regime a state sponsor is unquestionably a major impediment to business, however. The label itself sometimes gets in the way. This has been true with North Korea, despite a series of contacts with U.S. officials that gained momentum in 2000. Earlier in the year, Pyongyang had balked at following through on plans to send a high-level delegation to Washington for talks, saying that it should first be removed from the terrorism list.[10] North Korean leader Kim Jong Il specifically mentioned delisting as the key condition for improved relations.[11] North Korea's number two political leader, bound for a summit meeting at the United Nations in September 2000, returned to Pyongyang in a huff when a U.S. airline required him and his delegation—because they came from a listed country—to undergo body searches before boarding a connecting flight to New York.[12]

There are other, more serious, complications in the way the list—which treats state support for terrorism as a dichotomous proposition of being either on the list or off it, and which automatically attaches sanctions to being on it—works in practice. One complication is that other issues have, in effect, hijacked counterterrorism with regard to certain states on the list, as well as certain ones not on it. The formal designation as a state sponsor of terrorism has sometimes become just one of several penalties to be applied, withheld, maintained, or removed in managing troubled bilateral relationships, with decisions on use of this tool dependent less on terrorism than on other issues, events, and political realities. Cuba has stayed on the list not mainly because its scant lingering links with terrorism are troublesome but because of other political reasons that underlie a U.S. policy of continuing to ostracize Castro. Pakistan has stayed off the list not because it is doing less than any of the listed states to foster terrorism (untrue) but because imposing this additional penalty would have drawbacks in light of other U.S. interests in Pakistan and the U.S. stake in maintaining an even-handed approach toward South Asia as a whole.

In some cases counterterrorism *should* be subordinated to other interests that, for a given country or region, may be more important to the

United States. When counterterrorism is not just subordinated, however, but instead is manipulated as a tool for other purposes, there is a cost. The principal cost is to reduce the credibility of U.S. counterterrorist policy. It is understandable for questions to be raised, as they repeatedly are, about why a Cuba is on the list and a Pakistan is not. Incongruity between the list of state sponsors and actual patterns of state support for terrorism invites cynicism about the list and about whether the United States is sincere when it states that one of its tenets of counterterrorist policy is to "isolate and apply pressure on states that sponsor terrorism to force them to change their behavior," rather than this being a cover for pursuing other objectives.[13]

The conflation of terrorism with other issues also reduces the chance that state sponsors really will "change their behavior" regarding terrorism. If any positive steps a sponsor takes are likely to be trumped by continued U.S. grievances—and continued penalties or sanctions—arising from other issues, there may be little incentive to take those steps. This is especially true when the evident U.S. objective—as with Iraq—is to replace, or at least to outlast, the other regime. Being a target for removal trumps every other issue, terrorism included, and destroys whatever inclination there may be to offer cooperation, except where it may be tactically useful in buying time and maintaining power. Egyptian foreign policy adviser Osama al-Baz made this point about Iraq: "The Iraqi regime seems to hold the view that no matter what they do, they will be targeted by the United States. So they say, 'If the game is to topple us, then we'd be crazy to cooperate any further.'"[14] Similarly, Cuba's Castro could be excused for thinking that even if he expelled the remaining terrorist fugitives from Cuba, this would result in little or no change in U.S. policy toward Cuba. Any such thinking would be reinforced by the most recent major U.S. legislation on Cuba, the Cuban Liberty and Democratic Solidarity Act of 1996 (also known as the Helms-Burton Act), which explicitly states that neither Fidel Castro nor his brother Raul would be acceptable members of a transition government leading to greater democracy in Cuba, which the act posits as its objective.[15]

The fact that the listed sponsors of terrorism are many of the same states that are objects of containment and concern because of weapons proliferation, subversion, or other problems has encouraged the conceptual lumping of them together as "rogue states," or more recently, "states of concern." Such labels are convenient for mobilizing support to contain these states, but this kind of conceptual amalgamation can impede the formulation of discriminating, customized policies toward regimes that vary considerably with regard not only to terrorism but to the other problems.[16] Sometimes a state's support for terrorism is directly related to other problems in its behavior, making the conceptual link between issues appropriate for more than just sloganeering—for example, Iran's backing of terrorist groups being intrinsically related to its opposition to the Arab-Israeli peace process and its attempts to subvert moderate states in the Persian Gulf region. More often, however, the links between terrorism and the other objectionable behavior are much weaker.

A link that has been overemphasized is that between sponsorship of terrorism and the development of unconventional weapons. That most of the listed state sponsors also have known or suspected programs to produce chemical, biological, or nuclear weapons has frequently been noted but is not ipso facto a reason to consider chemical, biological, radiological, or nuclear (CBRN) terrorism to be the principal threat that they pose. States have indeed used chemical or biological substances in a terrorist mode to assassinate individuals (for example, Bulgaria's killing of dissident emigre Georgi Markov in London in 1978 using an umbrella with ricin in its tip, and Israel's unsuccessful attempt to kill Hamas official Khalid Mishal in Amman) and one of the state sponsors—Iraq—has used chemical weapons in a military mode to inflict mass casualties (in the Iran-Iraq war and against its own Kurdish population). But the often-postulated scenario of a state sponsor providing unconventional weapons to a client terrorist group is unlikely to materialize. The state would lose control over the matériel, an uncontrolled use of it by a group would serve no plausible purpose of the state, and sophisticated unconventional agents might be more traceable to their origin than the more mundane forms of assistance that sponsors usually provide to client groups. The danger of a state like Iraq someday directly employing unconventional weapons against U.S. targets is clearly real and acute, but that is a military problem that is separate from the terrorist problem of the state assisting terrorist groups or being involved in ongoing terrorist activity.

A more basic difficulty of the current system of designating state sponsors is that the automatic nature of the associated sanctions makes the list of sponsors a blunt and inflexible tool. The firm link between listing and sanctions influences decisions about listing and is part of what makes the list a distorted picture of where problems of state sponsorship of terrorism actually lie. States are kept on or left off the list more to subject them, or not to subject them, to sanctions than to make an accurate statement about current patterns of support to terrorism. In one sense this is an admirable exercise of discretion in what is, as the State Department periodically has to remind the world, a political decision by the secretary of state. But it contributes to the aforementioned problem of credibility and to the perception that the United States is applying its avowed counterterrorist policy inconsistently. For the states on the list, automatic sanctioning means a blanket approach when a detailed analysis of, and adjustment to, individual circumstances would be more appropriate.

The efficacy of sanctions has been extensively debated.[17] Two major lessons pertinent to the present subject can be drawn from that debate. One is that sanctions always entail costs, sometimes substantial costs, that should matter to the government imposing them. They include, but are not limited to, economic losses for one's own workers and businesses, hardships to citizens of the target country who suffer the impact of sanctions but are not able to change their regime's policies, frictions with other governments over differing policies toward the target country, and other unintended effects such as stimulating flows of refugees. The costs must be weighed against the expected benefit of even a successful application of sanctions. The other lesson is that, although sanctions can be useful in pursuing various foreign policy goals, their effectiveness is dependent on a host of variables such as the dependence of the target state on foreign trade, the responsiveness of its political system, the breadth of international support for the sanctions, and the importance to the targeted regime of the behavior the sanctions are intended to change. The wisdom of their use, moreover, depends not only on their anticipated effectiveness but also on what other policy options are available. An implication of these lessons is that any application of sanctions should be carefully considered and individually tailored. A one-size policy definitely does not fit all, and the common trait of having supported terrorism is not sufficient ground for imposing one.

It is impossible to measure accurately the effectiveness of sanctions that have been imposed to curb sponsorship of terrorism. One reason is the entanglement with other issues that have also been the basis for placing sanctions on the same states. Another reason is the long time that sanctions against most of the listed sponsors have been in effect, making it hard to distinguish responses to the sanctions from changes in policy that were really because of other events or altered circumstances. An informal look at the currently designated sponsors, however, provides only very modest support for the proposition that sanctions have helped to reduce terrorism. Sanctions have not led Iran to end its support to terrorism (or to change significantly some of its other objectionable external behavior), although evaluation of policies toward Iran is complicated by the fact that Tehran has simultaneously faced both sanctions from the United States and engagement by Europe.[18] Sanctions next door in Iraq—where they are multilateral, not just a U.S. measure—have had substantial material effects. But Saddam's Iraq is the perfect example of a ruthless and entrenched regime that passes on those effects to its populace while steeling itself to withstand the external pressure and to persist in the policies most important to it. The blame rests with Saddam for not permitting the UN-sponsored oil-for-food program to do more for the welfare of ordinary Iraqis. But the fact is that after years of sanctions, ordinary Iraqis remain poor, the regime exploits loopholes in the sanctions for the benefit of the security forces and the favored elite, and Saddam's political position has not crumbled.[19] The multilateral sanctions against the Taliban in Afghanistan have perhaps been in place too short a time to form a fair judgment about their effectiveness, but the signs so far are not favorable. A statement attributed to Taliban leader Mohammed Omar that was circulating in Pakistan in April 2000 said, "Even if the whole of Afghanistan is destroyed, we will never deliver Usama. A Muslim cannot deliver a Muslim to a non-Muslim." (A surrender of bin Ladin was the principal U.S. objective in pushing for the sanctions.) Sudan has made some cosmetic changes in its posture toward terrorists (and bin Ladin did stop residing in Sudan in 1996), but its cooperation with many terrorist groups continues.

The improvements in the behavior of other state sponsors cannot be attributed all, or even chiefly, to sanctions, given other influences on their policies. As was noted in chapter 3, the collapse of the USSR forced several erstwhile Soviet clients to moderate their behavior. Perhaps sanctions, by contributing to the penury that the withdrawal of Soviet aid helped to cause in a country like Cuba, hastened the economically motivated retrenchment that has included reduced involvement in terrorism. Even for these states, however, other factors are involved. For example, Syria (which has escaped most of the additional sanctions, beyond those directly attached to being designated a state sponsor, that have been applied to several of the other states) probably has been motivated at least as much by the diplomatic momentum of the Israeli-Palestinian peace process, and Hafez Assad's concern not to let terrorism by Syrian clients spoil his chance to recover the Golan Heights, as it has by sanctions or anything else. Fluctuations in the price of oil have also had at least as great an economic impact on some of the state sponsors as have sanctions.

Libya represents probably the best case of sanctions helping to shape a state sponsor's behavior on terrorism-related matters. As with Iraq, the sanctions against Libya have included multilateral ones (established through the UN Security Council resolutions cited in chapter 4) as well as those the United States has imposed unilaterally. The UN sanctions on Libya were less severe than those on Iraq, particularly since they did not embargo Libyan oil. In that sense the Libyan sanctions had less bite, but it also meant that they enjoyed reasonably broad international acceptance and that there was less debate about hardships being imposed and less "sanctions fatigue." The economic and political costs of the sanctions to the United States were moderate. Although it took several years to attain the result, there is little doubt that a desire to get rid of the sanctions was part of what motivated Qadhafi to surrender the Pan Am 103 suspects. This motive may also have been partly behind Libya's overall withdrawal from international terrorism.[20]

The Libyan case illustrates, however, the importance of distinguishing between sanctions themselves and the more general opprobrium with which they are associated. For Qadhafi, the latter has probably been more important than the former. He has always striven to play an international role well beyond Libya's borders. Being regarded as a pariah or a rogue impedes that; removing that stigma is thus likely to be more of a motive for him than removing a particular set of commercial restrictions. This is suggested by the greater emphasis that Libya has placed on terminating the UN sanctions even after those sanctions were suspended following the turnover of Fhima and Megrahi (meaning that termination would have more symbolic than practical significance) than on ending the U.S. sanctions that were still in effect.

Keeping in mind that each case is different, there are three general limitations to the use of sanctions in reducing state support to terrorism. The first two of these stem directly from the nature of terrorism.

First, it is often unclear what standards the target state should be expected to meet to end the sanctions, and whether such standards as do exist have been met. Even if a "zero tolerance" policy toward state sponsorship were advisable (and for reasons addressed below, it may not be), it may be hard to define zero. Does any presence of cells or members of a terrorist group in a country constitute support by that country? If so, then what about the cells of Hizballah, Hamas, and al-Gama'at al-Islamiyya that are present—as the director of the FBI publicly acknowledges—in the United States?[21] The answer to the latter question may be that members of those cells have not been proven to have committed a crime and in any event are being closely watched, but some of the listed state sponsors could give the same answer about cells on their territories. Even if there are agreed standards, determining whether they have been met is a judgment based in large part on intelligence that, for the reasons discussed in chapter 4, is often fragmentary and ambiguous. The absence of intelligence reports over a period of time regarding a particular state doing business with a particular terrorist group may mean that the state has stopped supporting the group, or it may mean that the relationship was well enough hidden that there just did not happen to have been any intelligence collected on it during the period. Intelligence reports that are more conclusive can rarely be shared with the public or with the targeted state. The uncertainty of the standards and whether they have been met is a reason that sanctions for this purpose are not backed up by credible threats of more forceful action if the target state does not comply—which is one of the things that students of sanctions point to as making sanctions more effective.[22] The option of military force arises when there is the clear offense of a major, recent terrorist attack for which a state has been proven responsible. Day-to-day support for terrorist groups and terrorist-related activity lacks such clarity.

Second, sanctions do little to degrade directly the capability of a state to practice or support terrorism. This distinguishes counterterrorism from certain other purposes for imposing sanctions—such as curbing the spread of weapons of mass destruction—with regard to which sanctions may have worthwhile effects even if they do not induce the target state to abandon its ambitions. The international pressure placed on Iraq, for example, has impaired its ability to procure advanced military hardware or to develop some unconventional weapons, despite Saddam's lack of repentance or cooperation.[23] With Iran, even though the sanctions are only unilateral, U.S. pressure against loans to Tehran (which has been part of those sanctions) has led Iran to reduce purchases of weapons, thereby reducing the military weight that Iran can throw around the Persian Gulf region.[24] Principally because supporting terrorism is cheaper than procuring an arsenal of advanced weapons, such measures do not directly affect sponsorship of terrorism as much—as the example of Iran indicates.[25]

Third, the U.S. policy of applying sanctions to countries it has designated as state sponsors of terrorism is out of step with the policies of most of its allies and most of the rest of the world. Even the multilateral sanctions regime against Iraq has developed cracks that, among the permanent members of the Security Council, have increasingly pitted the United States and Britain against a more skeptical France, Russia, and China. With Iran, the disagreements are deep enough that the Clinton administration never even seriously considered raising the issue of sanctions in a multilateral forum such as the Security Council.[26] Following suspension of the UN sanctions on Libya, European firms—backed by their governments—"practically trampled each other," as one observer put it, in rushing to sign deals with Tripoli.[27] As for Cuba, the United States has had to endure not only a lack of cooperation with its embargo but also an annual criticism of it in the UN General Assembly. The resolutions calling for the embargo to end have drawn increasingly broad support over the past several years. The one in November 2000 passed with 167 votes in favor, 3 (the United States, Israel, and the Marshall Islands) opposed, and 4 abstentions.

The specific implications for sanctions of this lack of support for U.S. policy are twofold. One is that sanctions tend to be less effective without broad support and compliance; unilateral sanctions are rarely effective.[28] The other is that for the United States to try nevertheless to use sanctions against this set of states entails an added political cost, particularly in frictions with its European allies. The worst tensions have resulted from unwise and unsuccessful legislative provisions—in both the Helms-Burton Act and the Iran-Libya Sanctions Act (ILSA)—that have attempted to extend the reach of unilateral U.S. measures by imposing secondary sanctions on foreign firms that do business with the targeted states. The European Union reacted to these laws by adopting regulations that would make it more difficult for their members to comply with the U.S. boycott.[29] A larger crisis was averted only when the Clinton administration, as part of an understanding reached with the Europeans in May 1998, agreed to waive, or continue to waive, certain sanctions in the two laws and to seek legislation permitting it to waive other provisions in the Helms-Burton Act.

The list of state sponsors, as it is currently structured and has generally been used, is inflexible not only about who goes on the list and the automatic application of sanctions but also in regard to getting off the list. As of 2000, states have been removed from it only twice, and neither of those deletions was actually a response to improved behavior. One was the removal of South Yemen in 1990, when it lost its independence by merging with the more populous and more moderate North Yemen. The other was the deletion of Iraq in 1982, a change motivated less by any alteration in Iraqi policy than by a U.S. tilt toward Iraq in its war against Iran.[30] (Iraq was placed back on the list after it invaded Kuwait in 1990.)

This stasis in the list contrasts sharply with remarkable change in the terrorism-related policies of several states on it. Syria has evolved from a direct practitioner of international terrorism as late as the mid-1980s (when, for example, its agents were attempting to bomb flights of El Al) to a major source of restraint on it—keeping its client groups from conducting operations abroad and prohibiting them from attacking civilians even in the Levant. North Korea has gone from killing much of the South Korean cabinet in 1983 and blowing up a civilian airliner with 115 people aboard in 1987, to reluctantly providing a home to a few fugitives and targeting the odd defector or two. Cuba has gone from an ambitious program of subversive violence in much of Africa and Latin America to a posture that is even more quiescent than North Korea's. And Libya has changed from a killer of hundreds of air passengers and backer of groups ranging from the Irish Republican Army to the Japanese Red Army, to a state with nothing more than a couple of residual links to groups it used to back. Even Iran, which is still more involved in international terrorism than most of these other states, has (since the first several years after its revolution) reduced its active subversion of neighboring countries and assassination of exiled dissidents. To point out such changes is not to argue that any particular state should have been delisted. It has probably made sense to keep Syria on the list until terrorism-related issues are resolved in negotiations with Israel, and to keep Libya on it until the Pan Am 103 trial is over and the victims' families have been compensated. But any structure for policy toward state sponsorship of terrorism that is unresponsive to changes this sweeping is insufficiently supple.

The Export Administration Act specifies that a state sponsor can be delisted if the president certifies to Congress that the state has not supported international terrorism for the preceding six months (or alternatively, that there has been a "fundamental shift in the leadership and policies" of the country and that it is not currently supporting terrorism) and that the state has provided assurances that it will not support international terrorism in the future. Any such certification is open to nit-picking as to whether there is *no* support whatsoever coming from the regime in question. The paucity of delistings is not just because of the legislative standard but also the demonization that tends to be associated with branding as a state sponsor in the first place and with the accompanying tendency to treat any regime so branded as an irreparable pariah. This tendency is part of what Robert Litwak has termed the "traditional Manichean streak" in American diplomacy, in which problems of international relations get viewed as moral struggles between good and evil.[31] It is politically hard to make any favorable gesture—and delisting would be a significant one—to any regime that has long been labeled as embracing the evil of terrorism and about which considerable rhetoric and resources have been expended in countering the evil behavior.

The difficulty in undesignating state sponsors is unfortunate, because whatever counterterrorist benefit flows from placing states on an official list and placing sanctions on them depends also on being able, when their behavior warrants, to remove them from the list and to remove the sanctions from them. Positive as well as negative inducements matter. With no possibility of change, there is no incentive to change. If U.S. policy is seen as in effect being "once a terrorist state, always a terrorist state," that is one less reason to become anything but a terrorist state. The logic applies at three levels. One is that of the individual leader of the state, who is looking for reasons to change or not to change his policies—or to sustain rewarded improvements in behavior, or to relapse into old ways if unrewarded. A second level is the internal politics of the targeted state. Factions favoring more moderate external policies are looking for evidence to support their argument that moderation brings benefits; their harder-line opponents are looking for any indication that the United States will always be hostile anyway. The first level is more applicable to a state like Libya, where there is no credible challenge to the supreme leader. The second is more pertinent to Iran, where there is genuine debate and struggle among elements with genuinely different views.

The third level is that of other governments, which observe U.S. policy toward the target state, draw lessons from it, and may adjust their own behavior in response. The other governments include not only ones that are not on the list of state sponsors and may be deterred from actions that would get them on it, but also ones currently on the list that are observing whether even improved behavior is sufficient to get a state off of it. Regarding the former, it is true that U.S. diplomats—in admonishing nonlisted governments with questionable terrorist-related behavior—have gotten rhetorical mileage out of the argument that "it's harder to get off the list than to get on it." But to the extent that designation as a state sponsor is seen as a one-way step, it is the atomic bomb of counterterrorist diplomacy. With the United States reluctant to use it because it is such a major and seemingly irretrievable measure, its deterrent value is minimal.[32]

Over the past couple of years the U.S. government has taken some tentative but welcome steps toward deossifying the list of state sponsors and sanctions against the listed states. A gradually increasing awareness of the limitations and full costs of sanctions—stimulated in part by the tussles with allies over Helms-Burton and the Iran-Libya Sanctions Act—has had a lot to do with this, as have the obvious changes in policies and politics of some of targeted states.[33] In April 1999 President Clinton exempted exports of food and medicine from the embargoes against Iran, Libya, and Sudan. In September 1999, the administration eased certain restrictions on trade with, and travel to, North Korea. In March 2000, in a major speech calling for a new chapter in U.S.-Iranian relations, Secretary of State Madeleine Albright announced that the import of certain luxury goods from Iran would no longer be banned, and that the administration would seek a legal settlement to free Iranian assets that were still frozen. Some momentum developed in Congress in the summer of 2000 to further ease restrictions on sales of food and medicine to several of the listed state sponsors, particularly Cuba.

Meanwhile, State Department Coordinator for Counterterrorism Michael Sheehan has pushed the sound concept that the list of state sponsors of terrorism ought to be neither frozen nor held hostage to other issues. For example, he told people on Capitol Hill that "if you have a problem with Cuba on human rights, get your own sanctions, don't use mine."[34] The annual report on international terrorism that his office released in April 2000 had promising language about the possible removal of states from the list of sponsors, which it described as "a primary focus of U.S. counterterrorist policy." The report declared that "if a state sponsor meets the criteria for being dropped from the terrorism list, it will be removed—notwithstanding other differences we may have with a country's other policies and actions."[35]

Fulfilling that promise will require overcoming the obstacles to change mentioned above, as well as more specific domestic political impediments addressed in the next chapter. The obstacles will be present to some extent with any system of designating supporters of terrorism; there will always be opposition to any positive gesture toward anyone or anything ever labeled as "terrorist." The designation of state sponsors would become a more flexible and useful tool, however, if it were decoupled from the sanctions that currently are automatically attached to it.[36] Such a revised system of designation would maintain the advantages of having an official list of state sponsors of terrorism (parallel to the advantages of designating FTOs): it would sustain attention to the problem of terrorism, help to bring counterterrorist considerations to bear in foreign policy decisions, and serve as a frame of reference in discussing counterterrorism with foreign counterparts. It would also continue to be a mark of opprobrium that, coming from the world's leading power, would be something worth avoiding even without material consequences directly linked to it.

Detaching the designation from the sanctions would lessen the most stultifying aspects of the current system. The list of state sponsors could be a truer picture of actual terrorist-supportive behavior because decisions about listing would not be surrogates for decisions about imposing sanctions. The complications that would arise from sanctions would no longer deter the United States from calling any state, even an otherwise friendly one, to account for such behavior. A reluctance, based on other grounds, not to confer rewards on a listed state would no longer deter the United States from removing the designation of state sponsor if the state's reformed policies warrant it. A more honest and credible list would be a more useful frame of reference in coordinating counterterrorist policies with allies. Most important, decoupling would recognize the need to tailor policies to the individual circumstances of each case. The current arsenal of sanctions could be available for use as a matter of executive discretion, but they would not be applied in blanket fashion and should not be applied without a careful assessment that particular sanctions were well-suited to the individual case.

With or without the reform suggested, U.S. policy toward each state sponsor needs to take account of all U.S. concerns—terrorism and other issues—in a troubled bilateral relationship, as well as the prospects for change (in policies or leadership) in the target state and all of the circumstances that make certain tools and strategies more, or less, promising in the case at hand. The positive incentives associated with strategies of engagement need to be considered as much as the negative incentives of sanctions and isolation. Overall there are almost certainly grounds for more engagement with the states designated as state sponsors of terrorism than has occurred so far.[37] "Overall," however, matters less than individual cases. Sometimes the impetus for engagement will come mainly from changes in the state's terrorist-related behavior; sometimes it will come from other considerations.

Libya exemplifies the former. The reform of its old terrorist ways has been sufficiently great that this improvement—along with ordinary U.S. interests in doing normal business with, and pursuing commercial interests in, most nations of the world—is reason enough to build on what has been accomplished so far on the Pan Am 103 case and to progressively engage Tripoli. Given that no Libyan alternative to Qadhafi is in sight, any refusal to do business with him would mean stagnation in relations with Libya for years to come.[38] Engagement would help as well with some of the remaining issues with Tripoli—particularly Libyan policy toward conflicts in Africa, where what is needed most is diplomatic coordination to ensure that Qadhafi's freelance peacemaking efforts do not complicate other efforts to resolve disputes.

Iran presents reasons for engagement *despite* continuing well-founded concerns about sponsorship of terrorism. There has been simply too much change in Iran—particularly an internal political evolution that has included the election of Mohammad Khatami as president in 1997 and a sweeping victory by reformists in parliamentary elections in early 2000—to let terrorism keep Iranian-U.S. relations in a freezer. The good internal political news from Iran has not yielded comparably good news on the terrorism front because the elements of the government responsible for supporting extremist groups and performing other terrorist-related activity—specifically, the Ministry of Intelligence and Security and the Revolutionary Guard Corps—are among the components that have been dominated by hard-liners and not controlled by the reformists. A real political struggle is going on in Iran, however, that has the potential to affect policy toward terrorism as well. This is that second level—debate among factions within the targeted regime—at which U.S. responsiveness or nonresponsiveness makes a difference. In Iran, a perception of nonresponsiveness and continual hostility from Washington has probably, at least until recently, strengthened the position of hard-liners in that debate by enabling them to argue that trying to please the Great Satan is fruitless.[39] Besides the internal political evolution, there are other considerations—including the sheer weight that Iran carries in its region, in energy matters, and in the Muslim world—to explore more positive and effective ways to deal with the continued terrorism problem than merely trying to isolate Tehran.[40] And as for internal politics, Iran is (despite the levers of power that its convoluted constitution lets the hard-liners hold) one of the more democratic states in its region and by far the most democratic country on the list of state sponsors of terrorism. It would be ironic and unfortunate if the question of internal democracy, which is the main issue underlying Cuba's continued place on the terrorist list, were to be nullified by true concerns about terrorism regarding another country on the list. The recent movement toward a more constructive relationship with Iran, represented by Secretary Albright's speech and the measures announced in it, is a necessary and appropriate response to the opportunities and the continued problems, including terrorist problems, that Iran presents.[41]

Each state sponsor presents a different mix of such opportunities and problems. Sudan, for example, may carry a risk—not present in either Libya or Iran—of fractionation and poverty someday leading it to become a "failed state" in which the government is incapable of meeting even minimum needs for public order. If this is a risk, international isolation of Sudan is more likely to exacerbate it than to alleviate it. And becoming a failed state might make Sudan even more of a haven for international terrorists than it is now. There has been little in Sudanese policy and politics to date, however, to provide a basis for improved relations with Washington.

Regardless of the blend of punishment and accommodation that characterizes overall relations with a state sponsor of terrorism, there are several principles that should govern the relationship as it pertains to terrorism itself. The theme of these principles is that the United States needs to *help* the other state to reduce its support of terrorism. The United States should try to make it easier, not harder, to shake the terrorist habit, especially inasmuch as there are apt to be other considerations and pressures that will make it hard enough as it is.

First, the unwavering U.S. objective should be to reduce the other state's practice of, and support for, international terrorism. The objective is not to pin a label of "terrorist" or "sponsor" on the other government; that is only a means, not an end. The objective is not to paint the regime as evil; that has the potential only for angering it, not for improving its behavior. The objective is not to get the other side to admit all of its past wrongdoing; that is likely to be unattainable, and does not change future policies. None of those things saves lives. Reducing support for terrorists and terrorist operations does.

Second, this objective and the specific changes expected from the other government should be communicated as clearly as possible to the other government.[42] One of the shortcomings of the European Union's "critical dialogue" with Iran, for example, has been the Europeans' vagueness in laying out goals and standards for improved Iranian behavior.[43] This principle is, in a sense, an argument in favor of engagement and direct dialogue, since nuances are often better communicated through give and take over a conference table than through public statements. Even public statements, however, can be clear and specific about the changes the United States seeks. When there is no direct private dialogue, the United States should consider initiating one. When it is the other side that refuses direct talks (for example, Iran), the United States should carefully examine what might lead the other side to change its mind.[44]

Third, the United States should expect only incremental improvement in the state sponsor's behavior and should be willing to reward such improvements incrementally. In any effort to improve someone else's objectionable behavior—whether a child's or a government's—there is always the question of whether to focus more on progress made or on problems that remain. With state sponsors of terrorism, to resist improving a relationship after a sponsor's performance improves, only because it retains some links to terrorism, would be shortsighted and inconsistent with the political realities that face almost any state sponsor. There are numerous reasons, ranging from bureaucratic inertia to practical problems in severing long-standing patron-client relationships, that a cold turkey approach to kicking the terrorism habit is unrealistic. While the United States should reiterate that no terrorism is acceptable, it should remember that the objective with a state sponsor is to *reduce* its support for terrorism. Reduction warrants a response. There are numerous incremental responses (for example, easing travel restrictions) appropriate for incremental improvements on the other side, while leaving room for further development of the relationship following further improvement in the behavior.

Fourth, in articulating which changes in terrorist-related behavior it wants to see, the United States should stress measures that would be most feasible for the state sponsor to take. Some steps are politically or practically more difficult than others. The easier steps—which can still demonstrate the regime's seriousness in improving its policies—should be insisted on first. Harder steps can wait until later. Some conceivable measures that would demonstrate seriousness may never be feasible. For example, to expect the dismantling of agencies or offices that conduct terrorism is apt to be unrealistic if they also serve other purposes, as most of them do. (Libya announced in 1992 that it was disbanding its Islamic Call Society, which has been a vehicle for exporting revolutionary violence. But the society, which is also an outlet for state-approved religious activity, continued.)[45] Client terrorist groups may be more expendable, but some aspects of cutting ties with them are more difficult than others. A relatively easy step (and a worthwhile one in terms of the immediate impact on terrorism) is to put the group on a short leash and try to prevent it from conducting terrorist attacks (as Syria already does with its clients). More difficult are expulsions of members and severing of all financial links to groups that have long depended on the sponsor for homes and livelihoods. Besides whatever sympathy a regime may have for the welfare of the group's members, it may face the risk of an angry terrorist group turning on its former patron (as the Abu Nidal organization has threatened to do against Libya). In some cases the United States may be able to facilitate patron-client divorces by working with the sponsor regime and perhaps third parties to resettle former members of the group who would otherwise be homeless and unemployed.

And fifth, natural linkages between reducing terrorism and getting what the target state wants from the United States should be exploited when possible. A safe, terrorism-free environment is a reasonable demand to make of a state that wants cooperation that would require Americans to work or travel on its territory. Such an environment can be made a condition for such measures as the lifting of restrictions on the use of U.S. passports to travel to the country.

Any rapprochement with a reforming state sponsor of terrorism will be a gradual, sometimes fitful process in which each bit of cooperation helps to build trust for the next step. One potential area of mutually beneficial cooperation is counterterrorism itself. State sponsors have terrorist enemies too. The Mujahedin-e Khalq, for example, has continued to conduct bombings and assassinations in Iran. The Qadhafi regime in Libya faces threats not only from its former client Abu Nidal but also from several small but violent Islamic extremist groups such as the Movement of the Islamic Martyrs and the Fighting Islamic Group, which has staged terrorist attacks against Libyan officials. Cuba suffered a string of small bombings against its tourist industry in 1997, with one of these attacks killing an Italian tourist.

There are several reasons for making at least limited counterterrorist cooperation (even just a modest exchange of information, within limits set by the sensitivity of the intelligence and the state of the overall relationship) one of the areas of incremental engagement with state sponsors. It demonstrates the U.S. commitment to oppose terrorism wherever it arises, no matter who the target is. It gives the other government a chance to demonstrate its counterterrorist bona fides even when this means doing so in concert with the United States. And some of the same terrorist groups that oppose these governments are anti-United States, or linked to ones that are (true, for example, of the radical Islamist groups that oppose the Qadhafi regime), so there may be some additional direct counterterrorist benefit. Even without a bilateral relationship that has developed to the point that a direct dialogue on counterterrorism is feasible, some tacit cooperation may be possible multilaterally. This has in effect occurred with the United States and Iran regarding the Taliban and its terrorist allies, which threaten the interests of both countries. UN Security Council Resolution 1267, which placed sanctions on the Taliban, cited the kidnapping and murder of Iranian diplomats in Afghanistan as among the terrorist offenses that led to the council's action.

For some of the same reasons, it would be a mistake for the United States to appear to condone or support terrorist groups opposed to a state sponsor, no matter how poor the U.S. relationship with that sponsor is. The one group that has presented such a problem in recent years is the Mujahedin-e Khalq, because of extensive lobbying, and financial contributions, by its members that have won the group support in the U.S. Congress. Several letters that have circulated on Capitol Hill—one in 1998 garnered the signatures of 220 members of Congress—have opposed the designation of the MEK as a Foreign Terrorist Organization and appealed to the administration to work with the group. Given the nature of the MEK, this support is surprising and—even bearing in mind that many of the congressional representatives were signing on the basis of incomplete information—indefensible. The MEK is a Marxist/Islamist group that was formed to oppose Western influence in the shah's regime. It conducted terrorist attacks against that regime and killed several U.S. military and civilian personnel working on defense projects in Iran. It supported the seizure of the U.S. embassy in 1979 and did not have a falling out with the clerical regime until the 1980s. Its consorting with the Iraqi regime in recent years has reduced what credibility it had inside Iran. It is properly designated as an FTO, and neither its past history nor its current methods give reason for the United States to use it as a foundation, or even a tool, in its policies on Iran. The congressional expressions of support for the group have been unfortunate detriments to counterterrorism and to the furthering of U.S. interests in Iran.

Enablers

The possibility of counterterrorist cooperation even with states currently listed as state sponsors underscores the point that the role of states in international terrorism is not a matter of clear distinctions between the good and the bad, between those that sponsor terrorism and those that oppose it. That any one state can be part of the problem and a potential part of managing the problem is true not only of those states currently on the list of state sponsors but also of some that are not. For a few of the latter, being part of the problem means not just failing to cooperate fully in countering terrorism but also doing some things that help enable it to occur. For various reasons these states have stayed out of the gallery of "rogue states" and off the terrorism list (although some might have had more trouble staying off a list that did not have sanctions automatically attached), and for most part they are rightly regarded as friends or allies of the United States. Listed or not, however, their enabling of terrorism needs to be addressed.

Two countries in particular are of concern. One is Greece, the only member of NATO to present difficulties of this nature (as distinct from disagreements with many of the other allies over counterterrorist strategy). There are two specific, and mostly unrelated, Greek terrorist problems. The one that has been around longer and has posed the more direct threat to U.S. interests (and has caused U.S. casualties) has been terrorism within Greece by leftists, embodied mostly in the groups November 17 and Revolutionary People's Struggle (ELA). The two groups—which Greek police believe have links to each other—are part of a still largely unfathomed Greek leftist underground that has also conducted attacks under other names, such as May 1 and Revolutionary Solidarity.[46] During the last twenty-five years, there have been more than 140 terrorist attacks in Greece against U.S. interests, including government officials and private businesses. European interests and prominent Greeks have also been frequently attacked. November 17, which has carried out most of the attacks, has killed twenty-two people, including four U.S. officials. In 1999 alone, there were twenty terrorist attacks against U.S. interests, part of an overall upsurge in Greek terrorism (partly stimulated by NATO's military action against Serbia) that made Greece second only to Colombia in the number of terrorist incidents in that year. It is not surprising that the State Department spends more for diplomatic security in Greece than in any other country.

Almost none of these terrorist incidents has been solved; almost none of those responsible has been caught or punished. That fact, along with the frequency and persistence of the violence, points to a problem that goes beyond questions of competence and commitment in combating terrorists to ones of sympathy and support for them. There are many specific reasons for Greece's dismal counterterrorist performance, including successful intimidation by the terrorists of would-be witnesses and the Greek media's emphasizing of civil liberties in a way that deters anything that could be called a crackdown. Underlying all of this, however, is a broad tolerance for what the terrorists do because of an admiration for much of what they stand for. They have acquired something of a Robin Hood aura and are thought of less in terms of their Marxism than as champions of the nationalist, anti-Turkish, anti-NATO, anti-U.S. themes that have a broader resonance in the Greek population. They also have shared experiences with the left side of the legitimate Greek political spectrum. The terrorist groups and the Panhellenic Socialist Movement (PASOK), which has been the governing party in Greece for most of the past two decades, can both trace their origins to the student opposition against the military junta that ruled the country from 1967 to 1974. The sympathy for the extremists extends well into Greek officialdom, and even when senior leaders genuinely want to make progress against terrorism, the response at lower levels is problematic.

The other, lesser, terrorist problem with Greece has been support for the Kurdistan Workers' Party (PKK). The involvement of Greek officials was highlighted by the fact that Ocalan, when he was captured in Kenya in 1999, had been enjoying the hospitality of the Greek ambassador in Nairobi. Help to the PKK has not entailed the same direct threat to Americans as the coddling of Greek leftists, but any support by one member of NATO for terrorism against another member is necessarily a matter of concern. For the Greeks, aiding the PKK has not had the same historical and emotional basis as sympathy for their own extreme left; instead, it is a matter of befriending the enemy of one's enemy. In that respect—and given the PKK's overall decline, and some warming of Greek-Turkish relations—it is a problem more likely to be ameliorated than the persistence of November 17 and the other Greek groups.[47]

Formal economic sanctions have not been used against Greece for its enabling of terrorism, nor should they have been. But many of the same points discussed earlier, about how the issue of terrorism should be handled with a listed state sponsor, apply as well to a case such as Greece. There is the same need to articulate clearly the changes that need to be made and to explain how persistence of terrorism will get in the way of other things that the offending government wants. One of those things is the spending of money by American businesses and, in particular, American tourists.

Some needed behavioral improvements, such as ending any further clandestine help to the PKK, would be difficult to measure and monitor, but the most needed improvement offers a clear and public set of benchmarks: namely, to solve the many unsolved cases of terrorist attacks in Greece, and to prosecute, convict, and punish the perpetrators.

The United States needs to continue shining a spotlight on the terrorist problem in Greece, although—as anywhere else—with enough attention to local sensitivities to avoid doing something counterproductive. In Greece, this means not saying anything about the extreme left that might make the United States appear to be on the wrong side of the old struggle against the colonels' junta. Discussions with the Greeks on counterterrorism need to steer clear of ideology and to stay focused on specific law enforcement measures that will improve the chances of cracking terrorist cases. The chances will improve partly by ensuring a role for U.S. experts and partly by establishing enough compartmentation on the Greek side to avoid—as has happened too often in the past—the blowing of counterterrorist operations through leaks by officials sympathetic to the terrorists.[48]

The other principal state that has been enabling terrorism while staying off the list of state sponsors—and that in several respects presents more difficult problems than Greece—is Pakistan. As with Greece, one of those problems involves support for terrorism against a regional rival: namely, Pakistan's backing of Muslim militants who conduct attacks in the Indian-controlled portion of Kashmir. Unlike Greek help to the PKK, however, what Pakistan is doing in Kashmir is not just a convenient way of making trouble for a neighboring foe. Rather, the fight for Muslim control of Kashmir is central to Pakistan's self-identity and its view of religion and politics on the South Asian subcontinent. Islamabad admits to giving only moral, political, and diplomatic support to fighters for what it considers the "liberation" of Kashmir, but the assistance is material as well.[49] Although both the claimed and actual emphasis of the militants' operations has been to attack Indian military targets, true terrorism—attacks on civilians—has been extensive. From 1995 to 1999 terrorist incidents each year in Indian Kashmir have numbered in the dozens, and casualties from them in the hundreds. The terrorism has touched American lives, such as with the kidnapping in 1995 of a group of hikers that included two Americans, one of whom escaped but the other of whom is still missing and probably dead.

The second terrorist problem with Pakistan, which is related to the first, is more obscure regarding exactly what the Pakistani government is doing but of even higher counterterrorist concern to the United States. That problem is the sympathy and support given to a variety of violent Islamic extremists in Pakistan itself and in neighboring Taliban-controlled Afghanistan. Within Pakistan, organizations with direct links to terrorism, like Maktab al-Khidamat, operate freely. They are most prevalent in the northwestern areas near Afghanistan, but the extremist violence can hit anywhere—as it did twice to Americans in Karachi, with the killing of two consulate employees in 1995 and the murder of four U.S. businessmen and their driver in 1997. What is occurring next door with the Taliban is of even greater concern, given Afghanistan's role as a home base for the export of terrorism. Pakistan spawned the Taliban, nurtured it, is one of only three countries that recognize it, and continues to support it in other ways.[50] The Taliban is a vehicle for Pakistan to realize its long-standing interest in having a friendly, or at least nonhostile, regime in Kabul, to minimize problems for itself that may come from that direction (such as any agitation for a greater Pushtunistan) and as strategic depth in its confrontation with India. More specifically—and this is how the problem in Afghanistan relates to the one in Kashmir—the Taliban and groups based in the territory it controls (including ones associated with bin Ladin) provide major support to the Kashmiri insurgency, in the form of both training facilities and manpower.[51]

The large stake and strong sentiments that the Pakistanis have in Kashmir and Afghanistan severely limit what the United States can accomplish regarding the problems of terrorism in those places, even with vigorous and imaginative diplomacy. Regarding Kashmir, keeping the terrorist issue in the forefront may help to keep the tactics of Pakistan's militant clients at least marginally less objectionable than they otherwise would be. But as with some other regional conflicts, terrorism is likely to continue as long as the broader dispute does. And even without terrorism, the Kashmiri pot would be kept boiling by continued guerrilla warfare against military targets and a military confrontation along the Line of Control, with periodic flare-ups such as occurred at Kargil in 1999. As for Afghanistan, the political and military environment has made it unrealistic to expect Islamabad to make bold counterterrorist initiatives, such as squeezing the Taliban sufficiently that it coughs up bin Ladin. Even if senior leaders could be persuaded to make the right promises, fulfillment of those promises would likely get snagged on pro-Islamist sentiments that exist at other levels of the Pakistani government and security services (somewhat akin to the problem of leftist sympathies in Greece). One basis for hope (other than the unlikely possibility of the Kashmir dispute somehow being resolved) is that Pakistani leaders may perceive that the radical monster they helped to create on the other side of the Khyber Pass is coming back to bite them, in the form of fundamentalist Deobandi groups and other extreme pro-Taliban elements expanding their influence throughout Pakistan, and not just in the Pushtun areas along the border. The increased Islamization of the Kashmiri insurgency—which may enjoy less international support the more it appears to be a jihad rather than a fight for self-determination—should also give Pakistani leaders pause.[52] U.S. diplomats can gently point out these realities while continuing to press for such actions as interdicting the flow of men and matériel across the Pakistani-Afghan border and closing the worst of the *madrassas*, the religious schools that are also often vehicles for organizing terrorism.

Major counterterrorist cooperation from Pakistan appears out of reach without such real or perceived changes in the environment. More modest measures, however, are not. This includes not only reining in client groups to reduce their most egregious operations (that is, to act somewhat more like Syria now does with its clients), but also other steps such as assistance in catching fugitive terrorists. Pakistan has provided the latter type of help in several important cases. One was the arrest of Ramzi Yousef in 1995 while he was staying at a guest house in Islamabad. Another was the capture of Mir Aimal Kansi in 1997. Pakistani cooperation in the latter case was more grudging than with Yousef, probably because of Kansi's Pakistani citizenship, his influential family ties, and some genuine support for what he had done. But after hesitating, the Pakistanis finally surrendered him to U.S. justice. Following the bombings of the embassies in Africa, Pakistan's arrest and prompt turnover of one of the suspects, Mohammed Sadeek Odeh (who had fled to Karachi on the day of the bombing) contributed significantly to the rapid solution of the case.

The ability of the United States to elicit more counterterrorist help than this out of Islamabad is further constrained by the fact that terrorism is not the only important U.S. concern about Pakistan, or even the chief one. More important is Pakistan's broader confrontation with India and, given the nuclear arsenals of both countries, a greater danger in South Asia than anywhere else of the first nuclear detonation in anger since Nagasaki. To press Pakistan harder on the terrorist issue (such as through formal designation as a state sponsor with accompanying sanctions) would complicate efforts to keep a lid on the South Asian conflict and, by reducing perceived U.S. evenhandedness toward that conflict, would have other costs in the

Muslim street and in Pakistan's thinking about what it needs to do to ensure its security. (An evenhanded approach that also designated India as a state sponsor for instigation of terrorist acts in Pakistan would cause even more complications for U.S. policy toward South Asia.) Pakistan exemplifies how strong concerns in the enabling state about the issues that underlie the terrorism, and strong concerns on the U.S. side about other issues, limit what can be achieved in counterterrorism.

There is no other case quite like Pakistan (or like Greece), but several other states exhibit a milder form of enabling behavior: namely, permitting terrorist groups to operate on their territories not because the government sees the terrorism as advancing its own interests (although a group may enjoy some sympathy in the country) but to avoid confrontations with the groups and to reduce the risk of terrorist attacks against its interests or on its territory. Some countries in the Persian Gulf region, as well as some other Arab states, exhibit this behavior. It ought to be easier to change enabling behavior when it is motivated by this kind of fear rather than by a Pakistani-style commitment to underlying causes, and in general it is. Besides using other carrots and sticks to induce the government to cooperate more with the United States than with a terrorist group, the United States can offer counterterrorist assistance to try to reduce the fears that led the government to accommodate a terrorist group in the first place. This means, however, surmounting an initial hurdle of concern about whether the costs of trying to contain a terrorist group (that is, suffering terrorist reprisals) will be felt before the benefits (eliminating the group's ability to strike back) are fully realized.

With each enabler, the United States should (as with sponsors) carefully assess the limits of what can realistically be accomplished in reducing the regime's tolerance for terrorist groups. Pressing beyond those limits may generate more friction than results. The primary U.S. goal should be to avoid terrorist attacks on U.S. interests in the state. Avoiding *any* terrorist attacks on its soil, including ones against U.S. targets, may be part of the tacit understanding that a regime has reached with a terrorist group. Such an understanding thus serves the primary U.S. goal, even though it may also mean tolerating commercial and other nonviolent activity by the group. Ideally, these other activities should also be quashed, because they can support the group's terrorist operations elsewhere. Politically and practically, it may not be feasible to do so. If it is not, then the nonviolent activities can at least be monitored.

Enablers include some of the grayest of the many gray areas of states both helping and hindering counterterrorism. That they have not been formally designated as state sponsors of terrorism should not dissuade the United States from calling them to account for policies and practices that facilitate terrorism. The State Department has increasingly been doing just that. The commentaries on Greece and Pakistan in the edition of *Patterns of Global Terrorism* released in April 2000 were pointedly critical. Those comments, together with the equally critical points that the National Commission on Terrorism made about Greece and Pakistan in its report released just a few weeks later, seemed to have gotten the attention of the Greek and Pakistani governments.

A reform of the designation system, along the lines suggested earlier, that would permit a more honest depiction of state behavior toward terrorism would help even more. A possible variation on that reform that might be especially applicable to enablers is to use something like section 330 of the Antiterrorism and Death Penalty Act, which provides for designating countries that are "not cooperating fully" with U.S. antiterrorist efforts.[53] The only countries that have yet been so designated are the seven on the list of state sponsors plus Afghanistan.[54] (Putting Afghanistan on one list but not the other involved legal hair-splitting. The AEDPA refers only to "countries" that are not cooperating fully, which technically does not raise the same problem of recognition of the Taliban as the statute for the state sponsors' list, which speaks of "governments.") The National Commission on Terrorism drew attention to this provision in the AEDPA and argued for its greater use. It urged that Greece and Pakistan be considered for the "not cooperating fully" designation and also that this category be used as a kind of halfway house for reforming state sponsors.[55] The latter suggestion has considerable merit in that it would move away from the all-or-nothing quality of the state sponsors' list and provide a way of reflecting and rewarding improved behavior without appearing to pardon remaining problems. The "not cooperating fully" list, however, shares with the state sponsors' list the disadvantage of having automatic sanctions—in this case, a prohibition on sales of arms or defense-related services. That is a significant impediment to designating a state like Greece, a NATO ally. It may also inhibit the designation of other states where nonlethal defense services such as an International Military Education and Training program could be useful in increasing U.S. influence and shaping the recipient state's behavior in desired directions. In response to the commission's report, Secretary of State Albright said that the administration would continue to press Greece and Pakistan on terrorism but was not considering sanctions against them.[56] As with the list of state sponsors, making any sanctions a matter of executive discretion would render this list a more useful tool and a more honest portrayer of places where there are terrorist-related problems.[57]

Cooperators

Chapter 3 mentioned the reasons the United States must rely heavily on foreign partners in counterterrorism. The discussion of intelligence in chapter 4 described some of the counterterrorist activity that is accomplished in liaison with foreign counterparts. The many liaison relationships that address counterterrorism (most of which are managed by the CIA, but with the FBI, State Department, and other agencies having pertinent ones as well) vary widely in effectiveness, for reasons of willingness and capability. The most effective partners are not necessarily developed countries or the biggest and most important U.S. allies. Developed countries such as the members of NATO do tend to have more highly skilled and professional security services than many other states. But the skills and knowledge required to contribute effectively to counterterrorism, especially with regard to specific terrorist groups, are often found just as readily in the services of less developed countries. Some of these countries have developed their knowledge the hard way, by being on the front line of conflict with the groups in question.

The same point applies even more acutely to the *willingness* of services to help. Some of the most unquestioning cooperators with the United States on counterterrorism are less developed countries. They often worry less about procedural niceties than their counterparts in more developed states and are more inclined to act quickly with less red tape. They are also likely to have acquired less of the institutional baggage that often accumulates in larger and older liaison relationships and that sometimes impedes cooperation between even close allies.

Fruitful cooperation on counterterrorism is often feasible despite significant disagreements on other subjects. As international terrorism, especially the radical Islamist variety, has affected an increasing number of states, there have been increasing opportunities for counterterrorist cooperation. These opportunities extend even to major U.S. rivals such as Russia and China. In Russia, the KGB foresaw as early as the 1980s the possibility of terrorism hitting the Soviet Union.[58] The possibility became reality in the 1990s, first with Russian citizens being killed by terrorists in Algeria and then with Chechen terrorism in Russia itself. The series of bombings of apartment houses in Russia in 1999 was a galvanizing event (and a rationale for a new Russian military offensive in Chechnya). After the second of the bombings, President Boris Yeltsin stated that "terrorism has declared war on Russia." Yeltsin's successor, Vladimir Putin, approved a new national security strategy in January 2000 that emphasized the fight against terrorism.[59] Russia has grown more concerned about links between the Chechen rebels and Afghanistan, where the Taliban has permitted the Chechens to open an embassy in Kabul. In May 2000, a Kremlin spokesman—citing intelligence that Taliban officials and bin Ladin had met with Chechen representatives and promised to send fighters and weapons to Chechnya—said that a Russian military strike against Afghanistan was a "real possibility."[60] Prior to a summit meeting between presidents Clinton and Putin in June 2000, U.S. and Russian officials issued a joint statement urging the Taliban to hand over bin Ladin and to dismantle the terrorist infrastructure on the territory it controls.[61]

Chinese concerns center around increased violence among the Uighurs of Xinjiang province and, to a lesser extent, other Muslim ethnic groups in China. Uighur militants have trained and fought in Afghanistan, and they maintain ties with groups in Taliban-controlled territory and perhaps with the Taliban itself.[62] A bomb that exploded on a bus in Beijing in March 1997—the first terrorist incident in the Chinese capital since the communists came to power in 1949—was, Chinese official believe, the work of Uighurs who used explosives from Afghanistan. A classified circular issued by the Ministry of State Security in December 1999 stated that the problem of Uighur and other Muslim violence would not go away and called for increased reporting on efforts by Islamic militants to infiltrate Chinese territory and to smuggle arms.[63]

The United States needs several forms of counterterrorist cooperation from foreign partners. Most important is a concerted effort to attack the capabilities of terrorist groups by dismantling their infrastructures. A related and equally important need is for intelligence, not only on the capabilities of terrorist groups but also anything that can be collected on their intentions. Other requirements are help in tracking down and capturing fugitive terrorists and the maintenance of adequate security for the embassy and other U.S. interests in the country. Cooperation is also needed on counterterrorist issues that go beyond the territory of the country in question; this mainly means supportive diplomatic postures on terrorist groups as well as state sponsors.

Inducing another state to help on these matters requires an understanding of how that country's leaders see the advantages and disadvantages of cooperating. What, in short, is in it for them? Most often the principal advantage is to reduce the chance of a terrorist incident on the country's own soil, with the danger of its citizens falling victim even if the United States were the principal target. A further incentive for helping to curb the activities of transnational terrorist groups—even if an attack in country seems unlikely—is for the government to better control its own territory. This is sometimes a factor when evidence surfaces of a group being engaged in smuggling, use of false documents, or other illegal activity. The opportunity to earn goodwill with the United States, and perhaps reciprocal favors on nonterrorist matters, is often a consideration. Finally—and foreign leaders and officials sometimes do seem to think this way—helping to fight terrorism and thereby to save lives is simply the right thing to do.

The potential disadvantages of cooperating are at least as numerous. Some of the same considerations mentioned in connection with enablers—fear of reprisals, and sometimes sympathy for causes a terrorist group espouses—may be causes of hesitation in moving against a group, even if there is no modus vivendi whereby the government deliberately allows the group to operate. Often the government does not want to do, or be seen to do, the United States' bidding because of the domestic political costs. A related reluctance is not wanting to cede any control to the United States over what many would deem to be an internal security or police matter. The concern may be that this constitutes an infringement of sovereignty or a tacit admission that one's own security services cannot handle the job. This kind of hesitation was seen in the Japanese reticence during the early days of investigating Aum Shinrikyo and has probably been a factor in the Saudis' refusal to completely share with the United States the results of their investigation into Khubar Towers. The cooperation requested by the United States may entail a drain on resources (such as in round-the-clock surveillance of suspect terrorists). Sometimes the government simply disagrees with the United States in its perception of the threat. And sometimes it agrees about the threat but disagrees about the U.S. way of handling it.

Besides the reasons that a government as a whole may hesitate to help, divisions within the government may slow or complicate cooperation. There are often battles over turf between intelligence and security services, or between an intelligence service and the police.[64] Sometimes different services in the same country do not communicate with one another effectively on terrorist matters. U.S. officials in multiagency bilateral consultations on counterterrorism have observed police and security officials on the other side of the table—who were not new to their jobs and, one would expect, had been working together for some time—exchanging business cards and evidently meeting for the first time. When the United States can get different parts of a foreign government to talk to one another on counterterrorism, so much the better. But trouble arises when rivalries are already sufficiently intense that cooperation with one service may mean resentment and closed doors in another one.

All of these considerations and complications need to be recognized in determining what approach would be most likely to elicit the desired cooperation from the other side. Just as in discussing terrorism with a state sponsor, the United States should assess everything that makes the other government tick when it comes to counterterrorism—and what other incentives can be brought to bear—in deciding what to demand, request, or offer, and how to couch its arguments. That means individually tailoring each cooperative relationship. The following three principles should be generally applicable, however, especially to partners in the less developed world.

First, emphasize the *shared interest* in combating terrorism. Governments should be persuaded to participate in this fight not primarily because the United States asks them to but because it is in their direct interest to do so to safeguard their own citizens. The bombing in Nairobi and the heavy Kenyan casualties it caused demonstrate how much third parties can share the suffering that terrorists try to inflict on the United States.

Second, emphasize *secrecy*. Most effective counterterrorist cooperation has a very low profile. That greatly lessens some of the principal concerns that may cause a state to withhold cooperation, such as the political cost of being perceived as following U.S. instructions. (It also serves the U.S. interests in concealing methods from the terrorists and not giving them further reason to retaliate against the United States.) Emphasizing secrecy means delivering it and not just promising it. Some of the sharpest setbacks in counterterrorist cooperation have resulted from leaks in Washington. The foreign partner's understandable reaction to some leaks has been to suspend operations against a terrorist infrastructure or to cut off intelligence from a source whom the leak jeopardized.

Third, offer *assistance* to the other government in developing its counterterrorist capabilities. In asking smaller and less developed partners to take steps that may mean taxing their skills and resources, not to mention accepting other risks, the least that the United States can do is to provide help that will make those steps more feasible and less taxing. The principal U.S. tool to do so is the Antiterrorism Training Assistance (ATA) program, which the State Department's Bureau of Diplomatic Security manages under policy guidance from the department's coordinator for counterterrorism. This program has trained more than 20,000 law enforcement officers, from more than ninety countries, in such subjects as rescue of hostages, protection for VIPs, detection of bombs, and airport and maritime security.[65] Other agencies also provide training relevant to combating terrorism, including the departments of Defense, Justice, Transportation, and Treasury, and the CIA. Pertinent training embraces not only such obviously terrorist-related subjects as detection of explosives but also other skills (such as those related to investigation and analysis) that are useful to a police or internal security service in attacking a terrorist infrastructure along the lines discussed in chapter 4. And assistance may include not just training but also equipment, organizational help, and intelligence. To ensure that such aid does not get siphoned off into other activities, it is sometimes appropriate to assist the foreign government in creating a dedicated counterterrorist unit to work closely with U.S. counterparts. The investment in resources can be significant, but so is the potential benefit for both parties. The foreign government gets greater ability to counteract not only terrorism but also other illegal activity within its borders. The United States gets a grateful and more able partner in attacking the capabilities of terrorist groups and an increasing stream of intelligence about the groups' activities. Both sides get a closer working relationship and habits of cooperation that pay dividends when a terrorist incident occurs.

This sort of assistance in building up capabilities is clearly less relevant to the Western allies, with whom the main problems in counterterrorist cooperation have involved not insufficient capability to police terrorist groups but rather differences over policy toward state sponsors, especially Iran. It is important to realize what does *not* underlie the allies' opposition (noted in the first section of this chapter) to U.S. attempts to isolate state sponsors. It is not a matter of being weak-kneed about terrorism in general. The Europeans (with the conspicuous exception of Greece) have actually been rather tough toward terrorist threats in their own countries and region, including the initiatives they took against the leftists in the 1980s and their posture toward groups like the ETA today.[66] It is also not a matter of being misinformed about what the state sponsors are doing. Even when the United States has used the most sensitive intelligence in briefing foreign ministers and heads of government, it has not swayed policies. In service-to-service discussions, U.S. intelligence officers have commonly found themselves in near-total agreement with allied counterparts on such subjects as Iranian support for terrorism, despite significant policy differences between their governments.[67]

The policies of the Europeans (and certain other allies, including Australia and Japan) toward state sponsors in general and Iran in particular instead reflects a combination of economic interests and tactical judgments about what is most likely to induce a state sponsor to improve. There is no question that trade, particularly in oil, weighs heavily on European policies toward Iran. Iran supplies about 15 percent of Europe's imported oil. Germany has the largest economic stake of any of the European countries in Iran: German exports to Iran in 1996 totaled about $1.3 billion, and nearly 170 German companies have local operations in Iran. Oil is also a significant factor in postures toward Libya, which supplies 51 percent of Italy's energy needs, 13 percent of Germany's, and 5 percent of France's.[68]

Important as parochial economic interests are, it would be a mistake to dismiss the European approach of "constructively engaging," rather than isolating or sanctioning, a state like Iran as mistaken and selfish because it is economically driven. At least incremental engagement makes sense, for the reasons adduced earlier in this chapter. Besides, any dwelling on economic motives may lead the Europeans to point out that the United States was willing to deal in Iranian oil and gas even after it had declared a policy of containing Iran, and that it changed course in 1995 (and canceled a deal that the U.S. firm Conoco had reached with the National Iranian Oil Company to develop gas fields in the Persian Gulf) only after being roundly criticized by Europe for hypocrisy.[69]

Whatever the merits of each side's brief in the European-American debate on this subject, neither side can "win" the debate. Whatever improvements occur in the behavior of state sponsors, the United States can attribute it to its sanctions, and the Europeans can attribute it to their engagement. The Europeans will not fundamentally change their policies toward state sponsors as a result of U.S. persuasion. Neither will they do so as a result of attempts to strong arm them through secondary sanctions like those in the Iran-Libya Sanctions Act and Helms-Burton. Such measures can be expected to elicit defensive responses, as they did with those two laws, not to mention causing other damage on trade issues.

The most significant disturbance—albeit a temporary one—to European policies toward Iran resulted not from U.S. pressure but from a judicial event involving terrorism within Europe: the prosecution (and conviction in April 1997) of an Iranian and four Lebanese for murdering three Iranian Kurdish dissidents at the Mykonos Restaurant in Berlin in 1992. Evidence presented during the trial traced responsibility for the killings to the highest levels in Tehran—the first time a Western court had documented the chain of command for an extraterritorial Iranian assassination. In connection with the case, the court issued a warrant for the arrest of Ali Fallahian, the Iranian intelligence minister and a former guest of the German government. In response to the Mykonos revelations, all of the members of the European Union except Greece recalled their ambassadors from Tehran, and the EU suspended ministerial visits to Iran. Khatami's election as president of Iran in mid-1997, however, caused relations to unfreeze fairly quickly. Ministerial visits resumed late in the year, and a head of government (the Italian prime minister) traveled to Tehran in July 1998.[70]

The improbability of major change in allied policies toward state sponsors—as indicated by the rapid repair of damage to European-Iranian relations from the Mykonos case—makes it advisable to look for ways to work with, not against, the Europeans on this subject. Uniformity of policies may be best, but if that is infeasible, harmonization of different policies is better than conflict over them. A lot can still be gained from dialogue with the allies on state sponsorship of terrorism. Neither side has a monopoly of wisdom or correct answers on the topic. A demonstrated willingness by the United States to consider strategies of engagement is also apt to give it more credibility, and more international support, when it calls for tougher measures against a state sponsor.[71] And if effective policies toward state sponsors require mixtures of engagement and containment, then a mixture of approaches practiced by the United States and Europe may not be all bad. If the mixture were a well-coordinated and consciously applied strategy—rather than, as it has tended to be, a symptom of divisions that the state sponsors can exploit—then both the carrots and the sticks might be more effective.[72] European initiatives toward state sponsors can have value for the United States in probing the sincerity and limits to change of the target state, while the possibility of future improved relations with the United States will continue to be a significant carrot in itself. Meanwhile, divergent diplomatic and trade policies toward a state sponsor need not impede practical cooperation, between U.S. and allied security services, to counter the terrorism that the state sponsor may practice or support. For the most part it has not impeded it, except for occasional constraints in sharing sensitive intelligence.

A final issue about cooperators arises not when a foreign government is less willing to go as far as the United States would in confronting a terrorist threat—as with European policies toward state sponsors—but when it goes *too* far, in the sense of using harsh measures that the United States would not. This problem occurs in the handling of individual terrorists, or suspected terrorists, and in certain policies toward domestic communities that have given birth to terrorist groups. The states involved include not only less developed countries where arbitrary extrajudicial measures taken in the name of security are common but also more advanced allies (notably Israel and Turkey) with well-developed legal systems.

The objectionable measures may include, in their mildest form, arrests or detentions of individual citizens and seizures of property, without such legal safeguards as demonstrations of probable cause or habeas corpus proceedings. More serious are indiscriminate actions that may hinder terrorist groups but also have a negative impact on the daily lives of many innocent people. Israel's periodic closings, in response to terrorist activity, of the borders between Israel and the Occupied Territories—which have prevented many Palestinian Arabs from commuting to their jobs—are an example. Another example is Turkey's evacuation of villages, and consequent generation of refugees, as part of its reclaiming of territory from the PKK. On a smaller scale, but even more abusive, is the use of torture as a method of interrogation. One might also include assassination, such as the Israeli examples cited in chapter 4.

These sorts of harsh measures cause two problems for the United States. First, they are an abuse of human rights. The United States has been outspoken about such practices even when they occur in the name of counterterrorism. The State Department's regular reports on human rights have described in detail, for example, the "serious human rights abuses" that Turkey has committed in its fight against the PKK, including torture, beatings, and extrajudicial killings (while also describing the PKK's atrocities).[73] It is not just the U.S. standards that are violated. In Sri Lanka, the country's own national human rights commission has documented the many cases of torture, detention without charge, and disappearances connected with the fight against the Liberation Tigers of Tamil Eelam.[74]

Second, harsh and indiscriminate measures can be counterproductive as far as counterterrorism is concerned. Populations whom such measures alienate and enrage are more likely to support violence, and this effect may outweigh whatever damage the methods inflict on the capabilities of terrorist groups. The frustration and hardship that Israel's border closings have caused Palestinians have probably had this effect on Palestinian views toward the terrorists and their methods.[75] Similarly, what has seemed at times to be Turkey's intention to repress not just the PKK but the Kurds as a whole has bolstered support for the PKK by making even a moderate approach toward Kurdish self-expression seem futile.[76]

Governments act in such counterproductive ways for any (or all) of three reasons. Their judgment may simply be mistaken about what is required to quell a violent resistance movement. They may be pressed by domestic constituencies (including ones inside the regime, such as the military) to act firmly against the resistance. Or other doctrines or objectives besides counterterrorism (ones which the United States does not share) may be shaping their policies. As an example of the last point, the harsh Turkish posture toward the Kurds and anything smacking of Kurdish self-expression has roots in dogma dating back to Ataturk that the Turkish republic is ethnically unified, and that there is thus no such thing as a distinct Kurdish community within it.

The objectionable methods of counterterrorist partners generally do not prevent the United States from cooperating intensively with them against terrorism, nor should they. The United States can do more to correct those methods by working together with the other government toward the common goal of stopping the violence, rather than cutting off cooperation. This is partly a matter of simple persuasion, with the United States pointing out not only what is right from the point of view of human rights but also what works from the point of view of counterterrorism. Sometimes this persuasion can play off of what elements inside the country are saying about human rights. The Israeli Supreme Court, for example, in a unanimous and significant decision in September 1999, banned the use of torture, which the Israeli security services had been employing for more than a decade to extract information from Palestinian prisoners. (Specific techniques included shaking the prisoner, depriving him of sleep, or forcing him into contorted positions.) A bill was subsequently introduced in the Knesset that would negate the court's decision by authorizing "physical pressure" in certain circumstances; proponents contend the "pressure" is sometimes required to learn of impending terrorist attacks. The United States rightly weighed in against the bill, a panel of experts that Prime Minister Ehud Barak appointed to study the matter was divided, and the legislative initiative appeared to bog down.[77]

To support its persuasion, the United States can—besides linking the issue of human rights with other incentives—shape counterterrorist assistance in ways that make the recipient less inclined to commit abuses in the first place. The $100 million in counterterrorist aid that the United States extended to Israel following the Sharm el-Shaykh summit in 1996 was designed to reduce Israel's reliance on the damaging border closures.[78] All of the courses in the ATA program include units that cover the international conventions on human rights and how they apply to the use of force in combating terrorism. Intelligence can be shared if it would be useful in, say, capturing a terrorist leader but withheld if it would be more applicable to indiscriminate military operations. Some help, however, could be used either for good purposes or, potentially, for abusive ones. That fact alone is not reason to withhold the help, although each case needs to be considered individually. It is usually beneficial, for example, to share information useful in capturing a terrorist leader even if, should the other country get possession of him first, he would not enjoy all the rights and safeguards that he would in the U.S. criminal justice system.

There are some methods relevant to counterterrorism that the United States has good reason not to use itself but that, if used by a foreign partner, need not be cause for concern, much less for an attempt to stop their use. In some cases it may even advance U.S. interests for the other government to use them. This principle is clearest with regard to the extradition or rendition of fugitive terrorists. The United States does not deliver fugitives (accused of any type of crime, not just terrorist ones) to another government without giving the individual a chance to appeal the transfer in court.[79] Yet, on several occasions the United States has taken delivery of a wanted terrorist in a quick, no-frills, no-court, unannounced rendition, with the foreign government simply handing over the prisoner on a tarmac (often in the middle of the night). From the U.S. point of view, this is the best way to receive a fugitive terrorist. It is faster, with less opportunity for something to go awry, than a long extradition process. The United States would not be seeking custody of the individual if it did not already have good reason to believe he had committed terrorist crimes, and he receives all the rights that any defendant does before he can be convicted in a U.S. court. The point is that the United States benefits from, and should encourage other governments to use, a method of handling suspected terrorists that it would never use itself.

This discussion of sponsors, enablers, and cooperators has shown how the distinctions among these categories are in many ways less important than the differences within each category or the common challenges of dealing with all of them. There are ample problems and opportunities with each category. With each, there is a need to carefully structure positive as well as negative incentives to try to modify a state's behavior in the direction of making the world less friendly to terrorists without doing violence to other values and objectives. And with each, the modifications will be incremental, and the results almost always less than what the United States would prefer. With state policies toward terrorism, there are no white hats and black hats. There are only varying—and often vexing—shades of gray. Each state is a different story of capabilities and constraints, intentions and frustrations, that are pertinent to terrorism and the effort to counter it. Lists and categories cannot completely tell those stories. The story of each state must be pieced together individually to construct sound counterterrorist policy toward it.

CHAPTER SEVEN

Publics

Counterterrorism includes the shaping of attitudes and intentions not only of terrorist groups and states, as discussed in the previous two chapters, but of whole populations or other elements in the private sector. The foreign and domestic sides of managing public opinion on this subject present different problems, but they are not unrelated, especially since messages intended for one audience are inevitably heard by the other.

Foreigners

The attitudes of foreign publics are important to terrorism and counterterrorism in several ways, even in undemocratic countries. First, popular sentiment constitutes part of the roots of terrorism. It affects the formation of terrorist groups, the willingness of people to join them, and the sympathy and support that constituent publics give to them. Second, it is part of the political environment that limits what foreign governments are willing to do in countering terrorism. And third, it affects the willingness of individuals to come forward and assist foreign authorities or the United States in catching terrorists or heading off planned terrorist operations.

Public diplomacy thus has a useful role in counterterrorism. That role entails explaining all aspects of U.S. counterterrorism policy, but a couple of themes need to be stressed. One is the shared nature of the threat, a theme also to be emphasized to governments. People need to be reminded that although the United States is the primary target, it is not the only one. They need to be told the truth about the rapaciousness and ruthlessness of terrorist leaders and about how terrorist methods often inflict suffering on the people whose interests the terrorists claim to be championing. And they need to have pointed out that, as in Nairobi, even a terrorist attack aimed at the United States can grievously harm others.

The other major theme is to clarify what U.S. counterterrorist policy is *not*. Misperceptions must be corrected. In fighting terrorists, the United States is not going after certain religions or nationalities, nor is it trying to undo revolutions. It is only going after a method. The principal misperception that needs to be countered is that the United States is hostile to Islam or to Muslims—a mistaken belief that flows partly from the fact that major targets of recent U.S. counterterrorist efforts have mostly been Muslims. Senior U.S. officials have usefully addressed this issue many times over the past several years.[1] The need to keep addressing this issue arises partly from the publicity given to fugitive terrorists and the U.S. determination to bring them to justice. A wanted poster that is circulated on a terrorist's own turf unavoidably draws attention to the conflictual side, rather than the cooperative one, between the United States and the country or region (or religion) with which the terrorist is identified.

This is certainly not a reason to discontinue publicity about fugitives, which has been a valuable tool in eliciting cooperation from informants and other individuals able to provide help in capturing them. That cooperation has been critical in several cases, including the arrests of Ramzi Yousef and Mir Aimal Kansi in Pakistan. Both of those cases were well publicized in the region (and with Yousef and the other World Trade Center bombers, throughout the world) through posters, leaflets, matchbooks, and other media. A reward of up to $2 million was offered for information leading to the capture of either fugitive. Yousef's arrest was made possible by a timely tip from an informant—just in time to nab the terrorist before he moved on, probably to Afghanistan and possibly to be out of reach for years.[2] The people who were instrumental in Kansi's capture not only knew where he was but also lured him to a location where he could be arrested.[3] In both cases the help came from walk-ins who, having been exposed to publicity about the fugitives, took the initiative in making contact with U.S. officials.

Several considerations have motivated such informants, including personal disputes, abhorrence of terrorism, and the prospect of a reward. Often a combination of motives is involved. The reward money was a major consideration in the Yousef and Kansi cases, although Yousef's betrayer also had misgivings about the terrorist planning in which Yousef continued to be engaged.

The attraction of money to foreign informants has made the rewards program one of the more cost-effective counterterrorist expenditures. The 1984 Act to Combat International Terrorism created the program, which is now called "Rewards for Justice" and has a maximum reward of $5 million. The State Department has also arranged with the Air Transport Association and the Air Line Pilots Association to each kick in another $1 million when there is a terrorist threat against U.S. civil aviation, making the maximum reward $7 million in such cases. Reward money has been paid (mostly in amounts far below the maximum) in some twenty terrorist cases over the past several years.

Careful attention to the framing and wording of messages conveyed to foreign audiences about terrorism is necessary to minimize the risk that publicity about fugitives will contribute to the broader misperception that the United States thinks of Muslims only as terrorists. Such attention to detail is also needed to minimize another hazard of the publicity—that of adding to the stature of the terrorist who is wanted. This has been a problem regarding Usama bin Ladin, given that his malevolent influence has rested partly on his wider reputation and name recognition and not just on his operational control of a group, and given also the heavy and narrow U.S. focus on him personally. Bin Ladin's public image is important to him, and he cultivates it skillfully. The controlled interviews at encampments in Afghanistan are part of this image making. So is the burnishing of his Afghan war record, which is widely perceived to have included significant experience in combat but actually was more related to logistical support.[4] The image that bin Ladin seeks to project is one of a leader who wields, and has earned, influence going far beyond al-Qaida. The propensity in the United States to describe sundry acts by Sunni extremists as "linked to" bin Ladin therefore plays into his hand—bearing in mind that, given the complex Islamist networks described earlier, a lot can be "linked to" bin Ladin for which he was not necessarily the driving force.[5] To be sure, bin Ladin is probably still the single most significant international terrorist threat to U.S. interests. But as far as public diplomacy is concerned, the emphasis should be on cutting him down, not building him up.

Again, this is not a reason to reduce publicity overseas about terrorists. If anything, there is room for a more extensive and vigorous public diplomacy effort on international terrorism—through speeches by U.S. leaders, broadcasts and publications, and all of the other means used for public diplomacy on other issues. Rather, it is a reason to be careful and sophisticated about everything that the United States says on this subject to foreign audiences, from wanted posters in Peshawar to presidential statements in Washington. Madison Avenue devotes extensive research and analysis to major advertising campaigns for commercial products to ensure that the desired messages, overt and subliminal, are conveyed. Selling counterterrorism to foreigners has some of the same challenges, including competitors (such as bin Ladin) who are trying to shape opinion in opposing ways and niche markets (such as potential informants) as well as larger general markets that need to be considered. The attention to detail and nuance that is common to commercial marketing needs to be applied to what the United States tells the outside world about terrorism, terrorists, and what the United States is doing about terrorism.

Americans

The American public, or segments of it, play several roles in counterterrorism. Most important is supporting U.S. counterterrorist programs. This means being willing to bear the costs, monetary and otherwise, of those programs. That support is now good. Resources devoted to counterterrorism since the mid-1990s have to some extent bucked the post–cold war downward trend in spending on national security matters.

Public support for counterterrorism has been comparably high at certain times in the past, such as the mid-1980s. The report of the task force on combating terrorism chaired by then-vice president Bush cited a poll in 1985 that showed that 78 percent of Americans considered terrorism "one of the most serious problems facing the U.S. Government," along with the budget deficit, unemployment, and strategic arms control.[6] That figure compares with the 79 percent of respondents who mentioned terrorism in a similar question in the poll by the Chicago Council on Foreign Relations that was cited at the beginning of this book. From the perspective of a decade and half later (and thanks partly to the economic boom of the 1990s), terrorism appears to be a more enduring concern than the other issues that most troubled Americans in 1985.

That comparison between two points in time masks considerable fluctuation, however, in public concern about terrorism and support for efforts to combat it. Concern about terrorism rises after major terrorist incidents, and even more so after series of incidents; it declines as time passes with few well-publicized attacks. Between the mid-1980s and the late 1990s there was a downturn of interest in terrorism and resources appropriated to fight it. Intelligence resources devoted to terrorism, for example, shared in the broader cuts to intelligence programs in the early 1990s, which in turn were part of still broader reductions in spending on defense and national security.[7] These cuts to counterterrorism continued as late as 1995. The Crowe panel that studied the bombings in Africa observed a parallel pattern regarding resources for embassy security. The panel was struck by how similar its conclusions were to those drawn by the Inman commission fourteen years earlier. "What is most troubling," the panel reported, "is the failure of the U.S. government to take the necessary steps to prevent such tragedies through an unwillingness to give *sustained* priority and funding to security improvements."[8]

Besides the temporary reduction of interest in terrorism, some of the cuts to counterterrorist programs resulted from the administrative fact that an ebbing budgetary tide lowers all boats. Comptrollers in such an environment impose across-the-board cuts or levy "taxes" to support unfunded agency or departmental requirements. Congress can protect favored programs somewhat by explicitly earmarking at least some of the appropriations for them, but even with such restrictions—and given that other money is fungible—creative departmental managers find ways to spread widely the pain of budget cuts. Adoption of the National Commission on Terrorism's recommendation that the national coordinator for security, infrastructure protection, and counterterrorism be given a greater say in budget guidance to agencies would reduce this problem.[9]

Although the bombing at the World Trade Center in 1993 began to raise public concern about terrorism, a critical mass of salient terrorist events—large enough to make a substantial difference in decisions on resources—did not begin to come together until 1995, with the bombing in Oklahoma City. After the attack on the military program office in Riyadh later that year, three incidents occurred in rapid succession in 1996: the bombing of Khubar Towers, the crash of TWA flight 800 into the ocean off Long Island (which a long investigation would eventually reveal had been caused by an accidental explosion in the plane's fuel tank but which at the time was generally assumed to be an act of terrorism), and a pipe bomb detonated at the Olympic Games in Atlanta (which had only minor physical effects but took place where high publicity was assured and further heightened American awareness of vulnerability to terrorism). This concatenation of jarring events brought the latest surge in American concern about terrorism, which—sustained by the bombings of the embassies in 1998—has carried into the beginning of the new millennium.

The actual threat that international terrorism poses to the United States in any given year, or on any given day, fluctuates **less** than the inevitably irregular pattern of terrorist incidents might suggest. More to the point, the threat fluctuates much less than the oscillating public concern about terrorism. A challenge for national leaders, therefore, is to elicit support for counterterrorist programs that is more sustained, at a more constant level, than has generally been the case. To some extent this can be accomplished within government (such as with greater use of multiyear appropriations). But because decisions on resources inside the government, and particularly in Congress, reflect public sentiment, the task is mainly one of educating the public and managing popular perceptions of terrorism. What political leaders say about the subject should reinforce several truths: that counterterrorism requires a long-term effort; that the absence of incidents over a period of time does not necessarily mean the threat has receded; and that the occurrence of several incidents within a short period does not necessarily mean that the threat has developed in ways that justify hasty new departures in counterterrorist policy. This task of managing popular perceptions is difficult. The tendency to overreact to shocking events, and to fall into complacency in their absence, is natural and inevitable. There will always be oscillations of public sentiment that swing beyond real changes in the threat, but leaders should at least try to damp the oscillations.

Another challenge in managing popular perceptions is that the simple themes that are most convenient in generating and maintaining broad support for counterterrorist programs tend to oversimplify the more complex realities of terrorism and what is needed to counter it. Of course, in counterterrorism—as with many other issues of public policy—the American public can support a policy without understanding all of the nuances and complications in executing it. But for a couple of reasons, the public needs to understand at least some of the complications about terrorism. One reason is that some of these complications directly affect ordinary citizens, not only in the sense of the different threats that may endanger them but also in the effects that security countermeasures have on their daily lives (not just on the use of their tax dollars). The other reason is that oversimplified public thinking can foment oversimplified public policy. This is especially true of actions taken by the public's elected representatives in Congress, but popular thinking about terrorism can constrain executive initiatives as well.

A topic that illustrates these and related problems—and where mood and oversimplification have probably most endangered balance and clear-headedness—is the threat of chemical, biological, radiological, or nuclear (CBRN) terrorism. The possibility of horrible new methods being used to kill large numbers of people has served as one of those simple themes that has helped to sustain support for counterterrorist programs, and in that sense it has brought some benefit to counterterrorism as a whole. There are several other reasons, however—besides the public's right to know what truly threatens it the most—that stirring up this worry has been detrimental.

First, it encourages skewed priorities and misdirected resources within counterterrorism. Appropriating more money for initiatives aimed narrowly at a chemical or biological threat, especially the worst case scenario of a mass casualty attack, may mean less money for efforts that combat terrorism in general (and that could save more lives). The General Accounting Office has observed, "By targeting investments based on worst case scenarios, the government may be over funding some initiatives and programs and under funding the more likely threats the country will face."[10] One facet of counterterrorism that may still be underfunded is the disruption of terrorist methods, which can consume significant resources in the form of assistance to foreign security services, and about which U.S. program managers were still having to make difficult, financially constrained decisions at decade's end. A point to remember is that some steps to counter the most catastrophic threats would not necessarily help to meet less catastrophic ones, which sometimes present qualitatively different problems.[11]

Second, the executive branch's need to be seen doing everything it can to combat possible terrorist use of unconventional weapons may incline it toward actions that compromise other interests, including other counterterrorist interests. The widespread worry over chemicals in terrorist hands was a backdrop to the decision to strike the al-Shifa pharmaceutical plant, for example, with the unfavorable political fallout described in chapter 4.[12]

Third, the rampant attention to the threat of biological or chemical terrorism, and the efforts to capitalize on this attention by some of those (both inside and outside government) with a fiscal stake in working on it, has started to generate cynicism as to whether all the talk about this kind of terrorist threat is motivated mainly by an interest in contracts and bigger budgets.[13] If this backlash helps to dampen some of the more excessive rhetoric about CBRN terrorism, so much the better. But the danger is that the skepticism may start to apply to counterterrorism in general, and to start the pendulum of public support for it swinging downward again.

Fourth, the publicity given to this subject has stimulated a surge in hoaxes. In 1999 the FBI investigated more than 150 threats allegedly involving anthrax and numerous others in which other biological, chemical, or nuclear substances supposedly were involved. The frequency of such threats is up sharply from the rate just four or five years ago. The FBI and other authorities have refined their response procedures to minimize the costs and disruptions from such hoaxes. Nevertheless, precautionary decontamination procedures and restricted areas established in response to CBRN threats carry greater potential for disrupting the communities where they occur than threats of conventional violence.

Fifth and most important, the heavy attention to the danger of mass casualties from biological or chemical agents will accentuate the psychological impact and fear (and in the worst case, possibly even panic) among the general population if an incident using them does occur. This is not to say that physical preparations to deal with mass casualty scenarios are not warranted. But as discussed in chapter 2, the direct physical effects of an unconventional attack are likely to be outstripped by the secondary psychological effects. Conditioning the public to be afraid of large numbers of people dying amplifies those secondary effects, and in so doing helps the terrorist achieve his desired result. It is helpful psychological preparation for the public to expect that some terrorists may try to use CBRN methods to achieve that result. It is unhelpful to lead the public to expect that a CBRN attack would probably mean thousands of people dying, rather than—as with all previous CBRN terrorism—far fewer casualties than that. Talking up the danger, in other words, has the counterproductive effect of making the danger even greater.

The way in which simple public moods and perceptions about terrorism can lead to oversimplified counterterrorist policies is most apparent when the policies become codified in legislation. Congressional action on counterterrorism has reflected two aspects of public attitudes about the topic. One is the broad, nonspecific sentiment of the general public in favor of fighting terrorism. The other is the influence of certain vocal minorities having strong interests in particular measures related to counterterrorism. Although what Congress has done over the past several years has assisted counterterrorism in numerous ways—by appropriating necessary resources, furnishing legal tools, and simply helping to sustain interest in the subject—its reflection of each of these two aspects has had less helpful sides.

The congressional response to the more general public sentiment on combating terrorism has ebbed and flowed along with the sentiment itself. Laws have tended to be written in bursts of enthusiasm, following major terrorist incidents, to "do something" about the problem. The haste with which some of this legislation has been written shows. During periods of high interest in terrorism, there is a push to do *more* of everything—more sanctions, more stringent requirements, heavier criminal penalties, wider application of existing rules—to satisfy a general desire to do more to fight terrorism, even if some of the measures adopted might not be well designed to reduce terrorism. This has often meant the enactment of blanket prohibitions and procedures, or other uniform policies, to tackle a problem that is anything but uniform.

An example of a seemingly unexceptionable—but damaging in its foreign ramifications—effort to impose uniformity (which also demonstrates the influence of domestic special interests) concerns the security of civil aviation. The Aviation Security Improvement Act of 1990 established a requirement for foreign air carriers serving U.S. airports to maintain a level of security similar to that provided by U.S. carriers serving the same airports. The Antiterrorism and Effective Death Penalty Act (AEDPA) amended this rule to require the foreign carriers' security measures to be not just similar but "identical" to those required of the U.S. airlines.[14] On the surface, this objective seems like a commendable effort to tighten security standards. But besides being an extraterritorial effort to tell foreign aviation authorities how to conduct their business, there is the practical problem of different methods being used at foreign airports. Many of the foreign measures may not be any better or worse than the U.S. measures, but they may be incompatible with them. The European Civil Aviation Conference promptly objected, pointing out these problems and others, including the confusion that would be caused by having one standard apply to carriers that fly to the United States and another to carriers at the same airport that do not, as well as the fact that implementing "identical" measures might lower the security currently provided by some carriers that serve dangerous areas. When the Federal Aviation Administration (which never wanted the amendment and would welcome its repeal because of the toxic effect it has had on relations with its foreign counterparts) dutifully published in November 1998 a proposed rule change to implement the new law, a new barrage of criticism came from foreign airlines, airport and transportation authorities, governments, and the International Civil Aviation Organization.[15]

Besides the other practical and principled objections, several foreign governments denounced the change as being motivated by the commercial interests of U.S. airlines that wanted additional requirements placed on their foreign competitors. The charge was supported by the fact that the new requirement would apply only to routes on which U.S. carriers competed and by the U.S. airlines' suggestion that identical standards could be achieved by *lowering* the ones imposed on themselves rather than raising the ones placed on foreign carriers. It is hard to disagree with the British government's description of the change as "complete nonsense in security terms."

The interests of deeply engaged minorities in the United States have mainly concerned policies toward state sponsors, and their influence has had the effect of constraining any openings toward those states and discouraging engagement with them. The American Israel Public Affairs Committee (AIPAC), for example, has been a force in favor of maintaining pressure on Iran (as has the Mujahedin-e-Khalq, thanks to the connections it has cultivated on Capitol Hill). The Cuban-American community centered in southern Florida has been a long-standing and well-known bastion of opposition to any rapprochement with the Castro regime. The principal instruments of that community's activism have been the Cuban American National Foundation and the Free Cuba Political Action Committee, with which it is associated. The families of the victims of the Pan Am 103 bombing are major players regarding policies toward Libya. Although not united into a single organization, the influence of the families has been remarkable for a group whose only defining characteristic is having been bereaved by a single incident. (As an example of the families' entrée into officialdom, they were given three seats—to accommodate each of the factions among them—on the White House Commission on Aviation Safety and Security that was formed in 1996.)

The effects of the general "do something about terrorism" sentiment and the more narrowly focused minority interests were seen in the latest burst of legislative enthusiasm in 1996, the year in which the AEDPA, the Helms-Burton Act, and the Iran-Libya Sanctions Act were all enacted. The political backdrop to this law writing was provided by the succession of terrorist-related incidents mentioned above and by the presidential campaign, in which terrorism became an issue.[16] The Clinton administration and the Republican leadership sparred over several aspects of it, and both were trying not to appear soft on it. The AEDPA was a huge omnibus bill that covered not only several of the topics addressed in earlier chapters but many others, including regulatory and law enforcement matters. The job of working this legislative leviathan into shape became increasingly rushed as lawmakers endeavored to have it ready for the first anniversary of the bombing in Oklahoma City.[17] Most of the debate in the latter stages of preparing the bill centered on the FBI's investigative powers and other domestic issues, with less attention to the international topics. Some of the international provisions that could have been designed better, such as those dealing with the designation of Foreign Terrorist Organizations, have been discussed in earlier chapters.

The Iran-Libya Sanctions Act (ILSA) and Helms-Burton also exhibited the same rush to "do something"—preferably something bold and sweeping—about terrorism, as well as showing the influence of the vocal minorities on policy toward the targeted states. Reservations about these bills, and sober considerations about exactly what they were likely to accomplish, were swept aside by the mood generated by the events of 1996. One key event influencing the enactment of Helms-Burton was not terrorism but rather the shooting down by a Cuban MiG-29 of two small planes flown by Cuban Americans over the Strait of Florida in February. (The planes belonged to the organization Brothers to the Rescue, which had earlier flown over Havana to drop anti-Castro leaflets.) After this incident, President Clinton—who had opposed some of the farther-reaching provisions of Helms-Burton—felt obliged to sign the legislation.[18] With ILSA, the mood of the moment was generated mainly not by anything Iran or Libya was doing but by the international terrorism that was presumed to have been involved in the crash of TWA 800. The bill was originally aimed only at Iran, but the parallels being drawn between TWA 800 and Pan Am 103 gave Senator Edward Kennedy, acting on behalf of families of Pan Am 103 victims, the opening to add Libya to the legislation.[19]

Hard-line sentiment against state sponsors—which reached a crescendo in the legislation of 1996—is one of those simple themes that is useful at times in mobilizing and sustaining public support for counterterrorism but has the disadvantage of constraining the president and his administration when a more complicated, less categorical approach may be more appropriate.[20] There is always political risk in being seen as compromising with a devil. Lest there be any doubt from the country-specific legislation as to what Congress expected from the president on this subject, section

324 of the AEDPA spelled it out: "The President should continue to undertake efforts to increase the international isolation of state sponsors of international terrorism, including efforts to strengthen international sanctions, and should oppose any future initiatives to ease sanctions on Libya or other state sponsors of terrorism."

Nonetheless, the American public's willingness to accept at least limited unfreezing of relations with reforming state sponsors of terrorism is probably greater than the words of Congress in 1996 would suggest. Attitudes (especially among the more informed parts of the public) seem to have moved slightly away from an unwavering hard line toward state sponsors of terrorism. This is partly because the events of 1996 have receded with the passage of time (or have been put into better perspective, as with the results of the investigation into TWA 800). It is partly because of the increased skepticism about how the United States has used economic sanctions. Regarding Iran, the well-reported electoral victories by reformists in Iran have made a difference. Regarding Cuba the tremendous public attention given to the custody case of Elian Gonzalez, the Cuban boy who was rescued at sea and whose mother drowned while they were attempting to reach Florida in November 1999, stimulated a more vibrant debate about U.S. policy toward Cuba than had been heard for years, with questions raised anew about the usefulness of the U.S. embargo. And although the general public's understanding of the patterns of international terrorism remains slight, the public probably does have a sense that terrorism is now a problem more characteristic of nonstate than state actors. This is largely because of the emergence of bin Ladin as the archterrorist enemy of the United States, taking a place in the public mind that in an earlier day would have been occupied by a Qadhafi or an ayatollah.

Moreover, despite the intensity with which some of the domestic interest groups involved hold to their positions, they do not constitute an insuperable obstacle to change in policies toward state sponsors. They are minorities, not an majority. Being seen as an obstructive, narrowly focused minority can become a political liability for some of them, as happened to the more militant part of the Cuban-American community in the Elian Gonzalez case. There are divisions even within the groups over the best tactics to use against the regimes in question.[21] And there are countervailing interests in the American business community, which sees economic opportunities being surrendered to the Europeans. Among the currently designated state sponsors, the greatest such opportunities are in

Cuba, because of proximity, and Libya and Iran, because of petroleum. On Cuba, at least, U.S. business is being heard from.[22] Agricultural interests have also showed influence in negotiations in Congress to permit exports of food to several state sponsors.

The government's management of public perceptions and sentiments about state sponsors needs to extend not just to the most incorrigible minority interests opposing engagement with state sponsors but to these other interests as well, and to the broader public. There are few foreign policy initiatives in which cultivation of public and congressional support is more important than the engagement of "terrorist states."[23] There will need to be more statements with the balance, candor, and salience of Secretary Madeleine Albright's speech on Iran, which spell out for foreign and domestic audiences the reasons a relationship is important and the remaining problems in it that need to be solved. Even if, as with Iran, the problems related to terrorism are still considerable and major departures such as a removal from the state sponsors' list are not imminent, it is never too soon to try to educate the public about the contours of a bilateral relationship and about what is lost as long as it remains sour. The process of changing public attitudes about relationships with reforming state sponsors—like the process of changing the relationships themselves—is necessarily slow and incremental.

The deeply committed minorities still need to be spoken to as well, of course. A group like the Pan Am 103 families needs to be part of the process not just because they would protest if they were not, but because of the moral claim that they always will have to be listened to, given the direct suffering that terrorism has inflicted on them. The message to be conveyed to the families—if improved Libyan behavior regarding terrorism warrants an improved U.S. relationship with Tripoli—should be grounded in an interest the families presumably share with their fellow citizens: to reduce the likelihood of similar terrorism in the future. Dialogue with the families should address how specific policies toward Libya would or would not advance that objective. If Libya cooperates with the trial of Megrahi and Fhima until its end, negotiates and pays monetary compensation to the victims' families, and stays out of the terrorism business, and if no alternative to Qadhafi as leader of Libya is in sight, then it is hard to envision how continued U.S. ostracism of Libya would reduce future terrorism. It might even increase it, by showing to Libya and to others—including other state sponsors—that even great improvement in behavior does not remove hostility from Washington. In those circumstances, any arguments in favor of the continued banishment of Libya would not be driven by the shared interest in saving lives from terrorism but by something else.

Americans who have fallen victim to international terrorism can affect U.S. foreign relations in another way, besides acting as a pressure group in the manner of the Pan Am families. One of the respects in which the AEDPA endeavored to do "more" to fight terrorism was to permit private citizens who have been victims to sue state sponsors in U.S. courts for damages.[24] The act thus created a new exception to the sovereign immunity that normally protects foreign governments from being sued. Several victims, or their families, have used this law to sue Iran for its support to groups that committed the terrorist acts that affected them. Tehran has not contested the suits, and some of the plaintiffs have won large judgments by default. The family of Alisa Flatow, an American college student who as a bystander in Israel was killed in 1995 by a bomb detonated by the Palestine Islamic Jihad, won a judgment of $247.5 million against Iran in 1998. Three of the hostages taken by Lebanese Hizballah in the 1980s (Joseph Cicippio, Frank Reed, and David Jacobsen) were awarded $65 million. Judgments against Iran in 2000 included: $324 million to Terry Anderson, the journalist whom Hizballah held longer than any other hostage (with an additional $17 million to Anderson's wife and daughter); $327 million to the families of Mathew Eisenfeld and Sara Duker, an engaged couple who were killed by a suicide bomb in Israel in 1996; and $355 million to the family of U.S. Marine Lieutenant Colonel William Higgins, whom Hizballah captured and killed in Lebanon in 1989.

These and other suits have raised the issue of seizing assets to make good on the judgments. An amendment that Congress enacted in 1998 provided the basis for such seizures but also gave the president the power to waive the law (as President Clinton immediately did) on grounds of national security. Secretary Albright stated in February 2000 that the administration was exploring options for helping the victims collect on their judgments.[25] At the same time, however, the administration was opposing a bill that would have curtailed the waiver power and opened up for attachment by the courts such foreign assets as the money remaining in an Iranian military sales trust fund dating back to the time of the shah.[26] In the meantime, victims have been in the position of being able to win judgments but not collect on them, and of feeling both supported and undercut by their own government.[27]

The issue pits sympathy for terrorist victims and a sense of retributive justice against the need for the executive branch to manage difficult bilateral relationships in a coherent and effective way, using all available tools. It is always hard to argue against making foreigners pay for suffering inflicted on innocent Americans. Negotiated monetary compensation is already an established part of coming to terms with previous terrorist acts. Examples include Libya's payment to the family of a police officer killed by gunfire from the Libyan embassy in London in 1984, the U.S. insistence that Libya provide similar compensation to the Pan Am 103 families, and the Palestine Liberation Organization's payment of an undisclosed sum to the family of Leon Klinghoffer, the American who was murdered by the hijackers of the *Achille Lauro*.[28]

Nonnegotiated seizure of assets, however, has potentially serious complications. There are issues of reciprocal obligations to protect diplomatic and consular properties, and possible jeopardy to U.S. properties overseas. Even if seizures apply only to financial accounts and not to property protected by treaty, it vitiates the program of blocking assets of terrorist states. If such assets are subject to attachment by private parties, then, in the words of Deputy Secretary of the Treasury Stuart Eizenstat, "The ability to use blocked assets as leverage against foreign states that threaten U.S. interests is essentially eliminated."[29] The basic problem is in leaving to individual citizens—and to the initiative and skill of their lawyers, and the case-specific decisions of judges—matters that unavoidably affect relations between the United States and a country like Iran, and that therefore are better left to negotiations between governments. Private citizens should not make foreign policy, even if they happen to be victims of terrorism.

The Clinton administration and members of Congress agreed in October 2000 on a bill that would have the judgments against Iran paid out of the U.S. Treasury, with the United States to seek reimbursement through the U.S.-Iranian claims tribunal or future negotiations with Iran.[30] That arrangement would either leave an innocent party (the U.S. taxpayer) footing a bill that was intended for someone else or have all of the same disadvantages of trying to collect directly from Tehran. A better way to eliminate the anomaly of people winning judgments but not being able to collect would be to repeal the provision of the AEDPA that created this exception to sovereign immunity in the first place.

Being a victim, or potential victim, of international terrorism is a respect in which members of the American public present certain other challenges to counterterrorist policy, beyond the ones just discussed of compensation and relationships with state sponsors. Most U.S. victims of international terrorism are in the private sector. More than two-thirds of the U.S. targets of international terrorism in 1999 (meaning persons who were killed, wounded, or kidnapped, as well as property that was bombed or set on fire) included businesses, and half of the rest were also in the private sector (such as tourists and missionaries). Protecting Americans from terrorism in the United States is a straightforward task of keeping citizens safe in their own homeland. Protecting private citizens abroad, however, where their presence is more often a matter of personal choice, is a more complicated issue. Americans do not *need* to be in all the hazardous places they go, and in which some of them become victims of terrorism. They could become victims anywhere, of course, but some places (say, Kashmir) are more dangerous than others, and terrorism against Americans would be less of a problem if fewer of them went to the bad spots. The U.S. public interest in what private citizens do overseas varies; it may be more apparent, for example, with a corporation marketing U.S. goods abroad (and thereby improving the trade balance) than with individual recreational travel. Given these considerations, what does the U.S. government owe its citizens in countering the terrorist threat against them abroad, and how active a role should it take in managing the risk in the private sector's activity overseas?

The main thing the government owes is the most complete possible information about threats in individual countries and regions. It discharges that obligation principally through the State Department's travel warnings, public announcements, and consular information sheets.[31] The government is obliged to find ways to convey the necessary information to members of the public even though some of the underlying reporting about terrorist threats is classified. In this regard, intelligence reports officers and other counterterrorist officials observe two rules. One is "duty to warn," which is the requirement to advise individual private citizens who may be targets of specific terrorist threats, and to give them any information about reported places or dates of attack, to enable them to make themselves less vulnerable. The other is the "no double standard" rule, which states that government employees who happen to have access to classified material or to those who handle it should not enjoy any informational advantage over the general public in planning travel. Counterterrorist officers scrupulously observe both of these rules, even though the latter one occasionally means telling an acquaintance in the next office, who has asked for inside guidance on whether a contemplated trip would be safe, to go read the latest State Department advisories.

Public consumers of the government's information about international terrorism need to be reminded of the limitations of that information. All of the caveats discussed earlier about the limits of counterterrorist intelligence and the resulting uncertainties in forecasting when and where terrorists will strike apply to public advisories at least as much as to classified assessments. Moreover, public advisories cannot and should not take the place of risk assessments that are inputs into decisions by American businesses regarding overseas ventures. Terrorism is but one of the political and economic risks involved in such decisions. It is an expense of doing business to calculate those risks (or to pay others to calculate them), and it is a business decision whether the expected return of a project makes it worthwhile to proceed despite the hazard of terrorism.

There is not much more that the U.S. government can do, beyond providing information (and, of course, continuing to act offensively to reduce international terrorism generally), to manage the vulnerability of the U.S. private sector overseas. This does not mean the government can ever take a hands-off approach to the risk its citizens face from terrorism abroad. There will always be an expectation for the government to do something whenever terrorism hits its citizens, no matter how well those citizens had been warned, and no matter how ill-advised it may have been for them to go where they went or do what they were doing. Any terrorist attack against Americans is a setback for counterterrorism and makes the United States look a bit weaker and more vulnerable, not to mention being a drain on the time and attention of government officials. The government thus inevitably shares in the risk assumed by its citizens abroad. In that sense it has an interest in discouraging endeavors that mean high vulnerability to terrorism, whether the activity is trekking in Kashmir or saving souls in a Colombian jungle. But there is no good mechanism for discouragement beyond the admonitions in the State Department advisories and the persuasion of consular officers or other officials. Part of being a free country is freedom to travel and work abroad. The secretary of state can ban the use of U.S. passports for travel to specified countries, but in many cases vulnerability to terrorism is a matter of what the traveler is doing once he or she is inside the country rather than just traveling to the country in the first place. Moreover, such bans, like the one that was in effect for Lebanon until 1997, are highly permeable barriers to travel and tend to be thought of more often as bargaining chips in dealing with the government of the country rather than as protection for U.S. citizens.

Another consideration is that the more special help that private citizens expect from their government (such as being rescued if they are taken hostage) the greater the potential for creating what economists call moral hazard—that is, a tendency of private interests to take chances they would not otherwise take because they see the government as covering some of the risk if things go bad. This does not seem to be a problem to date with terrorism. Most Americans taken hostage overseas are ransomed (by employers or families), not rescued. The private payment of ransom presents a different sort of problem, however, in that it is contrary to declared U.S. policy, risks encouraging more hostage taking, and provides support to groups that, like those in Colombia (where more Americans have been taken hostage over the past several years than anywhere else) have a political and true terrorist dimension and not just a criminal one. As objectionable as the payment of ransom may be, it would be infeasible to try to police it. Italy and Argentina have tried unsuccessfully to do so.[32] Some companies have come to see the occasional ransom payment as a cost of doing business (and retaining staff) in some parts of the world, and restrictions on payments would only tend to make them less likely to confide in the authorities and more likely to deal with the kidnappers in secret. The FBI, in working with employers and families on kidnapping cases in the United States and abroad, has stayed focused on the missions of getting hostages freed and pursuing any violations of U.S. law. If ransom gets paid, this means in effect condoning an action contrary to U.S. counterterrorist policy (a point that the State Department has raised with the FBI), but offsetting that drawback is the investigative advantage of getting all the information that the private parties in the case have to share.

The behavior of the American private sector overseas, as it relates to problems of terrorism, cannot be regulated; it can only be modified at the margins. It is one more example of governmental control being diluted in a globalized world, even on a matter as important, and as much a matter of national security, as one's citizens being struck by terrorism. The government can only use what mechanisms are available to it to try to cultivate a common view of the nature of the terrorist threat and of the approaches to be taken toward it, and to harmonize the private sector's security measures (which will always constitute a large proportion of the antiterrorist security provided to Americans overseas) with those of the government. One useful forum for doing this with American business is the Overseas Security Advisory Council, a public/private body that is managed on the government side by the State Department's Bureau of Diplomatic Security and includes, besides other government agencies that operate abroad, twenty-one private sector commercial organizations that represent more than 1,600 U.S. companies. The council is available to discuss not only the issues mentioned above but also other ways in which the policies and practices of American businesses operating overseas may affect U.S. counterterrorist initiatives. In a problem country like Greece, for example, it would useful if what U.S. companies say to Greek authorities complemented what the U.S. embassy is saying. Indeed, that is necessary if Athens is to be influenced in the manner suggested in chapter 6. There will be some resistance to this kind of coordination; companies do not want to be seen as lackeys of the U.S. government, and some companies that have suffered only moderate property damage in Greece seem to accept the occasional nonlethal attack as one more cost of doing business. The overall interests of the public and private sectors in international terrorism do run parallel, however, and coordination is worth the effort.

There is probably more that the United States could usefully do in communicating directly to public audiences, foreign and domestic, about international terrorism than what it has done so far. The importance of perceptions among foreign populations has become all the greater as terrorism has become less often a tool of state policy and more frequently a product of nonstate actors. The effects of popular sentiments on the ability of terrorist groups to operate are profound, ranging from the willingness of some individuals to volunteer for suicide bombings to the willingness of other individuals to volunteer information to the authorities. Public diplomacy that is energetic, continuous, and on the offense (as distinct from being only reactive or used to repair specific misperceptions) is an important part of counterterrorism.

The importance of communicating the right messages to the American public stems not just from public's role in paying taxes to support counterterrorist programs and in electing a Congress that passes laws that shape and constrain those programs but also from its role as a target of terrorism and the fact that so much of the impact of terrorism takes place in the minds of targets. "Target" in this instance means not just those who suffer the direct physical effects but also those whose emotions and perceptions the terrorist is seeking to influence. Assisting the public in keeping the terrorist threat in perspective, and in understanding at least some of its complexities, has become all the more important given the great attention to potentially more destructive forms of terrorism. The United States might draw a lesson or two from Israel, where public education about terrorism has received considerable attention. The International Policy Institute for Counter-Terrorism at Herzliya has an educational program that includes seminars for teachers, students, and civic leaders, and teacher training courses on countering the psychological effects of terrorism.[33] The milieu for terrorism in Israel is admittedly much different from that in the United States, and Israel has been forced to pay more attention to this matter because all of its citizens have been closer to the front line of terrorism. How one's public thinks, feels, and acts in the face of a terrorist threat, however, is important anywhere.

CHAPTER EIGHT

Lessons
and Futures

Sound counterterrorist policy requires a long and broad perspective. Awareness of past efforts to fight terrorism provides a sense of what is—and just as important, what is not—possible to accomplish in that fight. Sensitivity to other current national interests is needed to understand the immediate limits and complications of counterterrorism. An eye aimed at the future helps to prepare for threats yet to develop and possibilities yet to be exploited.

A Problem Managed, Never Solved

The long history of terrorism is reason enough to expect that it will always be a problem and usually a significant one. It is a product of such basic facts of human existence as the discontent that is sometimes strong enough to impel people toward violence, the asymmetries of the weak confronting the strong, and the vulnerability of almost every facet of civilization to physical harm at the hands of those who find a reason to inflict harm. If there is a "war" against terrorism, it is a war that cannot be won.

Counterterrorism, even though it shares some attributes with warfare, is not accurately represented by the metaphor of *a* war. Unlike most wars, it has neither a fixed set of enemies nor the prospect of coming to closure, be it through a "win" or some other kind of denouement. Like the cold war, it requires long, patient, persistent effort, but unlike it, it will never conclude with the internal collapse of an opponent. There will be victories and defeats, but not big, tide-turning victories. Counterterrorism is a fight and a struggle, but it is not a campaign with a beginning and an end.

Perhaps a better analogy is the effort by public health authorities to control communicable diseases. That effort, like counterterrorism, deals with threats that come in many different forms, some more virulent than others. Some of the threats are waxing; some are waning. Some are old; others are very new. Much of the challenge and the frustration comes from the fact that just as things are going well on one front—and occasionally even so well that a problem is eradicated altogether (smallpox, the Red Army Faction)—a different and perhaps even more threatening problem emerges (AIDS, al-Qaida). Attention and resources get shifted around as threats evolve, but the effort as a whole can never stop.

Analogies aside, a central lesson of counterterrorism is that *terrorism cannot be "defeated"—only reduced, attenuated, and to some degree controlled.* Individual terrorists or terrorist groups sometimes are defeated; terrorism as a whole never will be. Expectations must be kept realistic. Unrealistically high hopes for counterterrorism lead to impatience that in turn leads to sweeping (and thus perhaps satisfying) but not necessarily effective measures, such as some of the legislation enacted in 1996. Such hopes also encourage despair when they cannot be achieved. Each terrorist attack becomes that much more of a discouraging setback, and the dashed hopes assist the terrorist in damaging public morale. Moreover, unrealistic striving for zero terrorist attacks (which might mean retrenchment overseas to reduce exposure to terrorism) would be no better for overall U.S. foreign policy interests than striving for zero unemployment (which would exacerbate inflation) would be for U.S. economic interests. Counterterrorist programs will prevent many terrorist attacks but will not prevent them all. Terrorism happens. It should never be accepted, but it should always be expected.

The impossibility of winning a "war" or inflicting an overall defeat raises the question of what standards to use in assessing the success or failure of counterterrorist programs. Terrorist attacks, and people getting killed or wounded in them, are obvious and quantifiable indications of failure. But as noted, zero attacks would be an impossible standard. One could look at trends as a measure—that is, whether terrorism has been up or down lately—but the sporadic and uneven nature of terrorism means that short-term fluctuations have little significance, and the effects of other factors make longer-term trends only an imperfect gauge of the effectiveness of counterterrorist programs. One might also look at counterterrorist achievements such as renditions, prosecutions, or rolled-up plots, but this can never be more than a partial scorecard.

Although there is no simple standard, any assessment of counterterrorist policies should bear in mind that *the purpose of counterterrorism is to save lives (and limbs and property) without unduly compromising other national interests and objectives*. This principle has two elements, one narrow and one broad. The narrow one is that as far as counterterrorism is concerned, anything other than saving lives is but a means to that end. That goes for everything from prosecuting an individual terrorist to placing sanctions on a state sponsor. Some of those means may have come to be seen as ends in themselves for other reasons (such as the satisfaction of seeing justice done that comes from prosecuting a terrorist), but they are not counterterrorist ends. They are good for counterterrorism only if, given the circumstances in which they are used, they are likely to reduce terrorism and save lives.

The broad element is that counterterrorism constantly and inevitably impinges on other important U.S. interests, and so counterterrorist policy must be judged according not only to how many lives it saves but also to how little damage it does to those other interests. This objective is partly a matter of not letting the fear of terrorism, or measures taken to avoid it, so disrupt the other business of the U.S. government or of U.S. citizens that it constitutes a victory of sorts for the terrorists. This means, for example, not making U.S. elements overseas so preoccupied with protecting themselves against terrorism that what is supposed to be their primary mission becomes secondary. The chairman of the Joint Chiefs of Staff saw this happening to some extent to the U.S. military in the wake of the Khubar Towers bombing, given the heavy emphasis on force protection. To correct this imbalance, he issued reminders that the missions of the U.S. armed forces require them to go places and to do things that make some terrorism inevitable, and that the U.S. military "cannot afford to subscribe to a 'zero casualty' mentality."[1]

The broad element is also a matter of staying cognizant of the potentially detrimental side effects of counterterrorist measures and of employing those measures carefully and judiciously, with an eye toward all of the interests they affect. In the United States, awareness of counterterrorism's side effects has focused more intently on domestic concerns such as civil liberties rather than on the many ways in which steps taken in the name of counterterrorism can affect U.S. foreign relations, possibly to the detriment of other U.S. interests or even, in the long run, counterterrorism itself. Much of this book has been devoted to describing those potential effects. They range from resentment over the extraterritorial application of U.S. laws to perpetuation of myths about the anti-Islamic character of U.S. policy, and the rankling of allies—on whom the United States is dependent for so much besides counterterrorism—over what they perceive as obdurate policies toward state sponsors.

The integral link between counterterrorism and other aspects of foreign policy suggests an even broader standard for assessing the success or failure of counterterrorist policy. Besides such measures as plots foiled and fugitives caught, the success of any administration's counterterrorist policy should also be measured according to how more—or less—effective it makes that administration's overall foreign policy. It is a counterterrorist success, for example, if the United States elicits more forthright cooperation from a foreign government because effective counterterrorist work has made that government less afraid of terrorist reprisals for doing business with Washington. It is a success if U.S. diplomats feel safe enough in a terrorism-prone area to stay focused on their primary mission of advancing U.S. economic and political interests in the country to which they are accredited. And it is a success if the United States enjoys a positive image in a culture (for example, the Islamic world) because the problem of extremists in that culture has been handled in a deft way that does not antagonize the nonextremists, or if alliances are harmonious because policies toward state sponsors of terrorism are handled in a constructive way that influences the state sponsor's behavior without antagonizing the allies.

Recommendations

Some of the most basic and important aspects of good counterterrorist policy—such as a clear national commitment to counter international terrorism and the priority and resources that this effort warrants—are part of the general consensus on the subject and do not need to be restated again. But many pieces of advice have emerged in the preceding chapters—on ways to think about counterterrorism that are not so widely understood and accepted, and ways in which U.S. policies could be beneficially tweaked. The principal recommendations are summarized in the form of the following precepts.

Inject the counterterrorist perspective into foreign policy decision-making. Foreign policy should be made with the awareness that many aspects of U.S. foreign relations, although they may not carry the "counterterrorist" label, nonetheless bear on the threat that international terrorism poses to U.S. interests. U.S. initiatives overseas affect the resentments and motivations of those who might resort to terrorism. A U.S. posture overseas may entail increased vulnerability to terrorism (and in the worst case may involve a Lebanon-type trap in which withdrawals cannot be undertaken without the United States appearing to be defeated by terrorism). And the management of relations with many foreign governments whose cooperation is needed in combating terrorism has major consequences for the effectiveness of the whole U.S. counterterrorist effort. Other important U.S. interests—often more important than counterterrorism in any given case—are also at stake, but the question, "What are the implications of this for terrorism?" should at least be posed and analyzed as part of the decisionmaking process for many foreign policy issues. Those issues include any that involve a physical U.S. presence or a significant U.S. initiative overseas and any that have significant bearing on U.S. relations with a state that poses terrorist problems or is an important U.S. partner in combating terrorism.

Injecting the counterterrorist perspective is partly a matter of who participates in the decisions. The State Department's coordinator for counterterrorism should have a seat at more decisionmaking tables than has been true in the past. At the White House, the national coordinator for security, infrastructure protection, and counterterrorism should similarly have a voice in a wide range of issues (and not just on budgetary guidance). In large measure, however, keeping the implications for counterterrorism in mind is a matter of senior decisionmakers (and those who prepare their decision papers) remembering to do so.

Pay attention to the full range of terrorist threats. International terrorism's impact on U.S. interests covers a very wide range in terms of perpetrators, methods, and the interests affected. The United States cannot afford to focus narrowly on whatever segment of that range currently is in the headlines, given the diversion of attention and resources from other segments (or from terrorism as a whole) that entails. The United States should not become as preoccupied with any one terrorist as it has been with Usama bin Ladin (even given his considerable influence), because in the fractionated world of international terrorism no single individual is responsible for more than a small part of the mayhem. The nation should not be as preoccupied with any one scenario as it has been with mass casualty chemical, biological, radiological, or nuclear (CBRN) terrorism in the United States (even given the calamity that would be, if it occurred), because that is only one of many ways in which international terrorism can seriously affect U.S. interests, and it is not the most likely way. The allocation of counterterrorist attention and resources should be guided not only by the prospect of dead American bodies but also by the harm that international terrorism—by threatening foreigners—does to U.S. interests by wrecking peace processes or by destabilizing or intimidating otherwise friendly regimes. And the United States should look not only for the current bin Ladin but also for the *next* one, and for the circumstances that may cause such a threat to arise.

Disrupt terrorist infrastructures worldwide. Counterterrorism needs to be as far reaching, geographically and functionally, as international terrorism itself. With globe-girdling networks of cells, and peripatetic terrorists whom those networks support, most of the activity that could culminate in terrorist attacks on U.S. interests (including attacks in the United States) takes place far from U.S. shores, and most of it consists of such mundane but essential functions as recruitment, finance, and logistics. The United States should therefore devote a major effort to the piece-by-piece disruption of those terrorist infrastructures. It must rely on cooperative foreign governments to do most of this work, and it should take advantage of the enforcement by those governments of their own laws (including laws having nothing to do with terrorism) to make the terrorists' professional life as difficult as possible in as many places as possible. That this work is less visible and less publicly satisfying than the more dramatic counterterrorist measures the United States sometimes takes should not detract from the priority given to it.

Use all available methods to counter terrorism, while not relying heavily on any one of them. Even the disruption of terrorist infrastructures has shortcomings as well as advantages. The same is true of every other means available to the United States to combat terrorism. The shortcomings are found in basic elements of counterterrorism (such as attacking capabilities or influencing intentions), functional instruments (such as criminal law or military force), and more specific tools or policies (such as formally designating terrorist groups, or applying sanctions to state sponsors). The limitations may involve practical difficulties in implementation (for example, trying to identify terrorist financial accounts), undesirable side effects (for example, public resentment over a military strike), or the inapplicability of a measure to parts of the terrorist problem (true of many measures taken against state sponsors, which do not curb terrorism by independent groups). Some hoped-for effects may be inherently uncertain, such as the deterrent effect that a criminal prosecution may (or may not) have in the minds of other terrorists. Since no single measure can do the job, the United States must extract whatever advantage it can from each measure. This means the *selective* use of counterterrorist tools and instruments, bearing in mind the applicability—or inapplicability—of an instrument to a particular case. Anyone who promotes a single method or approach as the "key" to counterterrorism is selling not keys but snake oil.

The instrument of criminal law—even though it is enshrined in one of the basic tenets of current U.S. policy—should not automatically be given precedence over other instruments. A prosecution in a U.S. court should be viewed as one possible means rather than an end and should be foregone if in any case the use of other means (including, for example, the continued collection of intelligence on the activities of terrorists at large) seems likely to save more lives. The investigative resources of law enforcement agencies should be used to support not only criminal prosecutions but also other counterterrorist measures (such as administrative actions to interdict flows of money). And the United States should be open to seeing justice served in reliable foreign courts even for some terrorists who may have violated U.S. law.

Tailor different policies to meet different terrorist challenges.   A foolish consistency is the hobgoblin not only of little minds, as Ralph Waldo Emerson said, but also of insufficiently flexible counterterrorist policy. In some respects consistency in counterterrorism is indeed desirable, such as in upholding a reputation for firmness against terrorist coercion and in opposing terrorism no matter who is the victim (including adversaries of the United States). But beyond basic commitments, differences are at least as significant as similarities. The terrorist threat is not really "a threat" but rather a method used by an assortment of actors who threaten U.S. interests in varying ways and degrees. There are important differences in the roots of terrorism in various countries, the prospects for resolving conflicts with different terrorist organizations, the degree to which state sponsors are still behind terrorism, the salience of other issues in U.S. relations with states that sponsor or enable terrorism, and other pertinent variables. Such differences should form the basis for tailoring what is, in effect, a different counterterrorist policy for each group or state. Foreign terrorist groups are incredibly diverse—ranging from small bands of fugitives on the run like the Japanese Red Army to politically or militarily potent organizations like the Liberation Tigers of Tamil Eelam. The terrorist methods that each has used should be consistently opposed, and a counterterrorist technique or two (such as catching leading members of a group) might be applied to each, but almost everything else about dealing with them needs to be shaped to meet individual circumstances. Such tailoring may be complicated, difficult, and rhetorically unsatisfying (because it defies generalization), but it is necessary to make counterterrorism more effective and to protect other U.S. interests at stake.

Give peace a chance.   Although the objective regarding most terrorist groups should be to eradicate them, with others the most promising (or least unpromising) path toward ending the bloodshed is to enlist the group in a peace process aimed at resolving the underlying conflict. Determining whether this is so requires a careful assessment of the group's political and military strength, the nature of the issues and whether competing demands are bridgeable, and the availability of more moderate interlocutors to represent interests the terrorists claim to support. If engagement in a peace process seems more feasible than eradication, the United States should encourage the start of such a process or support—even indirectly as an interested outsider—any process that has already begun. The negotiations over Palestine and Northern Ireland (despite the continuing threat of renewed violence in both places) should serve as models of how much such peacemaking can curb terrorism. Colombia may some day become another example.

The legacy of a group's past terrorism, the disruptions caused by its more recent attacks, and even the abhorrence of terrorism that touches U.S. interests directly should not lead the United States to reject peacemaking with a group out of hand. Any road to peace that involves organizations that have used terrorism will be rocky. Infractions should be penalized as appropriate but not allowed to kill a process that otherwise still has a chance to succeed. The label "terrorist" should not be a permanent disqualifier for doing business with the United States or for being part of a U.S.-supported political process. Not only were Yasir Arafat and Gerry Adams leaders of terrorist groups; so were Menachem Begin and Yitzhak Shamir.

Legislate sparingly.   The need for well-tailored policies is one reason that legislation—which is inherently better suited to general rules than to specific applications—should play only a limited role in counterterrorist policy. The procrustean nature of much current U.S. counterterrorist law, with uniform penalties or restrictions placed on what are decidedly mixed bags of states or groups, has been its biggest drawback. Other disadvantages include the difficulty in responding quickly to changed circumstances when policies are codified in law, the unfortunate side effects of congressional micromanagement of matters like aviation security, and the defects that stem from the process by which U.S. laws on terrorism get written (that is, in fits and starts corresponding to the fluctuations in public concern about the topic, and with heavy influence by vocal minorities whose first concern is not counterterrorism). Because it needs to be flexible, U.S. counterterrorist policy should largely be a matter of executive discretion—and this includes the application of economic sanctions and most other counterterrorist measures that currently are constrained or required by law. Congress should refrain from enacting case-specific laws (such as the Iran-Libya Sanctions Act or Helms-Burton) in the name of counterterrorism. It should also resist the tendency to use the passing of still more laws as a gesture to respond to postincident bursts of public concern about terrorism.

Congress's legislative role in combating international terrorism, though limited, still has several important aspects. Besides providing the resources for a sustained counterterrorist effort, it is the job of Congress to declare objectives on matters such as human rights and to set the rules on subjects such as the extraterritorial activities of U.S. law enforcement agencies. Most important, it needs to keep the executive branch supplied with a full set of counterterrorist tools to apply at the latter's discretion, intelligently and flexibly, to individual cases. The International Emergency Economic Powers Act is a good model of such a tool-furnishing law. In the short term, legislation would be needed not just to give the executive branch more such flexibility but to undo some of the less helpful aspects of existing law, particularly on the topic of the next precept.

Keep terrorist lists honest.   Official U.S. lists of terrorist states or groups need to be accurate, complete, and up-to-date portrayals of what is really going on in international terrorism, as they currently are not. They need to be in order to keep U.S. counterterrorist policy credible, realize fully whatever value they have as incentives to improve terrorist-related behavior, and provide a fair and useful frame of reference in discussions of terrorism with foreign partners, the American public, and the groups and states that are on the lists (or should be). The lists should be about terrorism, not about other issues, as has too often been the case with the list of state sponsors. And the lists should be promptly changed when terrorist-related behavior changes.

The lists would be more likely to exhibit such truth and responsiveness if they were unshackled from the automatic sanctions, associated criminal penalties, and other measures to which they are currently bound by law. Decisions about whether a state should be designated as a state sponsor or as "not cooperating fully" on counterterrorism under the terms of the Antiterrorism and Effective Death Penalty Act should not have to be surrogates for decisions about sanctions. Decisions about designating Foreign Terrorist Organizations should not depend on the evidentiary problems that lawyers anticipate in defeating future legal challenges. The various sanctions and penalties should be retained as tools for the executive to use selectively, in cases when they—with other counterterrorist measures and bearing in mind other U.S. interests—seem most likely to be effective.

Encourage reforming state sponsors to reform even more by engaging them, not just punishing them. The United States should seize the opportunity provided by the substantial decline in state sponsorship of terrorism during the past several years to nurture even more improvement on this front, as well as to advance other U.S. interests in the states in question. This means not only keeping lists of state sponsors up to date but also using positive and negative techniques to move bilateral relationships in the desired direction. The economic sanctions and other negative measures on which the United States has primarily relied (and the limitations of which have been amply demonstrated) have a role, but their effectiveness as an inducement to better behavior depends on U.S. willingness to change them when the behavior that was the reason for enacting them in the first place has changed. The United States needs to demonstrate this responsiveness to keep the state directly concerned on the right path and to convince others that supporting—or reducing support for—terrorism makes a difference in what kind of relations they will have with Washington.

The United States should try to make it easier, not harder, for regimes trying to clean up their acts to clean them up further. This requires clear communication of what is expected, which is best done through direct dialogue. It also means not expecting the more difficult reforms to be accomplished quickly. And it means incrementally improving the relationship as terrorist-related behavior incrementally improves. Most important, the United States should avoid postures that lead decisionmakers on the other side (or in other countries) to conclude that relations with Washington will remain poisoned no matter how much support for terrorism is reduced.

Libya and Cuba are clearly candidates for better relations as far as issues (or rather, the paucity of them) of current support for terrorism are concerned. A similar statement could be made on terrorism and North Korea, with which there has already been engagement driven by concerns over weapons proliferation. Even when significant problems of support to terrorism remain (as with Iran), and major improvement in relations with Washington in the near term may not appear feasible, the same principles of structuring incentives to encourage, not discourage, incremental improvement apply.

Of every action (or inaction) regarding relations with state sponsors the question should be asked, "Is this likely to reduce terrorism?" The objective should not be to condemn people for the past but to save lives in the future. Changing a relationship with a foreign leader stained by sins of the past should not require any judgment that he has had a change of heart. What matters is change in his policies, and that might occur (as with Muammar Qadhafi or Fidel Castro) because the circumstances he faces have changed.

Help other governments to help with counter-terrorism. The dependence of the United States on a host of foreign governments for much of the counterterrorist work that needs to be done (especially the disruption of terrorist infrastructures) should be recognized in the management of relations with those governments. The needed cooperation often includes measures that are difficult or (from the foreign government's viewpoint) risky, and U.S. assistance and reassurance should be furnished to make the other government willing and able to act. The overall warmth of a bilateral relationship obviously affects willingness, but so do efforts to educate the foreign partner that terrorism is a threat to both countries. Training and other forms of practical assistance to police and security services enhance the ability of many foreign governments (especially in less developed countries) to help, and the United States should be generous in providing such assistance, through Antiterrorism Training Assistance courses and other departmental training programs. The concerns of cooperating governments about terrorist reprisals should be respected by preserving the secrecy of joint operations, even if this means resisting the urge to trumpet counterterrorist successes.

Work with, not against, allies. With most Europeans and other close allies, what is needed is not technical assistance and reassurance but rather more comity and coordination. The United States should respect (and even learn something from) different perspectives toward countering terrorism and not try to change allied policies that experience and deeply felt national interests dictate will not be changed. It should exploit ways in which policies that are not uniform may nonetheless be coordinated to mutual benefit, especially regarding state sponsors. The United States should also end the use of secondary economic sanctions—which have been ineffective and damaging to intra-alliance relations—in futile efforts to bend allies to its will. When the counterterrorist operations of allies raise human rights concerns (as they have at times with Israel and Turkey), the United States should work within the framework of continued close counterterrorist cooperation—one of the most effective channels the United States has for influencing human rights practices—to discourage such abuses.

Use public diplomacy to elucidate terrorism without glamorizing terrorists. The reaching out for foreign help and cooperation must extend not only to governments but also to their citizens. An active program of public diplomacy should explain why terrorism hurts the interests of those citizens and why U.S. counterterrorist efforts do not. The public diplomacy needs to be adroit, as well as active, to avoid the pitfall of making wanted terrorists appear more like Robin Hoods than like malign criminals.

Level with the American people. The strong domestic public support that is essential for effective counterterrorism—if the support is to be as sustained as it must be, and if public attitudes are not to exacerbate some of the less helpful policy tendencies—should be *informed* support. National leaders must resist the temptation to use emotional or simplistic themes that, although effective at drumming up support in the short term, may reduce the political room for maneuver when it comes to the more complex and delicate issues in counterterrorism. Instead of displaying a bag of sugar on television—as a senior government official once did—and speaking in exaggerated terms about how many people could be killed if it contained anthrax spores, it would be better to give Americans a sense of the different ways that international terrorism can directly affect their interests (which includes, among many other things, low-casualty as well as high-casualty CBRN attacks), and the less apparent but important ways in which it already affects their interests indirectly. Citizens have a right to know what to expect—not just any one way that terrorism could hurt them but the many ways in which it can and the relative likelihood of those different ways materializing.

American citizens, in their capacity not just as potential victims, but as taxpayers and sources of support for their government's policies, must become familiar with several other realities. One is surely the need for sustained, not sporadic, effort and resources to combat terrorism. Political leaders can help by saying more about the subject in the lulls between major terrorist attacks and not confining so much of their oratorical and legislative efforts to the aftermath of such incidents. Another reality is the need for flexibility. Sometimes the most promising way to reduce future terrorism is through the kind of measures, such as engagement of selected terrorist groups or state sponsors, that in a less educated perspective might be seen as going soft on terrorism. And yet another is that terrorism cannot be eliminated, that it will claim more victims, and that any attempt to achieve zero casualties would be in vain.

Remember that more is not necessarily better. U.S. counterterrorist policy needs to exhibit finesse and nuance, not just vigor and oomph. Both sets of characteristics are important, but so far responses to terrorism have emphasized quantity more than than quality. Much attention has been paid to making counterterrorist measures stronger, broader, or more numerous (whether the measures are sanctions, lists, criminal penalties, military strikes, or whatever). More needs to be paid to gauging how effective or applicable such measures are to individual cases.

A Cloudy Crystal Ball

So how might future developments in international terrorism affect the validity of what this book says? Counterterrorism surely needs to adapt to future changes in the threat, and successful anticipation of those changes would be useful. The heavy attention that has been given to possible terrorist use of CBRN or other unconventional methods—with scenarios being spun that go well beyond what terrorists are doing today—is, in a way, an admirable effort at that sort of anticipation. Perhaps the extensive discussion of that subject will help to avoid errors akin to the classic military planner's mistake of preparing to fight the last war rather than the next one. But there is an important distinction between the worst-case possibility of what terrorists *might* do and what they likely *will* do.

Anticipation of the specific materials that terrorists will use in their attacks (should we expect fertilizer bombs or nerve gas?) has some value in planning security countermeasures (such as in deciding what kind of protective gear to stock in embassies) and even more in planning to manage the consequences of a terrorist incident—particularly the low-probability, high-impact contingency of a CBRN attack that inflicts mass casualties. Such anticipation also underlies certain preventative measures, including steps to control the storage, shipment, or sale of nuclear, chemical, or biological materials (efforts that would be warranted in the interest of nonproliferation and not just of counterterrorism) and anything else intended to attack terrorists' CBRN capabilities directly (like bombing al-Shifa). This book describes, however, many other issues in counterterrorism—ranging from whether to bring criminal indictments against terrorists to how the United States should structure designations of foreign terrorist groups—that are important aspects of counterterrorist policy now, will continue to be important aspects of counterterrorist policy, and do not depend at all on whether terrorists are using gas or grenades.

Most counterterrorist measures that would be effective in *preventing* terrorist attacks are not dependent on judgments about the terrorists' modus operandi. Consider, for example, the contribution of intelligence. The intelligence community certainly does extensive work in attempting to track CBRN materials—work it would be doing anyway to support U.S. nonproliferation objectives—but its principal contribution to counterterrorism is to learn, through unilateral sources or foreign liaison, about the intentions and overall capabilities of terrorist groups. The intelligence sources that would be most valuable in preventing terrorist groups from attacking with unconventional means are the same sources that would be most valuable in preventing conventional terrorist attacks. The best counterterrorist use of the intelligence community, therefore, involves recruiting and exploiting such sources (and doing the other mundane but effective work described in chapter 4), rather than anything that comes under the CBRN label, even if one believes that CBRN terrorist attacks are a wave of the future.

Many other aspects of future international terrorism—such as which local conflicts will give rise to it, what belief systems will drive it, which regions or countries will be most plagued by it, and how current terrorist networks and patterns of sponsorship will change—would, if correctly anticipated, be at least as useful in guiding future counterterrorist policy as prognostications about the substances or methods that terrorists will use in their attacks. But while predictions about the latter have been plentiful and bold, forecasts about the former have been sparse.

A generous dose of agnosticism would be appropriate all around. One has only to look back, say, a decade to realize how difficult it is to forecast patterns of terrorism with even modest specificity. At the start of the 1990s, how many would have predicted the sidelining of most of the secular Palestinian resistance, the eclipse of most leftist terrorism, the entry of the Irish Republican Army into a peace process, the emergence of someone like bin Ladin, the terrorist significance of a place like Chechnya, the extent to which state sponsorship of terrorism would lessen, or the perpetration by a few unaffiliated terrorists of major attacks (World Trade Center and Oklahoma City) in the United States, which had been largely free of such misery? And as for terrorist methods, one could add to that list the sudden emergence of Aum Shinrikyo as a major factor in thinking about terrorism, and, after the attack on the Tokyo subway, the fact that this event did *not* inspire any similar incidents during the next half decade.

There are several reasons that strategic forecasting of terrorism—although it will never be as hard as anticipation of specific terrorist events—is difficult. One is the inherently sporadic nature of observable terrorist acts, which mathematicians would call "rare events" and which preclude the kind of precise analysis of trends that is possible with, for example, economic data. A second reason is the dependence of terrorism on the actions of a few individuals. Terrorism would look different, and the way Americans think about it would be much different, if there had never been an Usama bin Ladin, or a Ramzi Yousef, or a Timothy McVeigh, or a Chizuo Matsumoto (who later took the name Shoko Asahara and founded Aum Shinrikyo). This is not to say that the larger forces underlying the actions of these men were not at least as important, only that inherently unpredictable initiatives by individuals in making salient terrorist events happen are important too. As for larger forces—and this is the third reason forecasting of terrorism is so difficult—because terrorism is an epiphenomenon of broader political and social developments, to forecast terrorism requires the forecasting of many of those other developments. This means anticipation not only of epochal events like the end of the cold war but also political developments in many individual countries and diplomatic and military developments in many regional conflicts, not to mention other pertinent trends such as those involving technological change.

The difficulty of this kind of forecasting means it would be imprudent to base the planning of counterterrorist policy on any one image of the future, regardless of whether it is a reassuring image in which terrorism falls further into disfavor, a scary image of terrorists disseminating nerve gas and anthrax spores in American cities, or something in between. Counterterrorism is a matter of managing risks, not confronting certainties. Counterterrorist planners should think of possible *futures* of international terrorism, not any single future.

Sadly, this is not a prescription for rich and specific futuristic judgments about terrorism. Rich and specific means speculative, and it means little basis for confidence that the judgment will turn out to be true. One can have high confidence only in more general observations—bordering on the banal but perhaps still useful as reminders—about the future of international terrorism. One such observation is that terrorism in the years ahead will be a mixture of the old and the new, and it would be a mistake to ignore either. The heavy attention to possible high-tech methods of terrorist attack reduces the danger of overlooking the new. There are many other possible new elements of international terrorism, however, besides methods of attack. They may include new groups, new turns to violence by existing groups, new organizing ideologies, or new conflicts giving rise to terrorism. Counterterrorist officers and policymakers need to be alert to all of these possibilities. The old elements of terrorism are just as important to remember. Indeed, the persistence of many of the roots of modern international terrorism, and the tendency of most terrorists to be conservative planners who stick to familiar methods, mean that forecasts of the future that are simple projections from the present probably have as much chance of being accurate as do any others.[2]

Projecting from the present in this way—with all of the considerable caveats above, and bearing in mind that no single projection should be relied on—a few more observations about the future (looking ahead several years, if not several decades) can be ventured. One is the fundamental thought with which this chapter began: that terrorism will endure. That statement does not hinge on any vision of the larger world order. Terrorism is part of even the best known optimistic vision: Francis Fukuyama's contention that the evolution of human political and economic institutions is culminating in a victory for bourgeois liberal democracy. Ten years after first presenting his argument, Fukuyama defended it (in the face of criticism that pointed to voluminous evidence that the world is still conflict prone) by quoting what his earlier article had said about the "high and perhaps rising level of ethnic and nationalist violence" that would continue despite ideological convergence among major powers. An implication, Fukuyama had written, was that "terrorism and wars of national liberation will continue to be an important item on the international agenda."[3] Terrorism would have at least as great a role in less optimistic images of the future world order.

The continuation of terrorism is easier to anticipate than the forms of discontent that will sustain it at any given time. Even ethnicity—one of the least changeable of human characteristics that has served as a basis for organized violence, and one associated with much current terrorist capability and that Fukuyama believes will ruffle his otherwise consensual "posthistory" world—probably cannot be counted on as a consistent sustaining force. A leading student of ethnic conflict, Ted Robert Gurr, wrote in the early 1990s about a resurgence of ethnopolitics that had made it the dominant mode of conflict in most of Africa, Asia, Eastern Europe, and parts of Latin America.[4] Several years later, Gurr noted that the early 1990s had been a peak for ethnic warfare and that since then there had been, for various reasons, a trend away from confrontation and toward accommodation.[5] But Gurr observed that "since ethnic conflicts tend to end in compromise, disillusionment is inevitable," and that religious and class-based movements could well pick up some of the popular support that had been energizing ethnically based groups.[6] In short, the organizing ideas that underlie political violence, including terrorism, are always coming and going, but discontent and terrorism will continue.

Another reasonable expectation is that the United States will continue to be terrorist target number one. U.S. policies and the U.S. presence overseas can vary, but the United States' place as sole superpower, leader of the West, and principal exporter of modern culture do not seem likely to change.

The geographic breadth of terrorism and the number of countries that fall victim to it, however, is apt to be at least as broad as it is now. One reason is the increased porosity of borders associated with the trends that come under the label of globalization. Another reason is that there are further opportunities for terrorists to exploit the loosening of once rigid controls in formerly authoritarian states, particularly those of the former Soviet empire. Fukuyama's suggestion that a spread of liberal democracy may bring an increase in this form of violence is supported by the fact that terrorism has been more prevalent in free than in unfree societies. There will be many ways in which terrorism against non-U.S. targets will affect U.S. interests (including the threat it may pose to the stability of new liberal democracies). The good news, however, is that the more fellow terrorist targets there are in the world, the more potential counterterrorist partners the United States will have.

The decline in state sponsorship of terrorism during the past decade is likely to continue. A couple of the major roots of that decline are one-way developments: the end of the cold war and of Soviet patronage, and the maturation of revolutionary regimes whose own emergence was a response to archaic monarchical governments or neocolonial conditions that are unlikely to recur. Regimes like those in Iran and Libya have exhibited longitudinal, not cyclical, lives, with some of the same stages through which other revolutions have gone. Revolutionary fervor and the export of violence are most apparent in the early stages. With Iran, for example, much of Tehran's early efforts to foment similar Islamist revolutions in other states were based on the fear that the clerical regime would need to change its environment to survive—the same idea that, for the Bolsheviks, underlay Leon Trotsky's doctrine of "permanent revolution."[7] As a regime's longevity causes this fear to recede, it can afford to think about the quality, and not just the length, of its tenure, and what this means for improving relations with the outside world.

The principal uncertainty regarding state sponsorship is not recidivism by current or past sponsors but rather revolutions or coups elsewhere that might create new ones. A new revolutionary regime could be expected to pass through its own stage of high fervor, with the possibility that it would support terrorism outside its borders. Even such a disturbing entrant on the scene, however, would face some of the same incentives and conditions that have moved most of the existing state sponsors away from terrorism. These include the increased importance in a globalized world of having broad and normal economic relations, and the absence of the postcolonial, cold war–era political mood that once condoned revolutionary violence.

The practitioners of terrorism in the coming years will be at least as diffuse and numerous as they are now, not only because international terrorism is now more the business of groups than of states but also because the groups will continue to exhibit the fractionated, ad hoc, and organizationally confusing qualities that they have exhibited over the past few years. This trend, too, is rooted in larger—and unlikely to be reversed—trends, such as the revolution in information technology and increased ease in crossing international boundaries. There are likely to be more independent terrorist entrepreneurs like Ramzi Yousef, because these trends facilitate the organizing of even major terrorist operations without the backing of a large, established group.

As for methods of future terrorist attack, the plethora of attention to this one facet of the future of terrorism leaves little more to be said, beyond the points already made about it in chapter 2 and earlier in this chapter. The only additional observation is the somewhat obvious one that the longer the span of time being considered, the greater the chance that any particular technique will be tried. An event such as foreign terrorists attempting to use chemical or biological agents in an American city is more likely to occur in the next five years than in the next one year, simply because there are four more years in which it might happen. If it does happen, we should not be shocked, nor should we necessarily interpret it as marking a sea change in international terrorism.

Maybe these (very modest) forward-looking statements will turn out to be true; maybe they will not. Even if they do not, it should matter little if a robust, flexible, and adaptable counterterrorist policy is in place. Under such a policy, change in the pattern of international terrorism is part of the anticipated pattern. In terrorism, the United States needs to expect the unexpected.

Notes

Chapter One

1. Address to the nation by President Bill Clinton, August 20, 1998 (www.state.gov/www/regions/africa/strike/clinton980820.ahtr [December 7, 2000]).

2. Remarks by President Bill Clinton to the Fifty-Third United Nations General Assembly, September 21, 1998 (www.state.gov/www/global/terrorism/980921_pres_terror.htr [December 7, 2000]).

3. John E. Rielly, ed., *American Public Opinion and U.S. Foreign Policy 1999* (Chicago Council on Foreign Relations, 1999), pp. 15–16. The Chicago council's survey, which was conducted between October and December of 1998, may have partly reflected the recency of the bombings of U.S. embassies in East Africa in August of that year. But other polls throughout the late 1990s showed strong backing for counterterrorism. A *Time*-CNN poll taken in 1997, for example, revealed comparable levels of support for giving very high priority to "fighting international terrorism." See "Majority of Americans Support Strikes against Terrorist Sites," U. S. Information Agency report, August 25, 1998, p. 2 (usinfo.state.gov/topical/pol/terror/98082801.htm [July 24, 2000]).

4. Statement of FBI Director Louis J. Freeh before the Senate Judiciary Committee, September 3, 1998 (usinfo.state.gov/topical/pol/terror/98090301.htm [September 8, 2000]). These fugitive terrorists included Ramzi Ahmed Yousef, mastermind of both the World Trade Center bombing and an aborted plot in Manila to bomb eleven U.S.-flag jumbo jets out of the sky in early 1995; Mohammed Ali Rezaq, wanted for a hijacking and murder in 1985 and captured in Africa in 1993; Mir Aimal Kansi, who murdered two Central Intelligence Agency employees in 1993 and was caught in Pakistan in 1997; Tsutomu Shirosaki, a Japanese Red Army member who attacked the U.S. embassy in Jakarta in 1986; Mohammed Rashid, wanted for bombing a Pan Am airliner in 1982; several of Yousef's ac-

complices from the World Trade Center bombing and the Manila plot; and several of those involved in the bombings in Nairobi and Dar es Salaam.

5. Judith Miller and William J. Broad, "Exercise Finds U.S. Unable to Handle Germ Warfare Threat," *New York Times*, April 26, 1998, p. 1. The novel was Richard Preston's *The Cobra Event* (Random House, 1997).

6. Former deputy attorney general Philip B. Heymann assesses those concerns in *Terrorism and America: A Commonsense Strategy for a Democratic Society* (MIT Press, 1998), especially chaps. 7 and 8, pp. 105–51. Heymann concludes that existing authorities strike an appropriate balance, for the most part, between investigative needs and civil liberties. The National Commission on Terrorism that functioned in late 1999 and 2000 also addressed some of these issues. The commission did not recommend changes to either the attorney general's guidelines that govern FBI investigations or the statute (the Foreign Intelligence Surveillance Act) that covers electronic surveillance and physical searches of suspected foreign terrorists. It did conclude, however, that the guidelines needed clarification and that the statute had been applied in a cumbersome and overly cautious manner. See National Commission on Terrorism, *Countering the Changing Threat of International Terrorism* (Washington, June 2000), pp. 9–12.

7. See National Commission on Terrorism, *Countering the Changing Threat of International Terrorism,* pp. 4–5.

8. Department of State, *Patterns of Global Terrorism 1999* (2000), p. 2.

9. All but 22 of the 190 American deaths from domestic terrorism during the same period occurred in a single incident: the bombing in Oklahoma City. All statistics in this book on international terrorism are derived from the U.S. government's database on the subject, which is the basis for the statistics in the State Department's annual report *Patterns of Global Terrorism*. Statistics on domestic terrorism are from FBI data, which are reported annually in the FBI's report *Terrorism in the United States* (Washington).

10. See *The Protection of US Forces Deployed Abroad,* report to the President submitted by Secretary of Defense William J. Perry, September 15, 1996 (www.defenselink.mil/pubs/downing_rpt/report_f.html [July 24, 2000]), which incorporates the Downing Commission report on the Khubar Towers incident, and *Report of the Accountability Review Boards on the Bombings of the US Embassies in Nairobi, Kenya and Dar es Salaam, Tanzania on August 7, 1998,* submitted to the Secretary of State on January 8, 1999 (www.terrorism.com/state/accountability_report.html [November 2000]).

11. Two recent surveys of terrorism by long-standing experts on the subject are Bruce Hoffman, *Inside Terrorism* (Columbia University Press, 1998); and Walter Laqueur, *The New Terrorism: Fanaticism and the Arms of Mass Destruction* (Oxford University Press, 1999).

Chapter Two

1. Bruce Hoffman, *Inside Terrorism* (Columbia University Press, 1998), chap. 1. Another recent chapter-length discussion of definitions is in David Tucker,

Skirmishes at the Edge of Empire: The United States and International Terrorism (Praeger, 1997), chap. 2, pp. 51–69.

2. See, for example, the several articles on the subject in the autumn 1996 issue of the journal *Terrorism and Political Violence*, particularly Andrew Silke, "Terrorism and the Blind Men's Elephant," vol. 8 (Autumn 1996), pp. 12–28.

3. 22 U.S.C. 2656f (d).

4. For an argument that terrorism and crime should be kept conceptually distinct, see Phil Williams, "Terrorism and Organized Crime: Convergence, Nexus, or Transformation," in Brad Roberts, ed., *Hype or Reality: The "New Terrorism" and Mass Casualty Attacks* (Alexandria, Va.: Chemical and Biological Arms Control Institute, 2000), pp. 117–45. A contrasting view is in Roger Medd and Frank Goldstein, "International Terrorism on the Eve of a New Millennium," *Studies in Conflict and Terrorism*, vol. 20 (July-September 1997), p. 301.

5. Hoffman, *Inside Terrorism*, p. 43.

6. The discussion in chapter 4 on multilateral diplomacy addresses further what these rules, and recent modifications to them, imply for counterterrorism.

7. Assassination as a possible counterterrorist tactic is discussed in chapter 4.

8. Concurring opinion by Justice Stewart in *Jacobellis* v. *Ohio*, 378 U.S. 184, 197 (1964).

9. Quoted in Pamela Constable, "Kashmiri Rebels Pressure Pakistan," *Washington Post*, October 20, 1999, p. 23.

10. As Brian Jenkins has pointed out, this conception of terrorism does involve one value judgment: that an end does not justify the means. Brian M. Jenkins, "Terrorism: A Contemporary Problem with Age-old Dilemmas," in Lawrence Howard, ed., *Terrorism: Roots, Impact, Responses* (Praeger, 1992), p. 14.

11. International terrorism includes any incident that is terrorism under the statutory definition given above and that involves two or more nationalities when one considers the perpetrators, the victims, and the location of the incident.

12. Statistics are from unpublished FBI data.

13. Statistics on U.S. military casualties are Department of Defense data (web1.whs.osd.mil/mmid/m01/sms223r.htm [November 2000]).

14. Overseas Presence Advisory Panel, *America's Overseas Presence in the 21st Century* (Washington, November 1999), p. 38.

15. Peter D. Feaver and Christopher Gelpi, "How Many Deaths Are Acceptable? A Surprising Answer," *Washington Post*, November 7, 1999, p. B3.

16. General Accounting Office, *Combating Terrorism: Issues in Managing Counterterrorist Programs*, T-NSIAD-00-145 (April 6, 2000), pp. 3–4.

17. The most comprehensive study is Richard A. Falkenrath, Robert D. Newman, and Bradley A. Thayer, *America's Achilles' Heel: Nuclear, Biological, and Chemical Terrorism and Covert Attack* (MIT Press, 1998). Despite the somewhat ominous title, this is a well-researched work that lays out arguments both for and against the idea that terrorists are likely to employ unconventional weapons. A useful survey is Roberts, *Hype or Reality*, especially the chapter by Brian Jenkins, which summarizes points on which there appears to be consensus among most specialists. A recent book that touches on diverse aspects of the subject is Jessica Stern, *The Ultimate Terrorists* (Harvard University Press, 1999). Jonathan

B. Tucker, ed., *Toxic Terror: Assessing Terrorist Use of Chemical and Biological Weapons* (MIT Press, 2000), examines several past cases of attempted or reported terrorist use of chemical or biological substances. Reasons to be skeptical about the magnitude of an unconventional terrorist threat are discussed in David C. Rapoport, "Terrorism and Weapons of the Apocalypse," *National Security Studies Quarterly*, vol. 5 (Summer 1999), pp. 49–67; Ehud Sprinzak, "The Great Superterrorism Scare," *Foreign Policy*, no. 112 (Fall 1998), pp. 110–24; Jonathan B. Tucker and Amy Sands, "An Unlikely Threat," *Bulletin of the Atomic Scientists*, vol. 55 (July-August 1999), pp. 46–52; Brian M. Jenkins, "The Limits of Terror: Constraints on the Escalation of Violence," *Harvard International Review*, vol. 17 (Summer 1995), pp. 44–45, 77–78; Henry Sokolski, "Rethinking Bio-Chemical Dangers," *Orbis*, vol. 44 (Spring 2000), pp. 207–19; the exchange on "WMD Terrorism" in *Survival*, vol. 40 (Winter 1998–99), pp. 168–83; and part 1 of the *First Annual Report of the Advisory Panel to Assess Domestic Response Capabilities for Terrorism Involving Weapons of Mass Destruction*, December 15, 1999.

18. This is all the more true of acquiring a usable nuclear device or the fissile material necessary to make one, both of which—despite the breakdown of many of the controls in the former USSR—are still protected by significant safeguards. Partly for this reason, use of a device producing a nuclear yield is the least likely CBRN terrorist event. Use of radioactive material as a contaminant to be dispersed by a conventional bomb is more probable.

19. W. Seth Carus, "Biohazard," *New Republic*, vol. 221 (August 2, 1999), pp. 14–16.

20. See, for example, John Mueller and Karl Mueller, "Sanctions of Mass Destruction," *Foreign Affairs*, vol. 78 (May-June 1999), p. 44.

21. *Report of the Accountability Review Boards on the Bombings of the US Embassies in Nairobi, Kenya and Dar es Salaam, Tanzania on August 7, 1998* (January 8, 1999), Key Recommendations, sec. I.A.12 (www.terrorism.com/state/accountability_report.html [November 2000]).

22. FAA Notice 99-05, "Security of Checked Baggage on Flights Within the United States," *Federal Register*, vol. 64 (April 19, 1999), p. 19230. This cost estimate is a maximum, assuming a combination of profiling of passengers and matching passengers with their bags. Greater use of explosives detection machines (which are hardly inexpensive themselves) might reduce the cost.

23. Philip B. Heymann, *Terrorism and America: A Commonsense Strategy for a Democratic Society* (MIT Press, 1998), p. 16.

24. Barbara Crossette, "Fearing Terrorism, U.S. Plans to Press Sudan," *New York Times*, February 2, 1996, p. A6.

25. Steven Lee Myers, "At a Saudi Base, U.S. Digs In, Gingerly, for a Longer Stay," *New York Times*, December 29, 1997, p. A1.

26. See, for example, the research on ethnically based conflict reported in Ted Robert Gurr, *Minorities at Risk: A Global View of Ethnopolitical Conflicts* (Washington: U.S. Institute of Peace Press, 1993).

27. Khalil Shikaki, "The Politics of Paralysis II: Peace Now or Hamas Later," *Foreign Affairs*, vol. 77 (July-August 1998), pp. 35–36.

28. Ziad Abu-Amr, *Islamic Fundamentalism in the West Bank and Gaza: Muslim Brotherhood and Islamic Jihad* (Indiana University Press, 1994), p. 96.

29. Walter Laqueur, "Reflections on Terrorism," *Foreign Affairs*, vol. 65 (Fall 1986), p. 91.

30. Leonard B. Weinberg and William L. Eubank, "Terrorism and Democracy: What Recent Events Disclose," *Terrorism and Political Violence*, vol. 10 (Spring 1998), pp. 108–18.

31. Daniel Pipes, "It's Not the Economy, Stupid: What the West Needs to Know about the Rise of Radical Islam," *Washington Post*, July 2, 1995, p. C2.

32. Richard N. Haass, *Conflicts Unending: The United States and Regional Disputes* (Yale University Press, 1990), p. 53.

33. See Martha Crenshaw, "How Terrorists Think: What Psychology Can Contribute to Understanding Terrorism," in Howard, *Terrorism: Roots, Impact, Responses*, pp. 71–93; Jerrold M. Post, "Terrorist Psycho-logic: Terrorist Behavior as a Product of Psychological Forces," in Walter Reich, ed., *Origins of Terrorism: Psychologies, Ideologies, Theologies, States of Mind* (Cambridge University Press, 1990), pp. 25–40; Robert S. Robins and Jerrold M. Post, *Political Paranoia: The Psychopolitics of Hatred* (Yale University Press, 1997), chaps. 4 and 6; and Laqueur, *The New Terrorism*, pp. 93–96.

34. *The NewsHour with Jim Lehrer*, Public Broadcasting System, August 25, 1998.

35. See, for example, Richard Clutterbuck, "Negotiating with Terrorists," in Alex P. Schmid and Ronald D. Crelinsten, eds., *Western Responses to Terrorism* (London: Frank Cass, 1993), p. 285.

36. Thomas C. Schelling, "What Purposes Can 'International Terrorism' Serve?" in R. G. Frey and Christopher W. Morris, eds., *Violence, Terrorism, and Justice* (Cambridge University Press, 1991), pp. 31–32.

37. See Heymann, *Terrorism and America*, pp. 40–46; and Tucker, *Skirmishes at the Edge of Empire*, pp. 74–80.

38. Schelling, "What Purposes Can 'International Terrorism' Serve?" p. 25.

39. Fact Sheet on Funding for Embassy Security, Department of State, August 4, 1999 (www.usinfo.state.gov/topical/pol/terror/99080404.htm [October 2000]).

40. White House Fact Sheet on Embassy Security Funding, February 10, 2000 (usinfo.state.gov/topical/pol/terror/00021004.htm [November 2000]).

41. *Report of the Accountability Review Boards*, Introduction.

42. Walter Enders and Todd Sandler in "The Effectiveness of Anti-Terrorism Policies: A Vector-Autoregression-Intervention Analysis," *American Political Science Review*, vol. 87 (December 1993), pp. 829–44, analyze statistics on terrorist incidents to conclude that the fortification of diplomatic installations has reduced attacks on those installations but has led terrorists to conduct more assassinations instead. They reach a similar conclusion about the installation of metal detectors in airports.

43. Hoffman, *Inside Terrorism*, pp. 180–82.

44. Defense Science Board 1997 Summer Study Task Force, *DoD Responses to Transnational Threats*, volume 1: Final Report (October 1997).

Chapter Three

1. *Public Report of the Vice President's Task Force on Combatting Terrorism* (Washington, February 1986).

2. Walter Laqueur, *The New Terrorism: Fanaticism and the Arms of Mass Destruction* (Oxford University Press, 1999), pp. 29, 106; and Bruce Hoffman, *Inside Terrorism* (Columbia University Press, 1998), p. 83.

3. Michael Cox, "Bringing in the 'International': The IRA Ceasefire and the End of the Cold War," *International Affairs*, vol. 73 (October 1997), pp. 671–93.

4. John Kifner, "Police Seek Suspects Tied to Terrorism in Albania," *New York Times*, August 22, 1998, p. A7.

5. Bruce Hoffman, "Terrorism Trends and Prospects," in Ian O. Lesser, *et al.*, *Countering the New Terrorism* (Rand, 1999), pp. 15–20.

6. For further description of Afghanistan as a sanctuary and breeding ground for terrorists, see Michael Rubin, "South Asia: New Refuge for Middle East-Style Radical Terrorists," Policywatch 440 (Washington: Washington Institute for Near East Policy, February 2000); Ahmed Rashid, "The Taliban: Exporting Extremism," *Foreign Affairs*, vol. 78 (November-December 1999), pp. 22–35; and Rashid, *Taliban: Militant Islam, Oil and Fundamentalism in Central Asia* (Yale University Press, 2000), especially chap.10.

7. An overview of the Soviet bloc's support to terrorism is in Laqueur, *The New Terrorism*, pp. 158–68.

8. Steven Mufson, "A 'Rogue' Is a 'Rogue' Is a 'State of Concern'" *Washington Post*, June 20, 2000, p. A16.

9. Richard N. Haass, *The Reluctant Sheriff: The United States after the Cold War* (New York: Council on Foreign Relations, 1997), p. 42.

10. Policy toward state sponsors is discussed in chapter 6.

11. Bernard Lewis, "The Roots of Muslim Rage," *Atlantic Monthly*, vol. 266 (September 1990), pp. 47–60.

12. Samuel P. Huntington, "The Clash of Civilizations?" *Foreign Affairs*, vol. 72 (Summer 1993), pp. 22–49. Huntington's later book is *The Clash of Civilizations and the Remaking of World Order* (Simon and Schuster, 1996). All subsequent references to Huntington are to the book.

13. Huntington, *The Clash of Civilizations*, pp. 209–18.

14. See, for example, Stephen M. Walt, "Building Up New Bogeymen," *Foreign Policy*, no. 106 (Spring 1997), pp. 177–89; and the set of critiques in *Foreign Affairs*, vol. 72 (September-October 1993), pp. 2–26, especially the article by Fouad Ajami. Huntington's rebuttal to these critiques is in "If Not Civilizations, What?: Paradigms of the Post-Cold War World," *Foreign Affairs*, vol. 72 (November-December 1993), pp. 186–94.

15. Huntington, *The Clash of Civilizations*, pp. 264–65.

16. Olivier Roy, *The Failure of Political Islam*, translated by Carol Volk (Harvard University Press, 1994), p. 124, and on other points pp. 108, 112. See also John Esposito, *The Islamic Threat: Myth or Reality?* 2d ed. (Oxford Univer-

sity Press, 1995), especially pp. 201–04; Fred Halliday, *Islam and the Myth of Confrontation: Religion and Politics in the Middle East* (London: I.B. Tauris, 1996), p. 119; Graham E. Fuller and Ian O. Lesser, *A Sense of Siege: The Geopolitics of Islam and the West* (Westview Press, 1995), pp. 113–17; and Judith Miller, "The Challenge of Radical Islam," *Foreign Affairs*, vol. 72 (Spring 1993), p. 45.

17. Huntington argues that the mildness, or absence, of Muslim criticism of Islamist terrorism is evidence that the "quasi war" involves a whole civilization, not just a small, extreme minority. Huntington, *The Clash of Civilizations*, p. 217.

18. Data are from the Immigration and Naturalization Service (www.ins.usdoj.gov/graphics/aboutins/statistics/msrsep99/INSP.HTM [October 2000]).

19. State Department data.

20. Overseas Presence Advisory Panel, *America's Overseas Presence in the 21st Century*, Report of the Overseas Presence Advisory Panel (Government Printing Office, November 1999), p. 12.

21. Data from the *Defense Almanac* (www.defenselink.mil/pubs/almanac/almanac/people enlisted.html [November 28, 2000]).

22. Accountability Review Boards, *Report of the Accountability Review Boards on the Bombings of the U.S. Embassies in Nairobi, Kenya and Dar es Salaam, Tanzania on August 7, 1998* (www.terrorism.com/state/accountability [November 28, 2000]).

23. See, for example, Ivan Eland, "Does U.S. Intervention Overseas Breed Terrorism?" Foreign Policy Briefing 50 (Washington: Cato Institute, December 17, 1998); and Richard K. Betts, "The New Threat of Mass Destruction," *Foreign Affairs*, vol. 77 (January-February 1998), pp. 26–41. Betts adds the caveats that many extremists would hate the United States anyway, that there are other foreign policy interests worth pursuing, and that his analysis is not a case for isolationism. His main point is the very useful one that not all of the nation's important security interests complement one another.

24. Daniel Pipes, *The Hidden Hand: Middle East Fears of Conspiracy* (St. Martin's, 1998), pp. 111–12.

25. Fuller and Lesser, *A Sense of Siege*, pp. 39–40.

26. Quoted in Shireen T. Hunter, *The Future of Islam and the West: Clash of Civilizations or Peaceful Coexistence?* (Praeger, 1998), p. 13.

27. "Saudi Militant Is Said to Urge Forced Ouster of U.S. Troops," *New York Times*, August 31, 1996, p. 2.

28. Benjamin R. Barber, *Jihad vs. McWorld* (Times Books, 1995), p. 60.

29. Mark Juergensmeyer, *The New Cold War? Religious Nationalism Confronts the Secular State* (University of California Press, 1993), p. 23.

30. For example, Robert H. Bork, *Slouching Towards Gomorrah: Modern Liberalism and American Decline* (New York: ReganBooks, 1996), chap. 7.

31. Quoted in Pipes, *The Hidden Hand*, p. 216.

32. Joseph S. Nye, Jr., *Bound to Lead: The Changing Nature of American Power* (Basic Books, 1990), pp. 31–33. On the advantages to the United States of the worldwide spread of its culture, see also David Rothkopf, "In Praise of Cultural Imperialism?" *Foreign Policy*, no. 107 (Summer 1997), pp. 38–53.

33. Hoffman, "Terrorist Trends and Prospects," p. 35.

34. Huntington, *The Clash of Civilizations*, p. 58.

35. See Hunter, *The Future of Islam and the West*, chap. 1, esp. p. 56; Juergensmeyer, *The New Cold War*, pp. 160–64; Fuller and Lesser, *A Sense of Siege*, pp. 101–02; and Magnus Ranstorp, "Terrorism in the Name of Religion," *Journal of International Affairs*, vol. 50 (Summer 1996), pp. 41–62.

36. On the continuing significance of the Crusades in particular, see Esposito, *The Islamic Threat*, pp. 39–42.

37. Martin Kramer, "Ballots and Bullets: Islamists and the Relentless Drive for Power," *Harvard International Review*, vol. 19 (Spring 1997), pp. 16–19. See also Hunter, *The Future of Islam and the West*, pp. 12–20; and Fuller and Lesser, *A Sense of Siege*, pp. 27–43.

38. Pipes in *The Hidden Hand* provides numerous examples of this kind of misperception in the Middle East, most of which postulate some sort of malevolent conspiracy. On the tendency of religious extremists throughout the non-Western world to regard U.S. actions as part of a hostile plot, see Juergensmeyer, *The New Cold War*, p. 22.

39. For example, Ishaq Ahmad al-Farhan, "Can America Rule the World?" *al Dustur* (Amman), August 18, 1998, p. 25.

40. Ali Usman, "Beginning of Resistance against U.S. Hegemony," *Takbeer* (Karachi), May 6-13, 1999, pp. 13–15, translation in Foreign Broadcast Information Service, *Daily Report: Pakistan* May 6, 1999, p.10.

41. Robert W. Tucker, "Alone or with Others: The Temptations of Post-Cold War Power," *Foreign Affairs*, vol. 78 (November-December 1999), p. 16.

42. For an essay on this subject by an architectural historian, see Jane C. Loeffler, "Diplomacy Doesn't Belong in Bunkers," *Washington Post*, August 23, 1998, p. C4.

43. An example of a reasonable compromise between security and image is the new U.S. embassy in Ottawa. The building, which occupies prime real estate in the center of the city, presents a friendly, mostly glass face toward Parliament Hill. The glass is a false front that conceals the real wall, which has small windows. See Benjamin Forgey, "An Inviting Embassy with a Sense of Security," *Washington Post*, October 2, 1999, p. C1.

44. *The Protection of U.S. Forces Deployed Abroad*, Report to the President submitted by Secretary of Defense William J. Perry, September 15, 1996 (www.defenselink.mil/pubs/downing_rpt/report_f.html [July 24, 2000]).

45. Ibid.

46. Thomas W. Lippman, "Report on Terrorism Suggests Closing Some U.S. Embassies," *Washington Post*, January 9, 1999, p. A14.

47. *America's Overseas Presence in the 21st Century*, pp. 16, 27.

Chapter Four

1. The multilateral diplomacy of the time is described in Abraham D. Sofaer, "Terrorism and the Law," *Foreign Affairs*, vol. 64 (Summer 1986), pp. 903–06.

2. The issue of applying sanctions to state sponsors is addressed more fully in chapter 6.

3. Rosalyn Higgins, "The General International Law of Terrorism," in Higgins and Maurice Flory, *Terrorism and International Law* (London: Routledge, 1997), pp. 18–19.

4. Alex P. Schmid, "The Response Problem as a Definition Problem," in Schmid and Ronald D. Crelinsten, eds., *Western Responses to Terrorism* (London: Frank Cass, 1993), pp. 12–13.

5. Additional Protocol 1, articles 43 and 44.

6. Additional Protocol 1, article 51. For further discussion of these legal issues, see Geoffrey Best, *War and Law Since 1945* (Oxford: Clarendon Press, 1994), pp. 335–41; and Sofaer, "Terrorism and the Law," pp. 912–15.

7. *Counterterrorism and Infrastructure Protection,* testimony of FBI Director Louis Freeh, Hearings before the Senate Appropriations Subcommittee for the departments of Commerce, Justice, and State, the Judiciary, and Related Agencies, February 4, 1999, 106 Cong. 1 sess. (Government Printing Office, 1999), pp. 42–56.

8. Unpublished FBI data.

9. Ethan A. Nadelmann, *Cops across Borders: The Internationalization of U.S. Criminal Law Enforcement* (Pennsylvania State University Press, 1993), pp. 3-4, p. 105.

10. The 1984 act is 18 U.S.C. 1203; the 1986 law is 18 U.S.C. 2331. See *FBI Investigation into the Saudi Arabia Bombing and Foreign FBI Investigations,* testimony of Robert M. Bryant, assistant director, National Security Division, FBI, Hearings before the House Subcommittee on Crime, February 12, 1997, 105 Cong. 1 sess. (GPO, 1997), pp. 5–30; and Nadelmann, *Cops across Borders,* p. 157.

11. David A. Vise, "New Global Role Puts FBI in Unsavory Company," *Washington Post,* October 29, 2000, p. A30.

12. A former State Department counterterrorism coordinator has written about state-sponsored terrorism that when evidence is presented in open court, "the effect on popular attitudes and foreign policy making is clearly much greater than when only sensitive intelligence, which usually cannot be made public, is involved." Robert Oakley, "International Terrorism," *Foreign Affairs,* vol. 65 (January 1987), p. 621. Similar effects might ensue regarding non-state-sponsored terrorist groups. See also David Tucker, *Skirmishes at the Edge of Empire: The United States and International Terrorism* (Praeger, 1997), p. 81.

13. *Counterterrorism and Infrastructure Protection,* Hearings, pp. 42–56.

14. 18 U.S.C. App. III, sec. 1-16.

15. Title VII.

16. Nadelmann, *Cops across Borders,* p. 417; and Philip B. Heymann, *Terrorism and America: A Commonsense Strategy for a Democratic Society* (MIT Press, 1998), p. 54.

17. Heymann, *Terrorism and America,* pp. 52–53.

18. David Freestone, "International Cooperation against Terrorism and the Development of International Law Principles of Jurisdiction," in Higgins and Flory, *Terrorism and International Law,* pp. 44–45.

19. The extradition of fugitives who—like any terrorist—have acted for political reasons is one subject on which the United States has sometimes been less forthcoming than other countries. Most cases involving the United States in which extradition has been resisted or denied because the suspect's actions could be considered a "political offense" have been requests *from* a foreign country for extradition of someone in the United States, rather than U.S. requests to other states. Many foreign countries (particularly those with a civil law, rather than a common law, tradition) have been less cooperative than the United States, however, in extraditing their own nationals. See Freestone, "International Cooperation against Terrorism and the Development of International Law Principles of Jurisdiction," p. 46; Nadelmann, *Cops across Borders*, pp. 426–27; and Christopher H. Pyle, "Defining Terrorism," *Foreign Policy*, no. 64 (Fall 1986), pp. 63–78.

20. Roberto Suro and Pierre Thomas, "Freeh Criticizes Saudis on Bomb Probe," *Washington Post*, January 23, 1997, p. A8.

21. *Counterterrorism and Infrastructure Protection*, Hearings, pp. 42—56.

22. Consider this comment by the director of the Institute for Conflict Resolution in India, noting that more Indians than Americans have died from terrorism. "[The U.S. government's] evaluation of the magnitude and virulence of the terrorist offensive directed against America can only be justified in terms of the grossly skewed value attached to the lives of its own citizens in comparison to victims in other countries, and in particular, the Third World." Ajai Sahni, "Pax Americana and Islamic Threat," *Pioneer* (New Delhi), November 28, 1998, p. 8.

23. Karl Vick, "Strong Feelings Mark Albright's Visit to Nairobi," *Washington Post*, October 23, 1999, p. A17.

24. Rodney Tasker, "Thailand: Defused by Traffic—Foiled Bomb Plot Perplexes Authorities," *Far Eastern Economic Review*, March 31, 1994, p. 20; and William Branigin, "Thais Hold Iranian in March Bomb Attempt: Israeli Target Suspected," *Washington Post*, August 27, 1994, p. A15.

25. *Is a U.N. International Criminal Court in the U.S. National Interest?*, testimony of the chief U.S. delegate to the Rome conference, Ambassador David Scheffer, to the Senate Foreign Relations Committee, 105 Cong. 2 sess., July 28, 1998 (GPO, 1998), pp. 10–15.

26. *Patterns of Global Terrorism 1998* (Department of State, 1999), p. 22.

27. The FBI already considers some of its counterterrorist work to be intelligence gathering rather than criminal investigation and has different procedural rules governing each type of case. Even intelligence investigations, however, currently require specific information suggesting a violation of U.S. law.

28. A bibliography of recent work on "smart sanctions" is at www.smartsanctions.ch/papers.htm (October 2000).

29. IEEPA is 50 U.S.C. 1701–06.

30. 8 U.S.C. 2332d and 2339b.

31. Bruce Hoffman, "Terrorism Trends and Prospects," in Ian O. Lesser and others, *Countering the New Terrorism* (Rand, 1999), p. 24.

32. See departments of the Treasury and Justice, *The National Money Laundering Strategy for 2000* (www.treas.gov/press/releases/doc/ml2000.pdf [December 8, 2000]).

33. The connections of some terrorist groups to for-profit crime, however, do mean that interdicting the financial flows associated with that crime may indirectly affect the terrorists. The links between terrorist groups and narcotics trafficking—which are most conspicuous in, but not limited to, Colombia—are discussed in Stefan Leader and David Wiencek, "Drug Money: The Fuel for Global Terrorism," *Jane's Intelligence Review*, vol. 12 (February 2000), pp. 49–54.

34. Testimony of Louis Freeh.

35. All data on blocked assets are from Office of Foreign Assets Control, Department of the Treasury, *1999 Annual Report to the Congress on Assets in the United States Belonging to Terrorist Countries or International Terrorist Organizations* (March 1, 2000), pp. 8–11, 14–15.

36. White House Fact Sheet on President Clinton's Counterterrorism Funding Request, May 17, 2000 (www.whitehouse.gov/WH/New/html/2000531_9.html [December 8, 2000]).

37. National Commission on Terrorism, *Countering the Changing Threat of International Terrorism*, June 2000, p. 29.

38. *The National Money Laundering Strategy for 2000*, p. 72.

39. Bruce Hoffman, *Inside Terrorism* (Columbia University Press, 1998), pp. 72–73.

40. A chronology of the principal reported accomplishments of JSOC's Army component is at www.specialoperations.com/Army/Delta_Force/unit_profile.htm [December 8, 2000].

41. These and other Israeli rescue attempts are described in Eitan Meyr, "Israel, Hamas May Clash Over Kidnapping," *Jane's Intelligence Review*, vol. 12 (February 2000), pp. 28–30.

42. John E. Rielly, ed., *American Public Opinion and U.S. Foreign Policy 1999* (Chicago Council on Foreign Relations, 1999), p. 27.

43. Heymann, *Terrorism and America*, pp. 75–76.

44. An observation of Israeli terrorism expert Ariel Merari, cited in Ronald D. Crelinsten and Alex P. Schmid, "Western Responses to Terrorism: A Twenty-Five Year Balance Sheet," in Schmid and Crelinsten, *Western Responses to Terrorism*, p. 319.

45. Richard N. Haass, *Intervention: The Use of American Military Force in the Post-Cold War World*, rev. ed. (Brookings, 1999), pp. 56, 81.

46. Paul Richter, "U.S. Says Raids a Success, Warns of More Strikes," *Los Angeles Times*, August 22, 1998, p. 1.

47. James Risen, "Militant Leader Was a U.S. Target since the Spring," *New York Times*, September 6, 1998, p. 1.

48. James Risen, "Bin Laden Was Target of Afghan Raid, U.S. Confirms," *New York Times*, November 14, 1998, p. A3.

49. See Henry W. Prunckun Jr. and Philip B. Mohr, "Military Deterrence of International Terrorism: An Evaluation of Operation El Dorado Canyon," *Studies in Conflict and Terrorism*, vol. 20 (July September 1997), pp. 267–80; Walter Enders and Todd Sandler, "The Effectiveness of Anti-Terrorism Policies: A Vector-Autoregression-Intervention Analysis," *American Political Science Review*, vol. 87 (December 1993), pp. 829–44; and Hoffman, *Inside Terrorism*, pp. 192–93.

50. Raymond Tanter, *Rogue Regimes: Terrorism and Proliferation* (St. Martin's Press, 1998), pp. 164–65.

51. See Martha Crenshaw, "How Terrorists Think: What Psychology Can Contribute to Understanding Terrorism," in Lawrence Howard, ed., *Terrorism: Roots, Impact, Responses* (Praeger, 1992), p. 78; and Crelinsten and Schmid, "Western Responses to Terrorism: A Twenty-Five Year Balance Sheet," p. 319.

52. Jeffrey D. Simon, "Misunderstanding Terrorism," *Foreign Policy*, no. 67 (Summer 1987), p. 113.

53. Thomas E. Ricks and Robert S. Greenberger, "U.S. Adds Pressure on bin Laden," *Wall Street Journal*, August 25, 1998, p. A18.

54. Bradley Graham, "Bin Laden Was at Camp Just before U.S. Attack," *Washington Post*, August 29, 1998, p. A1.

55. For example, this statement by columnist George Will a year and half after the missile strikes: "There is reason to believe that [President Clinton] . . . bombed a country to distract attention from legal difficulties arising from his glandular life." George F. Will, "Sleaze, the Sequel," *Washington Post*, March 30, 2000, p. A21.

56. A good review—by a disinterested analyst—of the issues raised by information about al-Shifa is in Gavin Cameron, "Multi-track Microproliferation: Lessons from Aum Shinrikyo and Al Qaida," *Studies in Conflict and Terrorism*, vol. 22 (October-December 1999), pp. 292–93.

57. National Commission on Terrorism, *Countering the Changing Threat of International Terrorism* (June 2000), pp. 7–8.

58. Defense Science Board 1997 Summer Study Task Force, *DoD Responses to Transnational Threats*, Volume 1: Final Report (October 1997), pp. 37–38, C1-C2.

59. Frederic J. Frommer, "Arrests Bolster Backers of Law Requiring Tracking of Foreigners," *Washington Post*, December 26, 1999, p. A18.

60. Based on a total of 582.3 million passengers on domestic U.S. scheduled flights in 1999, according to data from the Air Transport Association (www.air-transport.org/public/industry/24.asp [October 2000]). The estimate of a 5 percent selection rate is in FAA Notice 99-05, "Security of Checked Baggage on Flights within the United States," *Federal Register*, vol. 64 (April 19, 1999), p. 19228.

61. Letter of transmittal to the secretary of state, January 8, 1999, accompanying the *Report of the Accountability Review Boards on the Bombings of the US Embassies in Nairobi, Kenya and Dar es Salaam, Tanzania on August 7, 1998* (www.terrorism.com/state/board_letter.html [October 2000]).

62. Department of Defense, *Report to the President and Congress on the Protection of U.S. Forces Deployed Abroad* (August 1996), annex A.

63. State Department data. Some other suspected terrorists were admitted for operational reasons—that is, to have the FBI monitor their activities in the United States to understand what they were doing and to lead to other suspects.

64. Statement by Director of Central Intelligence George J. Tenet to the Senate Select Committee on Intelligence, February 2, 2000 (www.odci.gov/cia/public_affairs/speeches/dci_speech_020200.html [October 2000]).

65. Speech by Director of Central Intelligence John Deutch at Georgetown University, September 5, 1996 (www.odci.gov/cia/public_affairs/speeches/archives/1996/dci_speech_090596.html [December 11, 2000]).

66. Section 324, Findings, of P.L. 104-132.

67. See, for example, Tim Weiner, "Rethinking the Ban on Political Assassinations," *New York Times*, August 30, 1998, sec. 4, p. 3; and Stuart Taylor, Jr., "Is the Assassination Ban Dead?" *National Journal*, vol. 30 (November 21, 1998), pp. 2758–59.

68. The fact that Israel used a chemical agent in the failed operation in Amman may also have reduced somewhat the disincentive for Hamas to use chemicals in future attacks against Israel.

69. Such a case is presented in Louis Rene Beres, "Assassination and the Law: A Policy Memorandum," *Studies in Conflict and Terrorism*, vol. 18 (October-December 1995), pp. 299–315. Some of the same legal arguments are made in Irwin Cotler, "Towards a Counter-Terrorism Law and Policy," *Terrorism and Political Violence*, vol. 10 (Summer 1998), pp. 1–14.

70. Ward Thomas, "Norms and Security: The Case of International Assassination," *International Security*, vol. 25 (Summer 2000), p. 129.

71. Brian Jenkins, "Assassination: Should We Stay the Good Guys?" *Los Angeles Times*, November 16, 1986, p. V-2.

72. See White House Fact Sheet, "Combating Terrorism: Presidential Decision Directive 62," May 22, 1998 (www.usinfo.state.gov/journals/itps/0798/ijpe/pj38trfx.htm [November 3, 2000]).

73. An example of a proposal for greater centralization is Ashton Carter, John Deutch, and Philip Zelikow, "Catastrophic Terrorism: Tackling the New Danger," *Foreign Affairs*, vol. 77 (November-December 1998), pp. 80–94. The article describes the DCI Counterterrorist Center as being "highly successful" but then proposes a change (essentially, moving the Center to the FBI) that would emasculate it by separating it from the CIA operational elements on which it depends for collection, foreign liaison, and covert action.

74. *Countering the Changing Threat of International Terrorism*, p. 16.

75. *Report of the Accountability Review Boards*, Key Recommendations, sec. I.A.13.

76. Nadelmann, *Cops across Borders*, pp. 474–75.

Chapter Five

1. See Magnus Ranstorp, "Terrorism in the Name of Religion," *Journal of International Affairs*, vol. 50 (Summer 1996), pp. 41–62.

2. The claim of responsibility for the East Africa bombings issued by the "Islamic Army for the Liberation of the Holy Places" did call first of all for the evacuation of Western forces from the Arabian Peninsula, but it also included such absurdly broad and invective demands as "halting the robbery and exploitation of the Muslims' wealth" and "halting the war of eradication launched by the

United States against the Islamic religion's tenets." The statement was sent to several news agencies in the Middle East. One place it was published was in *Al-Safir* (Beirut), August 11, 1998, p. 16; a translation is in Foreign Broadcast Information Service, TOT-225, August 13, 1998, p. 12.

3. *Counterterrorism and Infrastructure Protection*, testimony of FBI Director Louis Freeh before the Subcommittee for the Departments of Commerce, Justice, and State, the Judiciary, and Related Agencies of the Senate Appropriations Committee, February 4, 1999, 106 Cong. 1 sess. (Government Printing Office, 1999), pp. 42–56.

4. On the dimensions of the conflict with the PKK and its implications for Turkish foreign policy, see Simon V. Mayall, *Turkey: Thwarted Ambition*, McNair Paper 56 (Washington: National Defense University, January 1997), pp. 84–85; Henri J. Barkey and Graham E. Fuller, *Turkey's Kurdish Question* (Lanham, Md.: Rowman and Littlefield, 1998), especially chap. 6; and Heinz Kramer, *A Changing Turkey: The Challenge to Europe and the United States* (Brookings, 2000), pp. 38–39, 227.

5. The Turkish government rebuffed the gesture, arresting the eight and indicating that they would be treated like any other terrorists.

6. On Prabhakaran's objectives and the dim prospects for settlement as long as he is in control of the LTTE, see Chris Smith, "South Asia's Enduring War," in Robert I. Rotberg, ed., *Creating Peace in Sri Lanka: Civil War and Reconciliation* (Brookings, 1999), p. 37; and "Sri Lanka: City Slaughter," *Economist*, March 18, 2000, p. 41.

7. "The distinction between protest and rebellion is not absolute," Ted Robert Gurr has observed about ethnically based conflicts, not only because the political objectives of people with grievances are mixed but also because "their choice of strategies and tactics vary with circumstances, including the responses of their opponents." *Minorities at Risk: A Global View of Ethnopolitical Conflicts* (Washington: U.S. Institute of Peace Press, 1993), p. 93.

8. On the PKK's suspicions of the United States, see Barkey and Fuller, *Turkey's Kurdish Question*, p. 53.

9. Adrian Guelke, "The United States, Irish Americans and the Northern Ireland Peace Process," *International Affairs*, vol. 72 (July 1996), pp. 523–26.

10. *Counterterrorism and Infrastructure Protection*, Hearings.

11. See, for example, I. William Zartman, ed., *Elusive Peace: Negotiating an End to Civil Wars* (Brookings, 1995); Roy Licklider, ed., *Stopping the Killing: How Civil Wars End* (New York University Press, 1993); Richard N. Haass, *Conflicts Unending: The United States and Regional Disputes* (Yale University Press, 1990); and Paul R. Pillar, *Negotiating Peace: War Termination as a Bargaining Process* (Princeton University Press, 1983).

12. Kirk Semple, "Colombians March to Back Peace Talks," *Washington Post*, October 25, 1999, p. A20; and Karen DeYoung, "For Rebels, It's Not a Drug War," *Washington Post*, April 10, 2000, p. A1.

13. See I. William Zartman, "Dynamics and Constraints in Negotiations in Internal Conflicts," in Zartman, *Elusive Peace*, p. 3.

14. Daniel Byman, "The Logic of Ethnic Terrorism," *Studies in Conflict and Terrorism*, vol. 21 (April 1998), pp. 161–62; and Gurr, *Minorities at Risk*, pp. 69–70.

15. Graham E. Fuller and Ian O. Lesser make this argument about Islamist groups in *A Sense of Siege: The Geopolitics of Islam and the West* (Westview Press, 1995), pp. 119–23.

16. See *How Terrorism Ends*, Special Report of the U.S. Institute of Peace (May 1999), especially the contribution by Martha Crenshaw.

17. James Wilson, "AOL Chief Meets Colombia's FARC Rebels," *Financial Times*, March 4, 2000, p. 3.

18. Steven Dudley, "Colombian Citizens Join Peace Process," *Washington Post*, April 20, 2000, p. A30.

19. Polls have also revealed cynicism on the part of many Colombians about the Pastrana government's handling of the dialogue with the FARC. There is, nonetheless, strong popular support for some sort of peace process, as suggested by a series of pro-peace demonstrations in late 1999 that at one point involved several million Colombians. See "Colombia: No More!" *Economist*, October 30, 1999, p. 36. On the activity of the AUC, see "Dealing with Colombia's Death-Squads," *Economist*, April 8, 2000, pp. 35–36.

20. Gurr, *Minorities at Risk*, p. 69.

21. "Turkey's Kurds: Still on Their Feet," *Economist*, October 23, 1999, pp. 59–60.

22. The ETA announced in November 1999 that it was ending a cease-fire that it had observed for the previous fourteen months. The Spanish government said there would be no new talks with the ETA—an understandable and probably justified response, with or without a cease-fire. William Schomberg, "Spain Urges Isolation of Basque Guerrillas," *Washington Post*, November 30, 1999, p. A24; and "Spain and the Basques: Back to Bombs?" *Economist*, December 4, 1999, p. 48.

23. Zartman, "Dynamics and Constraints in Negotiations in Internal Conflicts," pp. 9–10.

24. On the Spanish government's posture toward Herri Batasuna, see Robert P. Clark, "Negotiations for Basque Self-Determination in Spain," in Zartman, ed., *Elusive Peace*, pp. 69–70.

25. Byman, "The Logic of Ethnic Terrorism," pp. 162–65.

26. Manoj Joshi, "On the Razor's Edge: The Liberation Tigers of Tamil Eelam," *Studies in Conflict and Terrorism*, vol. 19 (January-March 1996), p. 19; and Pamela Constable, "Tigers Hold Sri Lanka by the Tail," *Washington Post*, January 25, 2000, p. A15.

27. See Pillar, *Negotiating Peace*, p. 75.

28. "Northern Ireland: The American Connection," *Economist*, March 21, 1998, p. 68; and Jonathan Stevenson, "Northern Ireland: Treating Terrorists as Statesmen," *Foreign Policy*, no. 105 (Winter 1996–97), p. 128.

29. T. R. Reid, "IRA Quits Talks on Disarming," *Washington Post*, February 16, 2000, p. A19.

30. Stevenson, "Northern Ireland: Treating Terrorists as Statesmen," pp. 129, 134–36.

31. Title III, sec. 302.

32. *U.S. Counterterrorism Policy*, testimony of FBI Director Freeh before the Senate Judiciary Committee, Hearings, September 3, 1998, 105 Cong. 2 sess. (GPO, 1998), pp. 17–24.

33. "18 Accused of Aiding Hezbollah," *Washington Post*, July 22, 2000, p. A11.

34. *U.S. Counterterrorism Policy*, Hearings.

35. Title V, sec. 411.

36. See Michael Cox, "Bringing in the 'International': The IRA Ceasefire and the End of the Cold War," *International Affairs*, vol. 73 (October 1997), p. 687.

37. Department of State, *Patterns of Global Terrorism 1999* (April 2000), p. iii.

38. See press conferences given by Michael Sheehan, counterterrorism coordinator, on October 8, 1999 (www.state.gov/www/policy_remarks/1999/991008_sheehan_fto.html [October 2000]), and by Secretary of State Albright and Sheehan on May 1, 2000 (www.usis.it/file2000_05/alia/a005010a.htm [November 28, 2000]).

39. Department of State, *Patterns of Global Terrorism 1999*, pp. 90–99.

40. *Extremist Movements and Their Threat to the United States*, testimony of Michael Sheehan before the Subcommittee on Near Eastern and South Asian Affairs of the Senate Foreign Relations Committee, November 2, 1999 (GPO, 1999), pp. 8–12.

41. *People's Mujahedin Organization of Iran v. U.S. Department of State and Madeleine K. Albright, Secretary of State*, and *Liberation Tigers of Tamil Eelam v. U.S. Department of State*, both decided on June 25, 1999.

42. *Humanitarian Law Project, et al. v. Reno, et al.*

Chapter Six

1. 50 U.S.C. App. 2405 (6)(j).

2. *Anti-Terrorism and Arms Export Amendments Act of 1989*, P. L. 101-222.

3. See Raphael F. Perl, "Terrorism, the Future, and U.S. Foreign Policy," Issue Brief 95112 (Congressional Research Service, December 9, 1996).

4. The State Department's annual report, *Patterns of Global Terrorism*, summarizes terrorism-related issues and events pertinent to each of the designated state sponsors.

5. Steven Simon and Daniel Benjamin, "America and the New Terrorism," *Survival*, vol. 42 (Spring 2000), p. 62.

6. See *U.S. Foreign Policy toward Libya*, testimony of Deputy Assistant Secretary of State Ronald E. Neumann to the Subcommittee for Near Eastern and South Asian Affairs of the Senate Foreign Relations Committee, 106 Cong. 2 sess., May 4, 2000 (Government Printing Office, 2000); and a speech by Neumann

to the Middle East Institute on November 30, 1999 (http://www.mideasti.org/html/neuman-lib.html October 28, 2000]).

7. The somewhat reluctant manner in which North Korea has continued to support the Japanese extremists was revealed when a member of the Japanese Red Army was arrested in Cambodia in 1996 for counterfeiting. North Korea refused to intercede on his behalf even though the individual carried a North Korean diplomatic passport. Walter Laqueur, *The New Terrorism: Fanaticism and the Arms of Mass Destruction* (Oxford University Press, 1999), p. 182.

8. Robert S. Litwak, *Rogue States and U.S. Foreign Policy: Containment after the Cold War* (Washington: Woodrow Wilson Center Press, 2000), p. 76.

9. Remarks by Peter F. Romero, acting assistant secretary of state for Western Hemisphere Affairs, before the Council of the Americas, May 1, 2000 (http://www.state.gov/www/policy_remarks/2000/000501_romero_coa.html [October2000]).

10. John Pomfret, "North Korea Threatens to Skip Talks," *Washington Post*, March 29, 2000, p. A20.

11. Kyong Hwa Seok, "North Korea Issues New Offer for U.S. Relations," *Washington Post*, August 14, 2000, p. A18.

12. Colum Lynch and Don Phillips, "Angry Over Airline Search, North Korea Skips U.N. Summit," *Washington Post*, September 6, 2000, p. A1.

13. *Patterns of Global Terrorism 1999* (Department of State, 2000) p. iii.

14. Quoted in John Lancaster, "Egypt Urges Diplomacy, Not Force, in U.S.-Iraq Dispute," *Washington Post*, November 14, 1997, p. A35.

15. Title II, section 205(a)(7).

16. This is the major theme of Litwak's *Rogue States and U.S. Foreign Policy*. See especially p. 8 and the rest of the introductory chapter.

17. Major studies include Gary Clyde Hufbauer, Jeffrey J. Schott, and Kimberly Ann Elliott, *Economic Sanctions Reconsidered: History and Current Policy* (Washington: Institute for International Economics, 1985); David A. Baldwin, *Economic Statecraft* (Princeton University Press, 1985); and Richard N. Haass, ed., *Economic Sanctions and American Diplomacy* (New York: Council on Foreign Relations, 1998). Many of the analytic issues have been addressed in a running debate in *International Security* that began with an article by Robert A. Pape, "Why Economic Sanctions Do Not Work," vol. 22 (Fall 1997), pp. 90–136, and also includes Kimberly Ann Elliott, "The Sanctions Glass: Half Full or Completely Empty?" vol. 23 (Summer 1998), pp. 50–65; Robert A. Pape, "Why Economic Sanctions *Still* Do Not Work," vol. 23 (Summer 1998), pp. 66–77; correspondence by Baldwin and Pape in vol. 23 (Fall 1998), pp. 189–98; and an article by Baldwin, "The Sanctions Debate and the Logic of Choice," vol. 24 (Winter 1999-2000), pp. 80-107, which explores the analytical complexities—including the different ways of defining and measuring success—in assessing sanctions.

18. One respect in which Iran has reduced its involvement in terrorism has been its curbing of extraterritorial assassinations of dissidents in Europe. Its interest in maintaining economic ties with key European states has probably been a

factor. An additional explanation, however, is that Iran had simply finished killing most of the oppositionists it had targeted in Europe.

19. "Iraq and the West: When Sanctions Don't Work," *Economist*, April 8, 2000, pp. 23–25; and Ofra Bengio, "How Does Saddam Hold On?" *Foreign Affairs*, vol. 79 (July-August 2000), pp. 93–94.

20. On the advantages and effectiveness of the sanctions on Libya, see Gideon Rose, "The United States and Libya," in Richard N. Haass, ed., *Transatlantic Tensions: The United States, Europe, and Problem Countries* (Brookings, 1999), p. 157.

21. *Counterterrorism and Infrastructure Protection*, Hearings before the Subcommittee for the Departments of Commerce, Justice, and State, the Judiciary, and Related Agencies of the Senate Appropriates Committee, 106 Cong. 1 sess. (GPO, 1999), pp. 42–56.

22. See, for example, Elliott, "The Sanctions Glass," p. 58.

23. Daniel Byman, "A Farewell to Arms Inspections," *Foreign Affairs*, vol. 79 (January-February 2000), pp. 131–32.

24. Patrick Clawson, "Iran," in Haass, *Economic Sanctions and American Diplomacy*, pp. 94–95.

25. By inhibiting Iran's rebuilding of its conventional military capabilities following the revolution and the Iran-Iraq war, U.S. sanctions may have strengthened the position of Iranian hard-liners who favor unconventional tools of foreign policy, including terrorism.

26. Litwak, *Rogue States and U.S. Foreign Policy*, p. 67.

27. Rose, "The United States and Libya," p. 159.

28. Richard N. Haass, "Conclusion: Lessons and Recommendations," in Haass, *Economic Sanctions and American Diplomacy*, pp. 200–01.

29. Raymond Tanter, *Rogue Regimes: Terrorism and Proliferation* (St. Martin's Press, 1998), pp. 80–81.

30. Ibid., p. 104; and Litwak, *Rogue States and U.S. Foreign Policy*, p. 54.

31. Litwak, *Rogue States and U.S. Foreign Policy*, pp. 9, 63.

32. On the possibility of sanctions deterring objectionable behavior by third parties, see Elizabeth S. Rogers, "Economic Sanctions and Internal Conflict," in Michael E. Brown, ed., *The International Dimensions of Internal Conflict* (MIT Press, 1996), pp. 415–16.

33. On the rethinking about sanctions in both the Clinton administration and Congress, see Mark Suzman, "Tyranny of Sanctions," *Financial Times*, August 19, 1999, p. 14; Robert S. Greenberger, "U.S. Sees Limits to Economic Sanctions," *Wall Street Journal*, September 9, 1998, p. A2; and Nancy Dunne, "Sanctions Overload," *Financial Times*, July 21, 1998, p. 19.

34. Quoted in Barbara Slavin, " 'Terrorist State' List Should Be Flexible, State Official Says," *USA Today*, April 13, 2000, p. 14A. Sheehan later indicated (in a press conference on May 1, 2000) that his point applied to all of the state sponsors, not just Cuba.

35. *Patterns of Global Terrorism 1999*, p. iv.

36. The author is indebted to Meghan O'Sullivan for thoughts on this subject.

37. For a study of engagement—what it is, how it has been used in selected cases in the past, and where and how it can best be used in future relations with problem states—see Richard N. Haass and Meghan L. O'Sullivan, *Honey and Vinegar: Incentives, Sanctions, and Foreign Policy* (Brookings, 2000).

38. On Muammar Qadhafi's hold on power, see Milton Viorst, "The Colonel in His Labyrinth," *Foreign Affairs*, vol. 78 (March-April 1999), p. 73.

39. Gary Sick, "Rethinking Dual Containment," *Survival*, vol. 40 (Spring 1998), p. 16.

40. For a general argument that sanctions and containment have not worked and that a more accommodating policy toward Iran is required, see Sick's article as well as Zbigniew Brzezinski, Brent Scowcroft, and Richard Murphy, "Differentiated Containment," *Foreign Affairs*, vol. 76 (May-June 1997), pp. 20–30.

41. Besides ongoing terrorist activity, the bombing of Khubar Towers—and Iran's unwillingness to cooperate in the investigation of it—will be a cloud hanging over any effort to improve U.S.-Iranian relations. See Simon and Benjamin, "America and the New Terrorism," pp. 64–65.

42. As noted earlier, the nature of terrorism and of state support for terrorist groups presents some inherent ambiguities about standards of behavior and whether they have been met. This is mainly a problem, however, in determining whether a state has *ended* all support for terrorism—the kind of grand judgment that might be associated with a decision to end sanctions. The ambiguity is easier to manage with decisions on responding incrementally to a state that has *reduced* its support to terrorism—the focus of the third principle, in the next paragraph.

43. Johannes Reissner, "Europe and Iran: Critical Dialogue," in Haass and O'Sullivan, *Honey and Vinegar*, p. 43.

44. Following Secretary Albright's speech on Iran in March 2000, Tehran called her remarks positive but again rejected the long-standing U.S. offer to hold direct talks. An Iranian statement said a dialogue would be beneficial when conducted "under a normalized situation, devoid of pressure, allegations, and grandstanding" (quoted in John Lancaster and Helen Dewar, "Iran Rejects U.S. Bid to Open Official Talks," *Washington Post*, March 18, 2000, p. A14). There will be strong sources of resistance in Tehran to dealing with the Great Satan no matter what Washington does, but progress toward, for example, resolving the issue of frozen assets (to the extent that is possible without already having direct official talks) might help nudge Tehran toward a broad-based dialogue.

45. Department of State, *Libya Country Report on Human Rights Practices for 1998*, February 26, 1999.

46. *Patterns of Global Terrorism 1999*, p. 87.

47. Following the embarrassment of Ocalan's arrest, Greece's foreign minister, minister of public order, minister of interior, and intelligence chief resigned for their roles in aiding the PKK leader.

48. Greece initialed a Mutual Legal Assistance Treaty with the United States in May 1999. The Greeks have delayed signing a Police Cooperation Protocol, however, while trying to insert language that would weaken it.

49. The State Department's *Patterns of Global Terrorism* for 1999 (p. 8) states that "credible reports continued to indicate official Pakistani support for Kashmiri militant groups that engage in terrorism."

50. The other countries that have given diplomatic recognition to the Taliban are Saudi Arabia and the United Arab Emirates.

51. See Ahmed Rashid, "The Taliban: Exporting Extremism," *Foreign Affairs*, vol. 78 (November-December 1999), p. 28.

52. Ibid., pp. 27–28. Another basis for hope—which the United States can help to promote—is a possible settlement or at least cease-fire in the Afghan civil war. This might not change Pakistani thinking, but it would reduce the Taliban's dependence on bin Ladin and the other "Arab Afghans" who support it.

53. 22 U.S.C. 2781.

54. *Federal Register*, volume 62 (May 22, 1997), p. 28097, and subsequent annual renewals.

55. National Commission on Terrorism, *Countering the Changing Threat of International Terrorism* (Washington, June 2000), pp. 17–19.

56. "Proposal on Sanctions Rejected," *Washington Post*, June 5, 2000, p. A5.

57. The AEDPA does allow the president to waive sanctions for reasons of national interest but only with regard to specific transactions.

58. Laqueur, *The New Terrorism*, p. 162.

59. Martin Nesirky, "Putin Updates Russia's Security Strategy," *Reuters*, January 6, 2000.

60. Andrew Kramer, "Russia Threatens Afghanistan Attack," *Associated Press*, May 22, 2000.

61. Pamela Constable, "Russia, U.S. Converge on Warnings to Taliban," *Washington Post*, June 4, 2000, p. A23.

62. Rashid, "The Taliban," p. 31.

63. John Pomfret, "Separatists Defy Chinese Crackdown," *Washington Post*, January 26, 2000, p. A17.

64. Ethan A. Nadelmann, *Cops across Borders: The Internationalization of U.S. Criminal Law Enforcement* (Pennsylvania State University Press, 1993), p. 152.

65. *Counterterrorism and Infrastructure Protection*, testimony of Secretary of State Madeleine K. Albright before the Subcommittee on Commerce, State, the Judiciary and Related Agencies of the Senate Appropriations Committee, February 4, 1999, 106 Cong. 1 sess. (GPO, 1999).

66. Bruce Hoffman, "Is Europe Soft on Terrorism?" *Foreign Policy*, no. 115 (Summer 1999), pp. 62–76.

67. On the Europeans' agreement that Iran is a problem, see also Geoffrey Kemp, "The Challenge of Iran for U.S. and European Policy," in Haass, *Transatlantic Tensions*, p. 66.

68. Gil Feiler, "Counter-Terrorism and Commercial Interests: Do They Conflict?" *Terrorism and Political Violence*, vol. 10 (Summer 1998), p. 17; and Gahdat Bahgat, "Iran and Terrorism: The Transatlantic Responses," *Studies in Conflict and Terrorism*, vol. 22 (April-June 1999), p. 147.

69. See Bahgat, "Iran and Terrorism: The Transatlantic Responses," pp. 142–43; and Kemp, "The Challenge of Iran for U.S. and European Policy," p. 54.

70. Accounts of the Mykonos episode are in Bahgat, "Iran and Terrorism: The Transatlantic Responses," pp. 148–49; Laqueur, *The New Terrorism*, pp. 173–74; and Bruce Hoffman, *Inside Terrorism* (Columbia University Press, 1998), p. 194.

71. Haass and O'Sullivan, "Conclusion," in *Honey and Vinegar*, p. 162.

72. Such a mixed approach is endorsed in Hoffman, "Is Europe Soft on Terrorism?" p. 74; and, with regard to policy toward Iran, in Charles Lane, "Germany's New Ostpolitik," *Foreign Affairs*, vol. 74 (November-December 1995), p. 89. See also, however, the caveat by Richard Haass in *Transatlantic Tensions*, p. 237, that a "good cop, bad cop" arrangement works only if the good cop is willing to get tough when positive incentives do not bring the desired results.

73. Department of State, *Country Reports on Human Rights Practices*, Hearing before the House Subcommittee on International Operations and Human Rights of the Committee on International Relations, February 25, 2000, 106 Cong. 2 sess. (GPO, 2000).

74. Chris Smith, "South Asia's Enduring War," in Robert I. Rotberg, ed., *Creating Peace in Sri Lanka: Civil War and Reconciliation* (Brookings, 1999), p. 36.

75. Khalil Shikaki, "Peace Now or Hamas Later," *Foreign Affairs*, vol. 77 (July-August 1998), p. 35.

76. Henri J. Barkey and Graham E. Fuller, *Turkey's Kurdish Question* (Lanham, Md.: Rowman and Littlefield, 1998), pp. 45, 134.

77. Tracy Wilkinson, "Citing Terrorism Concerns, Israel May Return to Torture," *Los Angeles Times*, December 3, 1999, p. A5.

78. Simon and Benjamin, "America and the New Terrorism," p. 64.

79. The only exception was a case in 1864. Nadelmann, *Cops across Borders*, p. 437.

Chapter Seven

1. A useful early statement was a speech by Edward Djerejian, assistant secretary of state for near eastern affairs in the Bush administration, at Meridien House in Washington on June 2, 1992. For further discussion of U.S. statements on this topic, see John L. Esposito, *The Islamic Threat: Myth or Reality?* rev. ed. (Oxford University Press, 1995), pp. 246–47.

2. Philip B. Heymann, *Terrorism and America: A Commonsense Strategy for a Democratic Society* (MIT Press, 1998), p. 62.

3. Ibid., p. 26.

4. Mary Ann Weaver, "The Real Bin Laden," *New Yorker*, January 24, 2000, pp. 32–38.

5. The concept of bin Ladin being "linked to" terrorist acts has a tendency to get blurred into stronger, and perhaps unwarranted, statements about his responsibility for them. Even if government officials are precise in their statements, replays of what they say may not be. An example is a speech by President Clinton at the Coast Guard Academy in May 2000, in which he alluded to two successful disruptions of terrorist activity before the prior New Year holiday: the foiling of a plot in Jordan to bomb locations where Americans were expected to gather for the celebration, and the arrest of an Algerian attempting to smuggle bomb-making materials from Canada into Washington state. One newspaper account of the speech (*Washington Post*, May 18, 2000, p. A10) bore the headline "Clinton

Says Bin Laden Was U.S. Bomb Plotter" and reported in its opening sentence that "President Clinton said today that terrorist leader Osama bin Laden was behind efforts to plant bombs in the United States in the weeks before millennial celebrations, the first time he has publicly made such a charge." What the president actually said (and this was quoted later in the same article) was that the plot in Jordan "was linked to terrorist camps in Afghanistan and the organization created by Osama bin Ladin," and that in the incident along the Canadian border a customs agent had "discovered bomb materials being smuggled in to the U.S.—the same materials used by bin Ladin in other places." The full text of the president's speech is at www.state.gov/www/global/terrorism/000517_clinton_coastguard. html (November 28, 2000).

6. *Public Report of the Vice President's Task Force on Combating Terrorism* (Washington, February 1986), p. 17.

7. Spending for national defense reached a peak of $304 billion (in constant fiscal year 2000 dollars) in fiscal year 1989 and dropped to $266 billion by fiscal year 1996 before inching back up.

8. Letter of transmittal for the *Report of the Accountability Review Boards on the Bombings of the U.S. Embassies in Nairobi, Kenya and Dar es Salaam, Tanzania on August 7, 1998*, submitted to the secretary of state on January 8, 1999 (emphasis added) (http://www.terrorism.com/state/accountability_ report.html [October 2000]).

9. National Commission on Terrorism, *Countering the Changing Threat of International Terrorism* (Washington, June 2000), pp. 33–34.

10. General Accounting Office, *Combating Terrorism: Issues in Managing Counterterrorist Programs*, T-NSIAD-00-145 (Washington, April 6, 2000), p. 5.

11. See the *First Annual Report of the Advisory Panel to Assess Domestic Response Capabilities for Terrorism Involving Weapons of Mass Destruction*, December 15, 1999, pp. 35–36.

12. Jessica Stern, "WMD Terrorism: An Exchange: Apocalypse Never, but the Threat Is Real," *Survival*, vol. 40 (Winter 1998–99), pp. 176–79.

13. An example of such skepticism is Daniel S. Greenberg, "The Bioterrorism Panic," *Washington Post*, March 16, 1999, p. A21.

14. Section 322, which amends 49 U.S.C. 44906.

15. "Security Programs of Foreign Air Carriers," FAA Notice 98-17, *Federal Register*, vol. 63 (November 23, 1998), pp. 64764–769. The comments on the proposed change are at http://dms.dot.gov/search (November 28, 2000), docket 4758.

16. John Mintz, "Republicans Seize Upon Unusual Issue to Assault Clinton: Terrorism," *Washington Post*, August 25, 1996, p. A4.

17. The final congressional vote on the bill took place on April 18, the day before the anniversary. President Clinton signed it on April 24.

18. Ann Devroy, "Clinton to Tighten Sanctions on Cuba," *Washington Post*, February 27, 1996, p. A1.

19. See Gideon Rose, "Libya," in Richard N. Haass, ed., *Economic Sanctions and American Diplomacy* (New York: Council on Foreign Relations, 1998), pp. 142–44.

20. Some observers note an overall trend of Congress increasingly constraining the executive branch in foreign policy. See Sebastian Mallaby, "The Bullied Pulpit: A Weak Chief Executive Makes Worse Foreign Policy," *Foreign Affairs*, vol. 79 (January-February 2000), pp. 2-8.

21. Wayne S. Smith in "Cuba's Long Reform," *Foreign Affairs*, vol. 75 (March-April 1996), pp. 99-112, argues both that the political clout of the Cuban-American community is overrated and that about half of that community would favor some sort of dialogue with Castro, even though the great majority of Cuban-Americans are still strongly anti-Castro and skeptical that democracy could ever be achieved under him.

22. Charles Abbott, "Momentum Builds for Easing U.S. Embargo on Cuba," *Reuters*, May 19, 2000; Karen De Young, "Rifts in Hard Line on Cuba," *Washington Post*, February 21, 2000, p. A2; "Seven Hours with Fidel," *Economist*, October 30, 1999, p. 32; and Pamela S. Falk, "Eyes on Cuba: U.S. Business and the Embargo," *Foreign Affairs*, vol. 75 (March-April 1996), pp. 14-18.

23. See Richard N. Haass and Meghan L. O'Sullivan, eds., *Honey and Vinegar: Incentives, Sanctions, and Foreign Policy* (Brookings, 2000), especially Johannes Reissner's analysis of the European governments' failure to develop public support for their "critical dialogue" with Iran (p. 44); Leon V. Sigal's observations on how the lack of congressional support inhibited the executive branch's engagement of North Korea (p. 91); and the editors' general observations in their concluding chapter (pp. 165-66, 178-81).

24. Sec. 221, 28 U.S.C. 1605(a)(7).

25. Bill Miller, "Albright Seeks Ways to Help Terror Victims Collect Damages," *Washington Post*, February 17, 2000, p. A6.

26. Walter Pincus, "Bill Would Use Frozen Assets to Compensate Terrorism Victims," *Washington Post*, July 30, 2000, p. A2. See also a joint statement by senior officials of the departments of Defense, State, and the Treasury describing the administration's reasons for opposing the bill (www.treas.gov/press/releases/ps721.htm [November 28, 2000]).

27. See the frustration expressed by Alisa Flatow's father in Stephen M. Flatow, "In This Case, I Can't Be Diplomatic," *Washington Post*, November 7, 1999, p. B2.

28. Warren Hoge, "New Libyan Cooperation Leads to Renewed Ties with Britain," *New York Times*, July 8, 1999, p. A4; and Benjamin Weiser, "A Settlement with P.L.O. over Terror on a Cruise," *New York Times*, August 12, 1997, p. A6.

29. Quoted in Jonathan Groner, "Payback Time," *Legal Times*, June 5, 2000, p. 13.

30. Bill Miller, "Terrorism Victims Set Precedent," *Washington Post*, October 22, 2000, p. 1.

31. Available at www.travel.state.gov/travel_warnings.html (November 28, 2000).

32. Richard Clutterbuck, "Negotiating with Terrorists," in Alex P. Schmid and Ronald D. Crelinsten, eds., *Western Responses to Terrorism* (London: Frank Cass, 1993), pp. 278-79.

33. The institute's program is described at its website, http://www.ict.org.il (November 28, 2000).

Chapter Eight

1. Statement of General Henry H. Shelton to the House Armed Services Committee, February 9, 2000 (http://www.house.gov/hasc/testimony/106thcongress/ 00-02-09shelton.htm [July 24, 2000]).

2. See Brian M. Jenkins, "The Limits of Terror: Constraints on the Escalation of Violence," *Harvard International Review*, vol. 17 (Summer 1995), pp. 45, 77.

3. Francis Fukuyama, "Second Thoughts: The Last Man in a Bottle," *National Interest*, no. 56 (Summer 1999), p. 26.

4. Ted Robert Gurr, *Minorities at Risk: A Global View of Ethnopolitical Conflicts* (Washington: U.S. Institute of Peace Press, 1993), p. 91.

5. Ted Robert Gurr, "Ethnic Warfare on the Wane," *Foreign Affairs*, vol. 79 (May-June 2000), p. 52.

6. Ibid., p. 64.

7. On the early revolutionary zeal of the Iranian regime, see Shireen T. Hunter, *The Future of Islam and the West: Clash of Civilizations or Peaceful Coexistence?* (Praeger, 1998), p. 134.

Index